T. W. Walker
2071 Bonniebrae Dr
Lake Oswego Or 97034

T. W. Walker
2071 Bonniebrae Dr
Lake Oswego Or 97034

PAN/ORDNANCE SURVEY

THE MOTOR TOURING GUIDE TO BRITAIN WITH ORDNANCE SURVEY MAPS

BRITAIN

ON BACKROADS

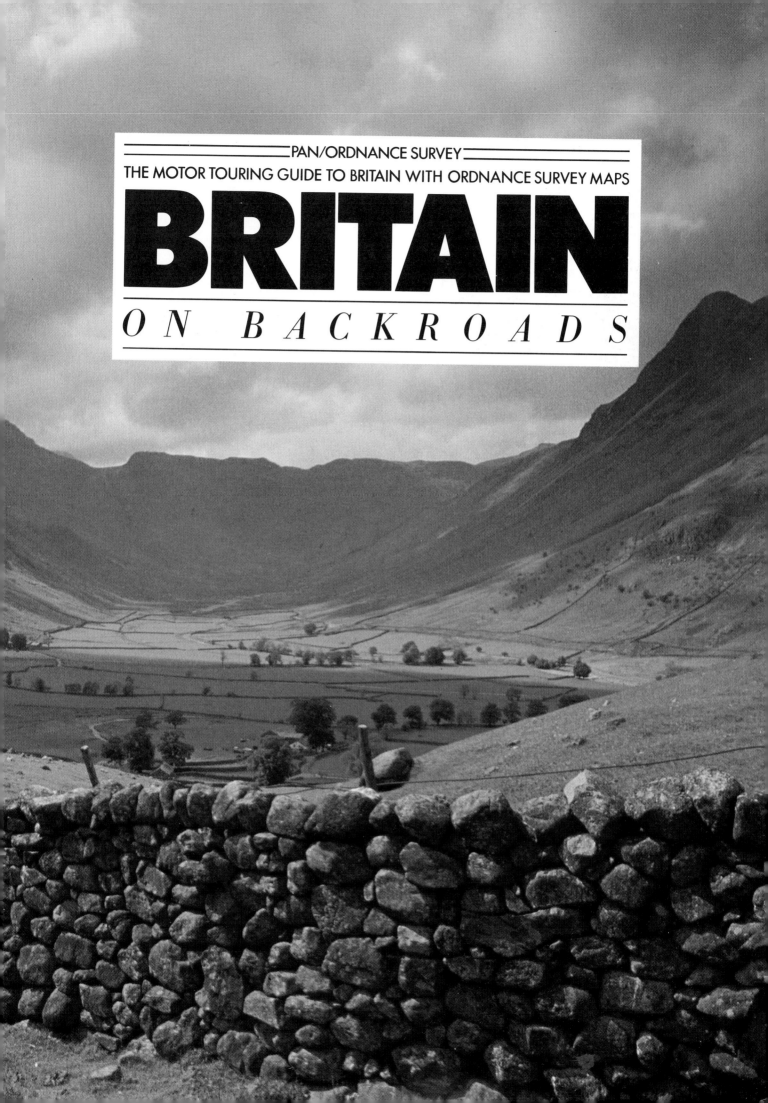

PAN/ORDNANCE SURVEY

THE MOTOR TOURING GUIDE TO BRITAIN WITH ORDNANCE SURVEY MAPS

BRITAIN

ON BACKROADS

First published 1985 by Pan Books Ltd, Cavaye Place, London SW10 9PG and Ordnance Survey, Romsey Road, Maybush, Southampton S09 4DH.
9 8 7 6 5 4 3 2 1

Conceived, designed and edited by Duncan Associates, 64, Fullerton Road, London, SW18 1BX with Mel Petersen & Associates, 5, Botts Mews, Chepstow Road, London, W2 5AG.

© Text and artwork, Duncan Associates/ Mel Petersen & Associates, 1985 (but traffic bottlenecks survey © The Royal Automobile Club, 1985).

© The maps in this publication are reproduced from Ordnance Survey maps with the permission of the Controller of HMSO. Crown Copyright Reserved.

ISBN 0 330 28579 3

Filmset, printed and bound in Great Britain by Hazell Watson & Viney Limited, Aylesbury. Member of the BPCC Group.

● Information on opening and closing times was correct at time of publication, but those who run tourist attractions are often obliged to change times at short notice. If your enjoyment of a day out is going to depend on seeing a certain place, it makes sense to check with the local tourist information office that you will gain admission.

● Some of the roads used for tours in this book are country lanes in the true sense: they are hedged, with zero visibility at corners; and sometimes they are too narrow for on-coming cars to pass. Please drive with appropriate care and attention, and at suitable speeds.

● Some of the roads used for tours in this book are in upland areas. During winter, they could be closed by snow. Consult one of the motoring organizations.

Edited by Gilly Abrahams

The contributors
Every inch of route in *Britain on Backroads*
has not only been carefully planned, but
driven by writers and local experts. The
editor thanks them for their remarkable local
knowledge, painstaking research, and the
hours spent not only at the typewriter, but
behind the wheel.

Routeplanner atlas
Bottlenecks survey by regional officers of The
Royal Automobile Club

Long-distance routes
Devised, driven and described by
Christopher Hall

Local tours
Land's End and Lizard; Bodmin and
Boscastle; Looe, Polperro and Mount
Edgcumbe: **David and Hilary Platten**
Totnes and Slapton Sands: **John Weir**
Bude and Bideford; Exmoor: **Brian Pearce**

Dartmoor: **Liz Prince**
Honiton, Exmouth and Lyme: **George
Pridmore**
Purbeck; Cranborne Chase; Salisbury,
Stonehenge and Wilton; The Mendips and
Somerset Levels: **Andrew Duncan**
Blackmoor Vale and the Dorset Hills: **Gilly
Abrahams**
New Forest: **Fiona Duncan**
South Downs: **Patricia Amos**
The Weald and the Cinque Ports; Chilterns
and Thames Valley; Constable Country; The
Suffolk Coast; The Leicestershire Uplands;
Norwich and the Norfolk Coast: **Richard
Beech**
Winchester and Selborne; The Surrey Hills
and North Downs; Cambridge, Ely and the
Fens; Lower Wye and the Forest of Dean:
John Nolan
Vale of White Horse; Cotswolds: **Linda Hart**
Pembrokeshire: **Brian John**
Brecon Beacons and Black Mountains: **Louise
Heinemann**
Mid Wales; Cadair Idris and Lake Vyrnwy;
Bala and Harlech; Lleyn and Snowdon;
Blaenau Ffestiniog and the Conwy Valley;

Anglesey and the Menai Strait: **James
Knowles**
The Upper Wye; The Shropshire Highlands:
Harry Baker
The Malverns: **Wilfred Harper**
Shakespeare Country: **Maurice Rotheroe**
The White Peak: **Neil Coates**
The Forest of Bowland; The South Pennines;
The Dales; The Dark Peak: **Colin Speakman**
The Lincolnshire Wolds; The Yorkshire
Wolds; The North Yorkshire Moors;
Teesdale; Alnwick and the Northumberland
Coast: **Bill Glenton**
Caldbeck, Buttermere and Derwent Water;
Windermere, Eskdale and Coniston Water:
Geoffrey Berry
Scotland – all tours: **Leslie and Adrian
Gardiner**

Further acknowledgements and a full list of
picture credits appear on page 240

Contents

Introduction

Y ou only have to do a drive from *Britain on Backroads* to rediscover what you always knew: Britain is quite startlingly rich in things to see and do; in history, in quirky fascination, and marvellous, infinitely beautiful and varied countryside. Moreover, Britain's network of country backroads is exceptional in its own right: the perfect partner for – the key to – that bounty of interest and scenery.

But before being carried away by the prospect, you could do worse than reflect on the experiences of Rat, Mole and Toad in Kenneth Grahame's *The Wind in the Willows* when they set out one day to sample the joys of the country byways. They were strolling quietly along a country road with their horse-drawn, canary-coloured cart when

'. . . far behind them they heard a faint warning hum, like the drone of a distant bee. Glancing back, they saw a small cloud of dust, with a dark centre of energy, advancing on them at incredible speed, while from out the dust a faint 'Poop-poop!' wailed like an uneasy animal in pain. Hardly regarding it, they turned to resume their conversation, when in an instant (as it seemed) the peaceful scene was changed, and with a blast of wind and a whirl of sound that made them jump for the nearest ditch, it was on them! The 'poop-poop' rang with a brazen shout in their ears, they had a moment's glimpse of an interior of glittering plate glass and rich morocco, and the magnificent motorcar, immense, breath-snatching, passionate, with its pilot tense and hugging his wheel, possessed all earth and air . . .'

Countless fans of Kenneth Grahame's classic regard that wonderful passage as nothing less than prophetic. It sums up, especially for the British, with their deep-rooted feelings about the countryside, the awful impact of the motor car on the sleepy, unspoilt world of the horse-and-cart; and it suggested the power of the alien machine to change an old way of life, indeed to alter the delicate natural balance of the countryside.

When the first edition of *The Wind in the Willows* was published, the age of the motor car was still dawning. Eighty-odd years later, few would deny the truth of Grahame's perception: the motor car has changed the countryside, and, come to that, the world.

However, like any generalization, it is not the full story. The actual outcome of the motor car's impact has, at any rate, been different to Grahame's dark observation about the car possessing 'all earth and air'. Indeed, there are several ways in which the motor car's impact has turned out not quite as badly as it might have done.

During the year in which *Britain on Backroads* was compiled, test-driven and written, the contributors and the editorial team who put the book together talked to dozens of people all round Britain professionally involved in managing the countryside. A broad, but clear consensus of opinion emerged that although some select country roads, particularly in beauty spots, come under appalling pressure from traffic at peak tourist periods, in general, the lesser A-roads, B-roads and unclassified roads of Britain carry less traffic than they did before the motorway system reached its present extent.

One other unexpected comment emerged: that easily the worst drivers on backroads today are not the visiting tourists, but the locals: the Mr Toads of the 1980s are, by consent, the 'young farmer' types. As one National Park official put it: 'They pass you at sixty on the narrowest country lane, but you can still identify them because of the sticker in the back window saying "Young farmers do it wearing wellies".'

Visitors are, by contrast, careful, if not dawdling drivers, and that, ironically, is often the greatest source of resentment against them. One of the most irritating, and potentially dangerous experiences of driving a narrow country lane with poor visibility is rounding a corner to find one must swerve to avoid a car pulled up half-on, half-off the road. No thought has been given to other traffic; the driver, his wife and children are happily picking flowers, or stroking a pony, or answering the call of nature, oblivious of the frustration and anger they have caused.

Country people, 'professional' and 'non-professional' alike, tend to agree that the most unforgivable – as opposed to the most irritating – crime of all is feeding animals. In areas like Dartmoor and the New Forest, where ponies and other creatures roam freely, feeding amounts quite simply to killing. The animals hang about the verges, attracted by the prospect of food; they don't, like humans, have road sense; inevitably, they lumber into the path of oncoming cars, particularly at night when they are blinded by headlights. In the New Forest, a pony is killed most nights on the roads during summer. If more people could witness the miserably distressing and unpleasant consequences of hitting an animal, there would be fewer such accidents.

There is one other perception of Kenneth Grahame's in *The Wind in the Willows* which still has remarkable relevance to driving on country roads. It is, of course, the character of Mr Toad himself; the observation that the excitement of the new, be it a new motor car or a lovely view, simply makes some people behave as if common sense never existed; perhaps even that they don't want it to exist. Carried away by the thrill of discovery, people – responsible ones at that – behave as if they had never considered the possibility of country lanes having poor visibility; or that 20 mph (32 km/h) is plenty fast enough to take blind corners; or that around any corner could be a hedge trimmer, or slow-moving tractor into which one could crash, or, swerving to avoid it, collide with an oncoming car. There are times when something of Mr Toad gets into the best of us: when we think it enough to hoot at a blind corner, and carry on without reducing speed; or when we park in a gateway, or in the only passing place on a narrow road; or tow a caravan down a backroad and then complain at being held up for hours when we meet a farm vehicle which is too wide to pass.

The spirit of *Britain on Backroads* is intended to be one of exploration; of meandering Britain's backroads slowly enough to assimilate the mood of a locality, but also alert enough to take in more than the casual passer-by. Being relaxed – but alert – was, in Kenneth Grahame's view, a great virtue; one which Rat and Mole, as opposed to Toad, possessed in abundance. It is the right approach to safely and considerately using a book such as *Britain on Backroads*.

Touring with *Britain on Backroads*

Happy motor touring depends on three things: planning where to go, and how to get there; actually getting there, with as much enjoyment, and as little frustration as possible; and having fun once you arrive.

The three sections of *Britain on Backroads* enables you to achieve each of these in turn.

The Routeplanner atlas section
The first section of the book is an atlas of England, Wales and Scotland on Ordnance Survey Routeplanner mapping.

At a scale of 1:625 000 – approximately one inch to ten miles (1 cm to 6.25 km) – it is designed specifically for route planning. It shows the motorway system, all the classified (A and B) roads, and some of the most important unclassified roads. In this book, it is complemented by an index of all place names plus grid references (pages 228–240) and a mileage chart (page 51).

The special feature of Routeplanner mapping is its depiction of primary routes – a national network of through routes complementing the motorway system. To travel on a primary route, using the mapping in conjunction with signposts, read the instructions on page 15.

Routeplanner mapping is not intended to give a complete coverage of the road system; it will not guide you all the way to a remote country cottage in a maze of backroads in the heart of mid-Wales. But it is the most useful, and up-to-date mapping available to the motorist who wants to plot the best overall routes; indeed, many drivers use these extremely popular maps and no others.

The Routeplanner atlas section in *Britain on Backroads* is enhanced by two useful additional features.

The first is a survey, conducted by the Royal Automobile Club's regional officers, of major **traffic bottlenecks**, with suggestions, where possible, on how to avoid them.

The second is another survey, carried out by regional contributors, of the most **attractive and interesting stretches** of the roads featured on Routeplanner mapping.

The long-distance routes section
Pages 54–99 of *Britain on Backroads* feature a unique network of long-distance routes extending over England, Wales and Scotland. They are alternatives to driving motorways and trunk roads – the answer, in fact, to many a modern motorist's prayer. They are travelling experiences in their own right: a way of exploring Britain. This section uses not Routeplanner but Routemaster mapping. At a scale of 1:250 000 – approximately one inch to four miles (1 cm to 2.5 km) –

this is the ultimate motorist's mapping, featuring Britain's road system in greater detail, and more comprehensively than any other cartography at the same scale.

The long-distance route network was devised, driven and written by an experienced traveller and writer who chose combinations of unclassified, A and B roads for interesting places *en route*, fine scenery and peaceful driving. The routes are intended to be as simple to follow as the roads themselves allow, and there are directions at key points.

The routes can be followed in part, or for their full length, and whatever your destination, you will discover that some or all of your journey could be taken on one of these routes: hints are given at the start of each route on convenient points to join or leave. Further details on using the section are given on pages 52–3.

The local tours section
The final section of *Britain on Backroads* is a collection of 60 local tours: the key to enjoying yourself once you have arrived. Wherever you are staying in Britain, or wherever you live, you will not be far from one of these figure-of-eight or circular tours, mostly designed to be driven either in a day if you are content to make only two or three stops including lunch, or in two days at a slower pace, stopping to see more sights.

The tours have been researched, devised, written and driven by local experts all over Britain with the object of giving an in-depth introduction to the area. You will find that driving them is a travelling experience in its own right, revealing the countryside in a way that will often surprise, and will certainly be of interest. The routes are largely made up of unclassified roads, linked with A and B road sections. Directions are given at key points for easy route-finding.

Around the routes are picked out an extraordinarily wide range of local sights and attractions: castles and great houses, churches and abbeys, pubs and restaurants, views, museums and exhibitions, walks and wildlife, local history and local excursions – indeed anything of interest to the visitor. No one would want, or have the time, to visit them all: the idea is to select, with the help of the accompanying text, those which interest you most, and then to explore in your own time.

Starting points are suggested for each tour, but you can join them and leave them where you wish. However, you are advised to follow the directions in the sequence given.

Combinations
Don't just use the three sections in isolation. They have been designed to work

together to make driving in Britain as worthwhile an experience as possible.

If, for instance, you cannot make up your mind where to rent a cottage for a summer holiday, or just for a weekend break, the local tours section will be as useful for planning as the Routeplanner atlas, for the text and pictures paint a stimulating and revealing picture of all the great, and many lesser-known, recreational areas in Britain.

Equally, you could use the long-distance section for planning a holiday by considering which destinations offer interesting alternative routes for the drive there and back. You might, however, want to take the first part of a journey quickly, and the second half at a more leisurely pace. For this, the fully indexed Routeplanner mapping will suggest the best prime route for the first half; then, by cross-referencing to the long-distance section, you can plan a leisurely alternative route for the second half. If, for example, the destination is the Pembrokeshire Coast, Routeplanner shows the standard fast route west – the M4 via the Severn Bridge. The long-distance section, however, offers an alternative route the whole way from London to Carmarthen; you could join it at M4 junction 18, or from the M6 junctions 11 or 13, and from there enjoy a magnificent run on backroads through the best scenery in south Wales.

Or, you might like to make a leisurely grand tour of the West Country, starting from Manchester. Starting nearby at Buxton is an alternative long-distance route which goes all the way to Bodmin. Once there, you like the idea of a different route home; looking in the local tours section, you see that there is a string of day drives all along the south coast from Cornwall to Sussex; you meander from one area to the other, making use of many of the roads indicated for the day drives, and pick up the long-distance route from Bournemouth to London. Cutting round London on the M25, you soon join the long-distance route from London to Buxton, and find your way home, still never seeing a trunk road or motorway service area.

Finally, don't just use *Britain on Backroads* in summer: going out in winter and autumn can be just as rewarding, and much more peaceful than during the holiday season.

Hints on map-reading
To get the best from the mapping in this book, first familiarize yourself with the symbols, colour coding and other cartographic features. For the Routeplanner atlas section, these are given on pages 14–15; for Routemaster mapping, used in the second two sections, see pages 12–13.

The colour coding makes the different status of the roads particularly clear; and the shading in hilly areas (designed to indicate the shadow cast by the setting sun) gives a fine impression of relief, indeed makes Routemaster rank among the most aesthetically pleasing cartography in the world.

The unclassified road network – backroads, byways or country lanes, call them what you will – are of course the key to exploring Britain in depth. They are distinctively marked by simple black lines with no coloured in-fill, and the book naturally uses them in large numbers for its routes. After them, the B roads (brown) are the next most widely used, then A roads with two or more digits. These, in contrast to A roads with a single digit (or a single digit and a T in brackets), are often relatively peaceful driving; they are not main roads, and, now that the motorway system is reasonably complete in Britain, they tend to carry relatively little traffic. Naturally, there are exceptions: in the mountainous areas of Scotland, all the roads may be A roads, none of them wide enough to allow two cars to pass, and always as quiet as country lanes in the heart of Devon. Conversely, in the West Country at the height of the holiday season, the B3311 between Penzance and St Ives can be bumper-to-bumper.

Routemaster is highly accurate mapping, a precision product based on detailed surveys: accurate measurement of the ground combined with aerial photography. Road bends only 200 yards (183 m) apart show up with clarity. However, it does not show quite all the unclassified roads, and the names of some small villages and settlements are omitted. In practice, this can be a help to the motorist: too much detail can confuse. On the other hand, it does require active map-reading.

That means, in essence, knowing where you are 'on the map' at any given moment. Understanding the implication of scale is the first step towards this: on Routemaster mapping, for example, a quarter of an inch on the map represents one mile on the ground, and for every mile you travel you should tick off mentally the appropriate portion of map. To do that, of course, you need a point of reference from which to start. This is generally easy when driving: obvious landmarks continually present themselves in the form of villages, side turnings and junctions. Not such obvious points of reference are rivers, railways, water and woodland areas, all shown on Routemaster mapping where they are of sufficient importance.

Perhaps one difficulty in using road maps stands out above all others. You are driving towards what appears on the map to be a crossroads, but on arrival you find

that it seems to be a T-junction, with no road continuing straight ahead. You stop, look right and left, and still see no continuing road; and, understandably, suspect you have lost your way.

In fact, you have come to staggered crossroads. The way ahead lies out of sight no more than 50 or 100 yards down the crossing road, possibly hidden by trees or buildings. The scale of Routemaster mapping can make such staggered crossroads difficult to identify at first glance; but often enough they are just discernible if you examine the mapping closely.

As the purpose of this book is to give you pleasure from driving, and leave you free to enjoy the sights along the way, there are ample route directions. The contributors' brief was to supply them at every point on a route where the way forward is not entirely obvious.

This book is intended to be complementary to, not a replacement for, a standard road atlas. *Britain on Backroads* is in fact the perfect companion for the hardback *Ordnance Survey Road Atlas of Great Britain*, which features the entire country on Routemaster mapping (4 miles to 1 inch scale). Those who find map-reading tricky may feel that the *1985 Ordnance Survey Motoring Atlas of Great Britain* is more convenient. It features the whole of the country mainly at the larger scale of 3 miles to 1 inch and is available in softback at £3.75. And if you enjoy walking, there is another ideal Ordnance Survey companion to this book: *Walker's Britain*, the complete pocket guide to rambling and walking. Its routes, and a wide range of accompanying points of interest, are featured on Ordnance Survey's Landranger mapping at a scale of 1:50 000, and it is published in softback at £5.95.

KEY TO THE SYMBOLS

Two symbol systems are featured on the Routemaster mapping in the local tours section. Those printed in **blue** are the Ordnance Survey's own symbols, standard on Routemaster mapping and showing a wide variety of tourist information.
Those printed in **black** are linked to textual comments written by the book's contributors and editors. An explanation of what they signify is given below; a key to the blue Ordnance Survey symbols is on page 13.

☆ Touring centre; place or route section of tourist interest

△ Outstandingly attractive or interesting stretch of road

▣ Excursion possible

✗ Picnic site

▯ Selected, recommended pub, either in its own right, or because it is on or near one of the routes

✗ Selected or recommended eating place, either in its own right, or because it is on or near a route

⁂ Viewpoint

⚲ Beach/swimming

❢ Walk, ramble or nature trail

⛪ Church; religious building

✝ Cathedral, abbey or priory

✿ Garden

➤ Nature reserve or other managed place; bird reserve

✠ Wildlife or animal interest – in the wild

▰ Zoo or wildlife park

✖ Insect or reptilian interest

◣ Aquarium

⛾ Country park

▦ House or building of historic or general interest

▦ Castle

ⲙ Monument managed by DOE

◗ Folly

⌒ Bridge

⌣ Industrial site, building; mechanical interest

⊼ Ruin or remains

✻ Prehistoric site, tumulus, earthwork or remain

✵ Windmill

▣ Local history or historical interest

⚔ Site of battle

▣ Museum, exhibition or display

⚒ Craft centre; local hand skill or craft display; local wares for sale

◊ Geographical or geological interest; fine landscape

▨ Cave

✿ Plantlife, flowers or botanical interest

♣ Tree(s); woods or forest

11

Key to Routemaster conventional symbols

RELIEF

Feet	Metres
3000	914
2000	610
1400	427
1000	305
600	183
200	61
0	0

·274
Heights in
feet above
mean sea level

Contours at
200ft intervals

To convert
feet to metres
multiply by 0·3048

HEIGHTS IN FEET

Kilometres
10   5   0   5   10   15
Miles
5   0   5   10

4 centimetres to 10 kilometres (one grid square)

1 kilometre = 0·6214 mile   1 mile = 1·61 kilometres

ROADS   ROUTES   STRASSEN
Not necessarily rights of way

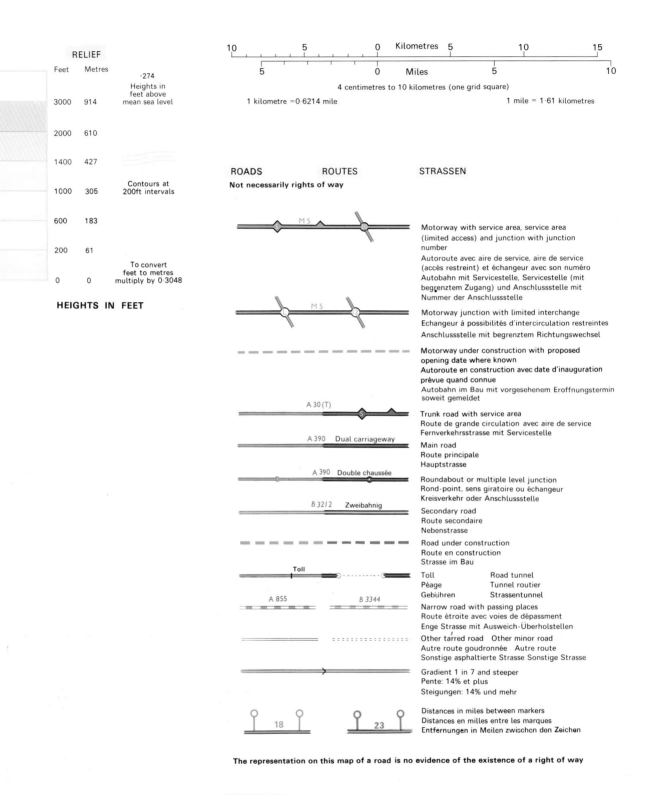

M 5 — Motorway with service area, service area (limited access) and junction with junction number
Autoroute avec aire de service, aire de service (accès restreint) et échangeur avec son numéro
Autobahn mit Servicestelle, Servicestelle (mit begrenztem Zugang) und Anschlussstelle mit Nummer der Anschlussstelle

M 5 — Motorway junction with limited interchange
Echangeur à possibilités d'intercirculation restreintes
Anschlussstelle mit begrenztem Richtungswechsel

Motorway under construction with proposed opening date where known
Autoroute en construction avec date d'inauguration prévue quand connue
Autobahn im Bau mit vorgesehenem Eroffnungstermin soweit gemeldet

A 30 (T) — Trunk road with service area
Route de grande circulation avec aire de service
Fernverkehrsstrasse mit Servicestelle

A 390   Dual carriageway — Main road
Route principale
Hauptstrasse

A 390   Double chaussée — Roundabout or multiple level junction
Rond-point, sens giratoire ou échangeur
Kreisverkehr oder Anschlussstelle

B 3212   Zweibahnig — Secondary road
Route secondaire
Nebenstrasse

Road under construction
Route en construction
Strasse im Bau

Toll — Toll   Road tunnel
Péage   Tunnel routier
Gebühren   Strassentunnel

A 855   B 3344 — Narrow road with passing places
Route étroite avec voies de dépassment
Enge Strasse mit Ausweich-Überholstellen

Other tarred road   Other minor road
Autre route goudronnée   Autre route
Sonstige asphaltierte Strasse Sonstige Strasse

Gradient 1 in 7 and steeper
Pente: 14% et plus
Steigungen: 14% und mehr

18   23 — Distances in miles between markers
Distances en milles entre les marques
Entfernungen in Meilen zwischen den Zeichen

The representation on this map of a road is no evidence of the existence of a right of way

RAILWAYS

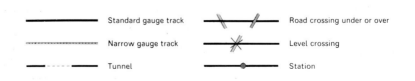

Standard gauge track   Road crossing under or over

Narrow gauge track   Level crossing

Tunnel   Station

WATER FEATURES

(boat)   (hovercraft)

Ferry routes for vehicles
(subject to change)

Short ferry routes
for vehicles

——— Canal

Lake

Marsh

Bridge   Ferry

Cliff

Slopes

Flat rock

Transport for vehicles

Light-vessel

Low water mark

Foreshore

High water mark

Dunes

ANTIQUITIES

⁂ Native fortress

⤩ Site of battle
(with date)

𝔪 Ancient Monuments and Historic Buildings in the care of the Secretaries of State
for the Environment, for Scotland and for Wales and that are open to the public.

Castle •   Other antiquities

CANOVIUM •   Roman antiquity

- - - - - Roman road
(course of)

BOUNDARIES

+ - + - + - + -   National

- - - - - - - { County, Region
{ or Islands Area

GENERAL FEATURES

Buildings

Wood

Lighthouse
(in use)

Lighthouse
(disused)

Windmill

Radio or TV mast

▲ Youth hostel

⊕ Civil aerodrome { with Customs facilities

✈ { without Customs facilities

Ⓗ Heliport

✆ Public telephone

✆ Motoring organisation telephone

+ Intersection, latitude & longitude at 30' intervals (not shown where it confuses important detail)

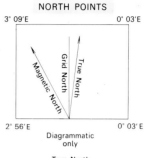

NORTH POINTS

3° 09'E   0° 03'E

Magnetic North   Grid North   True North

2° 56'E   0° 03'E

Diagrammatic
only

True North
Difference from grid north at sheet
corners is shown above

Magnetic North
About 5°W of grid north in 1986
decreasing by about ½° in three
years

PRIMARY ROUTES

These form a national network of recommended through routes which complement the motorway
system.
Selected places of major traffic importance are known as Primary Route Destinations
and are shown on this map thus PLYMOUTH Distances and directions to such destinations are
repeated on traffic signs which, on primary routes, have a green background or, on motorways,
have a blue background.
To continue on a primary route through or past a place which has appeared as a destination on
previous signs, follow the directions to the next primary destination shown on the green-backed signs.

TOURIST INFORMATION
RESEIGNEMENTS TOURISTIQUES
ALLGEMEINE TOURISTENANGABEN

✝ Abbey, Cathedral, Priory
Abbaye, Cathédral, Prieuré
Abtei, Kathedrale, Priorei

𝔪 Ancient monument
Monument historique
Altes Denkmal

Aquarium
Aquarium
Aquarium

Ⱥ Camp site
Terrain de camping
Campingplatz

Caravan site
Terrain pour caravanes
Wohnwagenplatz

Castle
Château
Schloss

Cave
Caverne
Höhle

Country park
Parc naturel
Landschaftspark

Craft centre
Centre artisanal
Zentrum für Kunsthandwerk

Garden
Jardin
Garten

Golf course or links
Terrain de golf
Golfplatz

Historic house
Manoir, Palais
Historisches Gebäude

ℹ Information centre
Bureau de renseignements
Informationsbüro

Motor racing
Course automobiles
Autorennbahn

Museum
Musée
Museum

Nature or forest trail
Sentier signalisé pour piétons
Wanderweg (Natur- bzw. Waldkunde)

Nature reserve
Réserve naturelle
Naturschutzgebiet

☆ Other tourist feature
Autre site intéressant
Sonstige Sehenswurdigkeit

✕ Picnic site
Emplacement de pique-nique
Picknickplatz

Preserved railway
Chemin de fer préservé
touristique
Museumseisenbahn

Racecourse
Hippodrome
Pferderennbahn

Skiing
Piste de ski
Skilaufen

Viewpoint
Belvédère
Aussichtspunkt

Wildlife park
Parc animalier
Tierpark

▲ Youth hostel
Auberge de jeunesse
Jugendherberge

Zoo
Zoo
Tiergarten

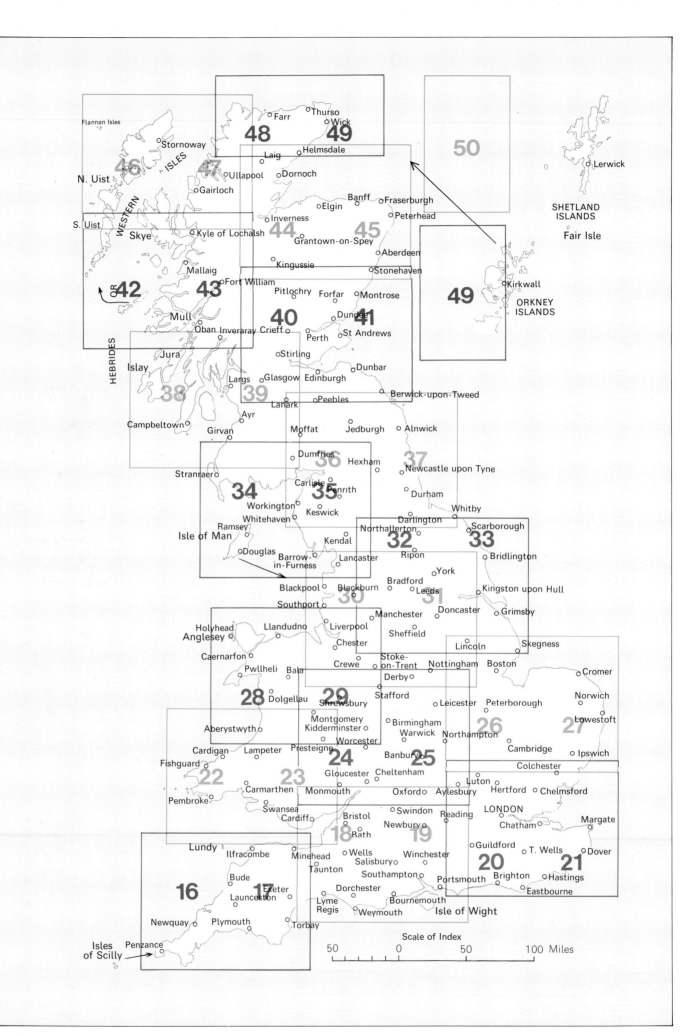

Flannan Isles

Stornoway

46 ISLES

47

N. Uist

Ullapool

WESTERN

S. Uist

Skye

Kyle of Lochalsh

Mallaig

42 OR

43

Fort William

Mull

Oban Inveraray Crieff

Jura

Islay

38

Campbeltown

HEBRIDES

Farr Thurso

48 **49** Wick

Laig Helmsdale

Dornoch

Banff Fraserburgh

Elgin Peterhead

Inverness

44 **45**

Grantown-on-Spey

Aberdeen

Kingussie Stonehaven

Pitlochry Forfar Montrose

40 Dundee

Perth St Andrews **41**

Stirling

Dunbar

Largs Glasgow Edinburgh

39

Lanark Peebles

Ayr

Girvan Moffat Jedburgh Alnwick

Dumfries **36** Hexham

Stranraer **34** Carlisle Penrith **37** Newcastle upon Tyne

Workington **35** Durham

Whitehaven Keswick

Ramsey Whitby

Isle of Man Kendal Darlington Scarborough

Douglas Northallerton **33**

Barrow- Lancaster **32** Ripon Bridlington

in-Furness York

Blackpool Blackburn Bradford Kingston upon Hull

Southport **30** Leeds **31**

Manchester Doncaster Grimsby

Holyhead Llandudno Liverpool Sheffield

Anglesey Chester Lincoln Skegness

Caernarfon Stoke- Nottingham Boston

Pwllheli Bala Crewe on-Trent Cromer

Derby Norwich

28 Dolgellau Shrewsbury Stafford Leicester Peterborough **26** Lowestoft

Montgomery Birmingham **27**

Aberystwyth Kidderminster Warwick Northampton Cambridge Ipswich

Cardigan Lampeter Presteigne Worcester Colchester

Fishguard **22** **23** **24** Banbury **25**

Gloucester Cheltenham Luton

Pembroke Carmarthen Monmouth Oxford Aylesbury Hertford Chelmsford

Swansea LONDON

Cardiff Bristol Swindon Reading Margate

18 Newbury **19** Chatham

Lundy Bath Guildford T. Wells Dover

Ilfracombe Minehead Wells Winchester **20** Hastings

Bude Taunton Salisbury Southampton Brighton

16 **17** Exeter Dorchester Portsmouth Eastbourne

Launceston Lyme Bournemouth

Newquay Plymouth Regis Weymouth Isle of Wight

Torbay

Isles Penzance

of Scilly

Flannan Isles

Gairloch

Lerwick

50

SHETLAND
ISLANDS

Fair Isle

Kirkwall

49 ORKNEY
ISLANDS

Scale of Index

50 0 50 100 Miles

14

Routeplanner Atlas

A complete road atlas at a scale of 1 inch to 10 miles (4 cm to 25 km), ideal for planning journeys: use it in conjunction with signposting (see instructions below) to follow 'primary routes' anywhere in the country.

The atlas also has two special features:

❶ TRAFFIC BOTTLENECKS
The numbers in circles are keyed to notes in the margins describing perennial points of traffic congestion. Traffic delays can, of course, build up unpredictably; featured here are the regular trouble spots identified by the RAC – usually places where roads cannot accommodate traffic volume during certain peak periods, or because of popular local events. Where possible, alternative routes avoiding the bottlenecks are described: follow the directions in conjunction with larger-scale mapping.

OUTSTANDING STRETCHES OF ROAD
Roads which are, in the opinion of *Britain on Backroads'* contributors, worth a detour, because they pass through exceptional scenery, or have special feature(s) of interest.

Scale 1:625,000 or about one inch to ten miles

Miles 10 0 10 20 30 40 50
Kilometres 10 0 10 20 30 40 50 60 70 80

1 mile = 1·61 kilometres

M8	Motorway with service area, service area (limited access) and junction with junction number	Autoroute avec aire de service, aire de service (accès restreint) et échangeur avec son numéro.	Autobahn mit Servicestelle, Servicestelle (mit begrenztem Zugang) und Anschlussstelle mit Nummer der Anschlussstelle
M9	Motorway junction with limited interchange (see diagram)	Echangeur à possibilités d'intercirculation restreintes (voir schéma)	Anschlussstelle mit begrenztem Richtungswechsel (siehe Nebenkarte)
M6 Mid 1986	Motorway, service area and junction under construction with proposed opening date	Autoroute, aire de service et échangeur en construction avec date d'inauguration prévue	Autobahn, Service-und Anschlussstelle im Bau mit vorgesehenem Eröffnungstermin
A6 / A516	Primary routes (see note below) / Main Road { Single and dual carriageway with service area	Itinéraires principaux (voir note ci-dessous) / Route principale { à chaussée unique et double avec aire de service	Durchgangsstrassen (siehe Änmerkung unten) / Hauptstrasse { Normale und zwei-oder mehrbahnige Strassen mit Servicestelle
	Main Road under construction	Route principale en construction	Hauptstrasse im Bau
	Narrow { Primary route / Main Road } with passing places	Etroite { Itinéraire principal / Route principale } avec voies de dépassement	Enge { Durchgangsstrasse / Hauptstrasse } mit Überholplätzen
B 6357	Other roads { B roads (majority numbered) / Unclassified (selected)	Autres routes { Routes B (la plupart portent des numéros) / Routes non classifiées - selectionnées	Sonstige Strassen { "B"-Strassen (grösstenteils numeriert) / nicht klassifizierte Strassen (Auswahl)
TOLL	Gradient (1 in 7 and steeper) and toll	Pente (14% et plus) et péage	Steigungen (14% und mehr) und Gebühren
AA...A RAC...R PO...T	Telephone call box	Téléphone	Fernsprecher
+·+·+·+·+·+·+·+	National Boundary	Limite d'Etat	Staatsgrenze
	County or Region Boundary	Limite de Comté	Grafschaftsgrenze
	Large Town Town Village	Localité importante Bourg Village	Grössere Stadt Stadt Dorf
⊕	Airport	Aéroport	Flughafen
	By sea { Internal ferry route / External ferry route	Par mer { Itinéraire intérieur pour bateau-ferry / Itinéraire extérieur pour bateau-ferry	Schiffahrtsweg { Fähre Inland / Fähre Ausland
	By Motorail (see diagram)	Par Motorail (voir schéma)	Per Motorail (siehe Nebenkarte)
Ferry	Short ferry routes for vehicles are annotated Ferry	Les courtes traversées en bac pour les véhicules sont indiquées Ferry	Kurze Fährstrecken für Kraftfahrzeuge sind mit Ferry bezeichnet
	Canal	Canal	Kanal
	Coastline, river and lake	Littoral, fleuve ou rivière et lac	Kuste, Fluss und see
427.	Height (metres)	Altitude (metres)	Höhe (in Metern)

Primary Routes. These form a national network of recommended through routes which complement the motorway system. Selected places of major traffic importance are known as Primary Route Destinations and are shown on this map thus DUNDEE. This relates to the directions on road signs which on Primary Routes have a green background. To travel on a Primary Route, follow the direction to the next Primary Destination shown on the green-backed road signs. On this map Primary Route road numbers are shown in green as indicated in the legend above and distances along Primary Routes, in miles, are also marked in green.
Motorways. A similar situation occurs with motorway routes where numbers and mileages, shown in blue on this map, correspond to the blue background of motorway road signs.

Itinéraires principaux. Ceux-ci constituent un réseau national d'itinéraires directs recommandés complétant le système d'autoroutes. On désigne par Destinations d'itinéraire principal, par exemple DUNDEE, les noeuds routiers de grande importance. Celles-ci sont indiquées sur les panneaux indicateurs qui placés sur les itinéraires principaux ont un fond vert. Pour suivre un itinéraire principal, il convient de suivre les indications relatives à la destination importante suivante figurant sur les panneaux à fond vert. Sur la présente carte, les numéros de route sur un itinéraire principal sont indiqués en vert ainsi qu'il est précisé dans la légende ci-dessus. Les distances sur les itinéraires principaux décomptées par milles sont également indiquées en vert.
Autoroutes. De même, dans le cas des autoroutes, les numéros et les distances figurent en bleu sur la carte, cette couleur étant la même que celle du fond (bleu) des panneaux indicateurs d'autoroute.

Strassen 1. Ordnung bilden ein nationales Netz empfohlener Durchgangsstrassen, die das Autobahnsystem ergänzen. Gewisse Orte, die von grösserer Bedeutung für den Verkehr sind-sogenannte Bestimmungsorte-werden auf dieser Karte folgendermassen gekennzeichnet DUNDEE. Diese Kennzeichnung entspricht den Hinweisen an den Schildern, die auf Strassen 1. Ordnung einen grünen Hintergrund haben. Will man seine Fahrt auf einer Strasse 1. Ordnung fortsetzen, so muss man den Hinweisschildern folgen, auf denen die Fahrthinweise zum nächsten Bestimmungsort auf grünem Hintergrund angegeben sind. Auf dieser Karte erfolgt die Numerierung der Strassen 1. Ordnung in grüner Farbe, wie in der Zeichenerklärung oben dargestellt. Ebenso sind die Entfernungen in Meilen auf Strassen 1. Ordnung grün beziffert.
Autobahnen. Bei Autobahnen lässt sich ein ähnliches Verfahren anwenden, wobei die auf dieser Karte in blauer Farbe markierten Strassennummern und Entfernungen den Autobahnschildern mit blauem Hintergrund entsprechen.

① **Traffic delays at Fraddon/Indian Queens particularly on Sat in Jul and Aug affecting motorists leaving Newquay and other north Cornwall resorts.** Try to leave early or delay start so as to arrive at congestion point outside the peak time of 9 am to 2 pm.
ALTERNATIVE Holiday Route indicated on the leaflet widely available at petrol stations. Holiday routes are clearly signposted at each junction by yellow signs bearing the legend HR. At the start of each route there are advance direction signs indicating the congestion points.

② **Traffic delays at Penzance Jul and Aug.**
ALTERNATIVE Holiday Route – see ① above.

③ **Delays, especially to through traffic on the A39 caused by the Royal Cornwall Show, usually the first weekend in Jun.**
ALTERNATIVE Avoid the A39 between Camelford and its junction with the A30 at Fraddon/Indian Queens. Instead use the B3266, A389 and A391 to pass between the A39 SW of Camelford and the A30 near the start of the Bodmin bypass.

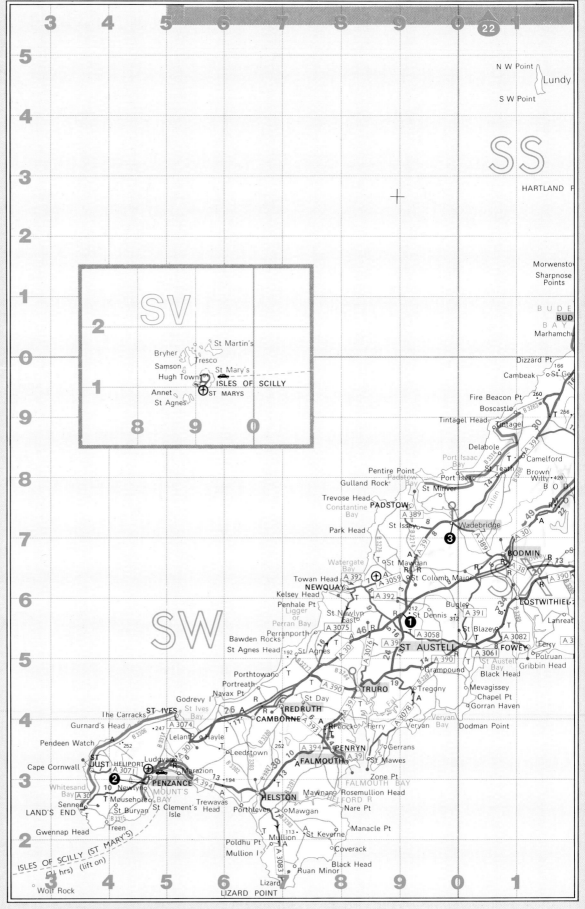

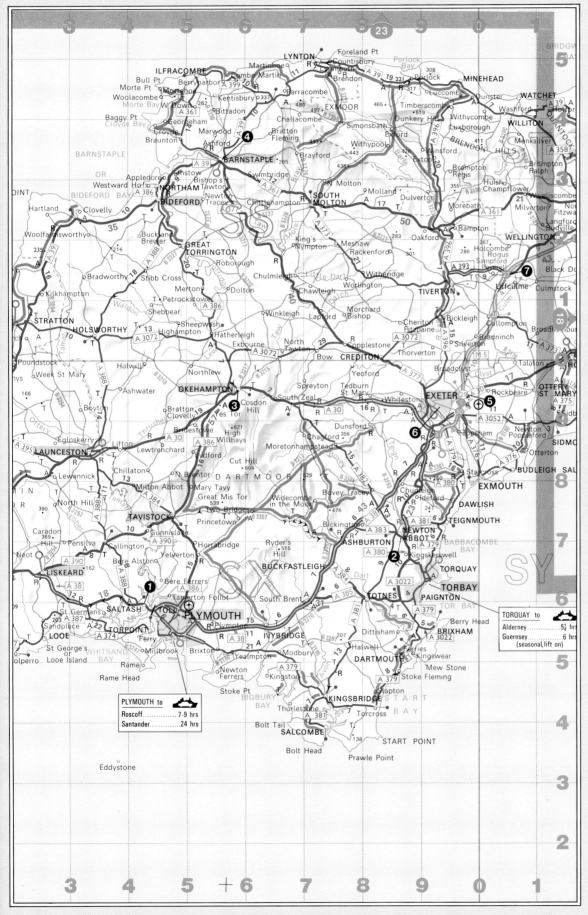

① **The Tamar Bridge on the A38 at Saltash just W of Plymouth is a bottleneck especially during peak periods.** Try to avoid, particularly between 10 am and 4 pm on Sat in Jul and Aug.

② **Traffic delays at Newton Abbot, particularly on Sat in July and Aug., affecting motorists leaving Torquay and other south Devon resorts.** Try to leave early or delay start so as not to arrive at the congestion point between the peak times of 9 am and 2 pm.

③ **Bottlenecks at Okehampton, also** ④ **Barnstaple and** ⑤ **on the A30 NE of Exeter.** ALTERNATIVE Holiday Routes indicated on the official leaflet widely available at petrol stations. (See ① on page 16.)

⑥ **Congestion on roads around the Devon County Show, Exeter, mid-May.** ALTERNATIVE Skirt Exeter area completely using the M5 between junctions 31 and 28.

⑦ **Heavy traffic on the M5 especially Jun, Jul and Aug, affecting traffic for the South West.** ALTERNATIVE for those going to north Devon and Cornwall: leave M5 at junction 27 and continue via Tiverton and Crediton.

TORQUAY to
Alderney...............5½ hrs
Guernsey...............6 hrs
(seasonal, lift on)

PLYMOUTH to
Roscoff.............. 7-9 hrs
Santander............24 hrs

① **M5 congestion, especially summer weekends, affecting southbound traffic.**
ALTERNATIVE Leave motorway at junction 14 and use the A38 to rejoin at junction 16; or turn right at Alveston, or Rudgeway, B4461 through Elberton to Aust roundabout and A403 coast road to Avonmouth to rejoin M5 at junction 18.

② **Delays at Wells during the holiday season can affect traffic bound for Glastonbury and the South West.**
ALTERNATIVE Use the A38 from Bristol and the A371/B3151 after Compton Bishop; if travelling N from the Yeovil direction, also use the B3151.

③ **Heavy summer traffic through Chippenham affects traffic bound for Devizes and beyond from the M4.**
ALTERNATIVE Avoid the A429 by taking the unclassified road linking M4 junction 17 with the A420. Continue through Langley Burrell, then B4279 and unclassified roads via Studley to the A342 for Devizes.

④ **Bottlenecks on the Severn Bridge, especially on Sat in Jul and Aug.**
ALTERNATIVE Holiday Routes on the official leaflet widely available at petrol stations. See ①, page 16.

⑤ **The Royal Bath and West Show, usually last weekend of May/first weekend in Jun, delays southbound traffic at Shepton Mallet.**
ALTERNATIVE Leave A37 at Farrington Gurney; A39 to Glastonbury; go south *after* the Northover roundabout on to the B3151, eventually rejoining A37.

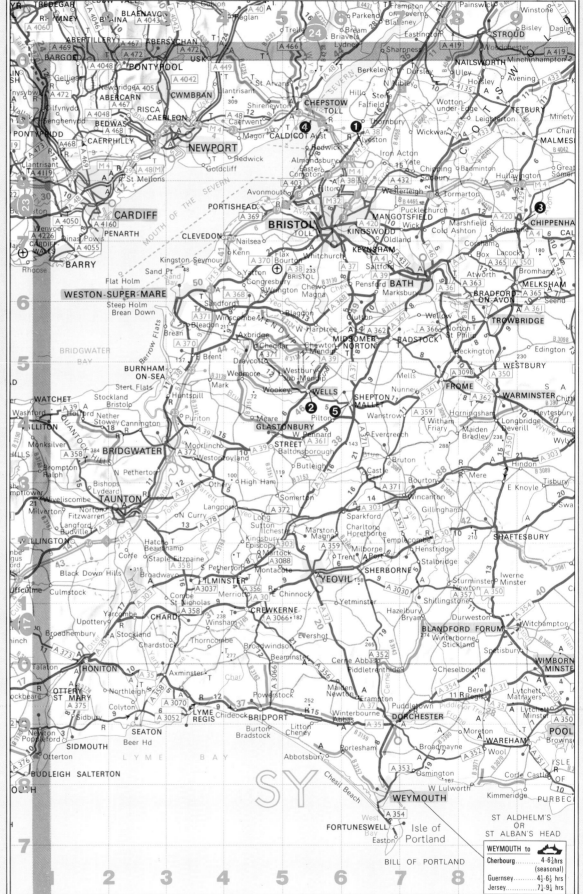

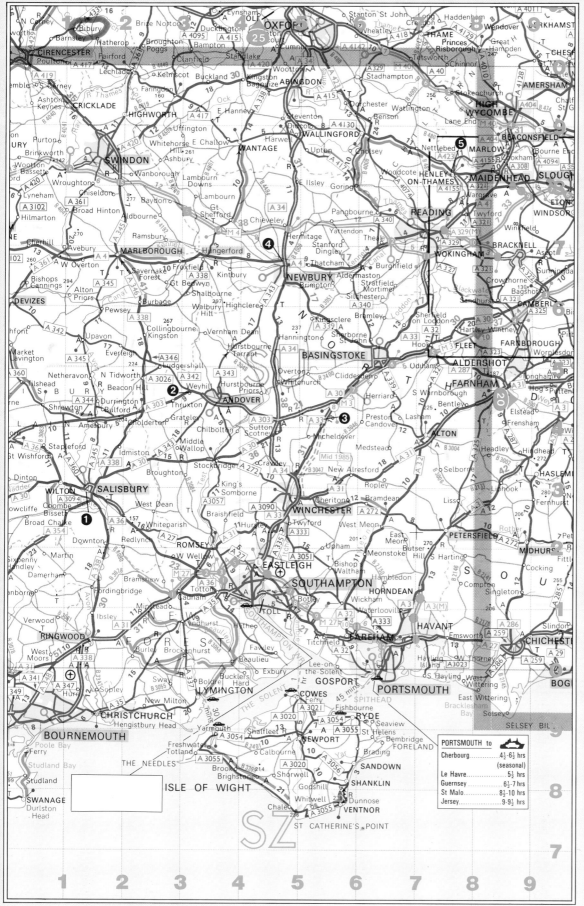

① **Congestion in Salisbury, summer.**
ALTERNATIVE Avoid the city centre completely by using the ring road; or skirt the town by using the pretty unclassified roads linking Winterbourne Earls, Old Sarum and Wilton. From Wilton use the A3094 via Netherhampton for access to the A354 or A338.

② **Delays during the holiday season affecting traffic at the Weyhill roundabout on the A303.**
ALTERNATIVE Leave A303 on Andover bypass and join the A343 to Middle Wallop (Salisbury road). At Middle Wallop turn right on to the B3084 in the direction of Tidworth and rejoin the A303 at Cholderton.

③ **Lengthy delays on the A33 S of Popham, affecting traffic for the New Forest/south coast.**
ALTERNATIVE Leave M3 at the A303/A30 and continue to Bullington Cross; turn left for Sutton Scotney. At Sutton Scotney join the A30 in the direction of Stockbridge where join the A3057. Continue through King's Somborne to Romsey, then use A31 (Cadnam/Ringwood road) and join the M27 at Ower. Or leave the A33 on the unclassified road for Micheldever, continuing to Sutton Scotney and from there as above.

④ **Congestion of A34 approaching Newbury; also around the race course, one weekend each month, Feb–Dec.**
ALTERNATIVE Unclassified roads between A4 and A34 via Donnington Castle and Snelsmore Common.

⑤ **Congestion of A423 in and around Henley-on-Thames during the Royal Regatta, end Jun/early Jul.**
ALTERNATIVE To S of Henley, use B481 to Rotherfield Peppard; unclassified roads to Shiplake; A4155 to Play Hatch; B3018/A4 N of Twyford via Hare Hatch to Maidenhead, and reverse. To N of Henley (going E) unclassified roads from Lower Assendon via Fawley and A4155 to Marlow; A404 to continue N or S.

① **Long delays in rush-hour on the A217 between Kingswood and Sutton.**
ALTERNATIVE Use M25 and A22.

② **Long-term delays caused by road works at junction of M25 and M20.**
ALTERNATIVE Use A2 and M2.

③ **Rush-hour queue on Putney Bridge and** ④ **A205 at Wandsworth.**
Avoid during rush-hour and at other peak times if possible.

⑤ **Dartford Tunnel congestion due to road works. Avoid in rush-hour if possible.**
ALTERNATIVE Use Woolwich ferry or other tunnels.

⑥ **Congestion on A41 at Berkhamsted,** ⑦ **Hemel Hempstead and** ⑧ **Kings Langley.**
ALTERNATIVE Use unclassified roads between Tring and Watford via Wigginton, Bovingdon and Chipperfield.

⑨ **Congestion on A412 at Slough,** ⑩ **Denham and** ⑪ **Rickmansworth.**
ALTERNATIVE (not suitable for large vehicles) Use A, B and unclassified roads via Yiewsley, Hillingdon, Ickenham and Northwood to get from the M4 at junction 4 (Heathrow) and the M1 at Watford. Or, the A416 between Berkhamsted and Amersham; A355 from Amersham via Beaconsfield to the M4 at Windsor.

⑫ **Congestion on the A1 out of London,** ⑬ **the M25 E from junction 23 and** ⑭ **on the A12 between Brentwood and Witham.**
ALTERNATIVE M1 out of London to Watford; E on A405 to Hatfield; A414 through Hertford to Ware; A10 N to Puckeridge and A120 E via Bishop's Stortford, Great Dunmow and Braintree; pass N of Colchester using A12.

⑮ **Congestion on the A406 (North Circular) at its intersection with the M1 – Staples Corner.**
ALTERNATIVE A1000 through Bushey, Elstree, Totteridge and Barnet.

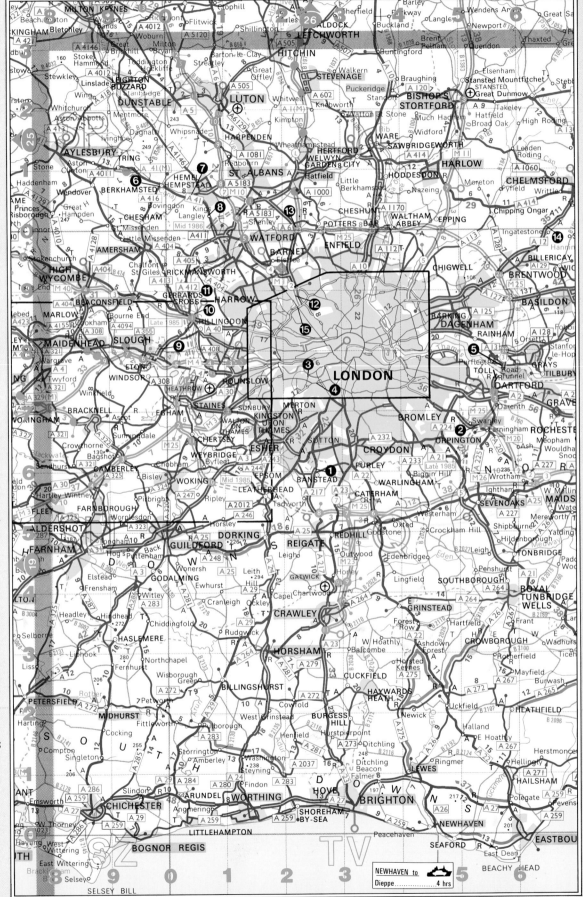

HARWICH to
Hook of Holland	6½-8½ hrs
Cuxhaven	20 hrs
Esbjerg	20 hrs
Hamburg	21 hrs
Gothenburg	24 hrs

SHEERNESS to
Vlissingen (Flushing)	7 hrs

RAMSGATE to
Dunkirk	2½ hrs

DOVER to
Calais	1½ hrs
Boulogne	1¼-1¾ hrs
Dunkirk	2¼ hrs
Ostend	3½ hrs
Zeebrugge	4 hrs

DOVER to
Calais	35 mins
Boulogne	40 mins

FOLKESTONE to
Boulogne	1¾ hrs
Calais	1¾ hrs
Ostend	4¼ hrs

① **Long delays, summer months on A299/A28 between M2 junction 7 (Brenley Corner) and Margate; also ② on the A253 approaching Ramsgate.**

ALTERNATIVE Use the A2 and A28 via Canterbury.

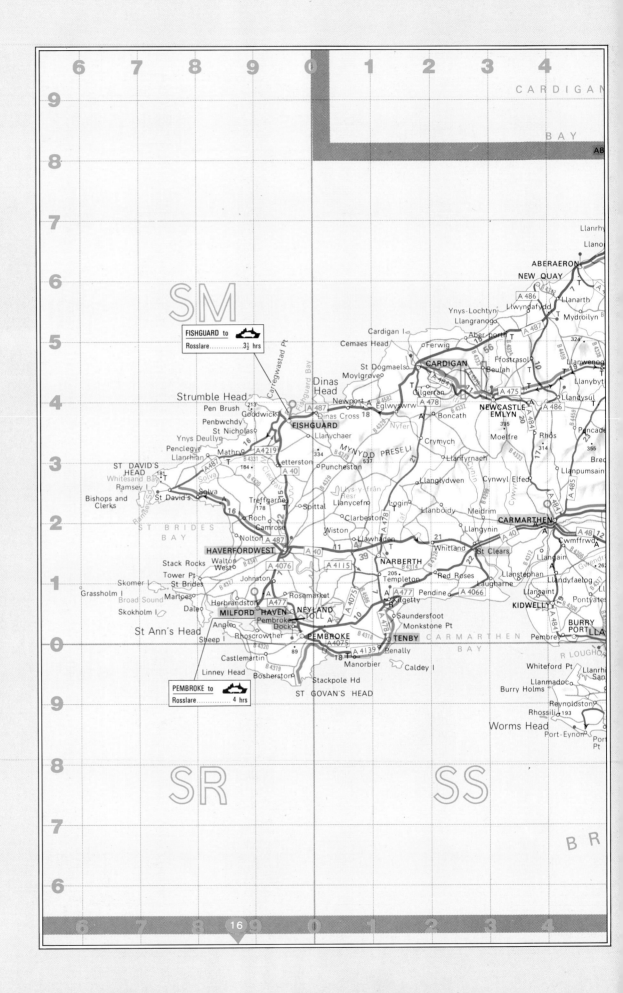

FISHGUARD to 🚢
Rosslare..............3½ hrs

PEMBROKE to 🚢
Rosslare.............. 4 hrs

SM

SR

SS

CARDIGAN

BAY

AB

Llanrhy
Llano

ABERAERON
NEW QUAY
A 486
Llanarth
Ynys-Lochtyn
Mydroilyn
Llangranog
Cardigan I
Aber-porth
A 487
Cemaes Head
Ferwig
56
St Dogmaels
Ffostrasol
Llanweneg
Moylgrove
Beulah
CARDIGAN
Dinas
A 484
A 475
Head
Cilgerran
Llanybyt
Newport
Eglwyswrw
A 478
NEWCASTLE
Dinas Cross 18
EMLYN
A 486
Strumble Head
Boncath
Llandysul
Pen Brush
Goodwick
A 487
A 484
Pancade
Penbwchdy
FISHGUARD
Crymych
Moelfre
Rhôs
St Nicholas
Llanychaer
Bred
Ynys Deullyg
MYNYDD PRESELI
Llanfyrnach
Llanpumsain
Penclegyr
Mathry
A 4219
Cynwyl Elfed
Llanrhian
334
A 485
ST DAVID'S
etterston
537
Llanglydwen
HEAD
184
Puncheston
A 40
Whitesand Bay
Solva
Llys-y-fran
Login
CARMARTHEN
Ramsey I
178
Resr
Llanboidy
Meidrim
A 48
Bishops and
St David's
Solva
Llanycefn
Llangynin
Clerks
16
Treffgarne
Spittal
Clarbeston
Wiston
Cwmffrwd
Roch
Camrose
Llawhaden
21
Whitland
St Clears
Llangain
Nolton
A 487
11
39
NARBERTH
22
Llanstephan
HAVERFORDWEST
A 40
A 4115
Red Roses
Laugharne
Stack Rocks
Walton
205
Templeton
Pendine
A 4066
Llandyfaelog
Tower Pt
West
A 477
KIDWELLY
St Brides
Johnston
Rosemarket
Kilgetty
Grassholm I
Broad Sound
Marloes
A 4075
Saundersfoot
BURRY
Skokholm I
Dale
Herbrandston
A 477
Monkstone Pt
PORT
NEYLAND
MILFORD HAVEN
TOLL
A 478
Pembroke
Pembrey
Angle
Dock
TENBY
CARMARTHEN
St Ann's Head
Sheep I
Rhoscrowther
PEMBROKE
BAY
A 4075
Benally
Whiteford Pt
Castlemartin
18
A 4139
Llanmadoc
89
Manorbier
Caldey I
Burry Holms
Linney Head
Reynoldston
Bosherston
Stackpole Hd
Rhossili
193
ST GOVAN'S HEAD
Worms Head
Port-Eynon
Port Pt

B R

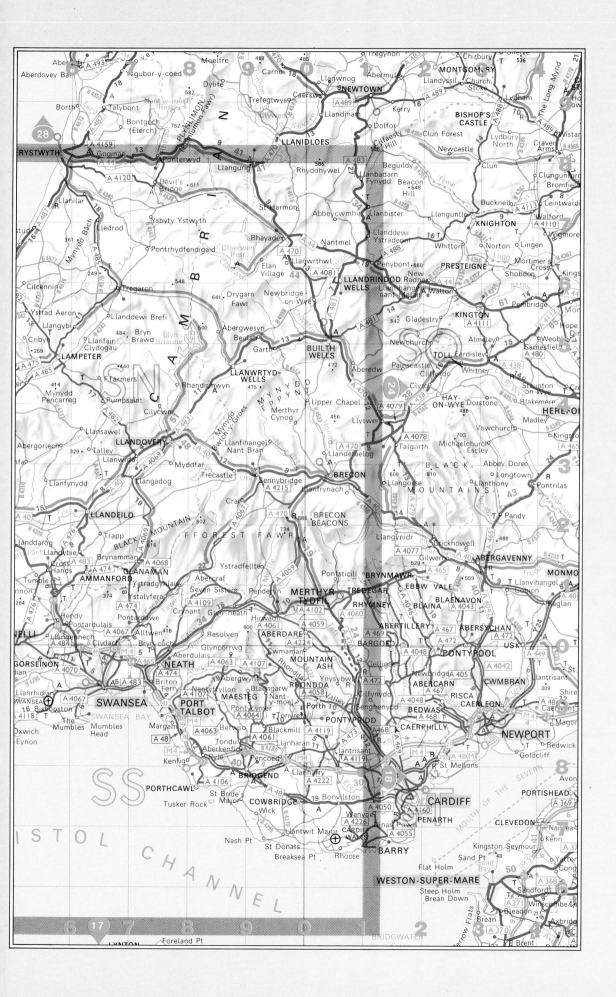

① **Congestion at the traffic lights on the junction of the A49/A44 (The Bargates), Leominster, especially heavy Bank Holidays and weekends through summer.**
ALTERNATIVE for north-southbound traffic B4362 from the A49 near Woofferton to Mortimer Cross; A4110 to Hereford.

② **Congestion at the junction of the A458/A454/A442, Bridgnorth, weekends and holiday periods.**
Avoid if possible, but this is not easy as all routes pass through Bridgnorth High and Low towns. Minor roads around the town are not recommended – in places they narrow to single track.

③ **Congestion in Bewdley most days of the week, particularly bad on summer weekends** – West Midlands Safari Park 1 mile (1.5 km) E of town. Streets into the town from W are particularly narrow.
ALTERNATIVE B4202 and A443 from E of Cleobury Mortimer to Ombersley and reverse.

④ **Heavy traffic through Stourport-on-Severn, summer weekends,** especially approaching on B4194 and B4195.
ALTERNATIVE Same route as for Bewdley, ③.

⑤ **Heavy traffic in Worcester most days of the week, not easily avoided if travelling west.**
ALTERNATIVE North- and southbound traffic should use M5. An attractive route round city (not suitable for caravans) to the SW uses the B4220/A4103/B4232/A4104 via West Malvern and Upton upon Severn to Pershore. The A443 and B4202 for Tenbury Wells and Ludlow, or the B4197/A44 to Bromyard are both attractive routes out of and around the city to the NW, recommended for caravans.

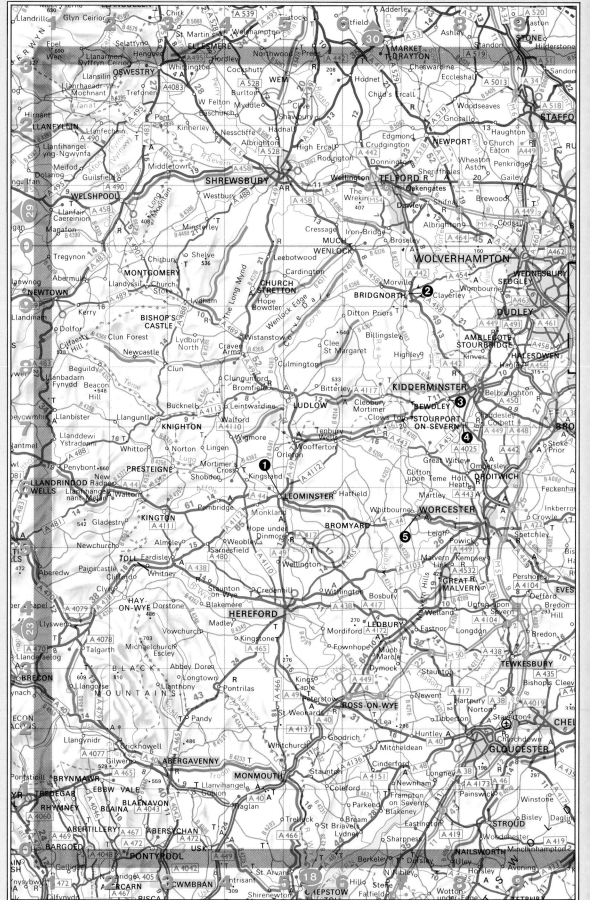

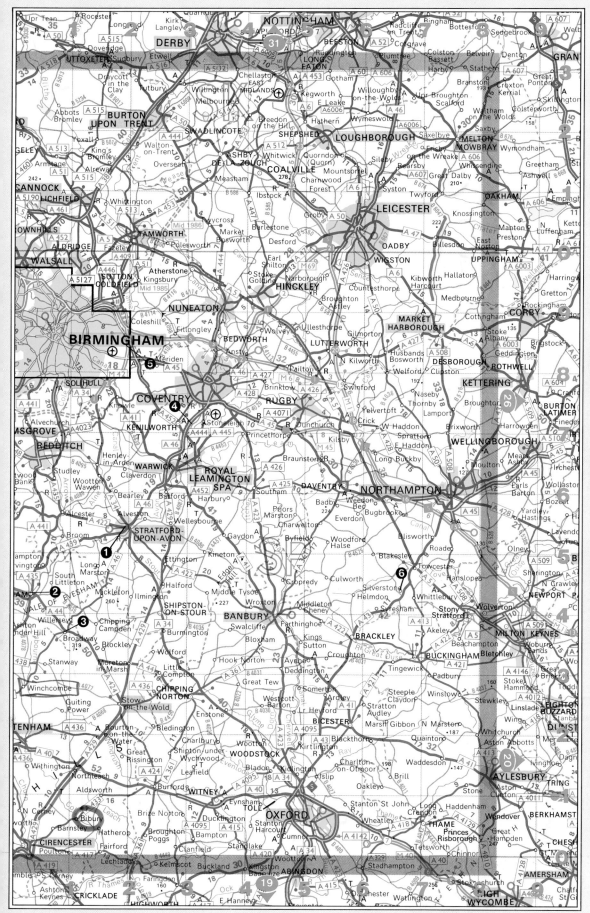

① **Heavy tourist traffic in Stratford-upon-Avon throughout summer.**
ALTERNATIVE Light vehicles can skirt the town to W by using the B4089 from Wootton Wawen and unclassified road via Temple Grafton, Welford-on-Avon and Long Marston to the A34 S of the town. Or, to E by A429 from Treddington at junction with A34; or by Foss Way.

② **Heavy traffic through Evesham in summer.**
ALTERNATIVE B4085/B4035/B4081 via Bidford-on-Avon and Chipping Campden.

③ **Heavy tourist traffic in Broadway through summer.**
ALTERNATIVE Same as for Evesham, ②.

④ **National Agricultural Centre, Stoneleigh:** heavy traffic on approach roads on the Spring Bank Holiday for Model Craft and Country Show: first week of Jul for the Royal Show and on Aug Bank Holiday for the Town and Country Festival.
ALTERNATIVE Use the A46 Warwick/Kenilworth bypass. Follow traffic direction signs and do not use minor roads – many will be congested with show traffic.

⑤ **The National Exhibition Centre, Marston Green:** regular events here bring heavy traffic on the M42/A45/A452, especially the Motor Show, held alternately in even-numbered years, ie **1986, 1988.** Avoid area if possible.

⑥ **Severe congestion on the A43 in and around Silverstone during race meetings, principally the British Grand Prix, biennially in Aug. and the Motor Cycle Grand Prix, annually in Aug.**
ALTERNATIVE Unclassified roads between A43 at Towcester via Abthorpe and Syresham to rejoin A43 S of Syresham.

25

① **Congestion on the A11 affecting southbound traffic.**
ALTERNATIVE Turn right off A11 at Worsted Lodge on to road signposted Babraham, cross junction with A1307, go through Babraham and follow this road to its junction with the A505. Turn right, pass Pampisford; at the junction with the A1301 turn left; continue via Hinxton to rejoin the A11 at Stump Cross. It is possible to do this diversion in reverse.

② **Delays at Norman Cross affecting northbound traffic on A1.**
ALTERNATIVE Going N, turn left off the A1 on to B660 to Glatton. Here turn right on to an unclassified road; at next T-junction turn right again, following signs for Elton. In Elton turn on to the B671 to rejoin the A1 at Wansford.

Main events causing local traffic congestion:

③ East of England Show, Peterborough, mid-Jul; ④ Imperial War Museum, Duxford, throughout season and particularly mid-Sept; ⑤ RAF Alconbury Air Tattoo, late Jul; ⑥ Cambridge Folk Festival, late Jul; ⑦ Spalding Flower Parade, Sat preceding 10th May, closes the town to traffic.

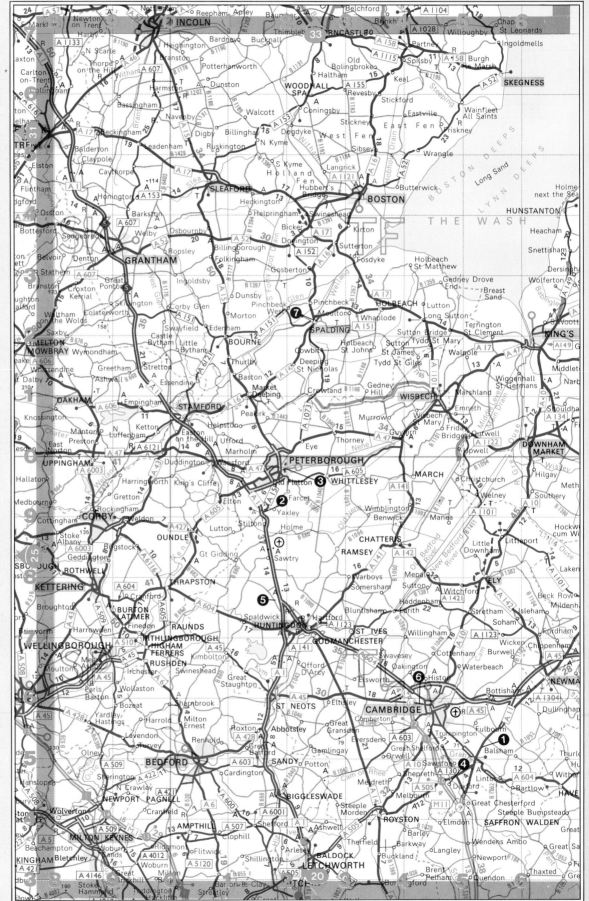

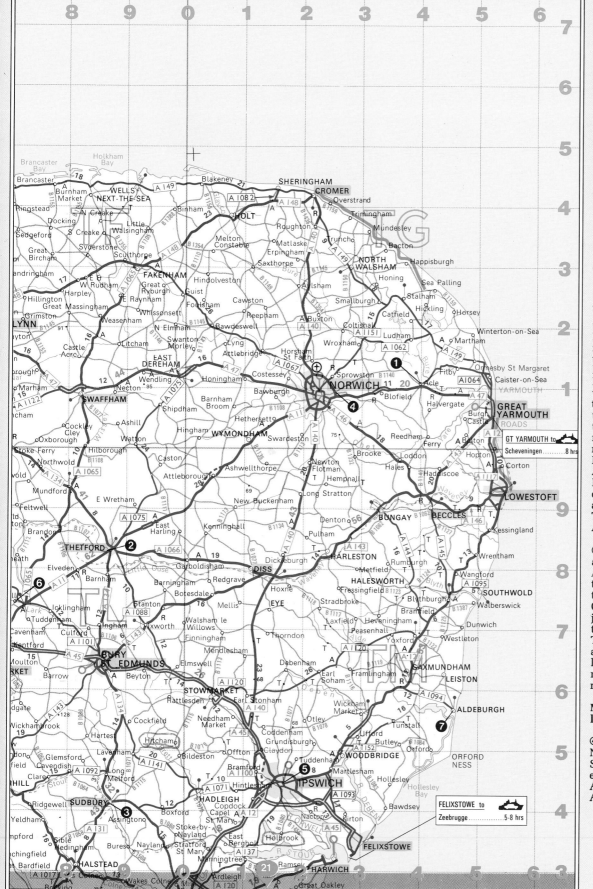

① **Congestion at Acle affecting eastbound traffic on the A47.**
ALTERNATIVE Turn right off A47 on to Brundall road, through Brundall and under railway bridge. Next left to Strumpshaw and continue to South Burlingham. At next crossroads after passing a post office turn left to Lower Green, cross the junction with the B1140 and turn on to the Halvergate road. Continue through Halvergate and on to road signposted Yarmouth. Follow it across Tunstall Marshes to the Stracy Arms and take the A47 to Great Yarmouth.

② **Delays in Thetford affecting traffic on the A11.**
ALTERNATIVE Travelling W turn left off the A11 on to the B1111 to East Harling. Continue to the next major crossroads and turn right on to a road leading through West Harling Heath to junction with A1066. Turn right through Shadwell and take next left to go through Rushford, over a river bridge and turn right for Euston. At Euston turn left on to A1088, then right to Barnham, after which cross junction with A134 and continue across Thetford Heath to rejoin A11; or reverse.

③ **Delays in Sudbury affecting through traffic.**
ALTERNATIVE Going S, turn left off A134 on to the A1141 through Cross Green to Lavenham. Then join B1071 and continue to junction with B1115. Turn right over heath and at next junction take the left fork along the Roman road to rejoin A134; or reverse.

Main events causing local traffic congestion:

④ Royal Norfolk Show, Norwich, end of Jul; ⑤ Suffolk Show, Ipswich, end of May; ⑥ Mildenhall Air Show, early Jun; ⑦ Aldeburgh Festival, Jun.

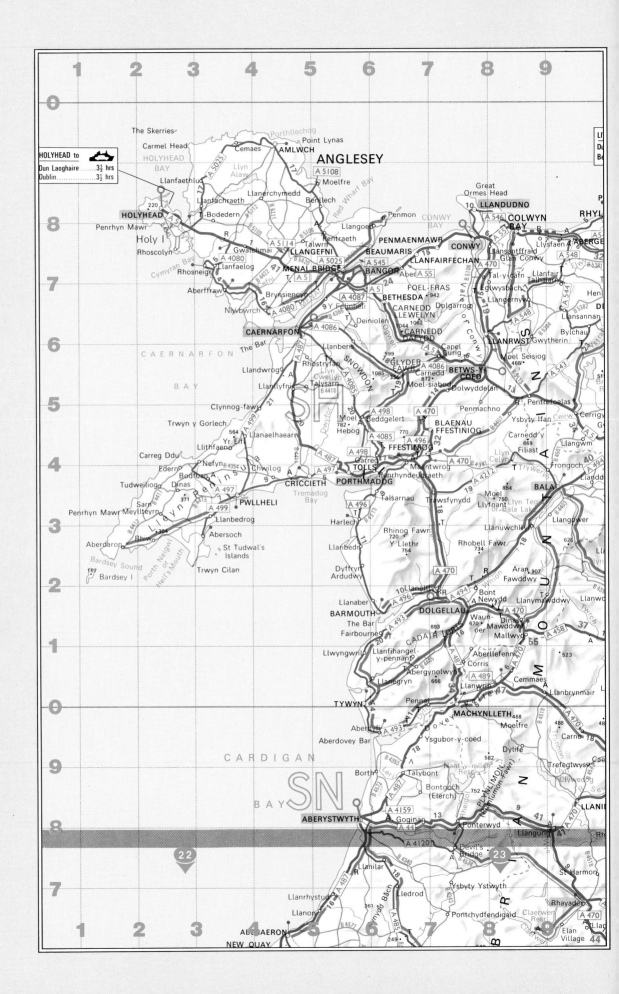

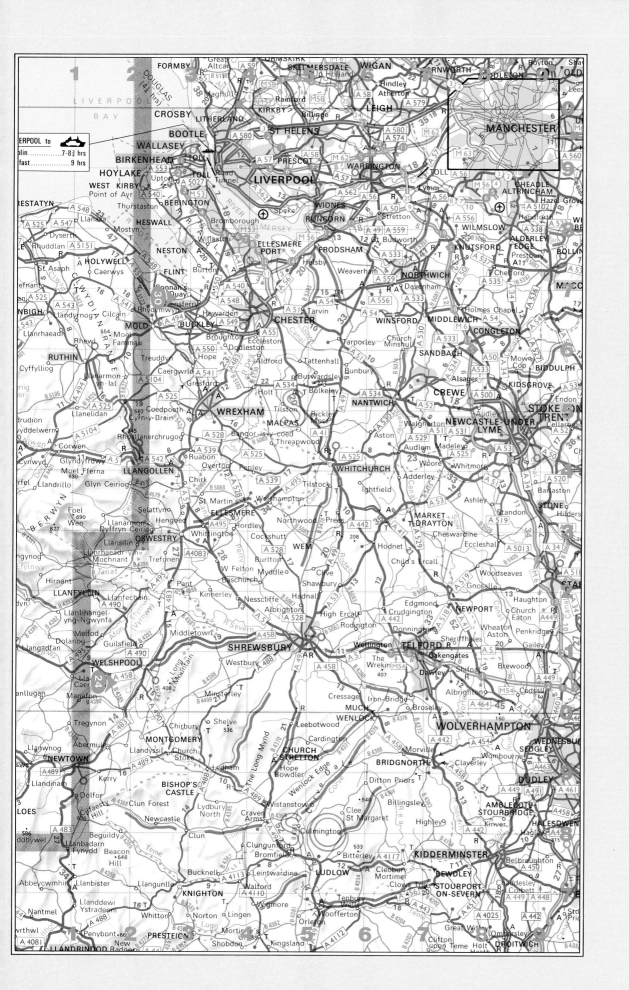

① **The junction of the M6 and M61 (M6 junction 30) cannot accommodate the volume of traffic passing through on Bank Holidays, Easter through to late summer, 10.30 am to 1.30 pm each holiday day. Northbound traffic going to the Fylde area is worst affected.**
ALTERNATIVE If traffic tails back S from M6 junction 28, Lancashire Police will filter traffic off to Lytham St Anne's and South Shore, Blackpool, via the A582 and A583. Similarly for M61 junction 8, via the A6 and A582. No alternatives viable from the S or SE.

② **Congestion at the junction of the M55 and A583 affecting traffic going W to the Blackpool area on Bank Holidays, Easter through to late summer, 11 am to 1.30 pm each holiday day.**
ALTERNATIVE Traffic to Fleetwood, Cleveleys and Bispham should leave the M55 at junction 3 to follow the A585 to Fleetwood; or the A585/586 to Cleveleys, Bispham and North Shore, Blackpool. No alternative possible for traffic heading towards the South Shore area. However, traffic from west Yorkshire, usually using the M62 and M61 could use the M65/A6119/A677 (Blackburn bypass) and A59, then continue via A5085/A583 to Blackpool (south) or A5085/A584 to Lytham St Anne's and Blackpool (south). Traffic for Fleetwood/Cleveleys could use M65/A6119 via Ribchester and Longridge to the A6, then by way of Churchtown and the A586 via Great Eccleston.

③ **Congestion on the M6 between junctions 32 and 30 affecting southbound traffic on Bank Holidays, Easter through to late summer, usually 6.30 pm to 9.30 pm and later.** No recommended alternative route: avoid at peak times if possible.

④ **Congestion on the M63 between junctions 1 and 7 and the M62 between junctions 12 and 17, during rush hours Mon–Fri.**

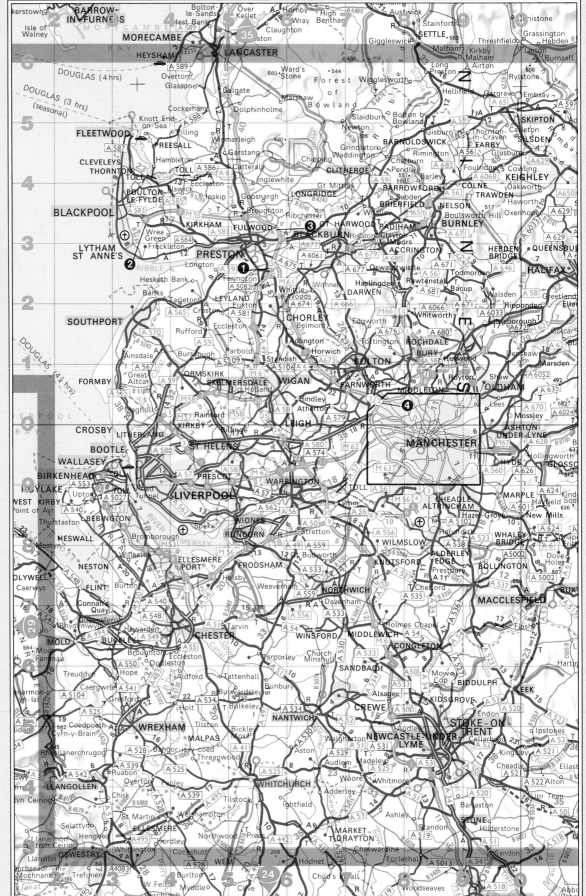

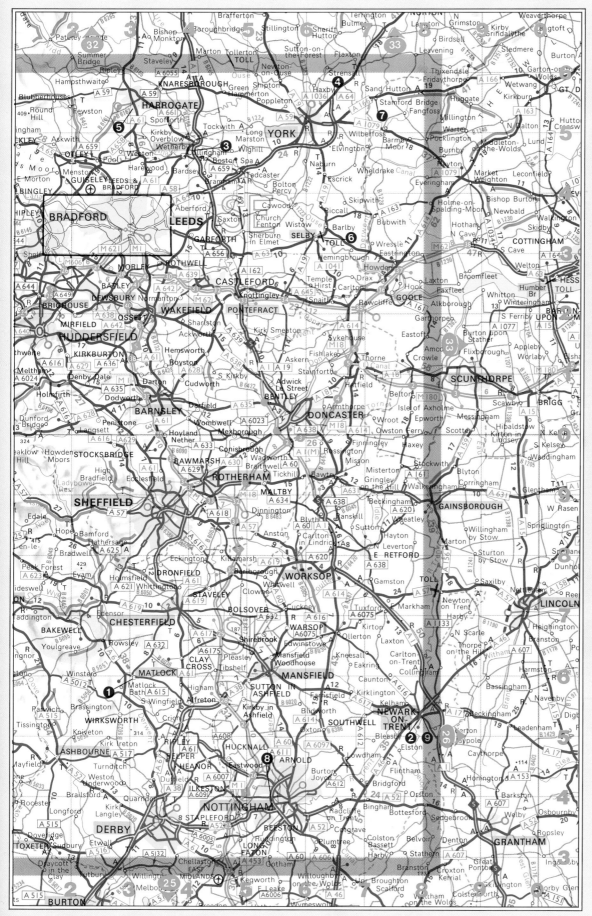

① Congestion at Matlock.
ALTERNATIVE Skirt the town to the SW by using the B5056 and B5023 between the A6 SE of Bakewell and the A6 just S of Duffield.

② Congestion in Newark.
ALTERNATIVE Skirt the city to the N using unclassified roads via South Muskham and North Muskham. Soon turn sharp right on to the A1; continue SE to junction with the A46.

③ Congestion at Wetherby Roundabout on the A1 throughout the year, but especially in summer and on race days – racecourse nearby.
ALTERNATIVE Unclassified roads to E via Thorp Arch, Cattal and Whixley; B6265 to rejoin A1 N of Kirby Hill. Or, if travelling W, use the A659 to Collingham and unclassified roads to link with the A661.

④ The A64 between York and Malton can become very busy, with congestion caused by dual carriageway becoming two-way traffic for several miles.
ALTERNATIVE Unclassified road N from York centre via Earswick and Flaxton to rejoin A64 SE of Flaxton.

⑤ Harrogate town centre is regularly congested.
ALTERNATIVE Skirt town to W using unclassified roads via Beckwithshaw and B6161 or to E via Knaresborough using the B6163 and B6165.

⑥ Queueing to pay the toll at Selby bridge can cause severe build-ups.
ALTERNATIVE Use the M62 or B1222 instead.

⑦ The bridge at Stamford Bridge is small and can cause hold-ups.
ALTERNATIVE Skirt town to N using unclassified roads via Buttercrambe.

Main events causing local traffic congestion:

⑧ The Goose Fair at Nottingham, Thur, Fri and Sat, first week in Oct;
⑨ The Newark and Nottinghamshire Agricultural Show, Fri and Sat, first weekend in May (showground on A46).

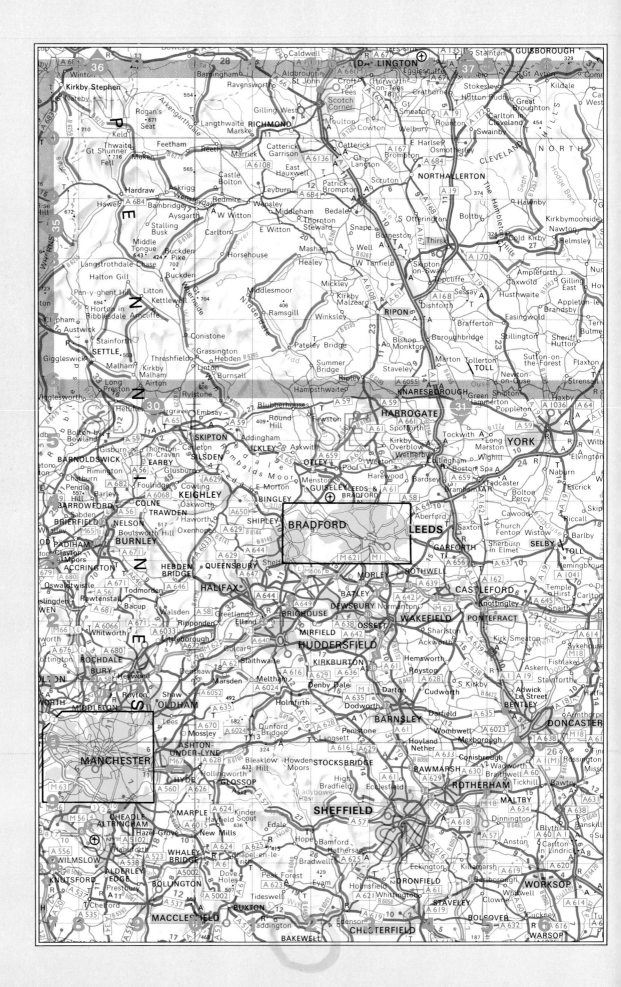

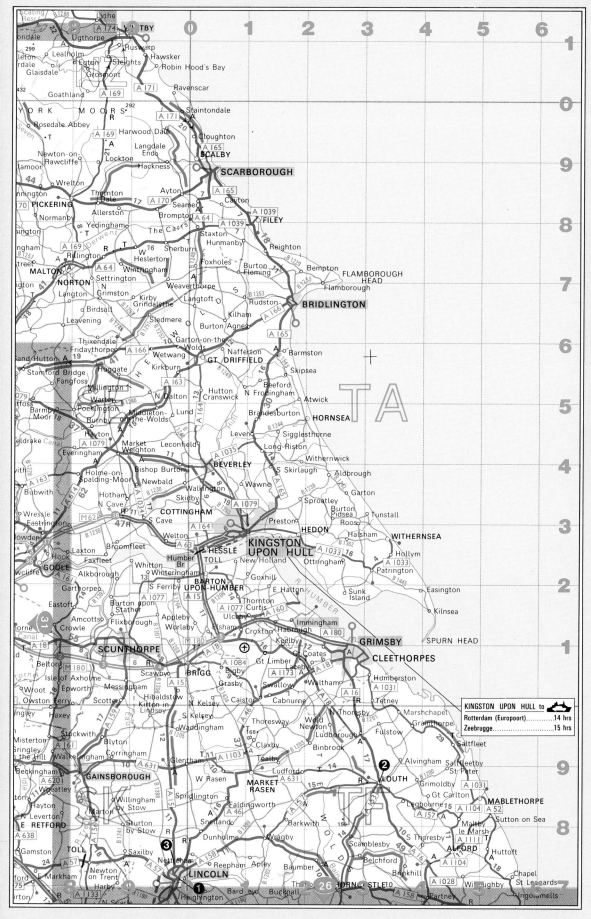

① **Congestion in Lincoln.**
ALTERNATIVE Skirt the city using the A1133 N from the A46 near Winthorpe; in Torksey, head E on unclassified roads via Bransby to connect with the A15 N of Lincoln. From there continue N on the A15 for Scunthorpe and Kingston upon Hull; turn E at Caenby Corner on to the A631 and A1103 to rejoin the A46 N of Market Rasen. A Lincoln bypass is due for completion May 1986.

② **Congestion in Louth affecting through traffic on the A16.**
ALTERNATIVE for southbound traffic: unclassified roads skirting Louth to the W from Ludborough on the A16 via Kelstern and South Ormsby, through the Lincolnshire Wolds to rejoin the A16 NW of its junction with the A1104; or reverse.

③ **The Lincolnshire Show, Wed and Thur of the third week in Jun,** takes place at the showground off the A15 N of Lincoln. Avoid neighbourhood if possible.

KINGSTON UPON HULL to	
Rotterdam (Europoort)	14 hrs
Zeebrugge	15 hrs

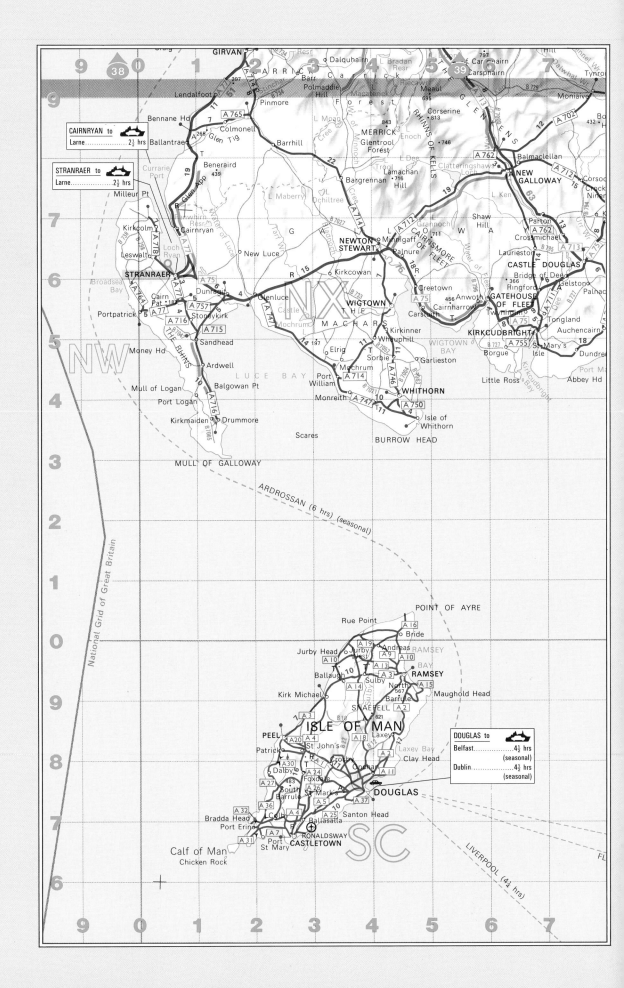

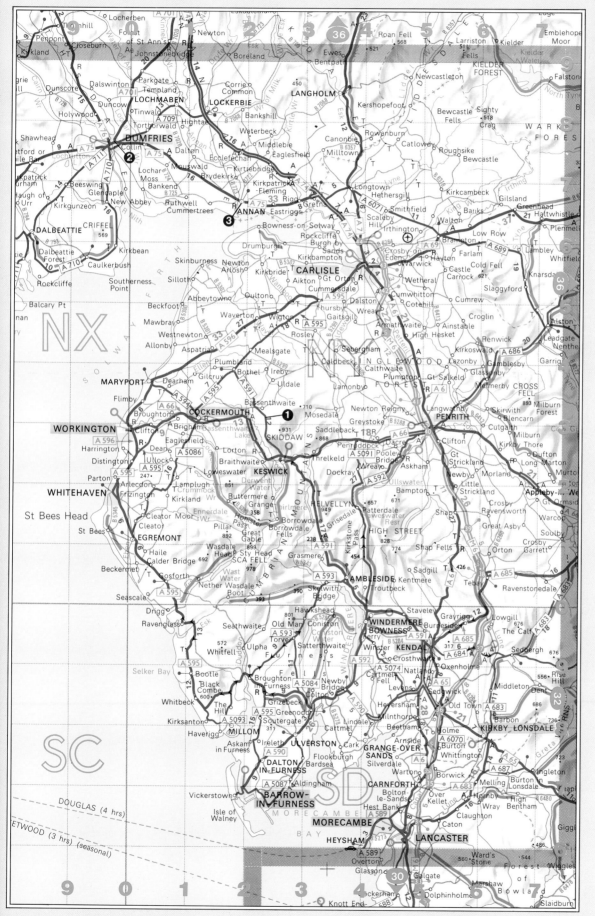

① **Six-fold traffic overloads roads in Cumbria during the holiday season.** Lake District geography makes it virtually impossible to improve the road system; patience is the only 'alternative'.

② **Congestion in Dumfries during the holiday season;** avoid if possible.

③ **Riding of the Marches, Annan, usually first weekend in Jul, causes local traffic congestion.**

① **A74 congestion during the holiday season.**
ALTERNATIVE B725 and B7020 via Lochmaben and A701 via Moffat; continuing if necessary on the B7016 via Biggar, the A70 via Carnwath, A743 via Lanark, A72 via Crossford to the M74 at junction 3.

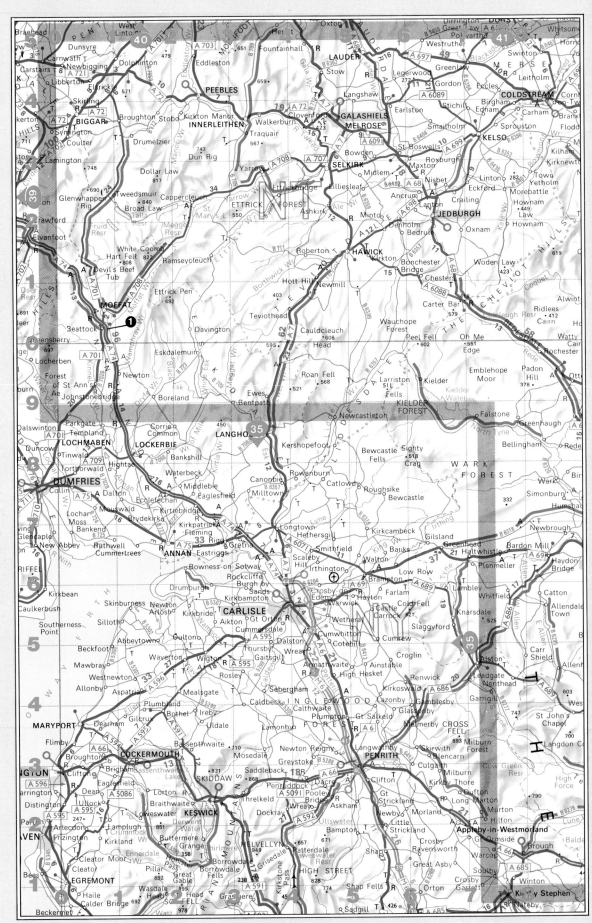

NEWCASTLE UPON TYNE to

Bergen	23½ hrs
	(seasonal)
Esbjerg	18-20½ hrs
	(seasonal)

① **At Stannington on the A1(M) a dual carriageway becomes two-way on a long slow hill climb. On holidays a tail-back can form here affecting northbound traffic.**
ALTERNATIVE Leave the A1 at Fisher Lane roundabout E of the Seaton Burn interchange, turn right at the roundabout on to the A1068, continue along the A192 N for 2 miles (3 km) and turn left at the junction to rejoin the A1 N of Stannington. (A Stannington bypass is planned).

② **Congestion on the A69 between Hexham and Newcastle caused by returning weekend and holiday traffic. Avoid at peak times, especially weekends in summer.**
ALTERNATIVE For traffic heading S of the Tyne: A695 to Gateshead to link with the A69 at Scotswood Bridge.

③ **The B6318, known locally as the Military Road, climbs and descends sharply.** The surface is good, but it is unsuitable for caravans.

④ **The Tyne Tunnel can be congested during rush-hour.**
ALTERNATIVE Use the B6127 through the city centre, and exit N using the central motorway system and the B6125. However, this route can also carry heavy commuter traffic. Through traffic bound for Scotland may find the A6127 from the Tyne Bridge via the A696 to join the A68 N of Otterburn is a useful alternative to the A1 Tyne Tunnel E coast route.

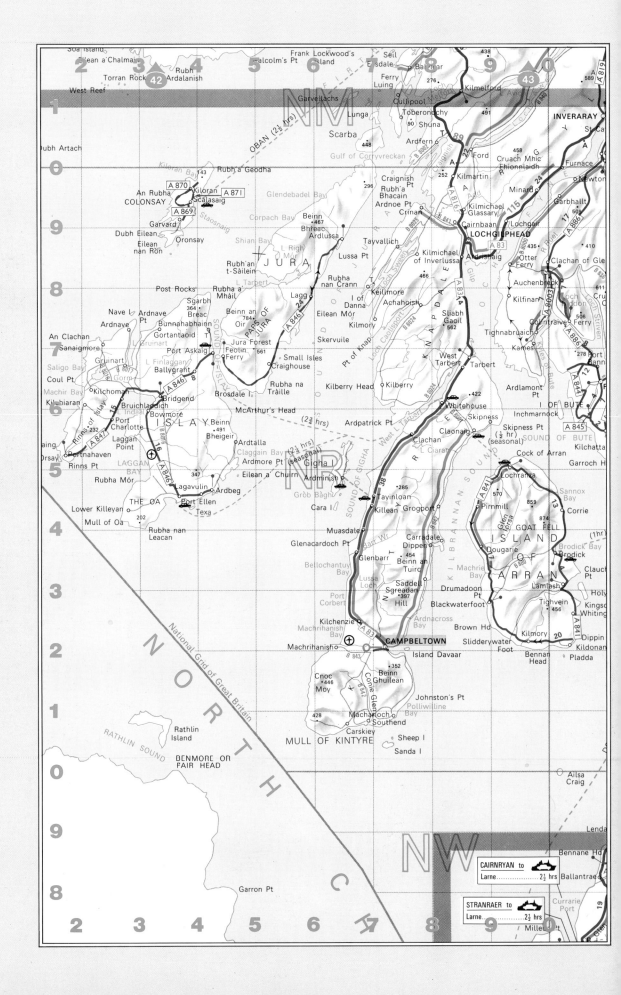

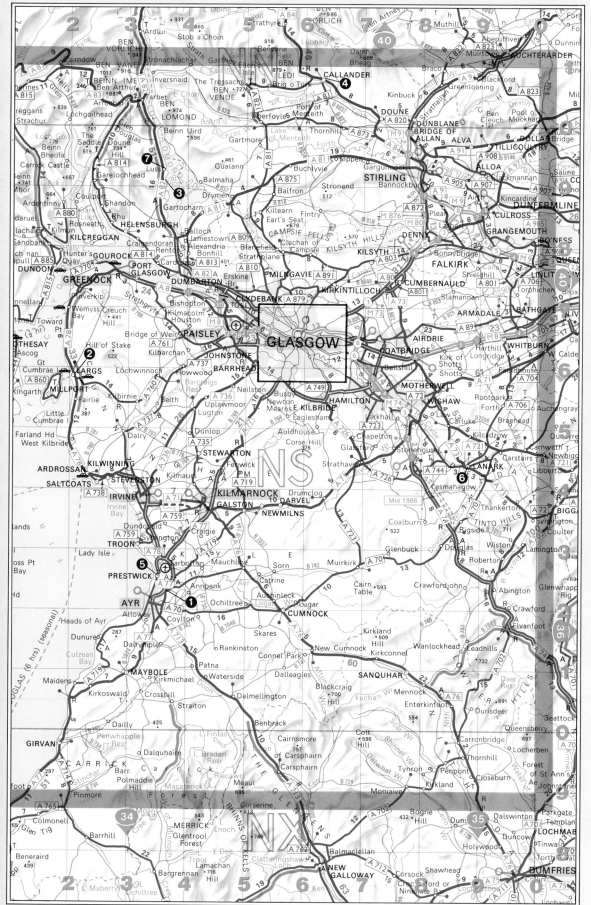

① **Congestion on the A77 during the holiday season.**
ALTERNATIVE B742, B730 and A719.

② **Congestion in Largs; avoid town if possible.**

③ **Congestion on the A82 along Loch Lomond during the holiday season.**
ALTERNATIVE A83, A814, B832 and B831.

④ **The A84 from Stirling via Callander to the west coast (Oban/Fort William) carries heavy traffic in summer and on some weekends the picturesque town of Callander may be a real bottleneck.**
ALTERNATIVE From Edinburgh take the A90 and M90, then the A823, A822 and A85 via Gleneagles and Crieff.

Main events causing local traffic congestion:

⑤ Prestwick Air Show, usually early Jun; ⑥ Lanimers Festival, Lanark, usually early Jun; ⑦ Highland Games, Luss, usually mid Jul.

① The A8 becomes very busy at the time of the Highland Show, Ingliston (usually the third weekend in Jun for five days) and on Sun in summer (Ingliston market).

ALTERNATIVE Traffic from Edinburgh bound for the M9 can take the A90 and A8000. If making for the M8, use the A71 and A899.

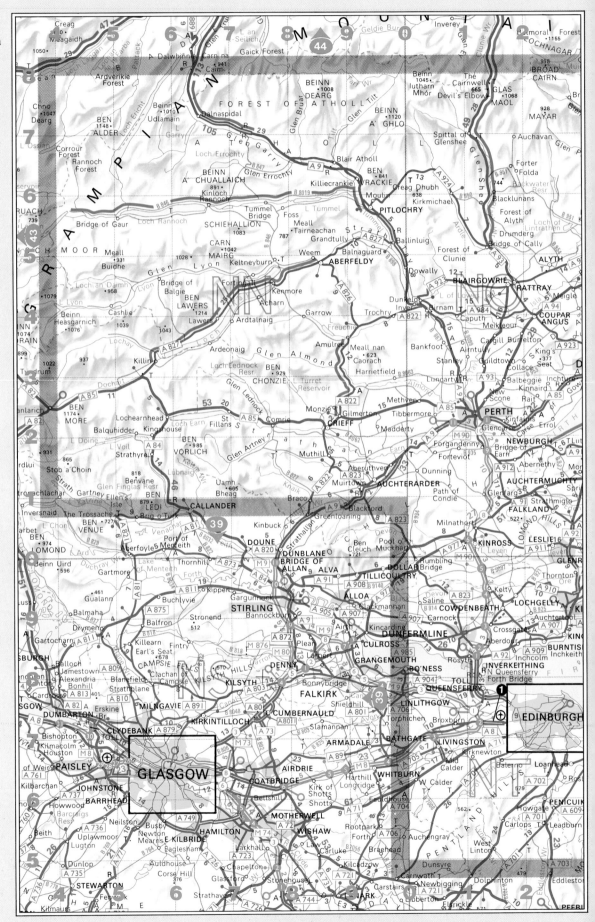

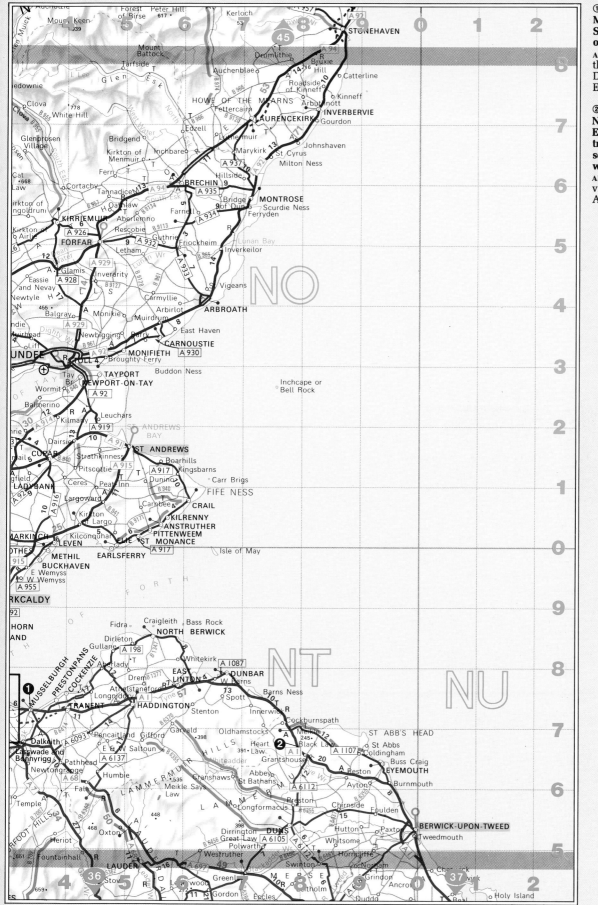

① **The A1 in Musselburgh (High Street) can be very busy on Sun in summer.**
ALTERNATIVE Skirt S on the B6414 and A68 via Dalkeith to reach Edinburgh.

② **The A1 between Newcastle and Edinburgh carries heavy traffic during the holiday season, particularly at weekends.**
ALTERNATIVE The A697 via Coldstream and the A68 from Carfraemill.

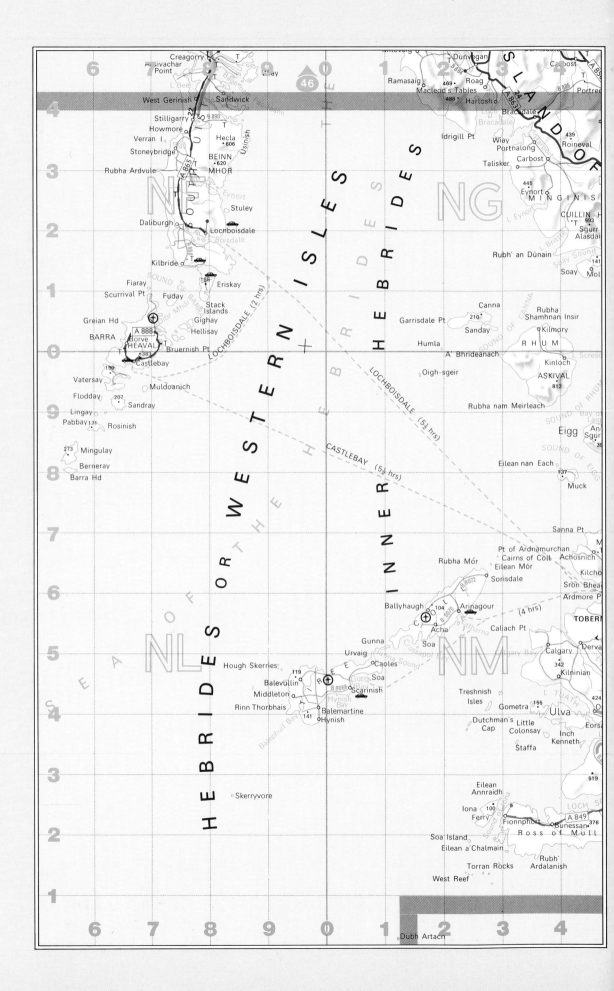

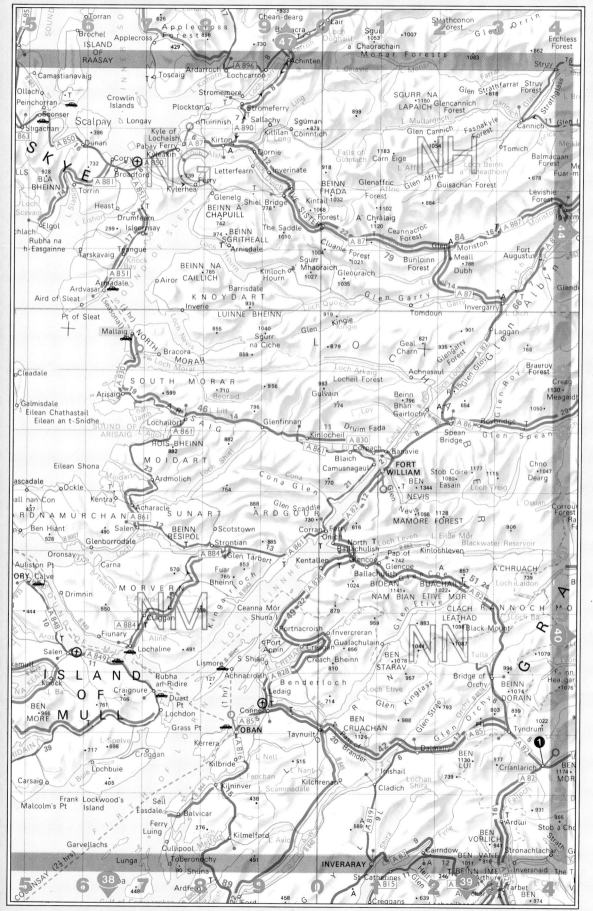

① **Congestion during the holiday season in Crianlarich, at the junction of the A85 and A82.**
ALTERNATIVE Skirt widely to the W, and enjoy some magnificent scenery: A83 and A819 via Inverary; A85 via Dalmally and B8074 through Glen Orchy to join the A82 S of Bridge of Orchy.

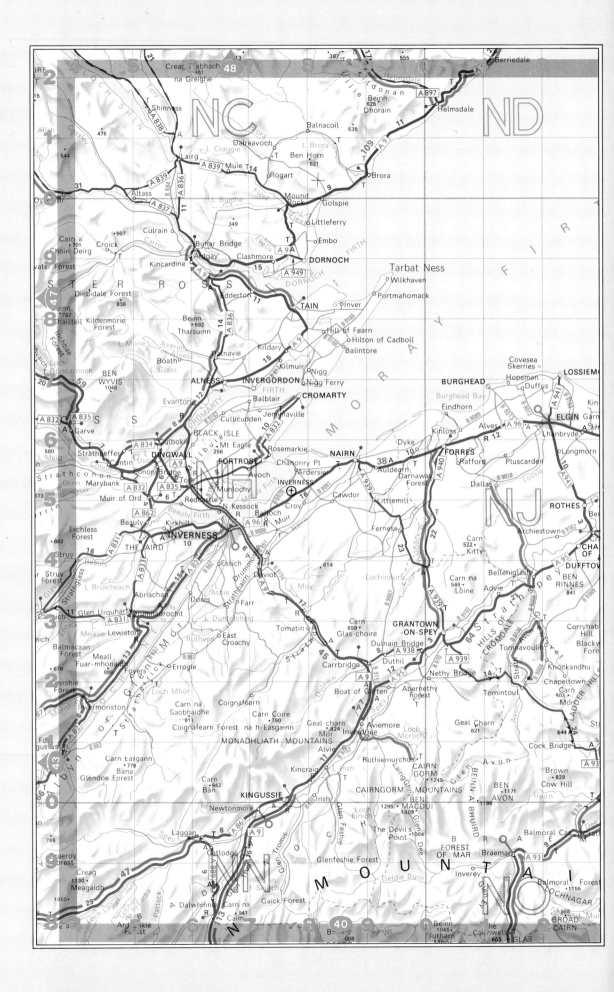

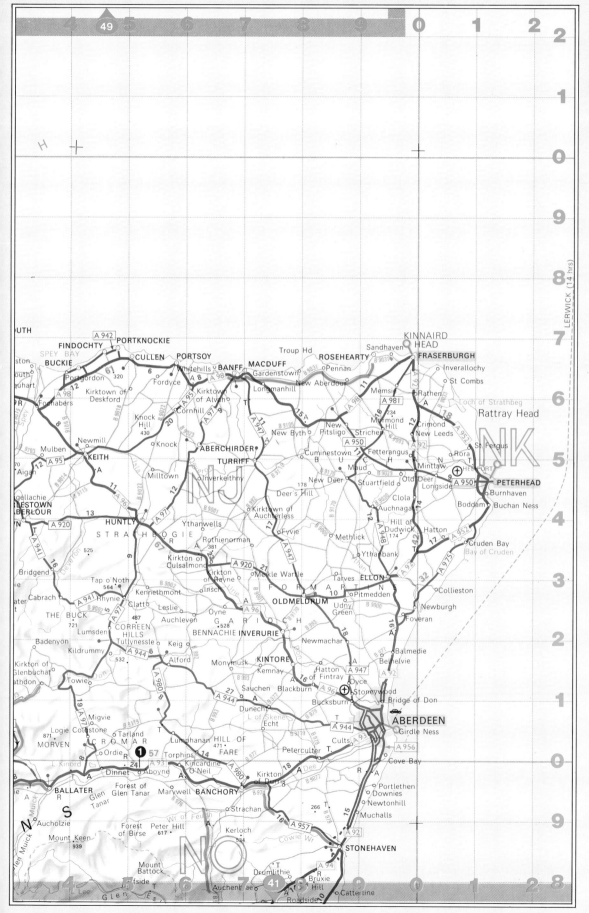

① **The A93 between Aberdeen, Braemar and Perth is an attractive, and popular, route in summer, and at the time of the Braemar Gathering (first weekend in Sept), it may be excessively busy.** ALTERNATIVE The A92 and A94 via Stonehaven, Forfar and Coupar Angus.

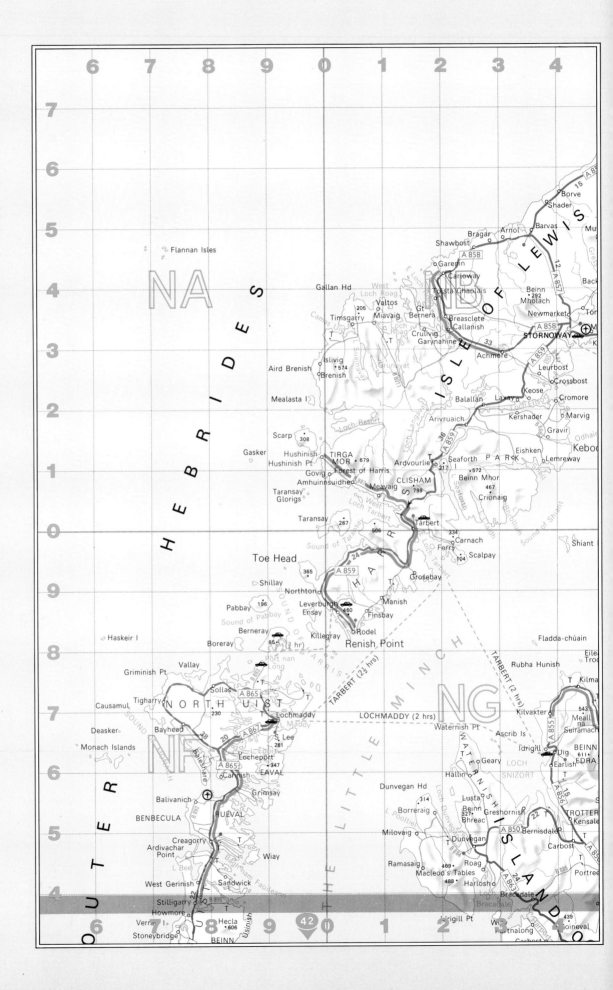

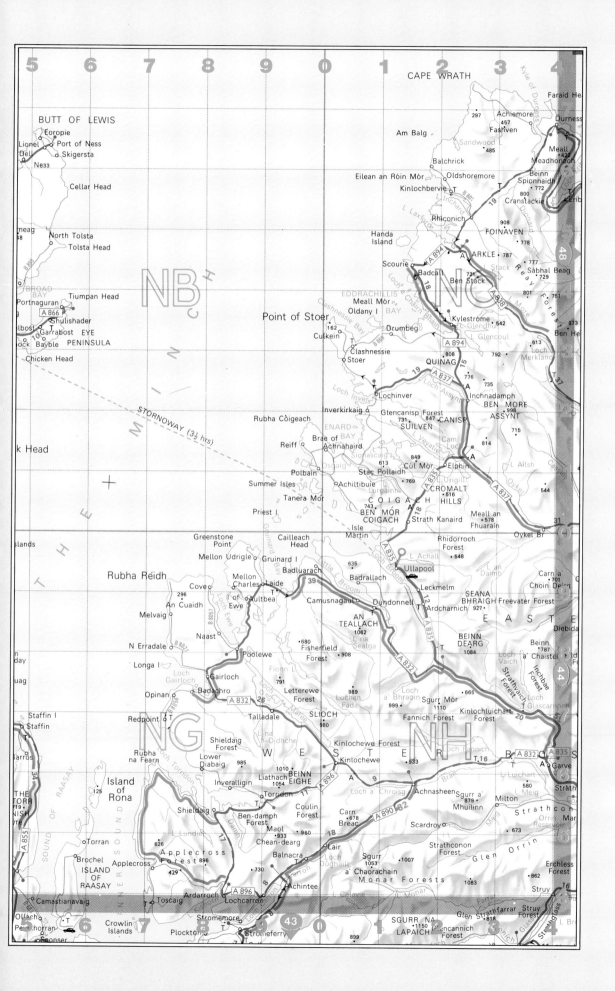

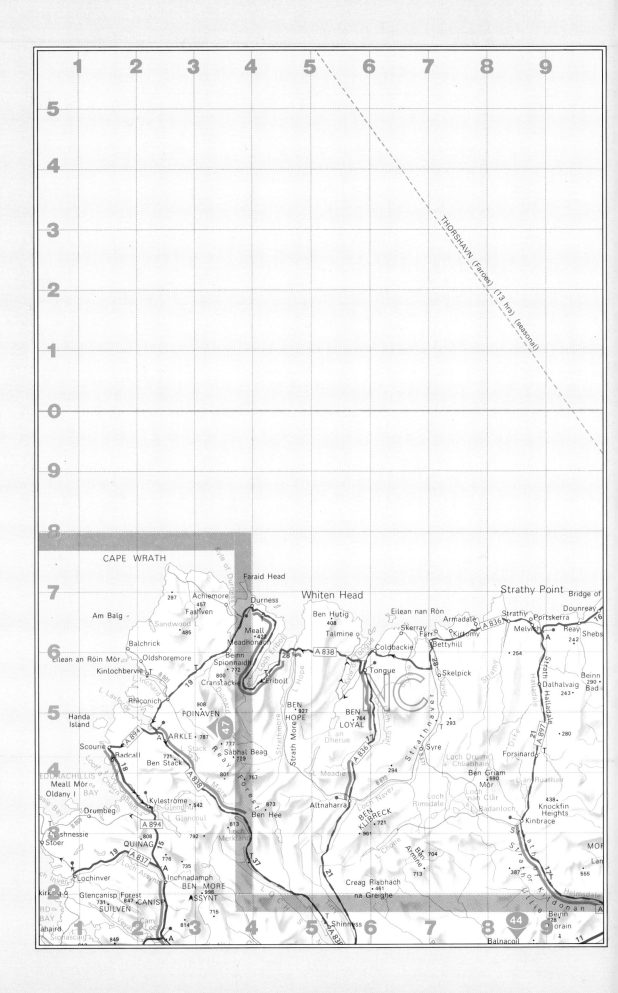

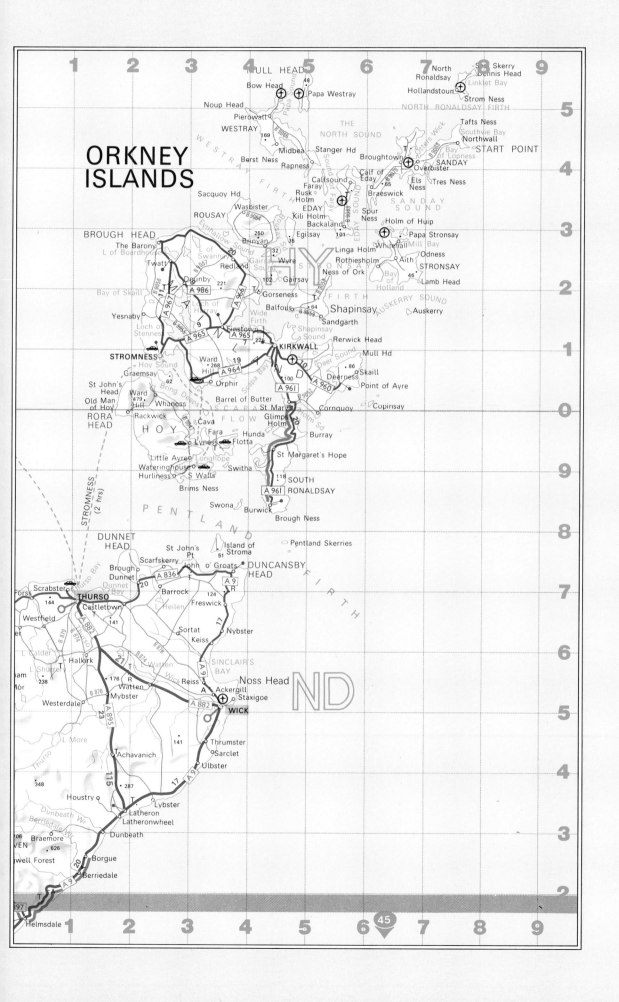

ORKNEY ISLANDS

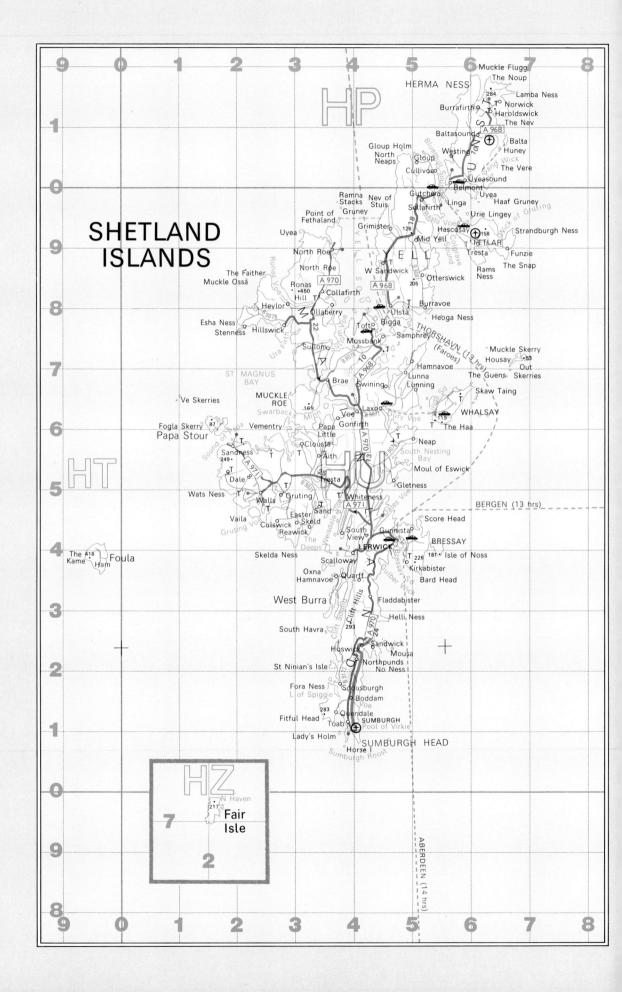

SHETLAND ISLANDS

Mileage Chart

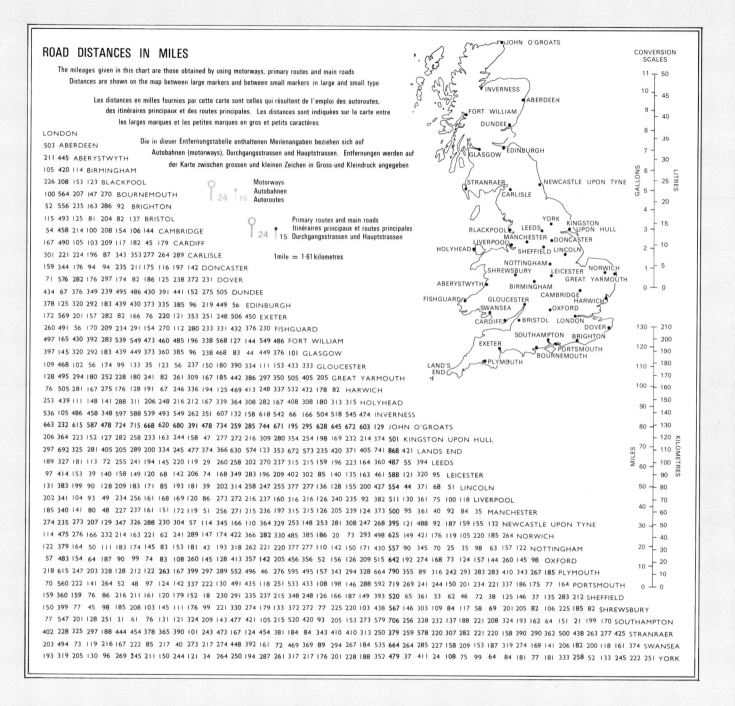

ROAD DISTANCES IN MILES

The mileages given in this chart are those obtained by using motorways, primary routes and main roads
Distances are shown on the map between large markers and between small markers in large and small type

Les distances en milles fournies par cette carte sont celles qui résultent de l'emploi des autoroutes,
des itinéraires principaux et des routes principales. Les distances sont indiquées sur la carte entre
les larges marques et les petites marques en gros et petits caractères

Die in dieser Entfernungstabelle enthaltenen Meilenangaben beziehen sich auf
Autobahnen (motorways), Durchgangsstrassen und Hauptstrassen. Entfernungen werden auf
der Karte zwischen grossen und kleinen Zeichen in Gross-und Kleindruck angegeben

Motorways
Autobahnen
Autoroutes

Primary routes and main roads
Itinéraires principaux et routes principales
Durchgangsstrassen und Hauptstrassen

1 mile = 1·61 kilometres

LONDON
503 ABERDEEN
211 445 ABERYSTWYTH
105 420 114 BIRMINGHAM
226 308 153 123 BLACKPOOL
100 564 207 147 270 BOURNEMOUTH
52 556 235 163 286 92 BRIGHTON
115 493 125 81 204 82 137 BRISTOL
54 458 214 100 208 154 106 144 CAMBRIDGE
167 490 105 103 209 117 182 45 179 CARDIFF
301 221 224 196 87 343 353 277 264 289 CARLISLE
159 344 176 94 94 235 211 175 116 197 142 DONCASTER
71 576 282 176 297 174 82 186 125 238 372 231 DOVER
434 67 376 349 239 495 486 430 391 441 152 275 505 DUNDEE
378 125 320 292 183 439 430 373 335 385 96 219 449 56 EDINBURGH
172 569 201 157 282 82 166 76 220 121 353 251 248 506 450 EXETER
260 491 56 170 209 234 291 154 270 112 280 233 331 432 376 230 FISHGUARD
497 165 430 392 283 539 549 473 460 485 196 338 568 127 144 549 486 FORT WILLIAM
397 145 320 292 183 439 449 373 360 385 96 238 468 83 44 449 376 101 GLASGOW
109 468 102 56 174 99 133 35 123 56 237 150 180 390 334 111 153 433 333 GLOUCESTER
128 495 294 180 252 228 180 241 82 261 309 167 185 442 386 297 350 505 405 205 GREAT YARMOUTH
76 505 281 167 275 176 128 191 67 246 336 194 125 469 413 248 337 532 432 178 82 HARWICH
253 439 111 148 141 288 311 206 248 216 212 167 339 364 308 282 167 408 308 180 313 315 HOLYHEAD
536 105 486 458 348 597 588 539 493 549 262 351 607 132 158 618 542 66 166 504 518 545 474 INVERNESS
663 232 615 587 478 724 715 668 620 680 391 478 734 259 285 744 671 195 295 628 645 672 603 129 JOHN O'GROATS
206 364 223 152 127 282 258 233 163 244 158 47 277 272 216 309 280 354 254 198 169 232 214 374 501 KINGSTON UPON HULL
297 692 325 281 405 205 289 200 334 245 477 374 366 630 574 123 353 672 573 235 420 371 405 741 868 421 LANDS END
189 327 181 113 72 255 241 194 145 220 119 29 260 258 202 272 317 315 215 109 390 487 55 394 LEEDS
97 468 102 56 174 99 133 35 123 56 237 150 180 390 334 111 153 433 333 GLOUCESTER
97 414 153 39 140 158 149 120 68 142 206 74 168 349 283 196 209 402 302 85 140 135 163 461 588 121 320 95 LEICESTER
131 383 199 90 128 209 183 171 85 193 181 39 202 314 258 247 255 377 277 136 128 155 200 427 554 44 371 68 51 LINCOLN
202 341 104 93 49 234 256 161 168 169 120 86 273 272 216 237 160 316 216 126 240 235 92 382 511 130 361 75 100 118 LIVERPOOL
185 340 141 80 48 227 237 161 151 172 119 51 256 271 215 236 197 315 215 126 205 239 124 373 500 95 361 40 92 84 35 MANCHESTER
274 235 273 207 129 347 326 288 230 304 57 114 345 166 110 364 329 253 148 253 281 308 247 268 395 121 488 92 187 159 155 132 NEWCASTLE UPON TYNE
114 475 276 166 232 214 163 221 62 241 289 147 174 422 366 282 330 485 385 186 20 73 293 498 625 149 421 176 119 105 220 185 264 NORWICH
122 379 164 50 111 183 174 145 43 193 318 262 221 220 377 277 110 142 150 171 430 557 90 345 70 25 35 98 63 157 122 NOTTINGHAM
57 483 154 64 187 90 99 74 83 108 260 145 128 413 357 142 205 456 356 52 156 126 209 515 642 192 274 168 73 124 157 144 260 145 98 OXFORD
218 615 247 203 328 128 212 122 263 167 399 297 289 552 496 46 276 595 495 157 343 294 328 664 790 355 89 316 242 293 283 283 410 343 267 185 PLYMOUTH
70 560 222 141 264 52 48 97 124 142 337 222 130 491 435 118 251 533 433 108 198 146 288 592 719 269 241 244 150 201 234 221 337 186 175 77 164 PORTSMOUTH
159 360 159 76 86 216 211 161 120 179 152 18 230 291 235 237 215 348 248 126 166 187 149 393 520 65 361 33 62 46 72 38 125 146 37 135 283 212 SHEFFIELD
150 399 77 45 98 185 208 103 145 111 176 99 221 330 274 179 133 372 272 77 225 220 103 438 567 146 303 109 84 117 58 69 201 205 82 106 225 185 82 SHREWSBURY
77 547 201 128 251 31 61 76 131 121 324 209 143 477 421 105 215 520 420 93 205 153 273 579 706 256 228 232 137 188 221 208 324 193 162 64 151 21 199 170 SOUTHAMPTON
402 228 325 297 188 444 454 378 365 390 101 243 473 167 124 454 381 184 84 343 410 410 313 250 379 259 578 220 307 282 221 220 158 390 290 362 500 438 263 277 425 STRANRAER
203 494 73 119 216 167 222 85 217 40 273 217 274 448 392 161 72 469 369 89 294 267 184 535 664 264 285 227 158 209 153 187 319 274 169 141 206 182 200 118 161 374 SWANSEA
193 319 205 130 96 269 245 211 150 244 121 34 264 250 194 287 261 317 217 176 201 228 188 352 479 37 411 24 108 75 99 64 84 181 77 181 333 258 52 133 245 222 251 YORK

CONVERSION SCALES

GALLONS — LITRES
11 — 50
10 — 45
9 — 40
8 — 35
7 — 30
6 — 25
5 — 20
4 — 15
3 — 10
2 — 5
1 — 5
0 — 0

130 — 210
— 200
120 — 190
— 180
110 — 170
100 — 160
90 — 150
— 140
80 — 130
— 120
70 — 110
— 100
60 — 90
50 — 80
— 70
40 — 60
30 — 50
— 40
20 — 30
10 — 20
— 10
0 — 0
MILES — KILOMETRES

Long-Distance Routes

A network of routes linking major population centres with major tourist destinations, avoiding motorways

Here is the way to travel round Britain on roads which make motoring a pleasure once more: to see and explore the country by car – rather than merely drive past it.
Four routes radiate out from London, and four from Buxton, in the heart of the north Midlands. Follow them in whole or in part, or link them to form grand tours.
Overall distances given for the routes are approximate.

53

London to Bournemouth/1

An alternative to the M3, A3, A31 and M27 connecting London with the New Forest and Bournemouth area

Distance: about 170 miles (273 km)
Guide time: 3½ to 4 hours

Access from main roads: M25 junction 10; A3 at Guildford and Haslemere; A31 or A33 at Winchester; A31 at Romsey; A31/M27 junction 1 at Cadnam

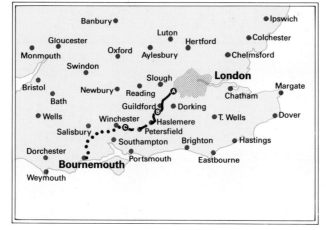

Route summary

Leave London by Putney Bridge; go straight ahead along Putney High Street and up Putney Hill to the A3 on the edge of Putney Heath. This – now converted to modern dual carriageway – is the old coaching road to Portsmouth. Stay with the A3 past Richmond Park and through the suburban vastnesses of New Malden and Tolworth to the first intimations of countryside around Esher and Cobham. Except in the rush-hour, you should reach Ripley within about 20 minutes of crossing the Thames. Leave the A3 at signposts for Ripley, and negotiate the roundabout, following signs for the village itself. In the village centre turn left on to unclassified roads across the ridge of the North Downs to Shere. Continue by the A25 and A248 to Wonersh, then unclassified roads to Hambledon (Surrey). Take the A283 south followed by the B2131 west to Haslemere, then the A286 south to Fernhurst. From there an unclassified road leads west to the A3 and Petersfield. Then take the A272 (signposts for Winchester) to the left turn (south) 3 miles (5 km) west of New Cheriton. You will find that this is almost all easy driving, except for the narrow lanes cut deeply into the hillsides between ③ and ⑤.

Map 1
Real country

Ripley is your first real breath of fresh air. The busy main road is left behind and here is a true village, with a broad high street, half-timbered coaching inns and what is said to be the biggest village green in England; certainly it is a notable cradle of Surrey cricket. Take the unsignposted left turn ① 25 yards (23 m) after the Ship Inn and, about half a mile (0.8 km) after crossing the A3, go right ② down Hungry Hill Lane.

Over the Downs

This road takes you up from the valley of the River Wey on to the chalk ridge of the North Downs. At East Clandon, just about the last village left on the suburbanized strip between Leatherhead and Guildford, turn right ③ (signposted Guildford) but then shortly left on to an unclassified road for Shere.

At the summit of the ridge the road crosses the ancient 'Pilgrims' Way', now part of the North Downs long-distance footpath. Whether pilgrims truly made this way or not, historians are uncertain; but there can be no doubt that many who trod this high, dry track linking the shrines of Winchester and Canterbury did so with a holy purpose.

Gunpowder valley

At the junction ④ turn right (signposted Shere and Gomshall) and, at the A25 right again. Shere, probably the most photographed village in Surrey (and that is saying something) is behind you. Follow west along the valley of the little River Tillingbourne and go left on the A248 for Albury, another pretty village among hills and woods. It has a ruined church whose 17thC rector, William Oughtred, invented the multiplication sign.

William Cobbett, the radical journalist and agitator, made one of his famous 'rural rides' through here in 1822 and justly praised the valley's beauty. But at Chilworth, the next settlement on the A248 (name not on map) he was less than pleased: 'This valley . . . has been, by ungrateful man, so perverted as to make it instrumental . . . in carrying into execution two of the most damnable inventions that ever sprang from the minds of men under the influence of the devil! Namely, the making of *gunpowder and bank-notes!!*' All traces of the bank-note factory have gone, but you still find the old sheds and rails of the explosives industry in the woods.

Heather and pine

Turning left on to the B2128, you enter a different sort of countryside. The chalk downs and the beeches on the north side of the Tillingbourne are left behind and the road now enters the greensand hills of Surrey, clad in pines and heather. The roads are narrow, often cut deeply into the hillsides and, like all these twisting Surrey backroads, to be enjoyed for their effects of leaves and light, rather than speed.

Wonersh is a very 'Surrey' village. The street gently curves, and the buildings are an undemanding *mélange* of sandstone, brick, half-timber and the tile-hung cottages common in this part of Britain. Turn right ⑤ at the signpost for Bramley, which is a centreless village.

Cross the A281 to the unclassified road opposite and, after about a mile, turn right and shortly left. At the B2130 ⑥ turn right (signposted Godalming and Guildford), then soon first left and left again. (*Now see Map 2.*)
Follow signposts to the scattered village of

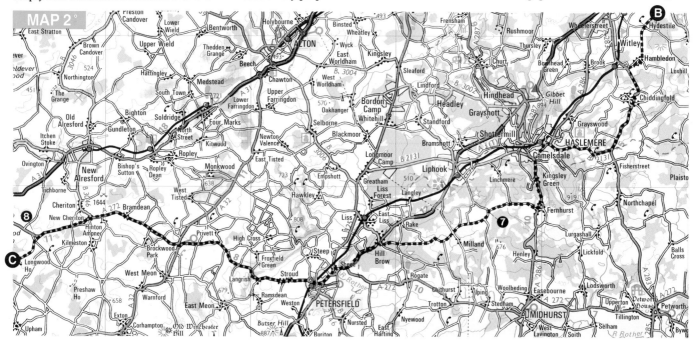

London to Bournemouth/1

MAP 1

Hambledon, set among a jumble of woods, heaths, ups and downs, with splendid and surprising views opening unexpectedly across the Weald to the North Downs. Just outside the village is Hydon Ball, a wooded hill with a memorial on top to Octavia Hill, one of the founders of the National Trust.

Old glass, and old iron

Turning right in Hambledon, go straight ahead to the A283, on to which turn left. Chiddingfold is a big village which was once the centre of the 'forest glass' industry that the Normans are said to have introduced – using the local sand, bracken and charcoal to make glass.

Turn right on to the B2131 for Haslemere. This is the last town in Surrey: a pleasant settlement where George Eliot and Sir Arthur Conan Doyle lived at different times, and where Tennyson is memorialized in a window of the church designed by the pre-Raphaelite, Burne-Jones.

The A286 south from Haslemere quickly takes you into Sussex and to the village of Fernhurst, marvellously positioned between Blackdown and Bexley Heath. Turn right in the middle of the village on to an unclassified road. You are now on the clay of the Weald, for centuries Britain's chief source of iron. The big wood to your left, about 1½ miles (2.5 km) west of Fernhurst, is Minepit Copse, one of many names hereabouts that recall the old industry.

At the T-junction ⑦ just beyond this wood, turn left (signposted Midhurst, Linch and Milland), then keep going straight ahead at all intersections until the A3 is reached, after a delightful run through woods, at Hill Brow.

You are now back on the old Portsmouth Road which you left at Ripley. Since then the route has crossed three distinct geological belts and contrasting scenery to match: the chalk of the Downs, the greensand ridge and finally the clay of the once-industrial Weald.

Into Hampshire

Turn left on to the A3 (signposts for Petersfield). At this point the road forms the boundary between Hampshire and West Sussex. A mile (1.5 km) before Petersfield you enter Hampshire, the county in which you remain for the rest of the drive.

Where the road crosses the River Rother, look left. The sharp line of hills some 3 miles (5 km) off is the escarpment of the South Downs.

All the bustle of the old times, when twenty-seven coaches a day pelted through, has gone from Petersfield, leaving agricultural peace, a handsome, mostly 14thC church and some exemplary Georgian houses. Now take the A272 (signs for Winchester) through respectable farmed countryside. Three miles (5 km) after Cheriton look carefully for a signpost to Owslebury, and ⑧ turn left.

● North Downs beauty spots are some of the most walked over and driven past in southern England: only the earliest risers encounter solitary, wistful scenes like this one at Box Hill, a few miles E of where the route crosses the downs. Nothing could be a greater contrast than the same place on a sunny Sunday in August, when you have to concentrate not to let the crowds distract you from the grandeur of this huge open space of down- and woodland. It takes its name from the numerous box trees.

London to Bournemouth/2

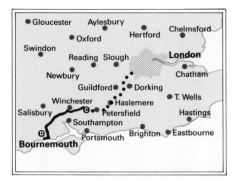

Route summary

The route leaves the relatively fast A272 in order to bypass Winchester to the south, at first on unclassified roads and then across the River Itchen in a short sequence of dual carriageways and main roads. After that you have plain sailing on the A31, and after Romsey, you pick up a parallel line of country lanes through some of the best New Forest scenery to Ringwood. The final stage is a pleasant run down the valley of the Hampshire Avon on the B3347 to Christchurch, which adjoins Bournemouth.

Map 3
The heart of Hampshire

Navigate these country lanes with care: the views of rolling chalk terrain and dominant beechwoods will be your reward. At the first junction after the A272 bear right and in a couple of miles (3 km) right again at the next intersection ⑨ signposted Winchester and Morestead. Turn right into that village, then

left ⑩ signposted Twyford. The road drops gently into the Itchen valley and the big, nothing-special village of Twyford. Cross the A333 ⑪ and go straight ahead on to the unsignposted road leaving Lloyd's Bank on your right. Go left at the roundabout ⑫ on to the A33. Follow signs ⑬ for 'non-motorway traffic', etc. and A31 Romsey. If driving the route in reverse, fork left off the A33 (here signposted Winchester) and, in 1½ miles (2.5 km), turn right, signposted A333.

Romsey

You are now clear of complications and the A31 takes you over the low watershed between Hampshire's two famous chalk trout streams, the Itchen and the Test. On the Test stands and has stood since Roman times, in one form or another, the ancient town of Romsey. This approach to it is somewhat undistinguished

until the first view of the Abbey, which lifts an otherwise run-of-the-mill country town right out of the ordinary. There was a nunnery here dating from Saxon times, but it was destroyed at the Dissolution. The towns' people of Romsey saved the Abbey that went with it by paying £100 to Henry VIII. We must praise their foresight: the purely Norman interior is dignified, calm and strong.

Through the New Forest

Leave Romsey by the A31 (signposts for Bournemouth), but about a mile out of town be ready for the unsignposted right turn ⑭ (approaching the crest of a hill), to East and West Wellow. (Florence Nightingale lies in the churchyard of East Wellow.)

At the staggered crossroads ⑮ continue on Ryedown Lane and at the next junction ⑯ keep left. The road brings you to a dangerous

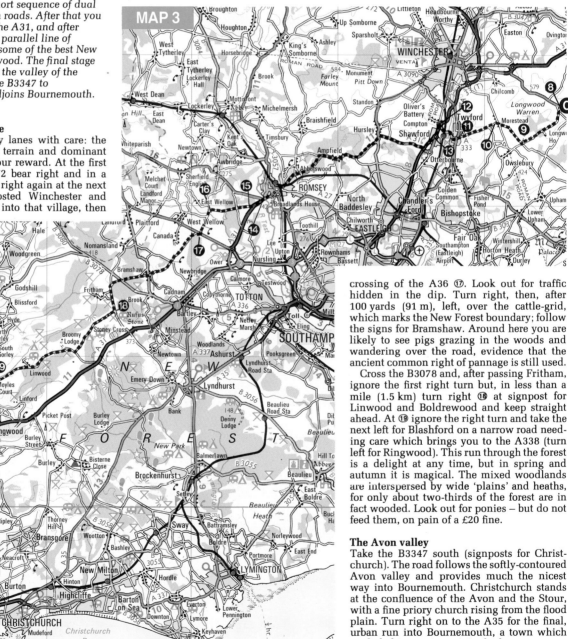

crossing of the A36 ⑰. Look out for traffic hidden in the dip. Turn right, then, after 100 yards (91 m), left, over the cattle-grid, which marks the New Forest boundary; follow the signs for Bramshaw. Around here you are likely to see pigs grazing in the woods and wandering over the road, evidence that the ancient common right of pannage is still used.

Cross the B3078 and, after passing Fritham, ignore the first right turn but, in less than a mile (1.5 km) turn right ⑱ at signpost for Linwood and Boldrewood and keep straight ahead. At ⑲ ignore the right turn and take the next left for Blashford on a narrow road needing care which brings you to the A338 (turn left for Ringwood). This run through the forest is a delight at any time, but in spring and autumn it is magical. The mixed woodlands are interspersed by wide 'plains' and heaths, for only about two-thirds of the forest are in fact wooded. Look out for ponies – but do not feed them, on pain of a £20 fine.

The Avon valley

Take the B3347 south (signposts for Christchurch). The road follows the softly-contoured Avon valley and provides much the nicest way into Bournemouth. Christchurch stands at the confluence of the Avon and the Stour, with a fine priory church rising from the flood plain. Turn right on to the A35 for the final, urban run into Bournemouth, a town which exploded into existence in the last century as a result of England's great love affair with healthful, salt-water bathing ●

London to Carmarthen/1

An alternative to the M4, M5 and M50, connecting London with south-west Wales.

Distance: about 130 miles (480 km)
Guide time: allow 10 hours – several sections of narrow, twisting roads.

Access from main roads: M40 junction 2; M4 junctions 9–18; M5 junctions 14–11; M50 junctions 1–4; A40 at Abergavenny, Brecon or Llandeilo.

Route summary
Leave London on the A40; if starting from central London, take advantage of the raised dual carriageway known as the Westway: the Marylebone Road actually leads into this remarkable piece of road-building in the vicinity of Paddington Station, and you can also join it from two further limited access junctions. Even in rush-hour, the traffic moves fast on the dual carriageway section; however, your pace will slow down at Acton where it ends.

Map 1
Leaving London
① Do not continue on the M40, but stay on the old A40, passing through the high streets of Gerrards Cross and Beaconsfield. The latter has an especially fine high street with a number of 18thC houses and a monument in the churchyard to Edmund Waller, the dashing Cavalier poet, who lived here.

Stay with the A40 beyond the town, then after nearly 2 miles (3 km), take the left turn signposted Bourne End and Marlow. The route is relatively suburbanized until Marlow, but none the less a pleasant route westwards compared with the motorway alternative. At Bourne End you approach the Thames, and from there until Henley-on-Thames you are driving a mostly delightful, if sometimes over-used road through respectable Thames Valley scenery. At Marlow the last signs of suburbia are left behind. This is your first riverside town of several on the route; it is a bustling place with its share of tourists, and like Beaconsfield, has some poetic associations: Shelley and T. S. Eliot both lived here.

● *Burnham Beeches, the popular beauty spot, is near the route – N of Farnham Royal on the A355.*

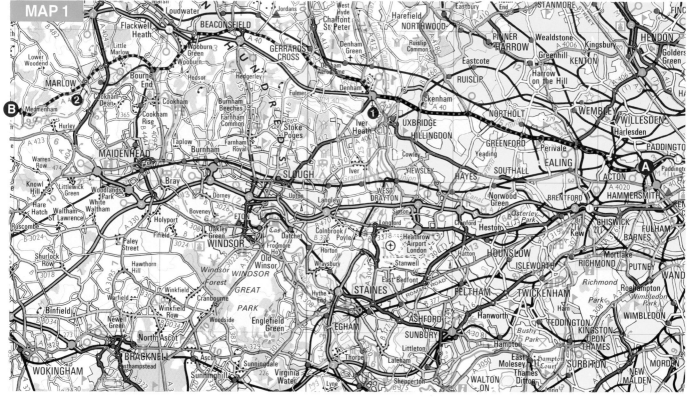

MAP 1

London to Carmarthen/2

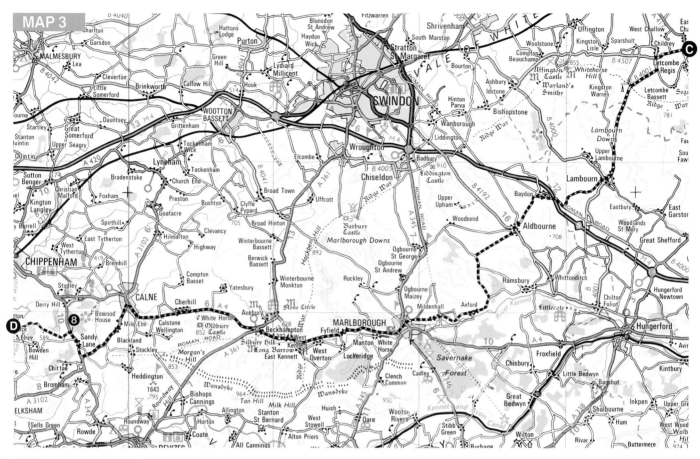

MAP 3

Route summary
From Marlow you continue along the Thames Valley on the A4155 to Henley-on-Thames. Then the route cuts across two hill ranges, the Chilterns and the Berkshire Downs, using mostly unclassified roads. A straightforward run along the Kennet valley brings you to Calne.

Map 2
Thames and Chilterns
At the central roundabout in Marlow ② the way is straight ahead on the A4155 to Henley. Despite A status, this is a sinuous road which needs care. It climbs up and down through woods with the river never far away to the left; but you will not see it properly until Henley. The town's one-way system (follow signs for Reading) takes you right beside one end of the famous Henley regatta course. At the bridge turn right up another wide high street (Henley has more than 300 listed buildings) and left at the traffic lights. As the street becomes sub-urban-Victorian, keep a sharp look-out for a right turn signposted for Harpsden ③. With the tower of Harpsden church in view, turn

right and follow this country lane straight ahead. It climbs gradually through woods and fields over another shoulder of the Chilterns.

Spring and autumn are the best times of year for this countryside. The first green of the beeches is incredibly delicate, and their autumn riot of red and gold equally beautiful in an entirely different way.

Three miles (5 km) from Harpsden church, at the T-junction ④ turn right (signpost for Sonning Common), then left after ¾ mile (1 km) and straight over the B481 on to another by-road. Keep straight ahead following signs for Kidmore End, which is built round a staggered crossroads ⑤. Again go straight ahead, leaving the church on your left. In about half a mile (0.8 km), just after the pylons, take the first right and drive very carefully. This lane is narrow; it twists and it has sharp gradients. At the A4074 turn right and follow it for about 2 miles (3 km). Then left (signpost for Goring) past a wood where the bluebells make a carpet in May.

The road drops to the twin Thames-side villages of Goring in Oxfordshire and Streatley in Berkshire. Boats are business here and, as you approach the junction with the A329, you may envy the freedom of navigators on the Thames.

Over the Downs
At the junction in Streatley ⑥, cross the main road and take the narrow street (signs for Newbury) opposite. This climbs steeply on to the Downs, a very different chalk landscape from that on the north bank of the Thames. After Aldworth take the right turn, signposted for East Ilsley. Until only fifty years ago this village was the scene of an annual sheep fair, sheep being the mainstay of the Downs until

they became arable. Many sheep were brought to the fair on the hoof along the ancient Ridge Way, which you will shortly cross. Follow signs for West Ilsley, Farnborough and then, turning right on to the B4494, Wantage. Cross the Ridgeway Path at the summit and drop down with superb views ahead. In Wantage go straight ahead at the A338 on to the B4507 ⑦. (*Now see Map 3.*)

In about 3 miles (5 km) go left on to the B4001 for Lambourn, which is on the southern side of the Downs. This is a small town almost entirely devoted to the racehorses whose gallops you have passed to the north. In the centre turn right, and almost immediately left. Follow signs for Baydon and Aldbourne; there turn left and then right for Axford, where you reach the Kennet valley.

Turn right for Marlborough, a gracious town with a Georgian flavour. Follow the A4 west, past mysterious Silbury Hill and the signs for ancient Avebury, to Calne. Leave the town on the A3102, meet the A342 and turn right. After ¼ mile (0.5 km) ⑧ turn left – signpost for Lacock.

The stretch of A4 west from Marlborough is marvellously atmospheric: passing Silbury Hill, and the vicinity of Avebury in particular, it does not need much imagination to sense that somehow the air is thick with the spirit of an ancient past. This part of the A4 is also to be enjoyed as a fine, fast country road.

● *Right, the famous landmark on Whitehorse Hill, S of the B4507: no one is sure of its date or manner of carving. The Ridgeway Path – an official long-distance walking route – passes close by.*

London to Carmarthen/2

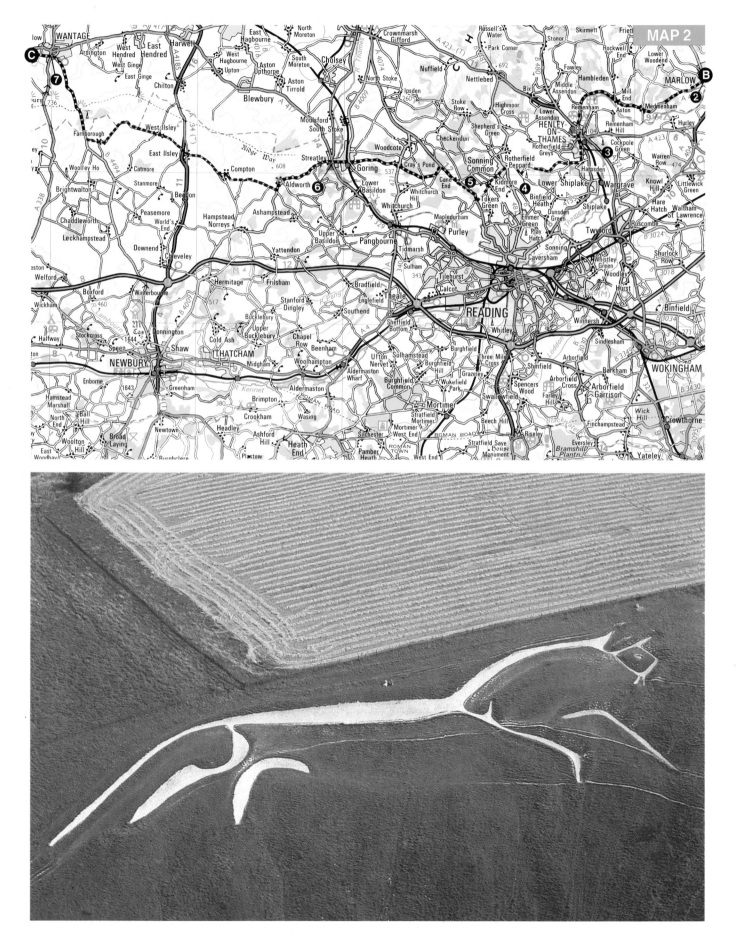

MAP 2

London to Carmarthen/3

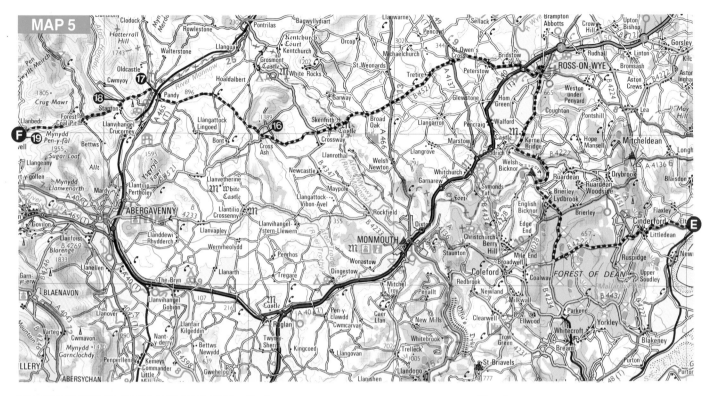

MAP 5

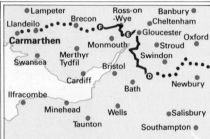

Route summary
Pleasant, not-too-demanding driving takes you northwards across Wiltshire to reach the Cotswold escarpment at Wotton-under-Edge. You follow the edge to Stroud and from there pass Bristol, cross the Severn and the Forest of Dean on A and B roads. From Ross-on-Wye onwards there are some stretches of A and B road driving, but there are also plenty of unclassified, narrow mountain-side lanes. They need care, time and attention, but they more than repay your trouble.

Map 4
Lacock and Chippenham
Lacock is one of the prettiest of English villages. It is wholly owned by the National Trust, as is the nearby Abbey which was converted to a private home after the original nunnery was suppressed in 1539.

At the A350 turn right (signposted Chippenham). The route, which has brought you more or less due west across Wiltshire, now turns north and north-west for the Cotswolds. But first there is the ancient market town of Chippenham to be negotiated: follow signposts for Cirencester until you reach the A420 (signposts for Bristol); there turn left. After just over a mile (1.5 km) on the A420, turn right ⑨ on to the B4039.

This road bypasses Castle Combe, which many say is the most beautiful village in the country; certainly it is among the most visited. Detour to the left at the sign ⑩ if you want to join the throng. The route is straight ahead on the B4039, over the M4 and so to your first village in Avon, Acton Turville. Here turn right ⑪ at the first fork and go straight over at the staggered junction, following the signs for Badminton on an unclassified road.

Through Avon
There are a few miles to go, mostly through the 'new county' of Avon, before you reach Gloucestershire and the true Cotswolds. Follow the road straight ahead, through some pleasantly rolling country, to Badminton, one of those villages which are obviously the 'capital' of a country estate. The Beauforts have ruled here for three centuries, and still do. Observe the ducal device which combines the heraldic symbols of England and France (there's grandeur), on the almshouses. Badminton House itself, built in the 17thC and

● *Goodrich Castle (1101), imposingly situated above the River Wye, is close to the route as it approaches Ross-on-Wye.*

greatly extended in the 18th, containing old masters and carving by Grinling Gibbons, lies east of the village.

Under the Cotswold edge
From Badminton follow the road straight ahead and over the A40 (signs for Hawkesbury Upton): take care, for this is a fast stretch. In Hawkesbury Upton also keep straight ahead, now following signs for Alderley, which lies just inside Gloucestershire. Bear right, for Wotton-under-Edge, an old and recognizably Cotswold town built from the limestone of which those hills are formed and named because it lies under their 'edge' or escarpment. Your road (turn left ⑫ on to the B4060 in the centre of Wotton) closely hugs this escarpment, with hills to the right and views over the Vale of Berkeley to the left.

Stroud and Gloucester
In Lower Cam turn right ⑬ (signs for Tetbury) on to the A4135 and after about a mile of urban driving take a left turn in Dursley, on to the B4066, signposted Stroud. Now you are once again clinging to the escarpment. This is a road to be driven slowly and for pleasure: every curve unfolds a new view of the hills or the plain to the west, and in any case, there are too many bends and gradients for fast driving.

   Eventually, the road plunges sharply into Stroud, an old wool town, originally crammed in the valley bottom, but later forced to expand up the hills. Turn left on to the A419 for Stonehouse.

Crossing the River Severn
Follow the A419 into Stonehouse and there turn right for Gloucester on to a road which takes you across the M5, after which you turn right on to the A38. At the third roundabout ⑭ take the A430 (signs for Tewkesbury) and in Gloucester ⑮ turn left following signs for Ross-on-Wye on the A40. About 2 miles (3 km) after crossing the Severn, take the A48 left, signposted for Cinderford. This winds through the flood plain of the Severn, orchards becoming more and more frequent. With the Severn in view on your left, take the right turn, the A4151, signposted Cinderford.

Map 5
The Forest of Dean
The road winds up between thickening woods to Cinderford, where you bear left and then right on to the B4226 which is signposted for Coleford and justly labelled 'scenic drive'. It takes you through the heart of the forest (many walks and picnic places) and past the Speech House, home of the Verderers' Court, but now an hotel. Panoramas over the forest are frequent. Not only timber is worked here, but also coal – some of it still won by free-enterprise miners operating their own 'dipples', as the drift-mines are known.

   At the crossroads in the valley below the Speech House, turn right on to the B4234 and then, when you reach the River Wye, beyond Lydbrook, turn right, following signs for Ross all the way. The road follows the meanders of the Wye for a mile or so, then cuts across wooded hills to Ross itself.

The Border
Ross-on-Wye is a busy town with many buildings in the pinkish local sandstone and some of the characteristic Herefordshire black-and-whites too. Pick your way through the central bustle, and across the Wye again, by following

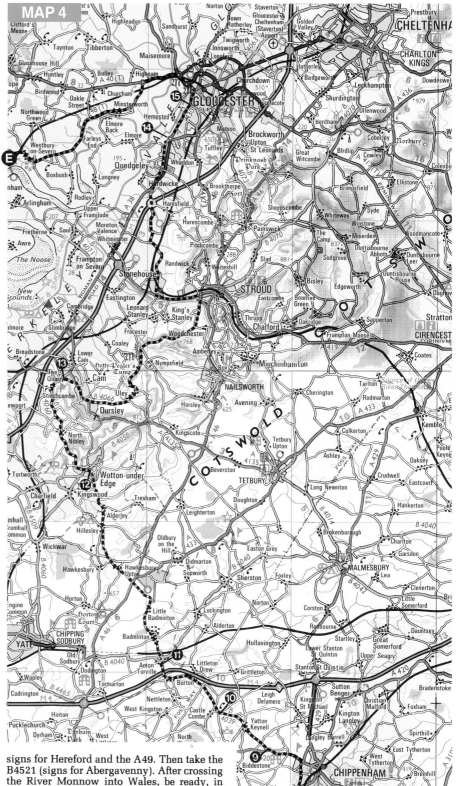

signs for Hereford and the A49. Then take the B4521 (signs for Abergavenny). After crossing the River Monnow into Wales, be ready, in about 5 miles (8 km) for a right turn ⑯ (sign for Pontrilas) just after the garage in Cross Ash. Now keep straight ahead through the lanes, ignoring signs for Grosmont and following those for Pandy, which is reached by a rough, steep hill. Turn right on to the A465 and almost immediately left (sign for Llanthony). Take the second left ⑰ after the railway and go straight ahead for ⑱ the B4423. Here turn left and then shortly right on a lane.

London to Carmarthen/4

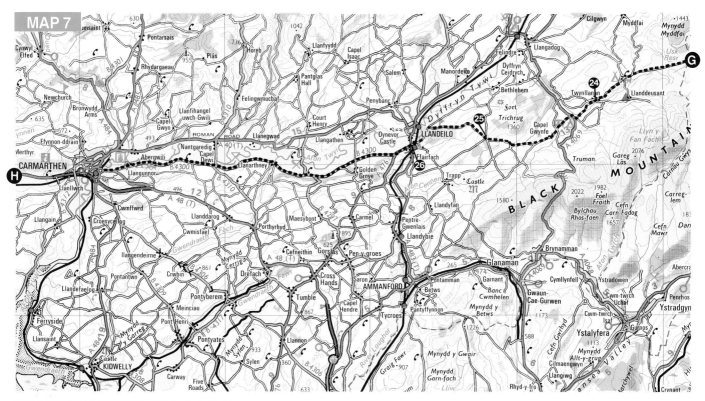

MAP 7

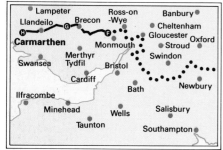

Route summary

You are now launched into the most testing and most spectacular section of the route. Between here and Carmarthen are long stretches of winding lanes along mountain sides; even the A and B roads will demand your concentration. The first section, on the B4558 between Crickhowell and Brecon, is relatively straightforward, but between Brecon and Llandeilo you will need to take your time. The final run from Llandeilo to Carmarthen is again quite easy, following the B4300.

Map 6
Under the Sugar Loaf
Your first lane, except for the care necessary on any road as narrow and winding as this, is pure joy. The main massif of the Black Mountains is the bulk to your right, while the Sugar Loaf, a National Trust property consisting of Old Red Sandstone rock, looms on your left. As befits a pass, you begin by climbing and then drop down after the watershed. At the junction ⑲ bear left and quite shortly right, following the signpost for Crickhowell. In this village, birthplace of Sir George Everest, for whom the world's highest mountain is named, ignore signs for Brecon, even though you are going there. Instead, bear left over the River Usk to the B4558 ⑳, signposted Llangynidr.

The Usk valley
This is another lovely road: it runs beside the Usk and the old Brecon and Abergavenny Canal all the way to Brecon. But the river is far from straight and the canal is following the contours, so there is not much room for both of them plus the road in what is anyway not a wide valley. Be ready for sudden corners where the road crosses canal or river.

Just before Brecon, turn left on to the town's bypass (the A40) which you last saw at Beaconsfield in London's green belt, but which you now encounter in the heart of the Brecon Beacons National Park. This 520-square mile (1,347 sq km) stretch of mountain scenery is in fact the nearest National Park to London.

Leave the A40 after a few hundred yards by the town centre road at the roundabout. It is worth stopping in Brecon as, architecturally, it is a jumble of every style of building from medieval to Victorian and later. It has a good parish church and, just outside the main part of the town, a priory church which is now a cathedral: both are built of the local sandstone and look magnificent in the evening light with the monochrome hills beyond. Being also the county town of Powys and the headquarters of the National Park, Brecon always has an air of busy purpose.

Through the Park
To leave Brecon, follow the signs for Llandovery and Merthyr Tydfil. At the roundabout junction with the A40, take the third exit, an unclassified road which climbs over Mynydd Illtyd and drops down to the A4215. Here turn right following signs for Llandovery.

Leaving Brecon, you have the Beacons on your left, but there are plenty more mountains within the National Park. As you travel along the A4215, the great chunk of mountain called Fforest Fawr lies on your left.

Where the A4215 enters Defynnog village, bear right (signs for Llandovery again), but just over the brow of the hill, take the left turn ㉑

between buildings: it is hard to spot. Follow this narrow lane around the contours of a small mountain, Fforest Fach. The road stays on the side of the hill above a valley. Ignore the first right and take the second ㉒ which dips sharply towards and across a stream and then climbs through woodland to a T-junction ㉓ where you turn right and follow straight ahead as the road drops into another valley, where you go left at another T-junction. From here (*now see Map 7*) go over the side of the Black Mountain for nearly 8 miles (13 km) to the hamlet of Twynllanan, where there is a complicated junction ㉔: essentially, you go straight ahead. Follow the lane down to the A4069, on to which turn right and then very shortly left up another steep twisting lane.

The next few miles of ill-signposted lanes require even more concentration than the last few. At the first crossroads, about a mile after leaving the A4069, go straight ahead. Rather more than a mile later, take the right fork and, after another mile, turn right at the cross. The next junction ㉕ gives you wide views ahead: go right and then, at the three-pronged fork, take the middle road.

The Tywi valley
The lane brings you quickly down to the gracious Tywi valley, with Llandeilo enjoying one of the finest sites of any small town in Britain – on a hillside in the middle of the vale.

Go under the railway and at the junction ㉖ take the A476 (signposted for Llanelli) but after one mile fork on to the B4300 which takes you all the way to Carmarthen, the capital of Dyfed, through the fertile valley of the Tywi ●

● *Right, Carreg Cennen Castle on its precipitous rock 300 feet (91 m) above the River Cennen.*

London to Carmarthen/4

London to Buxton/1

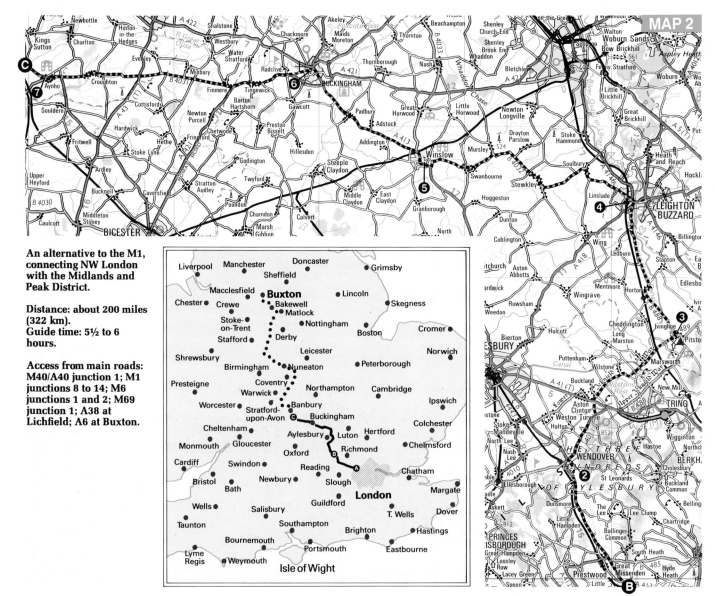

MAP 2

An alternative to the M1, connecting NW London with the Midlands and Peak District.

Distance: about 200 miles (322 km).
Guide time: 5½ to 6 hours.

Access from main roads: M40/A40 junction 1; M1 junctions 8 to 14; M6 junctions 1 and 2; M69 junction 1; A38 at Lichfield; A6 at Buxton.

Route summary
From the A40/M40 junction 1 take the A413 through Chalfont St Peter and Old Amersham to Wendover. Then the A4011 and B489 to Ivinghoe; B488 to Leighton Buzzard; B4032 to Winslow; A413 to Buckingham. From there take the A421 and B4031 to join the A41 at Aynho.

Maps 1 and 2
Through the Chilterns
The first 20 miles (32 km) of this route from the M40/A40 junction ① are a gentle climb through the Chilterns. The road goes through the wide high street of Old Amersham and bypasses the pleasant village of Great Missenden. Now the hills are higher, and hung with the beechwoods typical of this area. With the railway in a cutting on the left, you reach a point 508 feet (155 m) above sea-level and after that drop swiftly down the escarpment of the hills to Wendover.

Wendover to Leighton Buzzard
In Wendover ② turn right on to the A4011. This is a town that still lives up to its 18thC description, 'a pretty thoroughfare town, having two streets well built with timber' –

though there are rather more than two streets today.

The A4011 runs near the foot of the escarpment and after a wooded patch, wide views open up across the south Midland plain. You are in fact on the route of the Icknield Way, an ancient road that ran between Norfolk and Dorset. Turn left on to the B489 and follow it to Ivinghoe ③. The line of the Chilterns is clear to the right as you continue north-eastwards. As Ivinghoe Beacon comes into view so does an enormous cement works at Pitstone, a reminder that Chiltern means 'chalk'.

In Ivinghoe you take the B488 to the left ③. Now strike almost due north with the hills behind. This is a major transport corridor: running parallel are the main London–Birmingham railway and the older Grand Union Canal. The latter is so-called because it was created by the joining of no less than eight existing canals.

Into the heartland
At Leighton Buzzard ④ turn left on to the B4032. This launches you on a stretch of cross-country driving that will last to the northern edge of the industrial Midlands around Nuneaton.

The first watershed is at the straggly village of Stewkley. To the left (west) the streams run to the Thames, to the right (east) they run to the Ouse and The Wash. The road winds on – very much a country lane which has grown up only a little – to Winslow ⑤, a small country town with the air of having become stuck in the Edwardian era. Buckingham, a few miles further on, looks not much further advanced and ⑥ you must watch carefully for the turn on to the A421 (signposted Bicester) in the town centre.

Ironstone, and a battle
Taking the B4031 at Finmere we come to the adorable village of Aynho, where the gold flecked stone of the cottages reveals the local ironstone. Take the signposts ⑦ for Adderbury and Banbury, continuing through the ironstone belt.

● *Above right, the Chilterns near Watlington: these downs are classic chalk country, their tops clad with airy beech hangers. It makes fine walking, and footpaths are plentiful.*

London to Buxton/1

London to Buxton/2

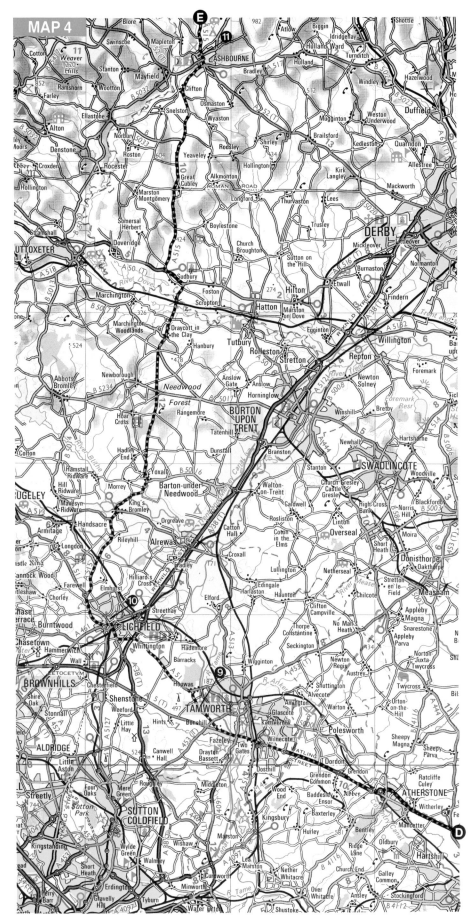

MAP 4

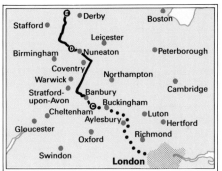

Route summary

Follow the A41 through Banbury, then take the A422 and an unclassified road to the B4086. Turn right on to the Foss Way and follow it in almost a dead-straight line to the A5, where turn left and continue to the A51, signposted Lichfield. From here take the A515 to Ashbourne, and from Ashbourne continue on the A515 following signs for Buxton. Prepare to turn right in just 2 miles (3 km) on to the B5056.

Map 3

Banbury and the Foss

In the bustle of Banbury ⑧ go straight ahead at the cross of nursery rhyme fame, then left on to the A422 (signs for Stratford). After signs for Upton House, take the unclassified road on the right. It runs along Edge Hill, beneath which was fought a Civil War battle with 3,000 casualties. At the B4086 turn left and go through Kineton (signs for Warwick) and continue to the intersection with Foss Way (signposted). Turn right.

Now, for 28 miles (45 km), you drive in an almost straight Roman line, hardly touching any settlements. This was the road the Romans used to serve their Trent–Severn frontier.

Watling Street

The A5 is another Roman road, as straight as the Foss you are now leaving. But the Foss successfully bypassed the west Midland conurbation, whereas Watling Street touches some dull urban driving between Hinckley and Nuneaton and through Atherstone.

Map 4

Tamworth

Tamworth ⑨ has more flavour of what a small Staffordshire town was once like. Bad new buildings do not obscure a big church, more than 60 yards (55 m) long, with a curious double spiral staircase in the tower. One staircase forms the floor of the other and the other the roof of the first. There is also a castle happily blending Norman, Gothic, Tudor, Jacobean and 19thC structures. The town is remembered because Sir Robert Peel (later Prime Minister) issued here the Tamworth Manifesto, regarded as the first modern election address.

Lichfield

Take the A51 from Tamworth to reach this town ⑩, dominated by the spires of its cathedral (known as 'The Three Ladies of the Vale') – unique, as this is the only English cathedral with three spires. It is also one of the smaller cathedrals, but the west front is dominant enough and the red sandstone is striking.

In Lichfield's Market Square are statues of Dr Johnson, the embodiment of English common sense, and his friend and biographer,

London to Buxton/2

James Boswell. Johnson's statue faces the building at the corner of Breadmarket Street which was his father's bookshop and is now his own museum.

Over the Dove

The A515 takes you more or less due north across a neglected slice of Staffordshire over the River Dove into Derbyshire and into Ashbourne ⑪ at the gates of the Peak District. North of Yoxall the remnants of Needwood Forest remind us that this was once the wild border country of the Kingdom of Mercia – a sharp contrast with the lush water-meadows of the little River Dove, the great Izaak Walton's favourite stream. Most people know the Dove higher up where it flows through the gorge of Dove Dale, but here it has its own gentleness and beauty.

Ashbourne

Now the route reaches its first Derbyshire town. It fairly earns its sobriquet, 'The Gateway to the Peak'. It lies in the valley of the Manifold and immediately to the north the hills of the Peak begin to rise with a sharpness not seen since Edge Hill.

Ashbourne itself is a pretty market town, less tourist-orientated than some of the similar spots in the National Park to the north. Its church ('The Cathedral of the Peak') has a spire some 215 feet (66 m) high. It contains a life-size, white-marble effigy of Penelope Boothby, a girl of five who died in 1791. The inscription proclaims that she spoke four languages.

If you go through Ashbourne on Shrove Tuesday, you will encounter its ancient football match played between residents of opposite sides of the Henmore Brook. Goals are 3 miles (5 km) apart and any number can play. The first goal wins, and may take a couple of days to score.

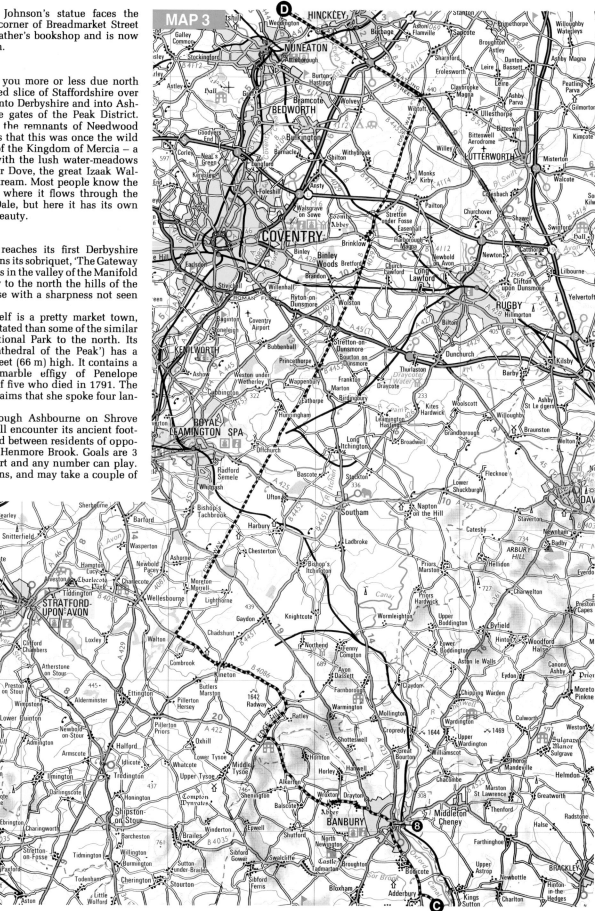

London to Buxton/3

MAP 5

Route summary

Two miles (3 km) after Ashbourne ⑪ turn right on to the B5056 and follow this to its junction with the A6 – about 12 miles (19 km). Here turn left, staying with the A6 through Bakewell, and continue through some superb country on to Buxton.

Map 5
Into the Peak

The Peak District is not named for any particular summit and, although hilly, it lacks sharply defined peaks. The name comes from that of a tribe which once inhabited the area.

The route now runs through a series of typically grey limestone villages. This southern part of the Peak is called the 'White Peak' from the glistening limestone of which its houses and walls are built. Much further north, beyond Buxton, is the 'Dark Peak', so-called for the local millstone grit. The whole area is in fact the southern terminus of the Pennine Hills – the 'backbone' of England which progresses more or less up the centre of the country as far as Northumberland, where the Cheviot Hills take over.

The National Park

At the A6, the route joins the valley of the Wye and this takes you into the heart of Britain's first National Park, established in 1951. The road passes Haddon Hall, a marvellous medieval 'great house' to which Elizabethans and Jacobeans added. Bakewell ⑫ is the headquarters of the National Park, as well as the home of Bakewell puddings and tarts. Beyond it the 12-mile (19-km) run to Buxton ⑬ is on arguably one of the most beautiful main roads in Britain. But concentrate: it twists and winds continuously through the superb woods and cliffs on either side.

Buxton is a gracious spa town, and 1,000 feet (305 m) above sea level, is sometimes said to be the highest town in England. It is also something of a national centre, which is why it has been chosen as a starting point for several of the long-distance routes in this book. Because the town sits close to the southern tip of the Pennines, travel in any direction quickly offers a change of environment: across the Cheshire Plain to North Wales or the Marches; north to the moors of Lancashire and Yorkshire; north-west for the Lakes and Scotland or east to the Dales and Scarborough ●

● *The village of Matlock Bath is not to be confused with Matlock the town and former watering place. Few English villages have such a dramatic setting, deep in a splendid limestone ravine cut by the River Derwent. A superb row of crags line the east bank.*

London to the North East/1

An alternative to the M11, A1 and A1(M), linking London with the North East.

Distance: about 350 miles (560 km)
Guide time: 10½ to 11 hours

Access from main roads: M11 junctions 6–13; A1 at Peterborough; M62 and A63 at Kingston upon Hull: A1(M) Scotch Corner.

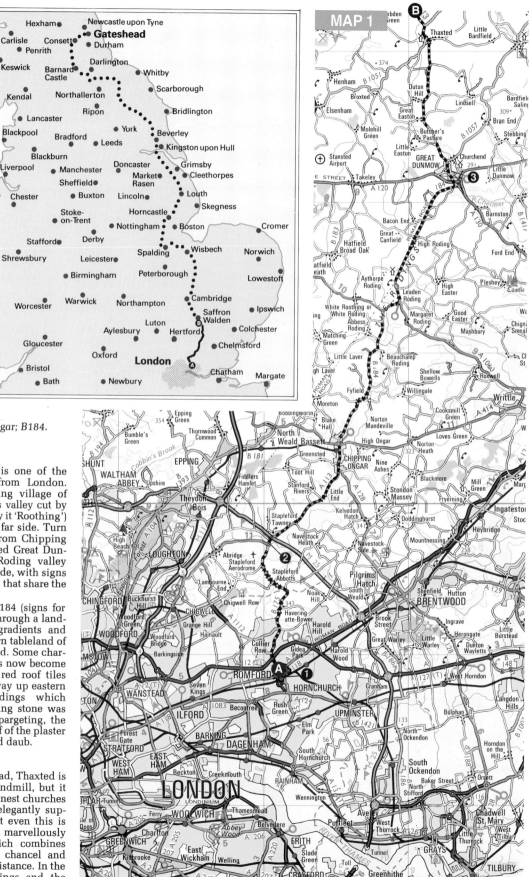

MAP 1

Route summary
B175 and A113 to Chipping Ongar; B184.

Map 1
The Roding Valley
Northwards from Romford ① is one of the pleasantest ways to escape from London. Immediately after the straggling village of Stapleford Abbotts, the gracious valley cut by the little River Roding (locals say it 'Roothing') opens up with the M25 on the far side. Turn right ② on to the A113 and from Chipping Ongar take the B184, signposted Great Dunmow. The road follows the Roding valley through easily rolling countryside, with signs left and right indicating villages that share the river's name.

In Dunmow ③ stay on the B184 (signs for Thaxted and Saffron Walden) through a landscape of perceptibly gentler gradients and bigger fields as the north-western tableland of Essex is reached beyond Thaxted. Some characteristic local building features now become noticeable: pantiles, the curly red roof tiles which are to be found all the way up eastern England; timber-framed buildings which betray the fact that here building stone was always hard to come by; and pargeting, the decoration by engraving or relief of the plaster which made snug the wattle and daub.

Thaxted
Approached by the Dunmow road, Thaxted is dominated by its old tower windmill, but it also possesses one of the very finest churches in Essex. Its graceful spire is elegantly supported by flying buttresses, but even this is outshone by the interior with a marvellously proportioned 14thC nave which combines with Perpendicular work, the chancel and arcades, to give a rare sense of distance. In the town, a wealth of fine buildings and the Guildhall owe their origin to the cutlery trade which flourished here between 1300 and 1500.

London to the North East/2

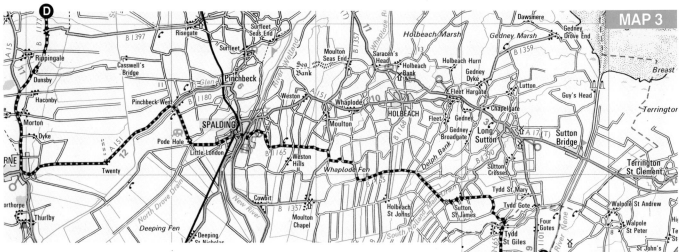

MAP 3

Route summary

After leaving the chalk hills a mile or so south of Cambridge, you now travel over some of the flattest land in Britain. On this section of the route you are never far from the Fens and, for a long stretch, you will be driving right across them. On the whole this means straight roads with good visibility. A look at the map will show you that the roads don't curve much, but they do have sharp right-angled bends – often coinciding with the crossing of a cut (drain) and a bridge. Be ready for these. Remember, too, that on either side of the road there is probably a ditch. It may not be readily visible – but fen-drivers assume it is there and make allowance when passing other vehicles. This applies even on classified roads.

Map 2
Saffron Walden

The name comes from the dried stigma of the saffron crocus, which was grown here and used to dye cloth. Making cloth was the town's chief economic activity in the late medieval period. Once one of the most important towns in Essex, it remains one of the most impressive architecturally. The strongest feeling of past power and glory lingers in the market place; some of the best pargeting anywhere is on the old Sun Inn in Church Street; and the church itself (almost the biggest in the county) is huge, Perpendicular, and lavishly decorated.

The Granta valley

Leave Saffron Walden by following signs ④ for Bishop's Stortford, but fork right (unclassified road) almost immediately. Pass the main entrance to Audley End and turn right on to the B1383 (signposted Great Chesterford).

This is the valley of the River Granta (or the Cam as it becomes after Cambridge). A couple of miles before Saffron Walden, you crossed the watershed of the lands drained by rivers such as the Roding and the Granta. The first flows south and south-east, but here you will see the Granta flowing north; it joins the River Ouse and eventually empties into The Wash.

Grantchester and Cambridge

At Stump Cross roundabout ⑤ turn left on to the A1301, a typically Cambridgeshire road through flat country dotted by villages of yellow brick and thatch. The first is Hinxton and the road bypasses Sawston, which has a respectable Elizabethan manor house and a village college, the first of a number built in the county during the 1930s as part of a notable experiment in rural education.

At the A10 ⑥ turn right then sharp left (signposted Grantchester). Cross the river into Rupert Brooke's village, past the old vicarage where he lived. Turn right for Cambridge after the church.

Cambridge has horrendous traffic (including thousands of students' bicycles); and a modern industry co-existing with seven hundred years of learning and a treasure house of architecture. The absolute must is King's College Chapel (seen across the Backs), where the Cam lazes between daffodils in spring, thronged by punts in summer.

On to the Fens

From the centre of Cambridge follow signposts for the A604 and Huntingdon. Less than half a mile (0.8 km) after crossing the river, take a right turn on to the B1049 (signposted Histon and Cottenham). Follow it across the A45 (Cambridge's northern bypass), through suburban Histon and out into the countryside beyond. Two or three miles (4 km) after Histon you reach the biggish village of Cottenham, set in what is still to some extent orchard country.

At the village of Wilburton with its good timber-framed houses ⑦ turn right on to the A1123, signposted for Newmarket and then, after just a few score yards, left on to the unclassified road (signposted for Wentworth).

Wentworth itself is a tiny lost village on what counts as a ridge in this part of the world.

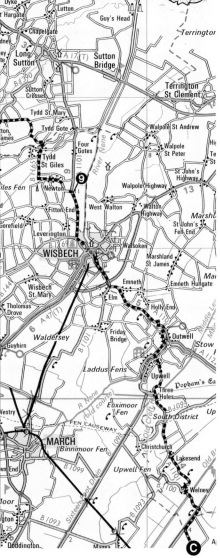

Pass it on your left and cross the A142 (signposted Coveney). This is a rather more sizeable place, also set on a ridge of dry land which reaches 45 feet (14 m) above sea level, and so gives a terrific panorama across the Fens. Ignore the signs for Ely and go north from the village on the very minor road to Downham. To do this you must make a right turn at the Way Head intersection ⑧. Downham is yet another built-above-the-Fen village, this time with views towards Ely, an island in the flood country. In Little Downham – to use the full name – go left on to the B1411, which after some zig-zags soon has you running beside the New Bedford River, cut by the Dutch engineer, Cornelius Vermuyden, in 1651, when his earlier effort about a mile to the west proved insufficient to carry the Ouse's flood waters off the Fens. (*Now see Map 3.*)

When you reach the A1101 turn left on to it, following signs for Wisbech, reached after 19 twisty miles (30.5 km). This town is the commercial hub of the bulb and seed-growing countryside around; it also possesses, in The

London to the North East/2

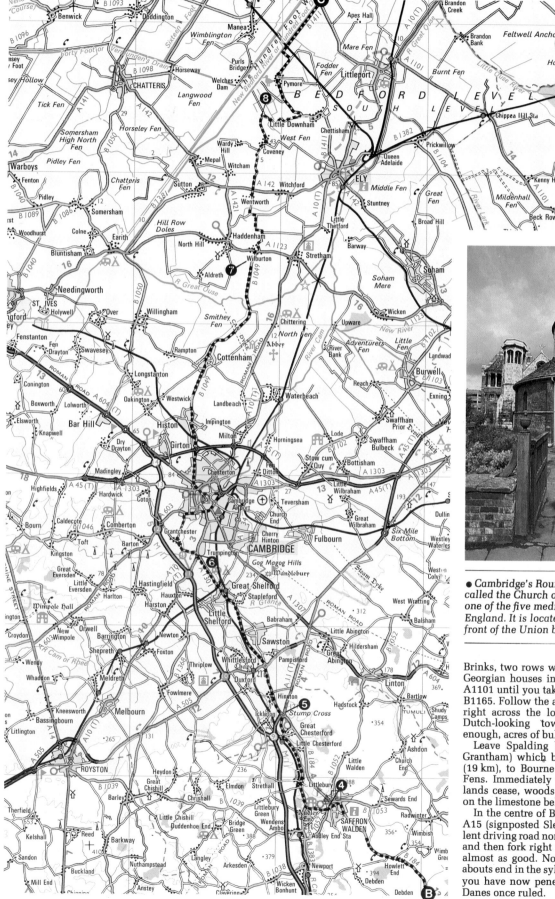

MAP 2

● Cambridge's Round Church – properly called the Church of the Holy Sepulchre – is one of the five medieval round churches in England. It is located off Bridge Street, in front of the Union building.

Brinks, two rows which are among the finest Georgian houses in Britain. Continue on the A1101 until you take the left turn ⑨ on to the B1165. Follow the angular course of this road right across the lower Fens to Spalding, a Dutch-looking town, with, appropriately enough, acres of bulb fields around it.

Leave Spalding by the A151 (signposted Grantham) which brings you, after 12 miles (19 km), to Bourne on the very edge of the Fens. Immediately west of the town the flat lands cease, woods appear and you are back on the limestone belt.

In the centre of Bourne turn right on to the A15 (signposted Sleaford). Follow this excellent driving road north for about 5 miles (8 km) and then fork right on to the B1177, which is almost as good. Note how the villages hereabouts end in the syllable '-by', a sure sign that you have now penetrated country where the Danes once ruled.

London to the North East/3

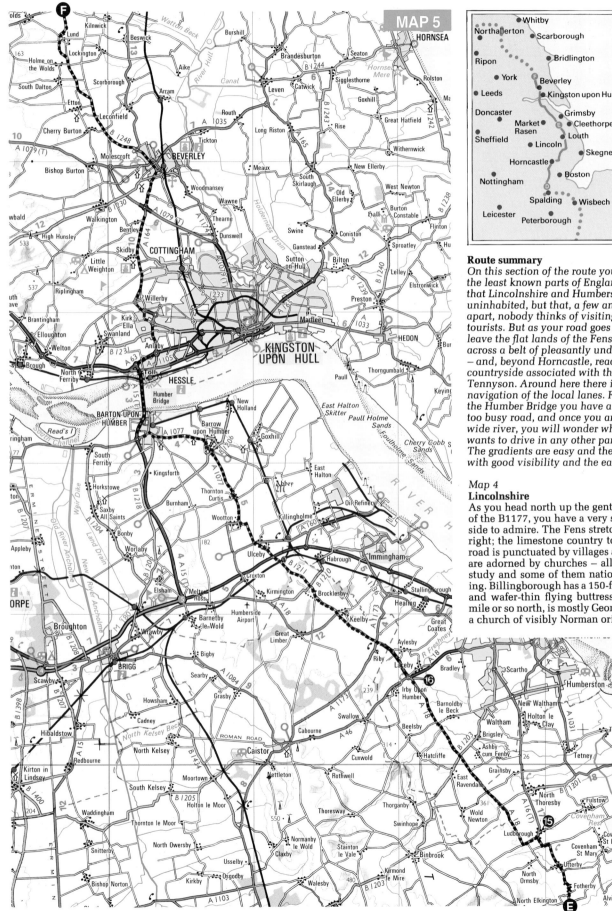

MAP 5

Route summary

On this section of the route you cross one of the least known parts of England. It is not that Lincolnshire and Humberside are uninhabited, but that, a few ancient cities apart, nobody thinks of visiting them as tourists. But as your road goes north you leave the flat lands of the Fens and swing across a belt of pleasantly undulating terrain – and, beyond Horncastle, reach the countryside associated with the poet Tennyson. Around here there is some tricky navigation of the local lanes. From Louth to the Humber Bridge you have a good and not too busy road, and once you are across the wide river, you will wonder why anyone wants to drive in any other part of Britain. The gradients are easy and the roads roll on with good visibility and the easiest of curves.

Map 4
Lincolnshire

As you head north up the gentle, easy driving of the B1177, you have a very simple countryside to admire. The Fens stretch away to your right; the limestone country to your left. The road is punctuated by villages and the villages are adorned by churches – all of them worth study and some of them nationally outstanding. Billingborough has a 150-foot (46-m) spire and wafer-thin flying buttresses; Horbling, a mile or so north, is mostly Georgian and boasts a church of visibly Norman origin.

London to the North East/3

Keep straight ahead across the A52, through tiny Swaton on the B1394 and on to Helpringham with another magnificently-spired church. But the finest is yet to be, at Heckington, which you enter after crossing the A17. In a county of great churches, this one, though only in a village, could serve a town. It is built of the local Ancaster stone, is 164 feet (50 m) long and its spire reaches 180 feet (55 m).

You drive north on the unclassified lane signposted for Howell, bearing right at the two junctions ⑩ and ⑪ until, on a road of typically Lincolnshire straights and angularities, you make a T-junction with the B1395 and turn left on to it. After about a mile you turn right on to the A153 (signposted Skegness) which will carry you across the barely perceptible valley of the River Witham as it flows southeastwards from Lincoln to the sea near Boston. You pass through Billinghay and just before you reach the river 3 miles (5 km) further on, there is a sign on the right for Dogdyke where the Dambusters were stationed – but you go straight on to cross the river at Tattershall Bridge.

Tattershall and Horncastle

From the bridge over the River Witham continue directly ahead on the A153 and into Tattershall. This town has a castle – a massive, lowering affair – built in 1445 for Ralph Cromwell, Treasurer of England. As you might expect in such flat country as this, the roof gives a magnificent prospect. The town's church is almost as impressive, and especially noted for its many brasses. Where the A153 bends to the right in the middle of the town, take the B1192 left (signposted Woodhall Spa) and then immediately the first turn right – an unclassified road.

This follows an almost identical course to the A153 which you have just left, but on the west bank of the River Bain and the old Horncastle Canal, instead of on the east. In the village of Kirkby on Bain, ignore signs for Woodhall Spa ⑫ and continue parallel to the canal. When about 3 miles (5 km) later you make a junction with the B1191, join it (signposted Horncastle).

Horncastle is your first town on the Lincolnshire Wolds, a range of low but delightful limestone hills, of which you will see plenty more between here and the Humber. Though small, Horncastle has a pleasingly urban feel. Its church (built in the greenstone local to the area) is definitely a town building. Leave the town on the A158 (signposted Skegness).

Tennyson country

A mile (1.5 km) beyond the boundary of the built-up area of Horncastle, in the hamlet of High Toynton, take the unclassified left turn and follow it as it curves round to the right. It takes you into the heart of the Wolds and of the Tennyson country – some of the most beautiful country in Lincolnshire and equal in quality to parts of the Chilterns and South Downs. However, the lanes are narrow and winding. Navigate carefully.

At the right turn signposted Greetham ⑬ go straight ahead; about half a mile later, go right and immediately left at the intersection ⑭. Keep straight on past the lane signposted for Ashby Puerorum, for the village of Somersby, where Tennyson's father was rector. Drive out of the village by following signs for Tetford, a lovely settlement, set in dimpled hills.

Leave Tetford by taking signs for Louth, which lead you away from the village by a sharpish hill and then over the crossroads at

the top. Continue over generously undulating countryside to the A16, on to which you turn left for Louth – a bustling rural centre with a delicately buttressed church.

Map 5
The Humber

You are now on the eastern flank of the Wolds which you follow by the A16 and then ⑮ the B1431. At the roundabout ⑯ take the A18 to Keelby and from there the B1211 to Ulceby. At Wootton you join the A1077 which takes you to Barton-upon-Humber and the Humber Bridge. On the other side follow signs for Beverley, a superb minster town which you reach by a straight run along the A164. Leave Beverley by the A164 (signposted Bridlington) but, just outside town, turn left on to the B1248. This is an excellent road, giving a real taste of the Yorkshire Wolds which lie to the left and to which you draw nearer.

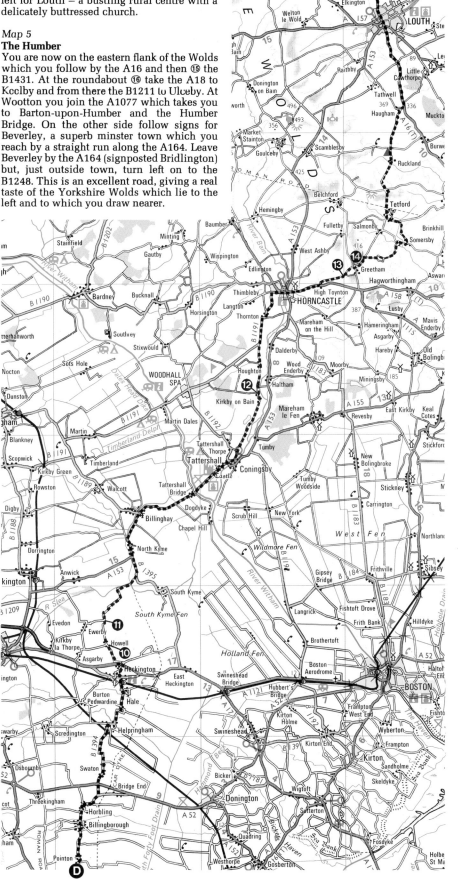

London to the North East/4

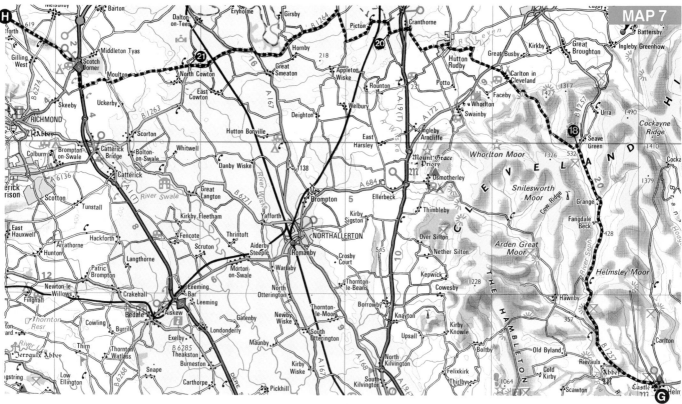

MAP 7

Route summary

The final stages of your route are up-and-down. On straight, easy B roads, you cross the northern arm of the Yorkshire Wolds and follow the line of the Howardian Hills across the vale beyond them. The going becomes more tortuous after Helmsley as you climb into the fastnesses of the North Yorkshire Moors, where the valleys are deeply incised. There follows a stretch of driving on mostly minor roads as you cross the plain – essentially the valley of the Tees – which separates the Moors from the Pennines. A length of fast Roman road takes you nearly to Barnard Castle. After that, you climb out of the Tees valley over the moors to Weardale on a sinuous B road. This is followed immediately by a similar exercise to take you from Weardale into the valley of the Derwent. You are then on the edge of the north-eastern conurbation and pick your way through industry to Newcastle. (From here it is a further 166 miles (265 km) to Edinburgh by the rather indirect main road route, the A1.)

Map 6
Norton

At the end of a very straight stretch of road you enter Norton, through which ⑰ you go straight ahead following signs for Malton, the adjoining town on the other side of the River Derwent. In crossing you pass from the old East Riding into the North Riding; but the modern boundaries have extended North Yorkshire further south.

Malton to Pickering

Malton is a spirited place and has been so for many centuries. The Romans were here. Old Malton, away to your right in the direction of Scarborough, has the remains of a 12thC church which was part of a priory. New Malton, in other words the main town through which your route goes, has a mainly Norman church right in the middle of the market-place. Here operates a major livestock market and here, too, the training of racehorses is an important activity.

Leave Malton by the B1257 (signposted for Helmsley). A pleasingly driveable road this, through a series of villages. It runs on a shelf of land with the wooded Howardian Hills on your left and the flood plain of the River Rye to your right. Several village names ending in 'street' indicate that you are still on a Roman route. It brings you, some 8 miles (13 km) from Malton, to Hovingham, certainly one of the prettiest villages in Ryedale. Here, too, there is evidence of the Romans, and another Saxon tower as well.

Vale of Pickering

Follow the road round to the right in the centre of Hovingham. As you leave the village, you begin on a section of the route in which the roads are nothing like so straight as those you have been following since crossing the Humber. You have first to get over the Vale of Pickering – the plain ahead as you leave

Hovingham. In the middle of it stands the low ridge of Caulkleys Banks with the tiny village of Stonegrave, overshadowed by a great church, at one end. Go straight through on the B1257, following signs for Helmsley. The terrain is fast becoming noticeably more hilly and more wooded. After Oswaldkirk the road bends right and points you directly towards the bulk of the moors, with compact Helmsley and its castle at the foot of their slopes.

Map 7
Moors and Pennines

Take the B1257 out of Helmsley (signs for Middlesbrough), which takes you through wooded valleys into the National Park. Be ready for a sharp left turn ⑱ on to an unclassified road some 10 miles (16 km) from Helmsley. This follows a stream valley and then climbs on to Cringle Moor and descends from there swiftly to Carlton in Cleveland. A few yards beyond Carlton church ⑲ bear left and go straight over the A172 to Hutton Rudby, where you follow the Crathorne signs. In this village you bear left over the A19 and then shortly right ⑳. At the T-junction beyond Picton turn right and, when you reach the B1264, turn left on to it. After about 5 miles (8 km) you reach the A167 on to which you turn right and then, in rather over half a mile (0.8 km), left on to the B1263. Follow this over the railway and, where the B road swings sharp left ㉑, take the unclassified road opposite (signs for Moulton). At the A1 turn right and drive north for a mile (1.5 km) to Scotch Corner. Here you go left on to the dead straight A66 for Barnard Castle.

Hills begin to rise distinctly on your left – outliers of the Pennine chain, which you will be among nearly all the way to Newcastle.

Over the Wolds

Continue on the B1248 to make a T-junction with the A166 in the village of Wetwang. Turn

London to the North East/4

left. The curious-sounding name probably means no more than 'the wet field'. Shortly after leaving its straight main street, turn right on to the B1248 again, following signposts for Malton. This straight road now lifts you over the Yorkshire Wolds, significant hills at the very end of the great chain of chalk uplands which crosses England from Dorset to Scarborough. It is a countryside of wide fields with a somewhat bleak feel to it, until you dive suddenly into a sheltering valley. As the road begins to drop towards the village of Wharram le Street, look out for the car park on the left ⑰, from which a path leads across just such a valley to the deserted medieval village of Wharram Percy. This is one of the most remarkable archaeological sites in England. The well-labelled mounds of the ancient homes and the ruined church compose a scene combining the eerie and the historic. But the route continues down the short hill to Wharram le Street (the latter part of the name indicating a Roman road), a village whose church has a tower of mixed Saxon and Norman work. Continue straight through, still following signs for Malton. You pass through North Grimston, one of the most charming of the Wolds villages, cosily tucked under the swelling hills.

● *Rievaulx Abbey – one of the loveliest ruins in Britain – seen from the E. It is just off the route, near Helmsley.*

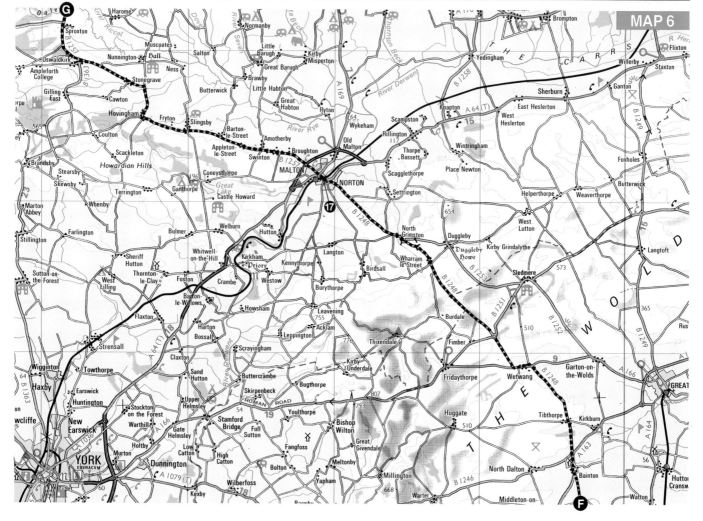

MAP 6

MAP 8

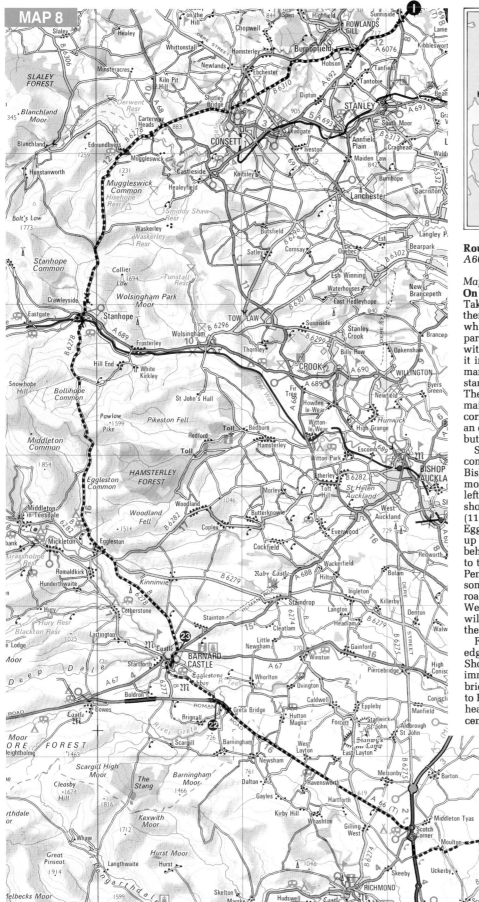

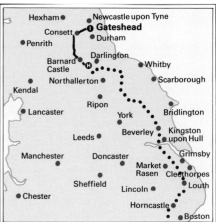

Route summary
A66, B6278 and B6310.

Map 8
On the flank of the Hills
Take the A66 to just beyond Greta Bridge and then turn right ㉒ on to the unclassified road which leads down to the River Tees and runs parallel to it. When you make a T-junction with the B6277, turn right on to it and follow it into the centre of Barnard Castle. This is a marvellous town. The ruined castle of its name stands on a dominating cliff above the Tees. The town itself has two splendidly generous main streets, Galgate and Market Place, at the corner of which is the big church. There is also an octagonal market cross. An air of judicious but unobtrusive design is the town's hallmark.

Setting off on your way again is a trifle complicated. Begin by following signs for Bishop Auckland – taking the A67. Rather more than a mile (1.5 km) out of town ㉓ go left on to the B6278. This climbs over a shoulder of hill and, after some 7 miles (11 km), brings you back into Teesdale at Eggleston. You stay on the B6278 as it climbs up into the hills, leaving the Tees finally behind you. This is a winding road. Don't try to take it too fast; enjoy the bracing air of the Pennines. Still more care is needed when, some 9 miles (14.5 km) after Eggleston, the road drops down a steep hill to Stanhope in Weardale. Follow the signs for Consett, which will take you through the village and up into the hills again – still on the B6278.

Follow the road over the A68 to the northern edge of Consett – a decaying steel town. In Shotley Bridge turn left on to the A69 and immediately right on to the B3610. Where this briefly rejoins the A69, continue on the B3610 to Burnopfield, where join the A692 for Gateshead and from there follow signs to the city centre ●

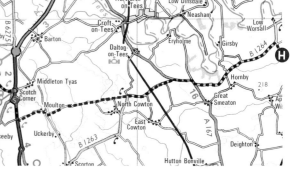

Buxton to Bodmin/1

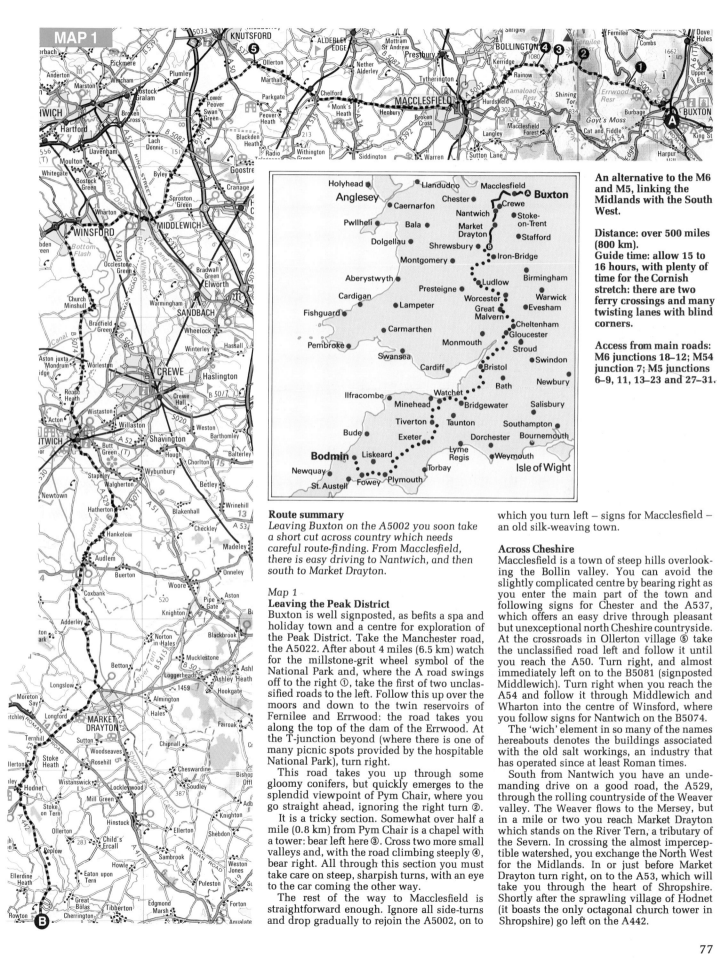

MAP 1

An alternative to the M6 and M5, linking the Midlands with the South West.

Distance: over 500 miles (800 km).
Guide time: allow 15 to 16 hours, with plenty of time for the Cornish stretch: there are two ferry crossings and many twisting lanes with blind corners.

Access from main roads: M6 junctions 18–12; M54 junction 7; M5 junctions 6–9, 11, 13–23 and 27–31.

Route summary
Leaving Buxton on the A5002 you soon take a short cut across country which needs careful route-finding. From Macclesfield, there is easy driving to Nantwich, and then south to Market Drayton.

Map 1
Leaving the Peak District
Buxton is well signposted, as befits a spa and holiday town and a centre for exploration of the Peak District. Take the Manchester road, the A5022. After about 4 miles (6.5 km) watch for the millstone-grit wheel symbol of the National Park and, where the A road swings off to the right ①, take the first of two unclassified roads to the left. Follow this up over the moors and down to the twin reservoirs of Fernilee and Errwood: the road takes you along the top of the dam of the Errwood. At the T-junction beyond (where there is one of many picnic spots provided by the hospitable National Park), turn right.

This road takes you up through some gloomy conifers, but quickly emerges to the splendid viewpoint of Pym Chair, where you go straight ahead, ignoring the right turn ②.

It is a tricky section. Somewhat over half a mile (0.8 km) from Pym Chair is a chapel with a tower: bear left here ③. Cross two more small valleys and, with the road climbing steeply ④, bear right. All through this section you must take care on steep, sharpish turns, with an eye to the car coming the other way.

The rest of the way to Macclesfield is straightforward enough. Ignore all side-turns and drop gradually to rejoin the A5002, on to which you turn left – signs for Macclesfield – an old silk-weaving town.

Across Cheshire
Macclesfield is a town of steep hills overlooking the Bollin valley. You can avoid the slightly complicated centre by bearing right as you enter the main part of the town and following signs for Chester and the A537, which offers an easy drive through pleasant but unexceptional north Cheshire countryside. At the crossroads in Ollerton village ⑤ take the unclassified road left and follow it until you reach the A50. Turn right, and almost immediately left on to the B5081 (signposted Middlewich). Turn right when you reach the A54 and follow it through Middlewich and Wharton into the centre of Winsford, where you follow signs for Nantwich on the B5074.

The 'wich' element in so many of the names hereabouts denotes the buildings associated with the old salt workings, an industry that has operated since at least Roman times.

South from Nantwich you have an undemanding drive on a good road, the A529, through the rolling countryside of the Weaver valley. The Weaver flows to the Mersey, but in a mile or two you reach Market Drayton which stands on the River Tern, a tributary of the Severn. In crossing the almost imperceptible watershed, you exchange the North West for the Midlands. In or just before Market Drayton turn right, on to the A53, which will take you through the heart of Shropshire. Shortly after the sprawling village of Hodnet (it boasts the only octagonal church tower in Shropshire) go left on the A442.

Buxton to Bodmin/2

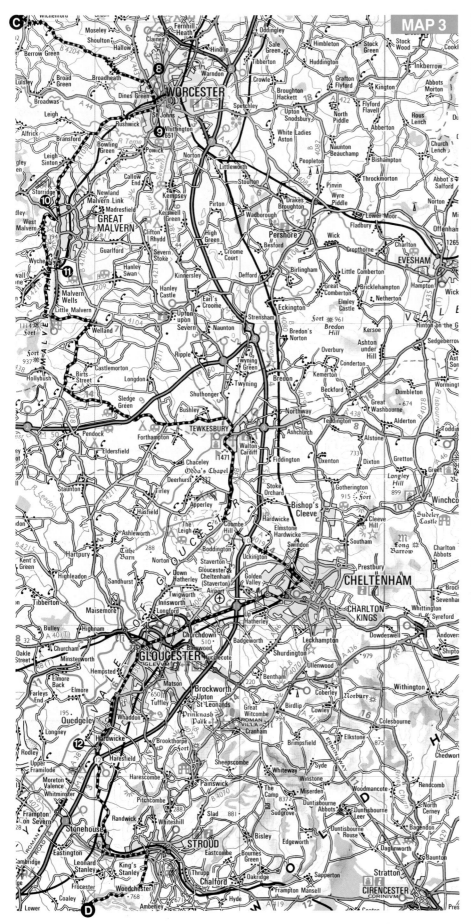

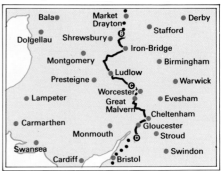

Route summary

The route picks its way through some attractive parts of Shropshire, then south via the Malvern Hills to the Cotswolds.

Map 2

Round The Wrekin

Now the countryside is becoming distinctly more hilly and you begin to get glimpses of The Wrekin ahead. This modest summit of 1,334 feet (407 m) is probably Shropshire's best-known landmark. At the roundabout ⑥ turn right on to the B4394 and follow this across the A5; it turns into the B4380 past the site of the Roman city, Viroconivm. For a time The Wrekin is dead ahead, but as the road winds its way into the gorge of the Severn you will have The Wrekin on the left. Go straight ahead as the road becomes the main street of Iron Bridge and you pass the famous bridge on the right – 'the stupendous iron arch' that spans the Severn, first of its kind anywhere; Iron Bridge is fast becoming one big museum of the early Industrial Revolution.

Carry on through the town and turn right over the river ⑦ at signposts for Broseley. This is another one-time centre of the iron industry, through which you follow signposts for Much Wenlock – a town with a still markedly medieval air and a ruined priory.

Shropshire

From Much Wenlock take the B4731 (signposted Church Stretton), which for 8 miles (13 km) runs along the foot of the famous limestone ridge, Wenlock Edge, then bears west to a Swiss-style holiday town, Church Stretton, nestled under The Long Mynd.

Leave the little town by the A49 (signposts for Ludlow and Worcester) but, after a quarter of a mile (0.5 km), turn right on to the beautiful B4370 which runs round the southern end of The Long Mynd. At the A489 turn left and follow to the A49, where you turn right.

You approach Ludlow, a marvellous old town, for centuries a strongpoint of the English defence of the Welsh Marches, with a view of the castle across the water meadows to the right. Ludlow itself, now happily bypassed, is still essentially a medieval market town with a church, the biggest in Shropshire: it sails above the huddled houses.

Follow the Worcester signs on the A49 out of Ludlow and, after about 6 miles (10 km), turn left on to the A456 which you take as far as Tenbury Wells. Here turn right (signs for Leominster) and then, immediately after crossing the river, turn left on to the B4204 ⑦ – an enchanting road that takes you up and down and in and out of the Teme valley.

Map 3

Worcester and the Malverns

Where the B4204 makes a T-junction with the

Buxton to Bodmin/2

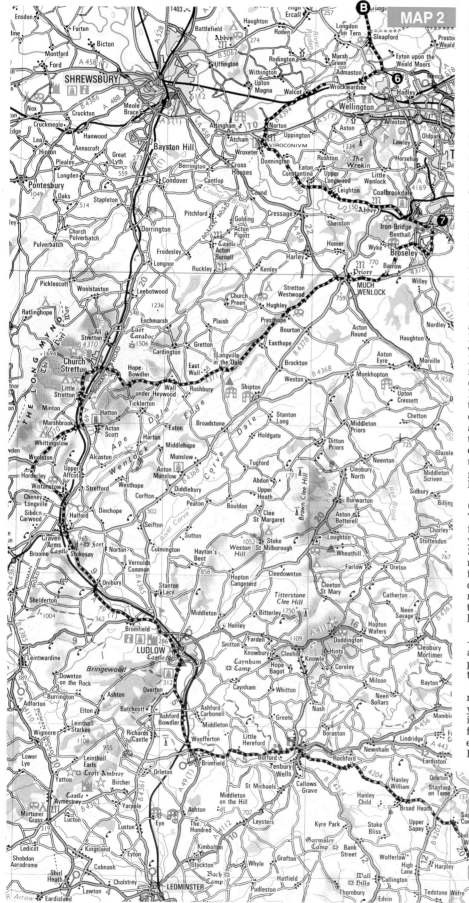

A443, turn right and skirt the city of Worcester. Do *not* cross the river ⑧, but follow signs for Hereford and the A449. This takes you past the county cricket ground and, glancing left, you will see the cathedral's 14thC tower beyond the River Severn. At the roundabout ⑨, go straight ahead, now on the A4103, for Hereford.

About 3 miles (5 km) from the built-up area you cross the River Teme for the last time and, as you rise gradually from its valley, you will see the line of the Malvern Hills ahead, another of those free-standing lumps like The Wrekin and The Long Mynd, which characterize this part of England. The Malverns are ancient volcanic rock, sheep-grazed common land and an exhilarating piece of public open space.

At Leigh Sinton, turn left on to the B road for the Malverns, of which there are at least five. You follow signposts for Link until you reach the A449. Here turn sharply right ⑩ now following signs for West Malvern on the B4219 and, very shortly, left on to the B4232, which takes you through West Malvern, perched (like all the settlements here) on the side of the hills. This road gives you a real feel of the Malvern Hills.

In the village of Wyche turn right and then almost immediately left ⑪ to stay on the B4232. When, after about two miles (3 km) of winding hill-driving, you reach the A449, turn left, and as you descend from the Malverns' ridge after about half a mile (0.8 km) turn right on to the A4104 (signposted Tewkesbury). Follow this road as far as Welland and there turn right on to the B4208. You are now driving parallel to the Malvern Hills once again. After about 6 miles (10 km) turn left on to the A438 and stay with this up-graded country road all the way to Tewkesbury – a town of old houses, narrow alleys and a glorious abbey church owning an enormous Norman tower.

Gracious towns
Take the A38 south out of Tewkesbury, bound for Gloucester. The Severn, in whose valley you remain until reaching the Cotswolds at Stroud, is away to your right. After about 7 miles (11 km) turn left on to the A4019 and follow it across the M5 into Cheltenham, one of the most gracious town centres in Britain, rich in Regency buildings dating from when the Duke of Wellington took the spa waters here and made the place fashionable.

Leave Cheltenham by the A40 for Gloucester – an altogether more ancient town, for it was a port in Roman times and is dominated by a powerful Norman cathedral to which a 15thC tower has been added.

Take the A430 south to the A38 and at the roundabout ⑫, turn left for Stonehouse, where you go left again on to the A419. As you run into Stroud, turn right on to the B4066 and follow it up a steep hill on to the Cotswold escarpment: hills on the left and the Vale of Berkeley to the right.

Buxton to Bodmin/3

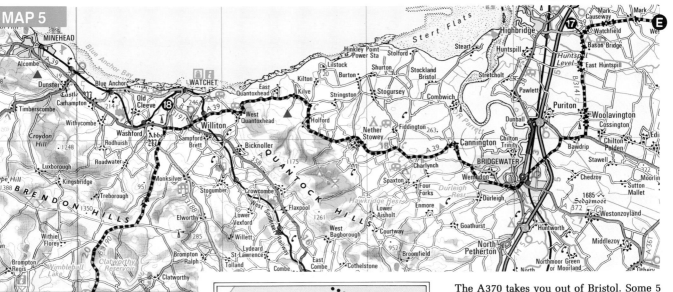

MAP 5

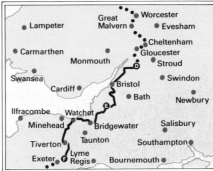

Route summary

Skirting Bristol by the relatively built-up but sensational road through the Avon Gorge, you enter the true West Country. Leaving behind first the Mendip Hills, then the Quantock Hills, head southwards, after Tiverton following closely alongside the M5.

Map 4
Cotswold to Bristol

No speeding on the B4066: this is a winding hillside road on which every bend needs to be driven. But it is rather fine, so enjoy it at a reasonable pace. In Dursley go right on to the A4135 and after about a mile (1.5 km) of urban driving, pick up the B4066 again, turning left on to it. It brings you down, over the M5, to the A38 where you turn left and, after little more than a mile, right on to the B4066 yet again. This brings you to the old market town of Berkeley, chiefly remarkable for its partly ruined 14thC castle still lived in by the Berkeley family.

Turn left in the centre of the little town and follow the B4509 back to the A38 where you turn right for a straight run to the northern outskirts of Bristol. You bridge the M4 and, as you approach M5 junction 16 take the right turn ⑬ signposted Over. In about 2 miles (3 km), where this road makes a junction with the B4055, turn left and join the M5 at junction 17 for a 4-mile (6.5-km) run to junction 18. Here leave the motorway following signs for the A4. This takes you along the bottom of the great Avon Gorge and under Brunel's famous suspension bridge. About half a mile (0.5 km) below the bridge, you reach a complicated junction ⑭ through which you must follow signs for the A370 and Weston-super-Mare.

The A370 takes you out of Bristol. Some 5 miles (8 km) out of town be ready for a roundabout ⑮ at which you turn left (signs for Chew Magna) on to the B3130. Follow this to the A38, a fast main road on to which you must turn right and, then, after about a quarter of a mile (0.5 km), left on to the B3130 again.

The Mendip Hills

Pure country driving, not fast, but rewarding, with a new view at every bend, lies ahead of you for some miles now. In the big village of Chew Magna, turn right on to the B3114 which takes you past Chew Valley Lake to the A368. Look carefully for the unclassified right turn ⑯ and follow it down to the A368, where you go right and immediately left on an unclassified road that climbs the Mendip Hills. When you reach the B3134, cross it to the B3371 (signposted Cheddar).

This road takes you over the bleak summit ridge of the Mendips and then descends the other side of the range through the towering limestone cliffs of the Cheddar Gorge. The Gorge demands careful driving, for the gradient is steep and the road winds, but there are parking places at which to pause.

Over the levels

In the village of Cheddar, take the signs for Wedmore and the B3151. There is a sharp transition from the hill country you have just crossed to the wide levels of the Axe valley. Beyond this, the road climbs a low ridge on which sits the wholly delightful village of Wedmore and its big church. Here you must turn right on the B3139 (signs for Burnham and Bridgwater) and back to the levels again. Your road has something of the feel of a causeway running above the area (which is liable to flooding), and it has more than its share of unexpectedly sharp corners.

Map 5
Bridgwater and the levels

In the village of Watchfield look out for the slightly unexpected left turn ⑰ on to the B3141 which, after a few flat miles, rises gently to Woolavington, a village on the low ridge of the Polden Hills. Beyond it, turn right on to the A39 and follow this road into Bridgwater, which you reach after crossing the M5. This is a decayed port, the River Parrett being tidal and subject to a twice-daily bore. Like Gloucester, it lost its trade to Bristol; but Castle Street

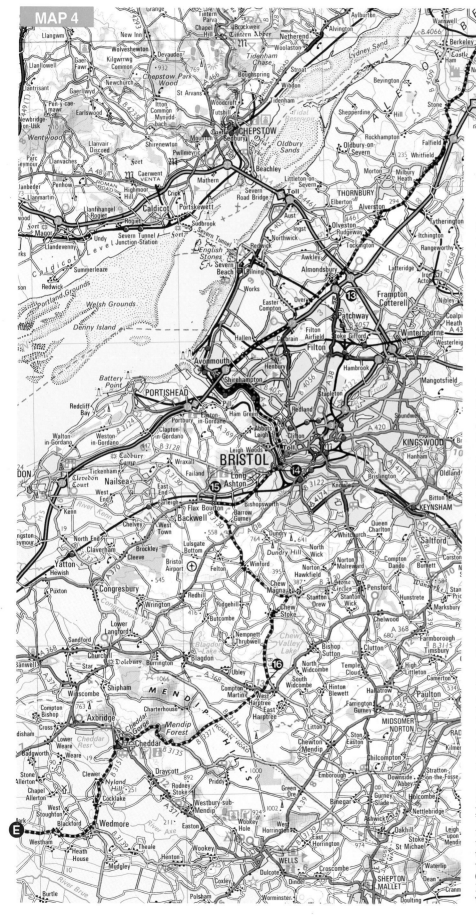

MAP 4

reminds of former eminence. In this town the Duke of Monmouth and his rebels spent the night before marching to Sedgemoor (east of the town) where they were routed by the army of James II in 1685.

Leave Bridgwater by the A39 (signposts for Minehead). You are on A and B roads for the rest of the drive through Somerset and across Devon to Exeter. But this is the South West, so the driving will not be effortless. The A39, now meandering westwards to the Quantocks, is a good example: a winding road with frequent villages and few bypasses.

The Quantock Hills
Nether Stowey, about 19 miles (30 km) from Bridgwater, is the biggest village hereabouts. William and Dorothy Wordsworth spent a year nearby when Samuel Taylor Coleridge was living here and writing *The Ancient Mariner*.

The line of the Quantock Hills now appears on your left: a chunk of Devonian rock (like Exmoor further ahead), sticking up from the Old Red Sandstone which lends its pink tone to so many churches in these villages, and which you see again in the Devon soil of the Exe valley south of Exmoor.

Minute as they are – 12 miles (19 km) long, 4 miles (6 km) across at their widest and a mere 1,261 feet (384 m) at their highest – the Quantocks are astonishingly beautiful. On this side they drop to the plain in narrow valleys filled with little streams and woods. On the west is a sharp escarpment.

The A39 takes you round the seaward end of the hills at West Quantoxhead. Follow it through Williton and just over a mile (1.5 km) later ⑱ take the left turn on to the B3190 (signposted Tiverton). This road climbs swiftly up to the ridge of the Brendon Hills, the eastern arm of Exmoor, and drops as rapidly on the other side, passing the southern end of the Wimbleball reservoir. Then you go up and over breezy Haddon Hill and cross the county boundary for your first Devon town, the somewhat drab Bampton.

Leave Bampton on the A396, which hugs the curves of the River Exe for 8 miles (13 km) to the altogether more bustling town of Tiverton. Here go left on the Taunton road (A373) which, after about 3½ miles (6 km), crosses the old Grand Western Canal, relic of the dream of linking Devon to the national waterway network. It never got further west than Tiverton, and now forms an isolated stretch of water.

In the village of Halberton, about half a mile (0.8 km) beyond the canal, look out for a right fork on to the B3391 ⑲, which quickly brings you to more lasting forms of transport, the Western Region main line and the M5. Go under both ⑳, then turn sharply right on to the B3181 (signposts for Cullompton). Negotiate its straggling and very narrow high street with care. Follow the B3181 (signposts for Cullompton) south for a few more miles to Broadclyst ('clyst' means a clean stream), where you follow the sign for Exeter.

Buxton to Bodmin/4

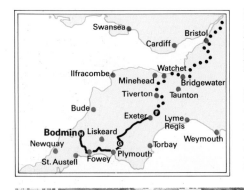

Route summary

Between relatively fast driving across Dartmoor and a similarly easy final run into Bodmin, you have to find your way through Plymouth and navigate a series of twisting Devon lanes.

Map 6
Through Exeter

The route through Exeter is best described by roundabouts. You enter the city on the B3181. About 2 miles (3 km) after crossing the M5 and after passing through suburban Pinhoe, you cross a railway and come to a fork. Take the right fork (signposted for the city centre).

After nearly 2 miles (3 km) of urban driving you come to a roundabout, from which you take the second exit (Western Way). Follow this road (it curves right) for about 500 yards (457 m) to the next roundabout ㉑ and here go straight across (ignoring signs for the M5 on your left). You are still on Western Way, and you follow it to a four-way intersection. Turn right into a one-way system.

Follow signs for Plymouth, Okehampton and Torbay (A377) until you have crossed the river. Immediately after the bridge turn right ㉒ and then in a few yards left on to Cowick Street, which is the B3212. The signposts are for Moretonhampstead and the road takes you past a railway station on your left.

Beyond the Exe

There is still a mile or two of urban driving before you are back in the Devon countryside, but Exeter and the River Exe are behind you and you are clearly pointed to the granite mass of Dartmoor. You will remain on the B3212 until almost the other side of the Moor.

The road goes under the roaring dual carriageway of the A30 and begins to climb through increasingly hilly and wooded countryside. The hills are steep and the corners sharp. Take it with care: it was not built for speed.

Dartmoor

You are now in a maze of sharply tiered hills, woods and streams. Where the road begins to drop steadily, with a stream on your right, be ready for the fork ㉓ and keep right on the B3212 past Dunsford. An easy loop of the

● *Fowey (pronounced 'Foy') quaintly sums up everyone's dream of a Cornish port. Its harbour can take ships up to 12,000 tons, and it was formerly a key port not just for Cornwall, but the whole country.*

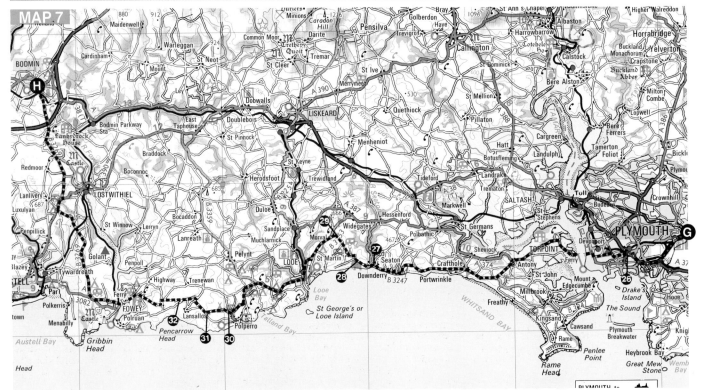

route will take you through this village of cream-washed and thatched cottages.

Continue on the B3212 beside the Teign and through Doccombe, until you drop into busy little Moretonhampstead. Still on the B3212, you notice that the moors now intrude more often into the field pattern until you are plainly on the Moor itself.

Driving across Dartmoor on this route is easy: just stick to the B3212. You will have plenty of time to take in the scenery of what has been called the last wilderness of southern England. The title is perhaps not quite just since man has long exploited the Moor; in fact, as numerous hut circles attest, since

Bronze Age times at least. Later came the tin miners and now the farmers with sheep and cattle. Admire the long tilts of subtle browns and greens and note how the granite thrusts itself up through the soil in dramatic 'tors'.

Princetown to Plympton

The road looks straight enough on the map, but is liable to sharp bends where it dips to cross streams, so take care. Four and a half miles (7 km) beyond Princetown and the gaol, turn left at a hotel (signposted for Meavy). Ignore two right turns for Meavy and follow your backroad right round a wood, then up a steep hill. Go straight on at the cross **24** and

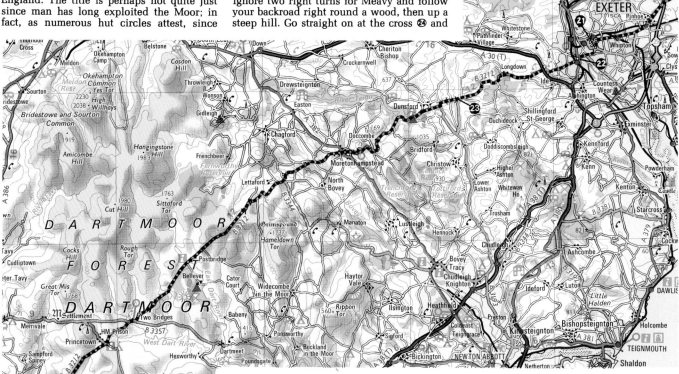

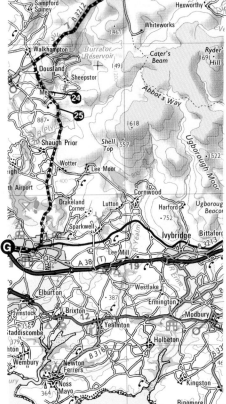

right at the next junction **25**; then straight on over the Plym and follow the signposts down to Plympton, with woods and fields gradually replacing the moorland. In Plympton turn right on the main street (signposted Plymouth).

Map 7

Plym, Plymouth and Tamar

Plymouth looks more complicated to navigate than is truly the case. You enter from Plympton and, immediately after crossing the Plym, turn left, ignoring the A39 on your left, and going straight ahead with the estuary on your left. As the road bears to the right (leaving the estuary) stay with it ignoring the A379 turn on your left. Keep straight on (signs for Saltash) until a big rotary around a church. Turn left here **26** along Exeter Street, past the bus station and take the third exit (Royal Parade) at the next rotary. Now go straight ahead (on the A374) and along Union Street. Cross a bridge and pass the hospital on your right: now watch for the left turn (signposted Ferry) which takes you down to and over the Tamar to Torpoint.

Cornish coast

From the ferry go straight ahead on the A374 (signposted for Liskeard), but in the village of Antony turn left on to the B3247. Follow this through Crafthole and Downderry to the beach at Seaton. Here, immediately after crossing the bridge, turn left **27** on to a by-road which

climbs sharply away from the coast. Take the first right, **28**. Now keep straight ahead, ignoring left and right turns, until your lane drops to the B3253 where you turn left **29**.

This drops you quickly to the A387 and the quintessentially Cornish fishing village of Looe: really the twin settlements of East and West Looe. Turn right to cross the river in the centre of the village and follow the A387 (signposts for Polperro). About 4 miles (6 km) from Looe, where the A387 drops into a sharp valley beside a stream, there are two right turns in quick succession: take the second **30** (signposted Lansallos) and go straight ahead up the left hand side of a valley. Above the valley go right at a T-junction **31**; ignore the left turn for Lansallos and go right half a mile (0.8 km) later and, in a few yards, left. Continue straight ahead for ¾ mile (1 km), then fork right **32**, following signs for Fowey. All these Cornish lanes need very cautious driving. Visibility around high-banked hedges is zero, and what looks like a farm road may be the route you want.

At Bodinnick, take the ferry to Fowey. The crossing only takes a couple of minutes, but look upstream (this is the Fowey River) rather than towards the sea: the winding, wooded banks offer a better view.

Your last stage is to follow the B3269 (except for a one-mile (1.5-km) stretch on the A390) into Bodmin. As you leave the coast the hills flatten and the Fowey valley winds away on your right ●

**Distance: about 130 miles
(209 km).
Guide time: allow four
hours.**

**Access from main roads:
M6 junction 19; M56
junctions 11–14; M53
junction 10; A55 S of
Chester.**

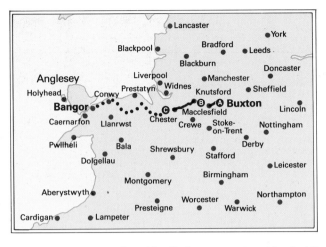

Route summary
*An exciting start to the journey takes you out
of the Peak National Park down to the
Cheshire Plain, where there is easy driving
on peaceful A roads to Chester.*

Map 1
The Peak District
Leave Buxton by the A5002 (signposts for
Manchester). Watch for the giant circle of
millstone grit marking the entry to the Peak
National Park, after a long, steady uphill climb,
about one and a half miles (2.5 km) from the
edge of built-up Buxton. Immediately after the
Park sign, the road swings right, but you go
sharp left ① and follow the backroad over open
moorland uphill.

In less than a mile you will find a laidout
parking space beside a small lake. There are
many such picnic places with simple wooden
tables in the area: the Peak Park Planning
Board takes very seriously its duty to provide
for its millions of annual visitors.

Immediately past the lake, fork right and
follow the road slantwise down the slope of
the hill towards the two reservoirs below –
Fernilee to the right and Errwood to the left.
Your road passes between the two stretches of
water on the embankment of the Errwood
Reservoir's dam. Beyond the water, gloomy
woodlands face you, but turn right at the T-
junction ② and climb swiftly through them to
Pym Chair – another parking space and a
marvellous viewpoint which gives a commanding panorama over the northern Peak
District, including Kinder Scout where ram-
blers and gamekeepers fought a famous battle
for access in 1932.

Go straight ahead down a moderately steep
slope until you reach the isolated Jenkin
chapel at a sharp bend. Bear left. As you climb
– very steeply – out of the second valley after
the chapel, you must swing sharply right ③,
ignoring a left turn. Now go straight ahead on
this road until you have dropped sharply
down to the A5002, on to which you turn left
(signposted Macclesfield).

Silk town
A short run brings you into Macclesfield, a
town of steep hills and much pleasant red
brick. It was founded on the silk industry and
is happily situated overlooking the Bollin
valley. Now you have properly entered
Cheshire: the corner through which you have
just passed is not typical.

The hilliness of Macclesfield is demonstra-
ted by the fact that you can either walk straight
into the church from the market-place or, on

another side, climb 108 steps to get in. And it
is worth it, not least for Burne-Jones's windows, made by his friend, William Morris.

A novelist's town
From Macclesfield take the A537 (signposted
Northwich). This is pleasant going – an A road
that has not forgotten its origins as little more
than a country lane. It leads you across the flat
lands of Cheshire, curving gently around the
southern edge of the Manchester conurbation
to which this county stands in the same
relation as Surrey to London.

Follow the A537 into Knutsford, where the
air of suburbia threatens to outweigh the old
world atmosphere which is its right. The May
Day celebrations here are said to be the oldest
in the country, and the name is said to derive
from the Danish King Knut (Canute). But
surely the town's major claim to fame is that
it is portrayed as Cranford in the novel of that
name by Mrs Gaskell, who lived as a child in
what is now called Gaskell Avenue.

Salt country
Take the A5033 out of Knutsford, across the
M6, and soon meet a T-junction with the A556,
on to which turn left. Follow this into Northwich – ignoring the left turn on to the A556:
Northwich is a town that deserves exploring.
Its motto is *Sal est vita* – 'salt is life' – which
may not appeal to modern heart surgeons, but
has been the making of this town which is
sited on top of Cheshire's salt-beds. Salt has
been won here since at least Roman times.
Here too, far more recently, Ludwig Mond and
J. T. Brunner launched the alkali works which
was the start of Imperial Chemical Industries.
The element 'wich' in the town's name, and
that of others such as Middlewich in the
neighbourhood, denotes the salt mines. Even
today, more than 4,000 million gallons of salt
are pumped out in a year.

Apart from salt, the town's most remarkable
industrial feature is the still-working Ander-
ton boat-lift. Built in the mid-19thC, this raises
and lowers boats weighing up to 100 tons (102
tonnes) between the Trent and Mersey Canal
and the River Weaver.

Delamere Forest
Leave Northwich by following the signs for
Chester. These take you to the roundabout
about 2 miles (3 km) west of the town centre
where the A556 (the Northwich bypass)
merges into the A54. Go straight ahead.

You now pass through what is – for Cheshire
– a belt of hill country. The hills, only a few
miles wide, divide the valley of the Weaver,
which you crossed at Northwich, from the
valley of the Dee, which you will cross at
Chester.

The forest is Delamere Forest – originally a
hunting preserve far more extensive than it is
today. The gradual extension of forests like
Delamere by the king was one cause of discon-
tent that led to the signing of Magna Carta.

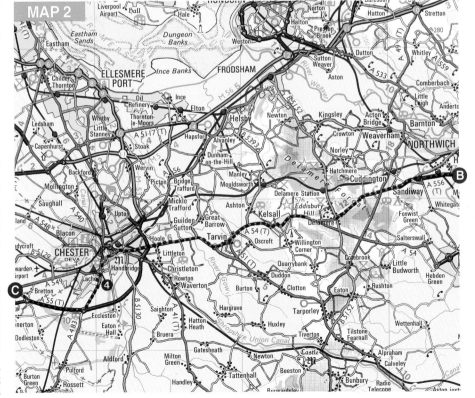

Buxton to Bangor/1

● Buxton's hotel district is in or around Eagle Parade, St John's Road, the Crescent and Grove Parade. Once famous as a watering place, this central arrival and departure point for the long-distance routes in this book is now a resort with a population of rather more than 20,000.

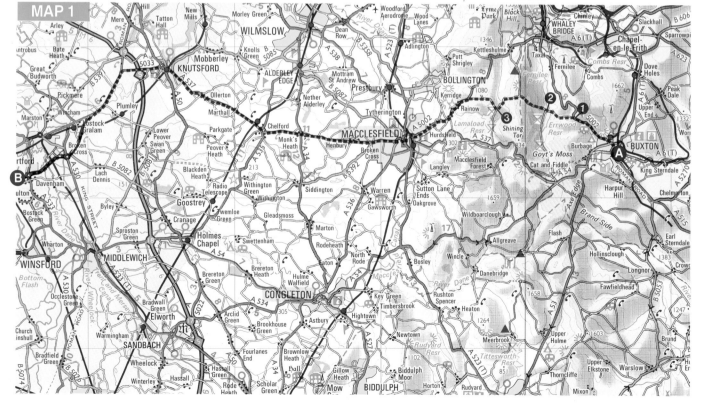

Buxton to Bangor/2

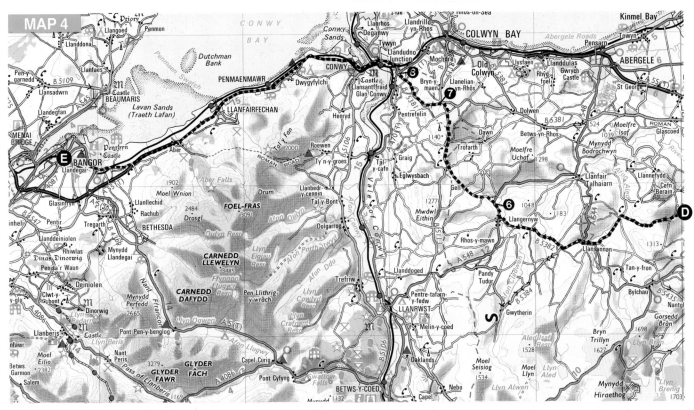

MAP 4

---

from that period. The Red Sandstone walls — stretching in a complete rectangle around the central city — follow the old Roman fortifications, but were remade in the 10thC, effectively enough for William the Conqueror to be held at bay here for several years after the Conquest.

Like all old medieval towns, Chester's centre is something of a maze for modern traffic. To avoid being trapped in the one-way system, the rule is to follow signs for Wrexham (not, despite your eventual destination, 'North Wales') and the A483. When you have crossed the river, you turn at the second roundabout ④ on to the A55 (now following signs for North Wales). After about 3 miles (5 km) you reach another roundabout, where you go left ⑤ on to the A549.

Bilingual road signs now proclaim that you are in Wales: in fact you crossed the border a mile before the last roundabout.

The Clwydians and the Vale

Keep straight west along the A549 through undistinguished Buckley and bear right on to the A541 (signpost for Mold just beyond the town). Go through Mold and now really begin to enjoy the drive. This is your way through the Clwydian Hills, which reach a height of more than 1,800 feet (549 m). You see them grow gradually before you, more pointed and more bosky as you go, until, a couple of miles after the village of Afon Wen, the A451 passes through what is almost a gorge to emerge with sudden and sweeping views across the Vale of Clwyd.

After crossing the River Clwyd, two miles (3 km) west of Bodfari, the A541 turns off to the right, but you continue more or less straight ahead on what is now the A543. Stay on this road up the climb into the centre of Denbigh, which stands on the edge of a limestone hill with a generous panorama of the vale you have just crossed. Go straight ahead through the town and, at the far end of the

market-place, fork right on to the B5382 (signposted Henllan).

Into the Hills

The route becomes progressively more beautiful, but also more challenging to drive. The B5382 has no pretensions, other than its Department of Transport number, to be anything more than a country lane over a steeply graded landscape. After Henllan (now see Map 4) it becomes increasingly twisty; in about a mile you first have the feel that you are entering mountain terrain as the slopes of Moel Fodiar, 2,280 feet (695 m), on the right, and Moel Tywysog, 1,313 feet (400 m) on the left, begin to crowd the road into a defile. You emerge from this into the valley of the Afon Aled, your road running to one side with lovely views of woods and hills to the right. In Llansannan you turn right for a brief spell on to the A544, but as the village ends, make a left turn on to the B5382 again.

Follow the B5382 all the way to Llangernyw and there turn right on to the A548 for about a mile. Watch carefully for ⑥ the unclassified road on your left signposted Trofarth. Take it. Follow signs for Trofarth and then for Eglwysbach until you reach the B5113, on to which turn right (signposted Colwyn Bay). In about two miles (3 km) be ready ⑦ to turn left (signs for Glan Conwy and A55) on to the B5381.

As this road drops towards Conwy you have your best views yet of the Snowdonia range (to the left), then of the sea and the Great Orme (ahead). At the roundabout ⑧ take the A55. The last lap is by Conwy Castle's walls, cliffs, and tunnel, then by the coast to Bangor ●

● Right, Conwy Castle, to many the most romantic of the great group of fortresses put up by Edward I in North Wales; its outer walls are 15 feet (4·5 m) thick.

Route summary

Chester to Bangor through North Wales is an exciting drive. The route avoids the dreary stop-go of the crowded coastal towns and, after a slightly industrial belt, crosses the Clwydian Hills and the Vale of Clwyd to reach Denbigh. There follows a stretch of hilly driving, when you always have the feeling that the hills may become mountains — but they never quite do. The road descends to the coast at Conwy and the final approach to Bangor is with the sea to the right and the Snowdonian mountains on your left.

Map 3
Across the Dee into Wales

As the A54 approaches Chester, you have your last views of characteristic Cheshire countryside: a pattern of still smallish fields (for this is dairy country), the hedgerows still rich in timber: Cheshire has always been a county of oaks rather than elms.

At Tarvin, the A54 merges with the A51, on which you go straight ahead. Chester is probably the best-preserved walled city in the country. The Romans settled it in the first century AD and the site has proved a rich store of coins and other archaeological finds dating

Buxton to Bangor/2

Buxton to Edinburgh/1

An alternative to the M6, A74 and A702 linking the Midlands with southern Scotland.

Distance: about 280 miles (451 km).
Guide time: allow eight hours.

Access from main roads: terminus of the M56 at Stockport or the M67 at Hyde; M62 junction 21; terminus of the M65 at Brierfield; M6 junctions 34–44; A708 at Mountbenger and A72 at Peebles.

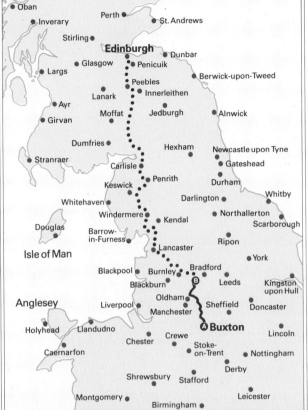

Route summary

Speeds on this route will vary a great deal. The southern end, mostly on classified roads, is relatively slow going through the fringes of the Manchester conurbation. On the other hand, you will be able to make surprisingly good time on the run north-east of Hebden Bridge – across the moors and through the Forest of Bowland. Again, once you are clear of Ambleside, you will pick up speed, except perhaps on summer weekends, to Penrith and Carlisle. Best of all, from the driver's point of view, is the stretch through Eskdalemuir Forest and across the Scottish Lowlands to Edinburgh. The roads are good, with excellent visibility, and there is little traffic.

The first part of the route follows the Pennines northwards. The main ridge of the hills lies to your right until, for a brief spell after Littleborough, you swing north-east and into Yorkshire on the other side of the watershed. This section is designed to avoid outright urban or motorway driving, and not to keep zig-zagging back and forth across the moors; a glance at the map shows that north–south roads are scarce: any route is therefore likely to be a compromise, and the one suggested here is certainly better than the alternatives further east or west.

Some urban driving is however unavoidable on the eastern side of the conurbation between Glossop and Littleborough. It is essential to pay close attention here to the map and the guidance in the text. Many of the junctions are complicated, and urban traffic signs are easy to miss.

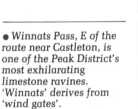

● *Winnats Pass, E of the route near Castleton, is one of the Peak District's most exhilarating limestone ravines. 'Winnats' derives from 'wind gates'.*

Buxton to Edinburgh/1

Map 1

The Peak District

Leave Buxton northwards by the A6 which is signposted for Chapel-en-le-Frith and Glossop. The route is through moorland country, but initially you are outside the Peak National Park, the tongue of land which encloses Buxton and Chapel being considered unworthy of such designation. In Chapel – an old market town whose church is unusually dedicated to St Thomas à Becket – you must be ready to leave the A6 by turning right ① on to the A624 (signposted for Glossop).

A fine stretch of moorland driving lies ahead. You climb first over Chinley Head, then drop to Hayfield and then – still on the A624 – you climb the spur of Burnt Hill with interesting views left over the huddled towns of the conurbation, before descending to Glossop. Hayfield and Glossop are Derbyshire by administration, but Lancashire by feel. The former is a great starting place for walks over Kinder Scout. Glossop is a Victorian mill town.

The Lancashire Pennines

You bypass the centre of Glossop by bearing left on to the A6016 ② and going straight ahead (signposted Oldham) as it becomes the A57. Through a mainly built-up area you cross the valley of the Etherow out of Derbyshire and into Greater Manchester. At the junction with the A628 ③ turn left and shortly right on to the A6018.

This, too, is a fairly urban road. About 4 miles (6 km) after joining it, be ready for an unobtrusively signposted right turn ④ on to the B6175 (signs for Millbrook). Follow this road across the A635 ⑤ to its junction with the A670 – probably the trickiest junction of the entire route. Turn left on to the A670 (signs for Delph) and then follow it immediately round to the right. The signposts here are for Delph, which you reach by making a sharp left turn ⑥ on to the A6052; it wriggles through Diggle to get you there.

Follow the A6052 into Delph and stay on it until – still in the village – you take the B6197 (signposted Shaw) on your left. After about 5 miles (8 km) of sharply curving road you reach a T-junction with the A663, on to which you turn right. Follow this through Milnrow, under the motorway and over the railway. Then, in a few hundred yards, go right ⑦ on the B6225 (signposted Littleborough).

This road reminds you that what the industrial settlements you have been driving through lack in charm, they more than compensate for in closeness to the open hills. You pass moorland and Hollingworth Lake on your right before dropping to Littleborough on the Rochdale Canal. Here ⑧ bear right on to the A58 (signposted Huddersfield).

The Moors again

A dramatic road lies ahead as the A58 gradually climbs out of Littleborough. After a wide series of curves it goes sharply up on to Blackstone Edge Moor where there is an official parking place, just where the Pennine Way footpath crosses the road. Blackstone Edge itself, 1,548 feet (472 m) high, with spectacular views across half Lancashire, is only a few hundred yards to the south. (The Roman road you see marked on the map runs straight over Blackstone Edge: you can still see the paving and a centrally placed gutter which was lined with turf so that horses should have adequate footholds on the steepest parts.) Follow the road past the reservoir and turn left on to the B6138.

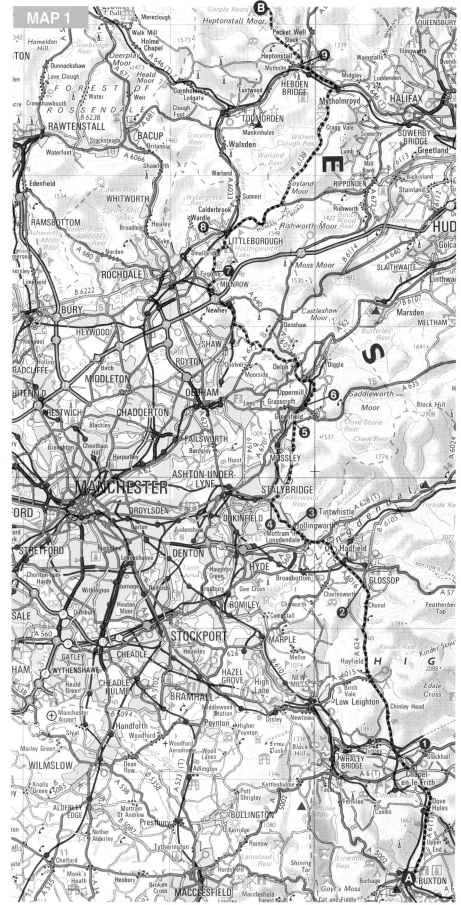

Buxton to Edinburgh/2

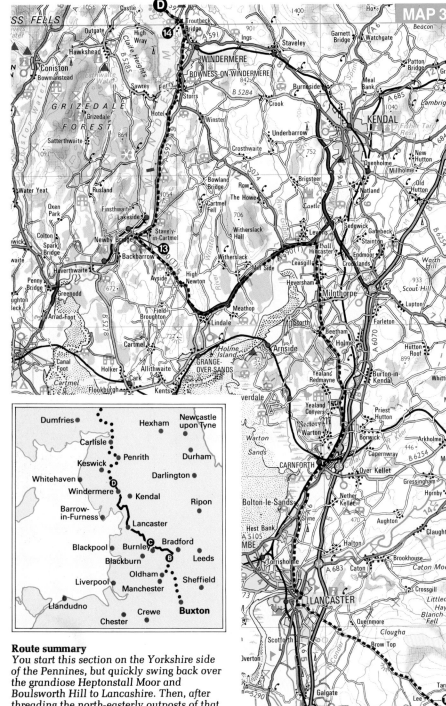

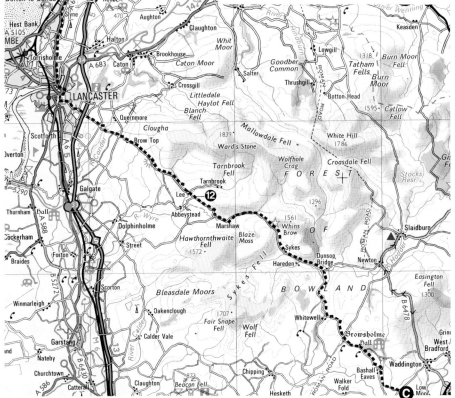

Route summary

You start this section on the Yorkshire side of the Pennines, but quickly swing back over the grandiose Heptonstall Moor and Boulsworth Hill to Lancashire. Then, after threading the north-easterly outposts of that county's industrial belt, you again strike into romantic territory, past witch-haunted Pendle, and on into country that really does seem wild – the Forest of Bowland.

You avoid the M6 by going straight into Lancaster and then heading north on the A6, a road which – unlike the motorway – conforms to the landscape instead of trying to dominate it.

The Lake District is best seen on foot. Traffic is always bad during the holiday season; the roads are rightly not improved lest they damage the delicately balanced scenery. But the A590 usually ensures a smooth entry to the National Park, with its landscape unique in Britain. In fact, this route has its own special charms.

Map 2
Yorks and Lancs

The B6138 descends swiftly to Mytholmroyd, a town squashed into its valley. Turn left at the main street on to the A646 (signposted Burnley) and follow this road into the next town – Hebden Bridge. This is equally 'squashed-into-the-valley', but you will also note how the houses cling to the surrounding hills. The steam-driven mills were built in the valley, next to water power, and the weavers' cottages had no option but to climb the hills.

You must go straight ahead in the centre of Hebden Bridge, following the A646, but about half a mile (0.8 km) from the centre, be ready for a sharp right ⑨ that goes up a wickedly steep hill to Heptonstall, a weavers' village on the edge of the moorland looking over Hebden Bridge and Hebden Dale. As this unclassified road curves around the hill, take the left fork at the chapel and go straight ahead through the main part of the village.

Twelve miles (19 km) of pure moorland driving lie ahead. The road is narrow and often steep. Take it easy, and take in the view. At first you run along the edge of the gorge of Hebden Water, on the other side of which lie the moors of the Brontë country. You dip to a bridge and a sharp curve; then go up and on past Widdop Reservoir, just beyond which you return to Lancashire. Boulsworth Hill comes into view to the right as the road drops from the Pennine spine. Bear left at the fork ⑩ (signposted for Burnley) and keep straight on to the roundabout ⑪ where you turn right. Go right at the following main junction and then left as Brierfield Station comes into view. This takes you over the M65 motorway. Reaching the T-junction with the A6068, you turn left (signposted Padiham).

Bowland and Lancaster

One and a quarter miles (2 km) along the A6068, take the unclassified road on your right

Buxton to Edinburgh/2

(signposted Sabden). This lifts you over the western shoulder of Pendle Hill; follow the road into Clitheroe, under its Norman castle, and here bear left on to the B6243 (signposted Longridge). A little way out of town, take the unclassified road on the right, signposted Bashall Eaves, which launches you on nearly 30 miles (48 km) of backroads through the austere moorland of the Forest of Bowland hills. (*Now see Map 3.*)

After Bashall Eaves, take the signposts for Whitewell and then for Abbeystead. But where that is signposted to your left ⑫ keep straight ahead and follow the road into Lancaster.

This is an ancient town with many fine buildings; its modern, industrial reputation is for furniture and linoleum. Look out for signs to the A6 and Carnforth, and you should navigate its old street pattern without any real problems.

Estuary and Lakes

The A6 takes you due north with Morecambe Bay to the left and the M6 to the right. There are too many settlements for fast driving until, 17 miles (27 km) from Lancaster, you turn left on to the A590, a modern road which sweeps round the southern fringe of the Lake District to Newby Bridge at the foot of Windermere.

Go right ⑬ on to the A592. Again, this is not a road for driving fast: it curves too much, and holiday traffic may be heavy. But it runs along the side of England's largest lake, busy with islands, passenger- and sail-boats. At Troutbeck Bridge you turn left ⑭ on to the A591.

● *Sheep pens on Red Spa Moor, which is crossed by the road between Heptonstall and Trawden. Here is typical South Pennine working terrain; it rubs shoulders with textile towns and mill villages, themselves reminders of a fading industrial era.*

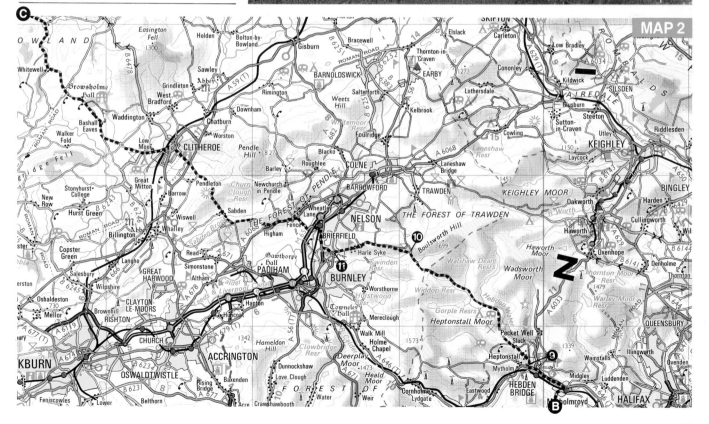

Buxton to Edinburgh/3

MAP 5

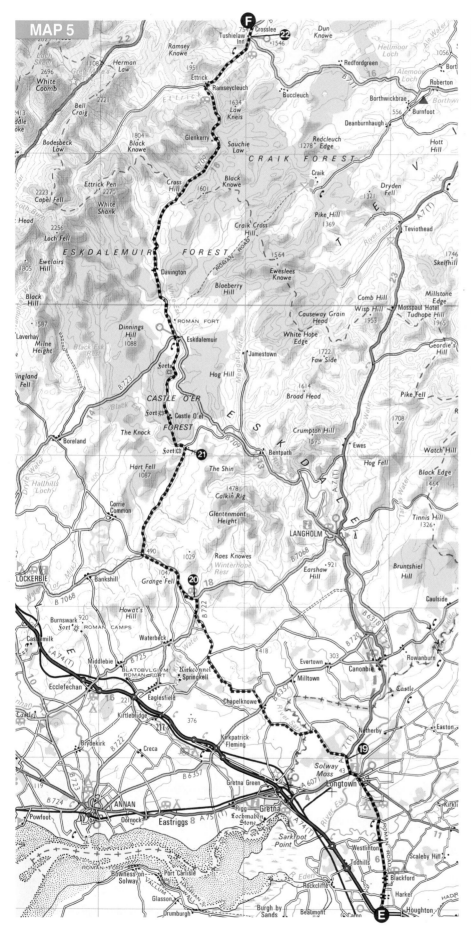

Route summary
On this section you have relaxed driving
ahead of you, to compensate for the winding
and often crowded roads of the Lake District.
Once out of that area, the running is almost
wholly on B or unclassified roads which will
present few problems. The gentler contours
ensure fairly straight roads and the relatively
sparse population means that the road
density is low – giving fewer junctions than
the earlier parts of the route.

Geographically, it is an interesting stretch.
You start it still in the Lakes, and then cross
a wide and little-known terrain to enter
Scotland. After that, the lowland hills begin
and you cut through immense forests –
Castle O'er, Eskdalemuir and Craik – which
have changed their face in recent decades.

Map 4
Helvellyn and Blencathra
Negotiate crowded and oversold Ambleside
by simply following A59 and Keswick signs.
Out of town the road continues to curve, and
overtaking is always risky. But the view
improves as you approach and pass (on your
left) the Wordsworthian village of Grasmere.
Now comes a steady climb up Dunmail Raise
with the slopes of Helvellyn ahead to your
right.

Over the summit, you drop quickly through
trees to the side of Thirlmere and run along its
bank until the A59 bears gradually away from
the lake and you take the right turn ⑮ on to
the B5322 – a charming road which drops
swiftly to a widening vale with superb panoramas of Skiddaw and Blencathra ahead.
Follow the road down to Threlkeld, where you
make a right turn on to the A66.

The Border
The A66 is a fine, speedy road, running at first
on the flanks of Blencathra. Gradually the
country becomes smoother and you turn left
⑯ on to the B5288, signposted Greystoke, a
sweet, stone village with a castle and a good
church. In the centre, bear right still on the
B5288, for Penrith. This is a very old town.
Note the fine, red sandstone church – a building material of which you will see plenty in
the next hour.

Leave Penrith on the A6 (signposted Carlisle) and glance to your left for a sight of
Blencathra and other peaks across the plain to
your left. Turn left ⑰ on to the B5305, a road
which runs easily across flattish countryside
decorated by pink farmhouses. At the B5299
⑱ turn right for the run into Carlisle – the
great border city: with its castle and solid

public buildings, very much a gateway. Take the signs for the A7 and the north, past the castle and over the River Eden.

Map 5
Through the forests

The A7 takes you due north out of Carlisle across the roundabout junction of the M6 and the A74. Stay with it until, a mile (1.5 km) after Longtown you take the left turn ⑲ on to an unclassified road signposted Chapelknowe. Keep following these signs at three junctions (between the first two of which you cross the River Sark, here forming the Border). At the B6357 go left and immediately right. Follow this unclassified road, taking signposts for Corrie at junctions, to the B722. Cross straight over, taking another backroad until, after about ¾ mile (1 km) you turn left ⑳ on to the B7068 (signposted Lockerbie).

After about 3 miles (5 km), turn right on to an unclassified road signposted Eskdalemuir; ignore the other road, signposted Corrie. The countryside is now distinctly a hill country – wide expanses of sheep-grazing. After some 5 miles (8 km) on this road, turn left at the fork ㉑ on to another unclassified road around which the conifer forests quickly close in to shut off the views. Insofar as you can make out geographical features under the dark green tree-blanket, you can tell you are following a river valley, in fact that of the White Esk.

The road climbs and winds beside the river until you reach its junction with the B709, where you turn left (ignore signposts for Moffat) at Eskdalemuir itself. Like all the settlements in this wide stretch of the Borders, it is a tiny place. Sheep never employ large numbers, and the highly mechanized forests which have taken over scarcely need more.

There are occasional gaps in the forest which enable you to see what this landscape used to be like. The best of these views come after the tiny hamlet of Davington. Now you can see occasional peaks, as yet unforested. But most of the hillsides are clothed in trees, divided only by the ruler-straight lines of the foresters' roads.

At the Tushielaw Inn bear left ㉒, staying on the B709 and then, after less than a mile, left again on a rising road: follow signs for Peebles.

● *Langdale Pikes, W of Grasmere, make a fine diversion. The higher one is called Harrison Stickle; the lower Pike o' Stickle.*

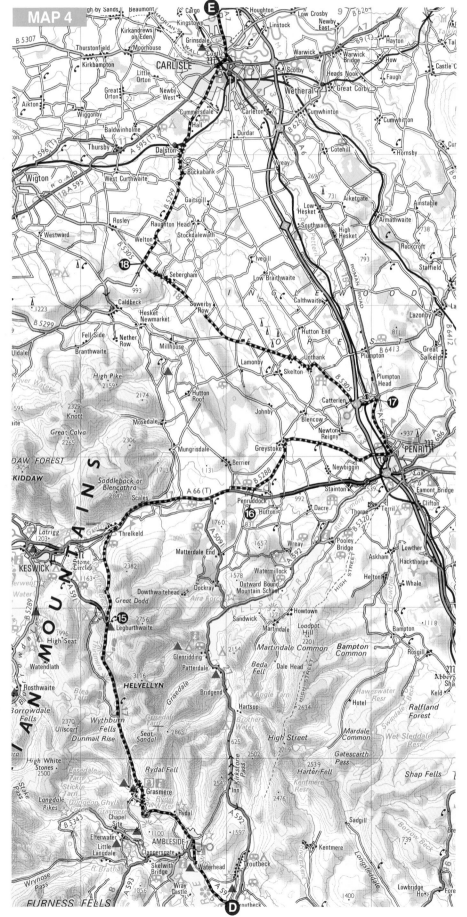

Buxton to Edinburgh/4

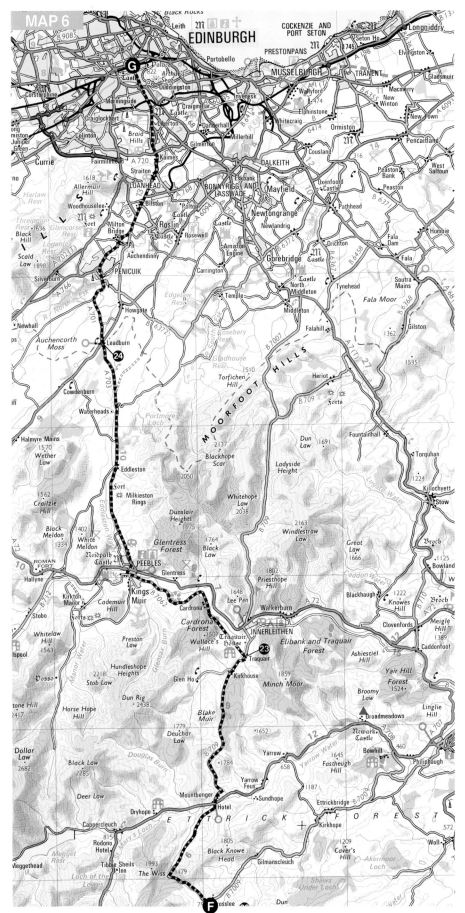

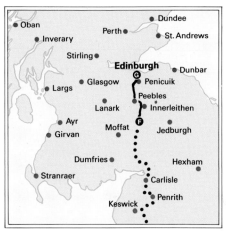

Route summary
B709 to Peebles and A703 to Edinburgh.

Map 6
The Valley of the Tweed

The 20 or so miles (32 km) to Peebles that lie ahead are through first-class scenery. Navigation is simple; the forests fall back and you have grand hill scenery to enjoy. The roads, though far from straight and sometimes steep, are not corkscrews either – easy to drive at a sensible pace.

You wind first round Black Knowe Head and then drop to a junction with the A708 at the Gordon Arms Hotel. A sign on it reminds you that this is one of Scotland's great literary landscapes: here in 1830 Sir Walter Scott and the Ettrick Shepherd (otherwise the poet James Hogg) met for the last time. You go straight across the A708, staying on the B709, which now ascends from the valley of the Yarrow Water, between fine and close-hugging hills, to cross the watershed to the River Tweed.

The scenery changes again when you turn left ㉓ on to the B7062 (signposted Peebles). This road follows the line of the Tweed which is on your right, with woods and hills to the left. The hills beyond the river and the busier A72 are the Moorfoots.

You are soon running into Peebles, the first town the route has touched since leaving Carlisle on the other side of the Border some 70 miles (113 km) back.

The town stands squarely on the Tweed – here a fast-flowing stream famous for its salmon; this is reflected in the town's motto: 'Against the stream they multiply', a reference to the fact that salmon swim upstream from the sea to breed in fresh water. The town is packed with historical memories, the most impressive being Neidpath Castle (a mile to the west): some of its 11-foot (3.6-m) thick walls can still be seen.

Edinburgh's countryside
For the last lap of the approach to Edinburgh, take the A703 from Peebles – a fine road with few bends running beneath the Moorfoot Hills, which are now on the right. To your left, and ahead, spreads a somewhat manicured, but gracious park-like landscape.

The A703 is a very driveable road. You join the A701 ㉔ and follow this through increasingly suburban terrain to Edinburgh. But another Edinburgh range of hills – the Pentlands – is on your left. This is the most crowded way into the city; but if you stay on the A701, you reach the centre at the east end of Princes Street ●

Buxton to Scarborough/1

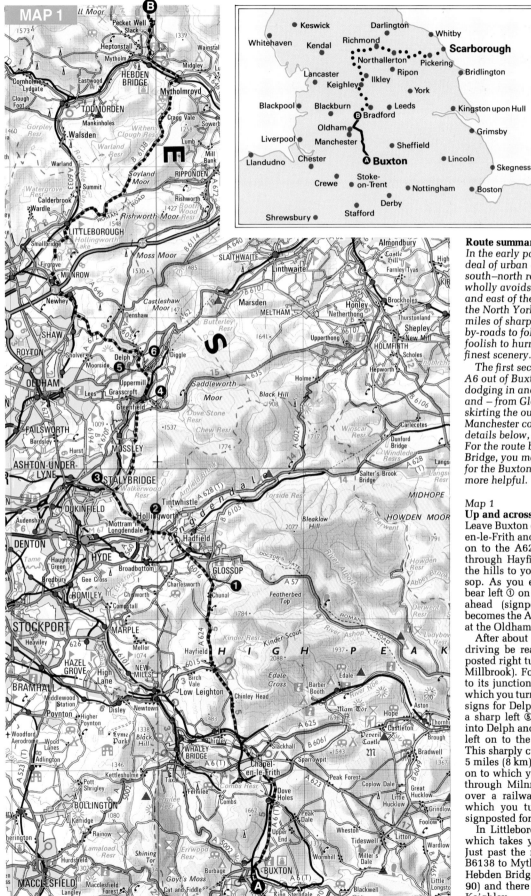

MAP 1

An alternative to the M1 and A64 linking the Midlands with the east coast of north Yorkshire

**Distance: 210 miles (336 km)
Guide time: allow 7 hours.**

Access from main roads: M62 junction 21; A16 E of Northallerton.

Route summary

In the early part of the route you have a good deal of urban driving to do. There is no south–north route up the Pennines which wholly avoids the conurbations to the west and east of them. In the Yorkshire Dales and the North Yorkshire Moors, you have many miles of sharply-bending and often narrow by-roads to follow. Anyway, it would be foolish to hurry through some of the north's finest scenery.

The first section of the route begins on the A6 out of Buxton, then follows other A roads, dodging in and out of the Peak National Park and – from Glossop to Littleborough – skirting the outermost fringe of the Manchester complex. Careful attention to the details below, and to signposts, is advised. For the route between Buxton and Hebden Bridge, you may find the fuller version given for the Buxton–Edinburgh tour (pages 88–90) more helpful.

Map 1
Up and across the Pennines

Leave Buxton on the A6 (signposts for Chapel-en-le-Frith and Glossop). At Chapel turn right on to the A624 and follow this (fine views) through Hayfield and past Kinder Scout (in the hills to your right after Hayfield) to Glossop. As you enter this Victorian mill town, bear left ① on to the A6016 and keep straight ahead (signposted for Oldham) where it becomes the A57. Bear right ② on to the A6018 at the Oldham signs.

After about 4 miles (6.5 km) of fairly urban driving be ready for an unobtrusively signposted right turn ③ on to the B6175 (signs for Millbrook). Follow this road across the A635 to its junction with the A670, a tricky one at which you turn left on to the A670 ④ following signs for Delph. You get to Delph by making a sharp left ⑤ on to the A6052. Follow this into Delph and, while still in the village, turn left on to the B6197 (signposted for Shaw). This sharply curving road brings you, in about 5 miles (8 km), to a T-junction with the A663, on to which you turn right. Stay on this road through Milnrow, under the motorway and over a railway, a few hundred yards after which you turn right ⑥ on to the B6225, signposted for Littleborough.

In Littleborough turn right on to the A58 which takes you dramatically into the hills. Just past the reservoir on your left, take the B6138 to Mytholmroyd where you go left for Hebden Bridge (further information, see page 90) and there turn right on to the A6033 for Keighley.

Buxton to Scarborough/2

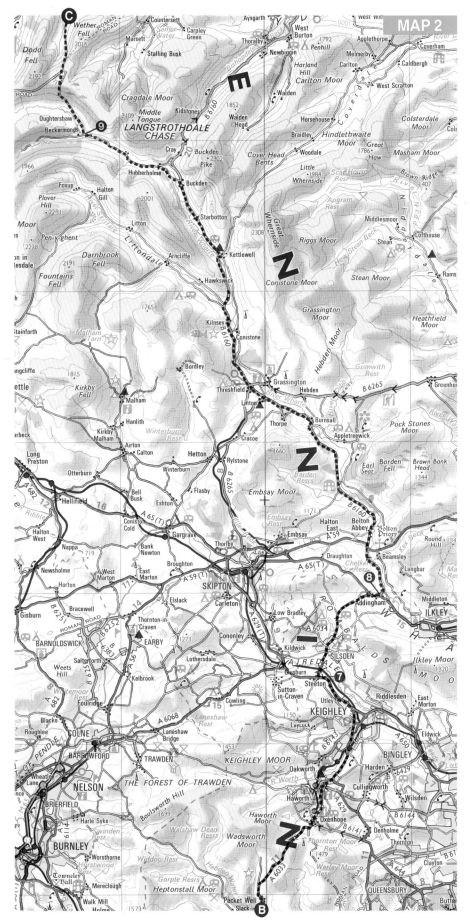

MAP 2

Route summary

The route starts in the South Pennines, where every valley has its own mill town or village. The first lift of moorland takes you over Wadsworth and Haworth Moors to Haworth where the Brontë sisters lived. After Keighley in the industrialized Aire valley, the road climbs over the lump of Rombalds Moor and drops into Wharfedale which you follow as it climbs into the hills for more than 20 unforgettable miles (32 km) of growing beauty.

North of Buckden a splendid moor road crosses into Wensleydale and, immediately, another like it leads into Swaledale which is followed nearly to Northallerton.

Map 2
The Yorkshire Dales

Your exit from Hebden Bridge is by the A6033 (signposted for Keighley), a right turn in the town centre. You climb fast and dramatically with views over the gorge of Hebden Water on your left and Wadsworth Moor opening ahead. You reach the village of Haworth, whose parsonage is revered by Brontë-lovers, about 6 miles (10 km) from Hebden Bridge. Be prepared not for an idyllic country spot, but a grey industrial village whose main street is cobbled and amazingly steep.

You drop now, turning left on to the A629 immediately after the village, down the valley of the little River Worth to Keighley, a much bigger place, but equally founded on textiles. Stay with the A629 as it swings north-westwards to follow the Aire valley. In Steeton ⑦ go right on to the A6034 (signposted for Ilkley). This road crosses yet another whaleback of moor and descends quickly into Wharfedale, where you turn right on to the A65 as though for Ilkley but, after about ¼ mile (0.5 km), go left on to the B6160 ⑧ (signs for Grassington).

The switchbacking over moorland is finished for a while. This is a twisting, not very wide road, which sticks to the valley-bottom, winding as the river winds, to be driven with love and care. It will take you past the Gothic ruins of Bolton Abbey, superbly positioned on a small bit of level land on the valley's edge, and through the exquisite stone villages of Grassington and Buckden.

Barely a mile after Buckden, turn left on to the unclassified road signposted for Hawes. This, too, is a superb drive – though in quite a different way from the route up the dale you have been following. Now the meadows of the valley-bottom beside the river give way to high, bare fells. The hills to your left are the very spine of the Pennines. Bear right for Hawes when your winding narrow road forks ⑨ in Langstrothdale. (*Now see Map 3.*)

As the road goes over the summit and begins to descend towards the little town of Hawes,

Buxton to Scarborough/2

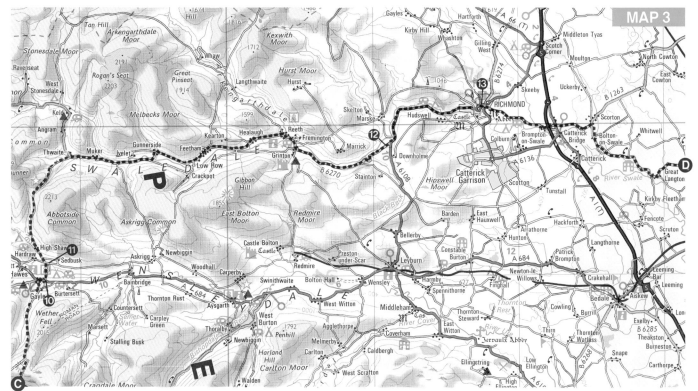

MAP 3

you have a spectacular panorama across Wensleydale. The fells on either side (Dodd Fell to the left and Wether Fell to the right) are classic limestone scenery – the bare moorland punctuated by occasional small, deciduous woods. All this is best seen on a day when a brisk breeze chases cloud-shadows across the hills.

Hawes

In the busy centre of Hawes, turn right on to the main street (A684). After some 650 yards (594 m), while still in the village, take ⑩ the first left. This road crosses the water-meadows of the River Ure. Where it begins to climb and makes a T-junction with another road, turn left and ⑪ in a few yards, right, following signposts for Thwaite and Keld. You go up through trees and climb gradually along the side of the fell with the land dropping to a beck below on your left.

The summit level on this road – and by now the hills stand up on both sides – is 1,728 feet (527 m) above sea level. This is the Butter Tubs Pass – a cosy name for a wild spot. The so-called 'butter tubs' are natural pits 50 to 100 feet (15 to 30 m) deep gouged from the limestone – easy to miss from the car.

The road goes full pelt down the very front of the fell with a sharp kink or two to jolt the unwary. Use your gears and brakes and take in the upper reaches of Swaledale as it unfolds below. At the bottom, turn right on to the B6270 which carries you gently down this lovely dale.

At the A6108 turn left ⑫ for Richmond, a lively town of alleys and squares guarded by the ruins of a great Norman castle. Pick out the B6271 in the centre ⑬ and follow it to Northallerton.

● *Far Withens, high on Haworth Moor, the isolated dwelling which could almost be Wuthering Heights.*

Buxton to Scarborough/3

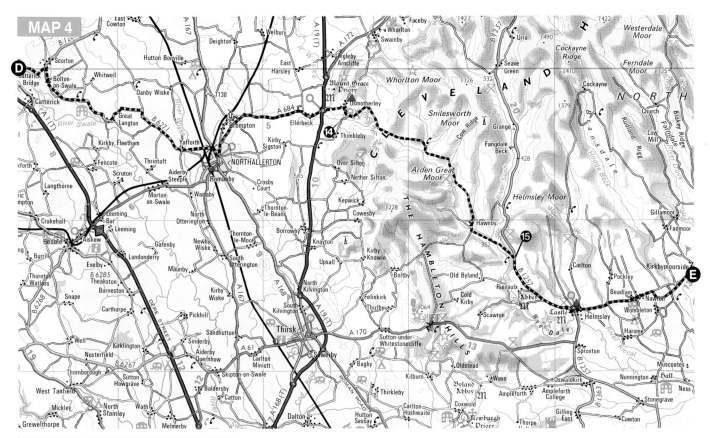

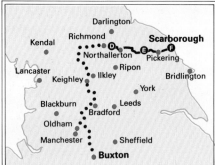

Route summary

For the last leg of the route you cross the narrow plain between the Yorkshire Dales and the Cleveland Hills, over which you climb on minor roads. After descending to Helmsley you have a straightforward run along the A170, which follows the southern edge of the North Yorkshire Moors for 30 miles (48 km) into Scarborough. This is a main road, but the only practicable west-east route; however, it has the great advantage of avoiding the A64 which in holiday periods bears a great weight of traffic from the Yorkshire cities to the sea.

You now make a transition from the scenery of the Yorkshire Dales to that of the North Yorkshire Moors – both National Parks. Both are limestone country, but of distinctly different types. Whereas the valleys of the Dales wind between shoulders of fell, those of the Moors are incisions into a flat tableland. Indeed, many of these gorge-like valleys were cut by overflows of water forcing their way through Ice Age ice. You will have a good insight into this as you drive from Osmotherley to Helmsley.

Map 4
Across the vale

Northallerton is the county town of north Yorkshire and retains a good-looking centre with many 17th–18thC buildings. It sits squarely in the fertile land of the Vale of Mowbray. Your exit is on the A684 (signposted for Middlesbrough). Follow this road for some 5 miles (8 km) to its junction with the A19 dual carriageway. Cross this, following signs for Osmotherley, a stone village of neat cottage terraces, cobbles and a market cross. Turn right at the church and keep straight ahead through the rest of the village.

Where the road out of Osmotherley forks ⑭, bear left on to a minor road which, after crossing a wooded valley, starts to climb steeply up the escarpment of the Cleveland Hills. You will have glimpsed the wall-like face of these hills as they rise from the plain at several points in the last few miles. Now you gain some 400 feet (122 m) in height in little more than a mile as the road curves around the valley of a small beck. Make time to stop where the road crosses open moorland on the top, and enjoy the view back across the vale. In anything like reasonable weather you will be able to see clearly the hills of the Yorkshire Dales rising around Richmond some 20 miles (32 km) away.

You do not stay on the top for long. The road quickly falls into a wooded valley, then goes up the other side to Hawnby Moor and the village of that name. Here, follow the signs for Helmsley which take you by steep and twisting hills over the River Rye, a few hundred yards after which you turn right (again signposted for Helmsley) ⑮ and go through the valley and its woods to make a right turn on to the B1257. This takes you straight into the town, past the turning for the ruins of Rievaulx Abbey.

The Scarborough road

Helmsley is a compact town set at the mouth of Ryedale, where the river of the same name breaks from the hills. It, too, has the remains of a castle, but its chief charm is the market-place, which is, in effect, the town square with the handsome Georgian Black Swan at one side. Leave the town by taking the A170 for Scarborough. This road now takes you all the rest of the way. It is an easy drive, with no problems other than the need to slow down through the frequent villages. The first of any size is Kirkbymoorside with its big market-place, shaped like a wide street rather than a square. (*Now see Map 4.*) Seven miles (11 km) further on is the town of Pickering.

Here is a place of charm with another wide-street market-place. Pickering, too, has its castle; it dates from the 12thC and has a complete circle of walls still standing. But the town's main interest is its geographical position at the head of the Vale of Pickering to the south and almost at the mouth of Newton Dale to the north.

Up Newton Dale runs a preserved steam railway line which offers a marvellously nostalgic, as well as beautiful, way (following a gorge) into the North Yorkshire Moors National Park. (The southern terminus is actually in Pickering.)

From Pickering continue east on the A170 to Scarborough. About 4 miles (6.5 km) along you come to the quite superlatively beautiful village of Thornton Dale. The main street is tree-shaded and a clean stream flows down one side: it has been called the prettiest village in Yorkshire. Indeed, most of the settlements on this final lap are worth a second glance.

You run into Scarborough itself by the back way past the railway station. The grandeurs of the cliffs, the castle headland and seaside architecture lie ahead ●

Buxton to Scarborough/3

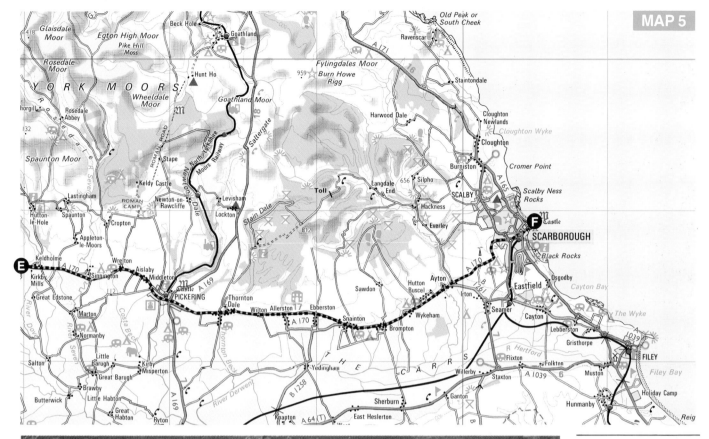

MAP 5

● The North York Moors
are essentially a plateau,
and ways up to it are
often steep and
spectacular. The
domesticated landscape
of farm buildings, stone
walls and green fields
gracefully gives way to
the bleaker, but grander
bracken and heather of
the tops.

Local Tours: Southern England

Twenty one- or two-day drives

Land's End and Lizard

West Cornwall's interior is surprisingly wild and empty, so Route One follows the coast: granite cliffs constantly buffeted by the Atlantic on the most western stretch contrast with the sub-tropical calm of secluded Penzance.

There are over two dozen notable prehistoric sites in Penwith district alone, lending the tour an element of mystery. Dating from much more recent times, the tall chimneys of the disused tin mines, so characteristic of much of Cornwall, can be seen from Carn Brea on Route Two, while Helston's award-winning leisure park brings the visitor face to face with twentieth-century technology.

Route One: 45 miles (72 km)
Directions in sequence from: Hayle
Direction of travel: anticlockwise

❧ **Hayle** Paradise Park has an internationally acclaimed collection of rare and exotic birds. Within the park, the Bird in Hand pub welcomes families and serves home-brewed real ale.

🏛 **Lelant** The Cornucopia Exhibition, with its displays of folklore, smuggling, shipwrecks, tin mining and famous Cornish buildings, portrays in models, paintings and landscaped gardens, some exciting glimpses of Cornwall's past.

☆ **St Ives** Twisting streets, granite steps cobblestones survive from the town's early days as a fishing port. Today, St Ives has a thriving community of artists, attracted by the special qualities of its light. Numerous galleries exhibit paintings and pottery. In the church, the huge *Madonna and Child* is by Barbara Hepworth, whose home was in the town. *Tourist information: tel. (0736) 796297.*

🌤 **St Ives** The headland beyond the harbour is known as The Island. This is the best point from which to view the panorama of St Ives Bay and Hayle Beach, with the famous Towan sand dunes behind.

● *The sands of Sennen Cove, NE of Land's End. The cove is reached down a narrow road from the village of Sennen, the westernmost village on the English mainland.*

① *Turn left by the tourist information office opposite the church on B3306, signposted Zennor.*

🌀 **Zennor** Zennor Quoit, an imposing Bronze Age tomb, can be reached easily by a track which leads off left from the road 1 mile (1.5 km) before the village. Large slabs of granite, set vertically, form rough walls surmounted by an even larger cap stone. The chamber thus formed was originally covered with earth. It is thought to be around 4,000 years old.

🏛 **Zennor** A museum displaying cremated bones, pottery and other artefacts from Zennor Quoit and other local, ancient tombs lies near the junction of the second turning to the village. *Open daily, May–Oct.*

🌀 **St Just** Carn Gluze, just west of the village, is an even more complex chambered tomb than Zennor Quoit.

☆ **Sennen Cove** A small fishing community with a pleasant pub, The Success, in a picturesque setting. On the cove, note the old cottages huddled under the cliff.

☆ **Land's End** Greatly restored, with all the old unsightly shacks removed, Land's End is now well worth seeing. The Visitor Centre presents two exciting exhibitions illuminating man's relationship with this rocky headland.

Local craftsmen make and sell their wares in the First and Last House. Good meals or light snacks are available in the Cornish Pantry or the Land's End pub. Extensive parking.

② *Turn right at Trethewey, signposted Porthcurno, and follow signs for Minack through the village and up the hill to the theatre car park.*

☆ **Minack** The open-air theatre enjoys a magnificent setting on the cliffs. Performances of plays and concerts are given throughout the summer and prove an unforgettable experience.

🌀 **Minack–Mousehole** At Boleigh, the road passes between the Merry Maidens and the Pipers (Bronze Age long stones). Legend has it that the 19 maidens and the two pipers who played for them were turned to stone for dancing on the sabbath.

③ *After passing the Merry Maidens, turn right down lane for the picturesque harbour of Lamorna; follow signs for Mousehole.*

☆ **Mousehole** With its tiny harbour and colourful fishing boats, the village (pronounced 'Mowsal') is one of Cornwall's most attractive ports.

△ **Mousehole–Newlyn** The coast road affords continuous magnificent views of Mount's Bay with St Michael's Mount (see below) on the far side.

☆ **Penzance** Elegant terraces, palm trees and an idiosyncratic Egyptian house (Chapel St.) all help to illustrate why the town was known as Cornwall's 'Brighton'.

From the centre, follow signs for Hayle round the one-way system.

🏰 **Marazion** St Michael's Mount, 2 miles (3 km) round the bay, is where Phoenician tin traders used to load their cargoes, two centuries BC, because the local inhabitants did not trust them enough to let them on to the mainland.

The castle, dating from the 14thC, is still lived in but is *open to the public: tel. (0736) 710507 for times.* From its ramparts there are superb views of the Cornish coast. To reach the Mount, either walk across the causeway or, if the tide is in, take a ferry *(regular service in summer).*

④ *Turn right on B3310 immediately after crossing the railway bridge; return to Hayle via A30.*

Route Two: 56 miles (90 km)
Directions in sequence from: Hayle
Direction of travel: clockwise

⑤ *Leave Hayle on B3302, signposted Helston. After turning left at Leedstown, follow signs for Redruth on B3280 and then B3297. After 2½ miles (4 km), turn left along unclassified road signposted Carnkie and*

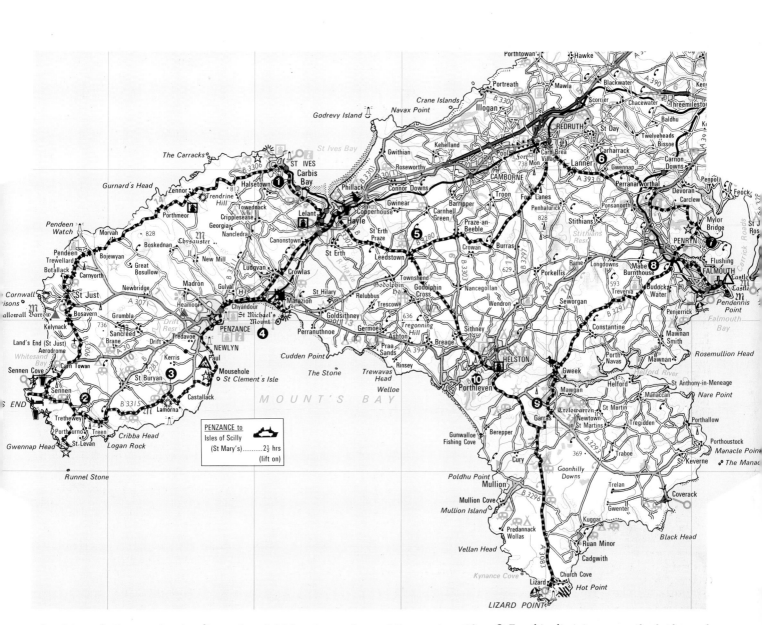

PENZANCE to
Isles of Scilly
(St Mary's)............2½ hrs
(lift on)

head towards the prominent radio mast. The track to the summit is in 1½ miles (2.5 km) on the right.

⚒ Carn Brea From the top of this long granite outcrop there are wide-ranging views of Camborne and Redruth. To the south can be seen over a dozen old mine pump houses with their characteristic chimneys.

▥ Carn Brea The southern slope is the site of what is perhaps the oldest factory in Britain. Here men of the New Stone Age reworked Old Stone Age tools to a new standard of polished efficiency.

✘ Carn Brea The castle, which once served as a lighthouse, is now a restaurant: lunches, dinners and summer cream teas.

⑥ *Two miles (3 km) past Fox & Hounds Inn (excellent food and real ale) turn left on to unclassified road signposted Perranwell and Bissoe. Turn right at sign for Perranworthal.*

At crossroads, turn right, signposted Falmouth. Turn right again at T-junction and after ½ mile (0.8 km) turn left, following signs for Mylor.

☆ Mylor A popular yachting centre with many small craft moored in the sheltered creek, or laid up in the boat yards.

⑦ *From the harbour, return up the lane and take the second turning on the right, signposted Penryn.*

☆ Falmouth A busy port with active dock-
⚓ yards, the town is also a popular seaside resort and has a long stretch of sandy beach. *Tourist information: tel. (0326) 312300.*

ጢ Falmouth Pendennis Castle, reached along
△ the lovely Castle Drive scenic route, was built by Henry VIII, *c.* 1540, with revenue obtained from the closure of the Cornish monasteries. *Open Mon–Sat, and Sun afternoon.*

⑧ *Returning up A39, turn left on B3291 signposted Gweek.*

➳ Gweek At the Cornish Seal Sanctuary, which cares for stranded and injured seals, knowledgeable staff guide visitors round the five special pools. The seals are victims of pollution and bad weather. *Follow signs from bridge, through housing estate.*

⑨ *For this diversion, cross the bridge and turn left on B3293 signposted St Keverne and Mawgan. In 2 miles (3 km) turn right on unclassified road, then left on A3083.*

ጢ Lizard The southernmost point of Britain; but Kynance Cove, with its curiously coloured serpentine cliffs and fascinating rock formations, is of greater interest and worth the short walk from the car park.

⚓ Lizard Housel Bay has a fine, safe bathing beach and makes a very attractive picnic spot. *Follow the signs from village.*

☆ Helston Helston Flora Day is on 8 May, when the locals dress up and dance in procession through the streets, and in and out of the houses, to the famous 'Furry Dance' tune.

▣ Helston The Aeropark (aircraft exhibition) and Flambards Village (reconstructed village) are on the Helston side of Culdrose Airfield. *Open Easter to Oct.*

⑩ *Turn left at the roundabout to town centre, then take A394, signposted Penzance. Once through the town, turn right on B3302.*

Bodmin and Boscastle

Along the north coast, the scenery is rugged and wild between the thriving little fishing ports nestled in sheltered coves. From here the tour passes through the strange and ever-changing landscape of the china clay country, where Cornwall's major industry can be seen at work from close quarters. Then follows the tranquil woodland beauty of Luxulyan Valley and Bossiney (both seen at their best from April to June when the hedges are filled with bluebells and campion), the grace of old stately manor houses and the isolated farmsteads and open country of Bodmin Moor.

Route One: 52 miles (83 km)
In sequence from: Wadebridge
Direction of travel: anticlockwise

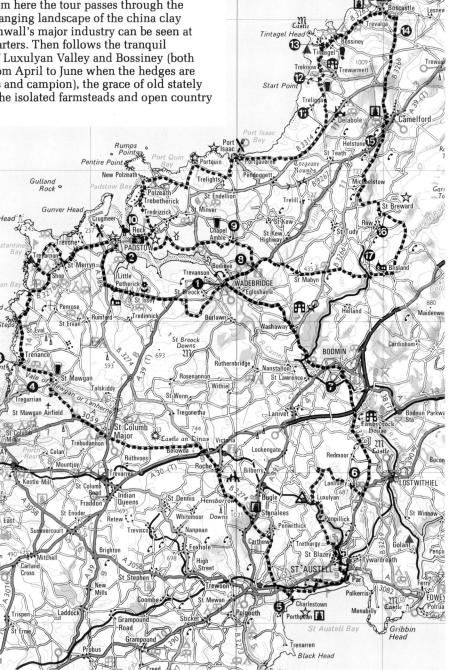

⌒ **Wadebridge** The multi-arched bridge over the River Camel is said to have been built with bales of wool in its foundations, to represent the source of the town's prosperity in medieval times.

① *Turn left at traffic lights on the west end of the bridge, into The Platt. Then first right into Polmorla Rd. and follow signs for Padstow.*

♨ **St Issey** A short diversion: turn left opposite the Ring o' Bells pub, for the cactus farm where many curious specimens are on sale.

🏠 **Little Petherick** The church of St Petroc Minor, on the right at the bottom of the hill, is worth a visit for its medieval font, old bench ends and unusually fine vestments.

☆ **Padstow** Originally called Petrocstowe after St Petroc, said to have arrived from Ireland floating on a millstone, this is a busy fishing port and popular holiday resort, which nevertheless manages to retain its old character. Extensive car parking at top of town and down by the harbour.

☆ **Padstow** For the May Day Obby Oss festival the town is decked with spring greenery and the local people, dressed in white, sing the age-old May Song and dance in company with the Oss, a weird black monster which parades round the town.

🕊 **Padstow** The tropical bird gardens at the top of the town house many exotic species in beautiful garden surroundings. There is also an extensive display of butterflies.

✗ **Padstow** Amongst the many attractions of the town there are several good restaurants. Try Rojano's in Mill Square for special occasions, or The Taste Bud in Market St. for salad lunches.

② *From the main car park above the town, turn right and follow signs for Newquay. Popular bathing beaches, a fine golf course and Trevose Head with its lighthouse, open to the public, are all signposted off to the right along this road.*

🥾 **Bedruthan Steps** Fine views of the coast down to Newquay may be had from various points along this part of the road.

③ **Mawgan Porth** *Just before the bridge, turn left along the Vale of Lanherne towards St Mawgan Village.*

🍷 **St Mawgan** The Falcon Inn serves good food outdoors in summer, or beside a log fire in winter.

④ *To leave the village, proceed up the hill keeping the church on the left. At St Mawgan airfield, turn left, and left again on to A3059. At roundabout, take exit signposted Castle an Dinas.*

🏵 **Castle an Dinas** The Iron Age hill fort with its massive triple ramparts, makes an excellent picnic spot.

🥾 **Roche** On leaving the village, note the ruins of the old hermitage on the prominent outcrop of Roche Rock, to the left.

🏛 **Hensbarrow–Penwithick** Here the route passes through the strange white landscape of the clay workings.
The Wheal Martyn China Clay museum, which traces the history of the industry, is reached by a 2-mile (3-km) diversion along the A391.

☆ **Charlestown** On the far side of St Austell, this harbour is a rare survival of a Cornish Georgian village, and was the setting for the *Onedin Line* television series.

🏛 **Charlestown** The Visitor Centre contains museums of shipwreck and rescue, with audio-visual presentations of the town's history.

⑤ *From the harbour, follow signs for Par along A3082 (A390) to St Blazey. At traffic lights, turn right past the church, following signs for Liskeard, then turn left, just before level crossing, on to unclassified road signposted Luxulyan. After ½ mile (0.8 km) turn right, following sign to Prideaux and Luxulyan valley.*

△ **Luxulyan valley** The woodland drive is particularly beautiful in spring, when bluebells carpet the ground. Just past the viaduct is a small car park for woodland walks along the river.

⑥ *Keep right, following signs for St Blazey and Fowey. Turn left at junction with A39, signposted Liskeard, and left again on to B3269, signposted Bodmin.*

🏛 **Lanhydrock House** A 17th-C manor house with fine gardens. The Long Gallery has a magnificent ceiling depicting Old Testament scenes. *Open daily, Apr–Oct.*

⑦ *Follow signs through Bodmin to Wadebridge, forking right on to A389 by the clock tower at the end of the town.*

🏛 **Pencarrow** In the grounds of this Georgian house you may pick your own soft fruit in season. The Cornwall Crafts Association has a gallery and shop in the stables.

Route Two: 38 miles (61 km)
In sequence from: Wadebridge
Direction of travel: clockwise

---

⑧ *Take A39 signposted Camelford and after 1½ miles (2.5 km) turn left on to unclassified road signposted Chapel Amble.*

🍺 **Chapel Amble** A pleasant village with a good pub, the Maltsters Arms, serving meals and bar food.

⑨ *Turn left just past the post office, and follow signs to Rock.*

☆ **Rock** This is the premier sailing centre for north Cornwall. The Quarry car park at the end of the road gives access to the beach and walks among the dunes. A passenger ferry service to Padstow operates from the beach during daylight hours.

⑩ *Returning up lane from car park, turn left at sign for Polzeath and keep to coastal road at each junction.*

☀ **Polzeath** The car park at the end of the road through the village gives access to the cliff footpaths out to Rumps Point, affording magnificent views of cliff scenery.

☆ **Portquin** The legend is that when all the fishermen from the village were drowned in a storm, their distraught widows deserted the village, leaving their houses with dinner still on the tables. Ruins of fishermen's cottages can still be seen.

☆ **Port Isaac** Unlike Portquin, this fishing village, with its picturesque harbour and narrow streets, still thrives. Parking is available on the harbour beach, depending on the tide. The Port Gaverne Hotel, just beyond the village, has a fine restaurant.

🪨 **Delabole** Famous for high quality roofing slate, the Delabole quarry is claimed to be the biggest man-made hole in the country.

⑪ *On entering the village, turn left at the sign for Trebarwith Village. The lane beyond the village is steep and narrow with a hairpin bend, left, at the bottom, for Trebarwith Strand.*

🍺 **Trebarwith Strand** The Mill House Inn serves excellent food all year round.

⑫ *Turn left by the Mill House Inn, up the steep lane signposted Treknow, and left at the T-junction on to B3263.*

🏰 **Tintagel** Although famous for its associations with King Arthur, the castle on the headland is actually Norman and was previously the site of a Celtic monastery. The extensive ruins are worth visiting.

🏛 **Tintagel** The Old Post Office is a well-preserved example of a 14th-C manor house.

⑬ *To leave Tintagel, turn right at the T-junction opposite King Arthur's Hall and follow B3263.*

❗ **Bossiney** From the car park, walk down to spectacular Rocky Valley with its ruined mill house and Phoenician rock carvings in the cliff behind the building, or up through the woods to St Nectan's Kieve – a curiously formed waterfall.

☆ **Boscastle** The narrow twisting inlet protects the harbour from storms but must have proved a dangerous entrance for the old sailing luggers that used this coast.

🏛 **Boscastle** The Witches' Museum beside the harbour displays a macabre exhibition of the history of witchcraft. *Open Apr–Oct.*

● *'The Hurlers', one of the ancient stone circles which dot the wilderness of Bodmin.*

⑭ *Leave Boscastle by returning up the hill round the hairpin bend. Turn left at the junction with B3266 signposted Camelford. On entering the town, turn left to remain on B3266.*

🏛 **Camelford** The North Cornwall Museum and Gallery, passed on the left, houses a number of agricultural exhibits from the 19thC and earlier. The Camel Art Society also exhibits paintings by local artists.

⑮ *At the main road, turn right along A39 signposted Wadebridge. On reaching the Camelot Garage, fork left along B3266, signposted Bodmin. After 3 miles (5 km) turn left following signs for St Breward.*

☆ **St Breward** The maze of lanes criss-crossing this part of Bodmin Moor are all well signposted, making it possible to explore some attractive moorland scenery without getting lost. The area is dotted with lonely farmsteads and wild ponies can often be seen.

⑯ *After driving through the village, turn right at the telephone kiosk, following signs for Blisland.*

🪨 **Blisland** This claims to be the only Cornish village with a proper green.
Do not miss the church of St Protus and St Hyacinth which has a carved wagon roof, granite columns which lean at astonishing angles and a highly decorated screen.

⑰ *Passing the Royal Oak pub, fork left at the post office and continue down the hill, following signs for St Mabyn and Wadebridge, over a level crossing and bridge.*

Looe, Polperro and Mount Edgcumbe

signs for Pont. At village, turn left, following signs for Lanteglos Highway and Bodinnick Ferry. This service operates daily until dusk throughout the year.

☆ **Fowey** Pronounced 'Foy', this attractive town surrounds a busy harbour used by fishermen and yachtsmen, as well as by larger ships loading china clay for export. Regatta and carnival in mid-Aug.

☆ **Fowey** The diversion to Gribbin Head is clearly signposted and passes Menabilly House, home of Daphne du Maurier and featured in her novel *The King's General*.

⚥ **Gribbin Head** Park in designated field at the end of the lane for a short walk to Gribbin Head with panoramic views of St Austell Bay.

☆ **Golant** Riverside parking in this area.

✗ **Golant** The Cormorant Restaurant offers a wide variety of dishes in luxurious surroundings. Gentlemen will need ties.

☆ **Lostwithiel** Once the capital of Cornwall, this ancient riverside town has a church with a remarkable Breton-style spire, and a main street lined with buildings dating from medieval times to the 18thC.

🜨 **Restormel Castle** Situated above the town (follow signs to Ancient Monument), the castle was built by Robert of Mortain, the stepbrother of William the Conqueror, in an attempt to control the local populace.

From the ramparts at the top of the castle's circular stone keep there are views of the surrounding countryside.

③ *Turn left off A390 on to unclassified road signposted St Neot.*

🚌 **St Neot** The most outstanding aspect of this typical moorland village is its church: the stained-glass windows, dating from the 14thC, are renowned for their brilliant colour and quality.

④ *On leaving the village, follow the signs through narrow lanes for Dobwalls.*

🚇 **Dobwalls** The Old Slate Caverns are still lit, as they were when being worked, by burning tapers supported on wall brackets. Warm clothing is required for the underground tour.

☆ **Dobwalls** The Forest Railroad Park is well signposted from the village. Model locomotives take visitors over miles of track; *open daily Easter to Sept.*

S outh-east Cornwall has a colourful past. Towns pillaged and burnt in the Hundred Years War with France, spectacular Plymouth Sound where the great Elizabethan fleets of Drake and Raleigh found shelter, the rich estates of the great mansions, and the fishing villages such as Polperro, Cawsand and Kingsand.

Both routes offer glorious views from the headlands but explore inland too. Route One takes in the lush Fowey valley, while both routes touch on the edge of the wild Bodmin Moor with its Arthurian associations and ancient stone crosses.

Route One: 34 miles (55 km)
In sequence from: Liskeard
Direction of travel: anticlockwise

☆ **Liskeard** A market town with narrow, steep streets and several handsome buildings which have survived in spite of the developers.

🎵 **St Keyne** The Paul Corin Musical Collection, near the station, features fairground and street organs in working order. *Open May–Sept.*

☆ **Looe** A tourist-oriented town with excellent facilities and beautiful surrounding countryside. *Tourist information: tel. (050 36) 2072.*

Ⅴ **Looe** The Woolly Monkey Sanctuary (fol-

low signs on approach to the town) accommodates a colony of monkeys breeding in near-natural conditions.

☆ **Polperro** Shoals of visitors come to photograph this picturesque fishing village, where the local industry is much in evidence.

🏛 **Polperro** At the centre of the village, in the Old Forge, the model village depicts in miniature many traditional features of old Cornwall. *Open mid-Mar to Oct.*

① *From the village, keep left, following signs to Polruan.*

⚥ **Polruan** Worth pausing in the main car park to take in the view of Fowey harbour and the ruined castle.

② *Turning right from the car park, follow*

Route Two: 48 miles (77 km)
In sequence from: Liskeard
Direction of travel: anticlockwise

---

⑤ *Two miles (3 km) along A38, turn right on to B3252 signposted Looe. After 2½ miles (4 km) turn left at sign for Hessenford and Widegates. Follow signs for Hessenford on to A387.*

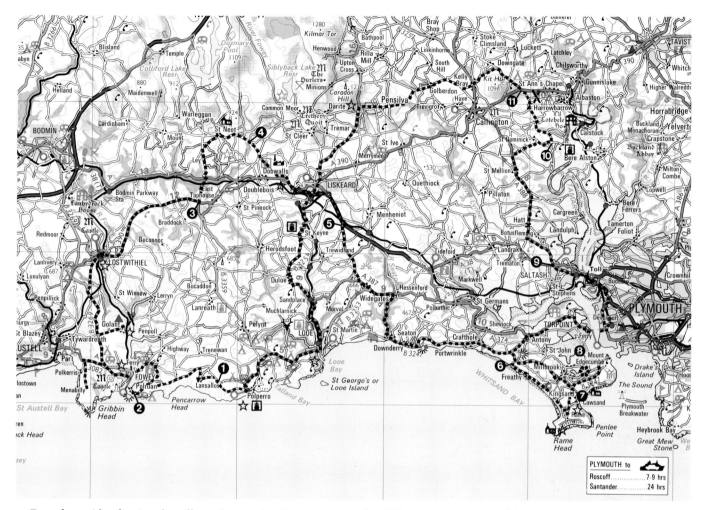

PLYMOUTH to [ferry symbol]
Roscoff............7–9 hrs
Santander.............24 hrs

Downderry After leaving the village, the road follows the line of the cliff top, giving sweeping sea views.

Millbrook From the village there are superb views of Plymouth Sound.

⑥ Turn right off B3247 on to unclassified road signposted Freathy Cliff.

Rame Head A clearly signed diversion from the cliff road gives access, through narrow lanes, to the church and coastguard station with parking area adjacent. Electricity has not yet been brought to the church, which is still lit entirely by candles.

☆ **Rame Head** Records show payments of watchmen at the headland as early as 1486, and it was used as a point for warning and celebratory beacons in Tudor times.

☆ **Cawsand and Kingsand** Twin villages, but until 1844, Kingsand was in Devon – the boundary stone can still be seen outside the Halfway Hotel. There is traditional rivalry between the villages, both of which were established in Elizabethan times, when Plymouth merchants built pilchard cellars along the beach and caused an influx of people into the area. Later, smugglers prospered in both villages.

Before Plymouth's breakwater was built, the bay provided anchorage for the Fleet.

⑦ On leaving the village, turn right at the junction signposted Maker, Mount Edgcumbe and Cremyll.

Maker The 15th-C church tower has a varied history: during the Civil War it was fortified and was captured by Parliamentary forces in 1644. In the 18thC the tower was used as an Admiralty signalling station.

✿ **Mount Edgcumbe** The estate is best known for its extensive gardens, formally planted with ornamental trees and rhododendron walks. Extensive views of Plymouth Sound and Drake's Island enhance the beauty of the park, which is open all year and especially attractive in spring and autumn.

⑧ The ferry runs 24 hours a day all year. After crossing, follow signs to Saltash.

Saltash On crossing the Tamar suspension bridge (without having to pay the toll when driving in this direction, as only those leaving Cornwall are charged), note Brunel's 19th-C railway bridge to the left. Warships of the Royal Navy can usually be seen at anchor in the estuary below the bridge.

⑨ Avoid turning into Saltash itself. One mile (1.5 km) after crossing the bridge, turn right on to A388, signposted Callington. This is an inconspicuous turn with no advance warning.

Shortly after passing St Mellion golf course, turn right at sign for Cothele House and Quay. Follow signs for house, through narrow lanes.

Cothele House Little has been altered at this splendidly atmospheric medieval house which was begun in the 15thC. Even the furniture, armour, tapestries and needlework have always been here.

There is also much to see in the extensive grounds including unusual shrubs, a medieval dovecote, the old manorial waterwheel restored to working condition, a blacksmith's and a wheelwright's shop. *House open daily Apr–Oct; gardens open all year.*

Cothele Quay There are 18th-C and 19th-C bridges, a shipping museum and a restored Tamar sailing barge.

⑩ Turn right from the car park by the house and left at the T-junction, following signs for Harrowbarrow.

✗ **Harrowbarrow** Good food in pleasant surroundings at the Carpenter's Arms.

⑪ Turn left on to A390 and then right on to B3257 signposted Launceston.

At Kelly Bray turn left, then almost immediately right, following signs for Golberdon. After passing through Meaders, take left fork signposted Pensilva.

☆ **Pensilva** On leaving the village the route passes over open heathland, typical of Bodmin Moor, with distant views of Liskeard.

Totnes and Slapton Sands

The heart of south Devon is an area of great beauty, diversity and interest; the roads follow the gentle folds of the landscape which give way to moors to the north and sea and estuary in the south and east. Soil and climate have made this part of Devon a very rich farming area, but the pattern of the landscape is still much as it was in the fifteenth century.

The tour has been planned to include extensive views of the countryside as well as a generous glimpse of the coast, and involves a 1½-mile (2.5-km) drive along a pebble ridge road, literally at sea level.

● *Lower Ferry, Dartmouth: this lovely estuary is one of the best protected on the south coast – all but completely landlocked.*

Route: 85 miles (136km)
Directions in sequence from: Totnes
Direction of travel: anticlockwise

☆ **Totnes** The core of this pleasant town (one of the oldest municipal boroughs in England) has a wealth of interesting buildings. Worth parking and strolling up the main street to the Butterwalk (antiques and craft shops). *Tourist information: tel. (0803) 863168.*

Totnes Overlooking the town is the circular Norman keep of Judhael's Castle which stands on the site of a much older motte and bailey. *Open Mon–Sat, and Sun afternoon.*

Totnes The Elizabethan House contains museum that, in addition to the usual displays, has a computer exhibition. *Open Mon–Sat, Mar–Oct; reduced hours in winter.*

① *Starting from The Plains, on the west bank of the river at the end of the town, follow signs to Buckfastleigh (A384) and Kingsbridge (A381) for ½ mile (0.8 km). At traffic lights, just beyond railway, bear left (A381 to Kingsbridge) and shortly first right (signposted Avonwick) along B3210.*

Totnes–Avonwick The road follows a ridge above the valley of the Harbourne river, a valley of gentle slopes overshadowed in the distance by the southern flanks of Dartmoor with Beara Common rising to 1,020 feet (311 m).

② *Just after crossing the bridge spanning the river, bear left at garage and follow signs to Ugborough.*

☆ **Ugborough** A quiet village with slate-hung houses, gospel hall, and a large and interesting church which occupies the site of a prehistoric camp.

The short detour to the village is recommended, if only for the view over the rooftops from the churchyard.

☆ **Ugborough–Ermington** Just before Ermington, after crossing the bridge over the River Erme, bear right immediately for Ludbrook Trout Farm. Fresh and smoked trout can be bought here, and visitors have the option of catching their own fish. *Open daily.*

Ermington Nestling against the hillside, the village is worth a visit for its crooked and twisted church spire.

③ *Continue along this scenic valley to Hollowcombe Cross. Turn left here for Modbury (A379) and left again at T-junction. The entrance to Flete House is opposite.*

Ermington Flete House, surrounded by woodland, stands in a commanding position above the river. Originally an Elizabethan manor house, it was much altered in the 19thC, but retains a Gothic style.

During World War II the house became a maternity home for the Plymouth area, and around 10,000 babies were born here. *Open Wed and Thurs afternoons (2–4) summer only.*

☆ **Modbury** 'Even when Plymouth was a furzy down, Modbury was a busy town.' Today, Modbury has a main street that goes down one hill and up another: an unspoilt vista with touches of Georgian elegance. The 20thC is represented by the conspicuous television aerials mounted on long poles to obtain better reception in this area of hill and combe.

Modbury The road out of town offers a fine view of St George's church and, eventually, of the South Hams on the right and Dartmoor to the left.

④ *Follow A379 for 1½ miles (2.5 km) then bear right at crossroads for Bigbury-on-Sea (B3392).*

Bigbury-on-Sea Worth looking inside the church to see the unusual and long commemorative verse to John and Jane Pearse, who died in 1612 and 1589 respectively.

☆ **Bigbury-on-Sea** Much holiday trade paraphernalia here, but Burgh Island is of considerable interest. At low tide it can be reached across the sand; when the tide is in, a 'sea tractor' runs a ferry service.

The building on the crest of the island was once a huer's hut for the lookout who raised the hue and cry when a shoal of pilchards was sighted.

Bigbury-on-Sea From the island there are superb views of the mouth of the River Avon and dramatic cliff scenery.

Bigbury-on-Sea Burgh Island's pub, The Pilchard, is reputed to be one of the oldest in Devon; the food here is excellent.

⑤ *Retrace route along B3392, and follow road to Aveton Gifford. (The short cut along unclassified road from Bigbury looks tempting but is a tidal road and can only be used at low tide. If at all in doubt, use B3392.)*

Aveton Gifford Pronounced 'Orton Jifford', the village has one of south Devon's oldest churches. Although modernized after being hit by a bomb during World War II, the church merits a visit for its two-storeyed 13th-C porch.

☆ **Aveton Gifford** Just past the village, the A379 crosses the water meadows of the River Avon on a medieval causeway.

⑥ *Two miles (3 km) from the village, at roundabout, carry straight on taking B3179 (signposted Salcombe) for a further 2 miles. At major junction bear left, following A381 through West Alvington to Kingsbridge.*

⑦ *On entering the town, turn left at bottom of hill (signposted Plymouth /Totnes) and continue up the main street (Fore St.). Car park half-way up on left.*

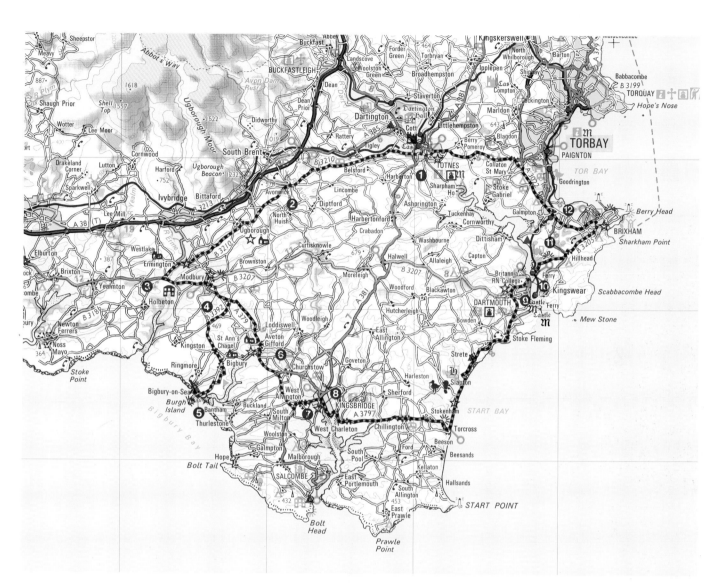

☆ **Kingsbridge** The main feature of the town is The Shambles, a fine market arcade supported on broad granite pillars and dating, in part, from 1585.

⑧ *To return to route, follow one-way system, bearing right at Duncombe St. (signposted Salcombe/Dartmouth) and then left for Dartmouth (A379) at junction.*

⚓ **Torcross** From here the view is unique, with lake, reed bed and shingle ridge in the foreground, and sea beyond.

Torcross lies at the southern end of the long (2½ miles/4 km) pebble ridge known as Slapton Sands, and is set perilously close to the sea.

☆ **Slapton Sands** Trapped behind the ridge are the waters of Slapton Ley, the largest natural freshwater lake in Devon. A lane leading to the village of Slapton separates the open lake from a silted-up area which is a valuable habitat for wetland and other bird species.

✦ **Slapton Sands** A field centre in the village provides information on local walks and wildlife.

▣ **Slapton Sands** A tall stone obelisk on the right of the ridge commemorates the use of the area in late 1943 and early 1944 for beach landing practice prior to the Normandy invasion.

⑨ *Bear right at junction with B3207 and follow road into the town centre.*

☆ **Dartmouth** Surrounded by hills and woodland and edged by one of the country's most beautiful rivers, the town has many interesting buildings, in particular the merchants' houses (1635–40) in the Butterwalk.

▣ **Dartmouth** Not surprisingly, in a town dominated by the Royal Naval College and with a long history as a port, the museum (in the Butterwalk) contains many maritime exhibits. *Open 11–5 Mon–Sat, May–Oct; 2.15–4 rest of year.*

▣ **Dartmouth** Newcomen, inventor of the atmospheric steam engine, was born here. One of his original engines can be seen working at the Newcomen Engine House (adjacent to the Butterwalk). *Open Easter to Oct.*

𝔪 **Dartmouth** The castle, 1 mile (1.5 km) south of the town, is a 15th–16th-C coastal fort. *Open Mon–Sat, and Sun afternoon.*

⑩ *Follow signs to Kingswear and Paignton and road markings to Higher Ferry and Paignton (A379). The ferry runs a continuous daily service. Closed to vehicles first two weeks in March.*

⚓ **Dartmouth–Brixham** Half-way up the hill (A379) look to the left: glimpses of the deep cleft of the River Dart can be seen through the woods of Waterhead Brake.

⑪ *At the top of the hill, just past the garage, bear right. Follow B3205 to Brixham.*

☆ **Brixham** A fishing town of largely unspoilt character. The harbour dominates the scene and numerous boat trips are available from here.

⚓ **Brixham** For an unrivalled view of the harbour, visit Breakwater Beach on the north-western edge of the town. *To reach the beach, bear left at T-junction at bottom of hill, and follow the waterfront for ¼ mile (0.5 km). Car park on left.*

⑫ *From the town centre, take the A3022 to Paignton. After 3 miles (5 km) ignore right turn to Paignton and continue along A3022 for about 2½ miles (4 km). At major junction, bear left for Totnes (A385).*

109

Bude and Bideford

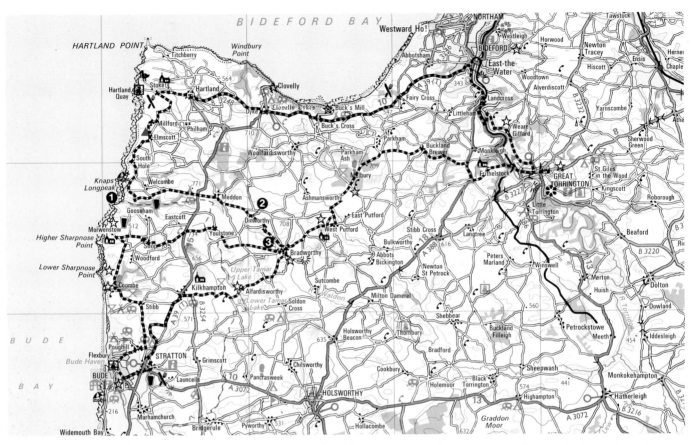

I n terms of distance from cities and public services, this is one of the most remote corners of England. The coastal area has some busy tourist attractions, but for the most part this region is quiet and unspoilt. Inland there are peaceful villages, lush pastures and leafy lanes. The north-facing coastline has little fishing villages and wooded cliffs. The west-facing coastline, however, faces the full onslaught of Atlantic gales. It is a dramatic coast of contorted rocks, shipwrecks and bracing winds, and a walk along the coast path between Hartland and Bude is guaranteed to be memorable.

Route One: 54 miles (86.5 km)
In sequence from: Bideford
Direction of travel: anticlockwise

☆ **Bideford** This historic port on the River Torridge was prominent in Tudor times, and has many associations with the Grenville family. Little to see of its history
⌒ except the remarkable medieval bridge with its 24 arches of different spans. There are pleasant sloping streets with some elegant houses and the tree-lined quay still handles some coastal trade.

✗ **Fairy Cross** The 17th-C mansion of the Pyne-Coffin family is now the Portledge Hotel, where restaurant or buffet meals may be followed by a stroll round the lovely grounds.

☆ **Buck's Mills** Just north of Buck's Cross, an attractive group of thatched cottages borders a stream running to the cliff edge. The village lacks the harbour and cobbled street of Clovelly, but is more peaceful.

☆ **Clovelly** The main street of this utterly charming village is traffic free: cars must be left at the cliff top, so be prepared for a steep walk down to the harbour. (The return journey can be made by Land-Rover.) Avoid peak periods; Clovelly is the area's chief tourist attraction.

🏰 **Stoke** St Nectan's church has the highest tower in Devon, a fine Norman font and a delicately carved medieval screen.

🏛 **Hartland Quay** A small museum of shipwrecks (open daily in summer) is appropriately sited on this rugged coastline of jagged rocks.

➤ A pleasant 1-mile (1.5-km) walk leads to Speke's Mill Mouth waterfall and nature reserve. This can also be approached from Kearnstone, 1½ miles (2.5 km) south of Stoke.

✗ **Hartland Quay** The hotel, converted from the Harbour Master's house and workers' cottages, has shipwreck relics in the Green Ranger bar. Bar food available all year.

🏖 **Welcombe Mouth** A rough and narrow track from crossroads ½ mile (0.8 km) north of Mead and ¾ mile (1 km) west of Welcombe leads to a small car park beside a waterfall dropping to a pleasant beach.

① Continue uphill, following the coast to Mead. The roads to Welcombe are difficult and it is advisable to avoid the village.

🍺 **Darracott** The Old Smithy Inn, dating from medieval times, has much atmosphere and is said to be haunted by a man in armour. Real ale, bar food and restaurant (evenings only).

② After Meddon take the second turning on right for Loatmead. Here turn left and then first right for Dinworthy and straight on through this hamlet for Bradworthy (see Route Two).

🏰 **West Putford** St Stephen's church escaped Victorian restoration and has retained the atmosphere of the 18thC. It has uneven walls, a chancel floored with Barnstaple tiles and a rare, oval Norman font.

☆ **West Putford** The Gnome Reserve has a remarkable collection of garden gnome figures, most of which are for sale. Not everyone's taste, but different. Open Easter–Oct; closed Sat.

☆ **Powler's Piece** Crossroads where detours can be made ¾ mile (1 km) to south-east for Common Moor, an attractive area of heath and scrub, and ¾ mile (1 km) north-west for Melbury Woods, a Forestry Commission plantation with picnic area and nature trail.

● *The North Devon coast at Hartland – its ruggedness an appropriate match for the treachery of the local waters. This grandiose scenery runs more than ten miles (16 km) from Hartland Point to Lower Sharpnose Point.*

Frithelstock Adjoining the church are the peaceful and beautiful ruins of a medieval Augustinian priory.

☆ **Great Torrington** Apart from a few elegant houses, it is a rather dull-looking town in a grand setting. From the central car park (where once a castle stood) there is a splendid view of the River Torridge far down below, and of the strip fields which were originally part of a leper colony.

✿ **Great Torrington** One mile (1.5 km) southeast on B3220 the Rosemoor Garden Trust has several types of gardens, a semi-natural woodland area and an arboretum, all part of the grounds of a small 18th-C house. Unusual plants, including old-fashioned roses, are on sale. *Open daily Apr–Oct.*

Great Torrington From Dartington's modern, ugly factory comes high-quality, stylish, hand-blown glassware. Interesting displays and guided tours. Factory shop and pleasant cafeteria. *Open Mon–Fri.*

The factory is off School Lane, which is opposite the parish church, and is well signposted.

☆ **Weare Giffard** Strange to think that this attractive, straggling village on the east bank of the Torridge was once a busy port, the only signs of which now are the rows of lime kilns on the riverbank. The big house seen from the road is Weare Giffard Hall (private), famous for its great hall.

Bideford Half a mile (0.8 km) from the outskirts of the town, a lay-by on the right affords a fine view down the Torridge estuary to Bideford Long Bridge.

Route Two: 27 miles (43 km)
In sequence from: Bude
Direction of travel: anticlockwise

☆ **Bude** Small seaside resort with several large hotels and guest houses. Good sandy beaches, popular with surfers, and many other sporting facilities. There is an old canal, formerly used for carrying beach sand inland for agricultural purposes. *Tourist information: tel. (0288) 4240.*

Bude On the wharf by the canal, Bude and Stratton Historical and Folk Exhibition has many nautical displays. *Open afternoons, daily, Easter–Sept.*

Stratton At The Tree Inn, the 13th-C Galleon Room (à la carte menu) has beams made from timbers of wrecked ships. There are several bars serving excellent food.

Kilkhampton St James's church has a richly decorated Norman doorway and exceptional 15th- and 16th-C woodwork in the roof timbers and bench ends. There are also monuments to the Grenville family.

☆ **Tamar Lakes** Two modern reservoirs formed by damming the River Tamar, which divides Cornwall from Devon. The upper lake has facilities for sailing, boardsailing, canoeing and fly fishing. The lower lake is quieter, more attractive and good for bird-watching.

☆ **Bradworthy** This old village is built round a large square, once used for fairs and markets. From the outskirts of the village

there are views across to Dartmoor and Bodmin Moor.

③ *Turn right at the top of the square, then fork right and straight on for Blatchborough and Youlstone.*

☆ **Morwenstow** The 19th-C theologian, poet and eccentric, the Rev. R. S. Hawker, lived here. His rectory has chimneys shaped like the towers of his churches. It is worth the walk to Vicarage Cliff where his hut, made of driftwood, can still be seen.

Morwenstow St Morwenna's church is not to be missed. Its special features include a Norman doorway, superb Norman arches (one of which has a weird 'beak-head' ornament), and a Saxon font. In the churchyard, the figurehead of the *Caledonia* marks the grave of her shipwrecked crew.

Morwenstow The Bush Inn serves real ale, bar food and excellent evening dinners.

☆ **Composite Signals Organization Station** Satellite tracking station with several dish-shaped aerials. Fine view south along Cornish coast beyond Bude to Tintagel, Pentire Point and Trevose Head.

☆ **Coombe** Attractive ford with thatched cottages can be reached by turning left at the bottom of the hill. Return and continue on previous road. *Turn first right for Duckpool with its car park and pebbly beach (detour of 1 mile/1.5 km). Return and continue across bridge.*

After ¼ mile (0.5 km) turn left for another short detour to Stowe Woods, where there is a car park, picnic area and nature trail.

Dartmoor

Three distinct areas are explored on this tour. Route One goes through the rich red land of the Exe Estuary. From Exeter, the road leads back inland across the tree-capped Haldon Hills: here are splendid views and forest walks.

Route Two crosses the eastern part of Dartmoor, which offers the most spectacular tors (outcrops of rock) and the moor's best-known village.

Although this tour ventures into some fairly out-of-the-way places, it avoids the very narrowest lanes that are difficult for drivers to negotiate.

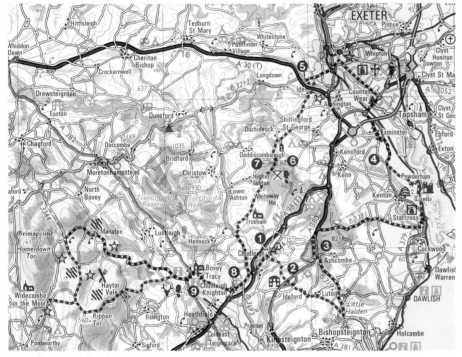

🏠 **Bovey Tracey** Climbing the hillside above the River Bovey, this little town has a church that is notable for its 15th-C stone and wood carving. The screen, with its painted birds and grapes, is delightful. Note also the fox and duck misericord, and the south porch boss of four heads joined together at the neck.

① In Chudleigh, turn right just past the zebra crossing, down Clifford St., signposted Ugbrooke House, Ideford and Teignmouth.

🎣 **Chudleigh** At the bottom of Clifford St., The Wheel craft centre is open daily.

🏛 **Ugbrooke** The stately home of the Cliffords was originally built around 1200, but was redesigned by Robert Adam. Visitors see fine furniture, paintings, embroideries, a dolls' house, and a collection of early gramophones. Open June–Sept, 2–5.30.

② Continue along the same road, beneath the separate carriageways of A380, and through Ideford and Luton. At Little Haldon, turn sharp left (signposted Exeter) and left again on to B3192.

DARTMOOR PAST AND PRESENT
Dartmoor is the nearest thing to a wilderness in southern England, but it abounds in traces of man and his work. Isolation has preserved an unusual number of prehistoric remains – stone circles, standing stones, burial chambers and hut circles, dating from as early as 1800 BC, litter the whole area. From more recent times, there are the spoil heaps and gulleys left by the tin miners who operated here from the 12th to the 15th C.

Today army firing ranges make large tracts of northern Dartmoor inaccessible. If you plan to wander in the vicinity of the Okehampton ranges, check firing times first by ringing Plymouth (0752) 772312, or enquire at a local post office.

🏞 **Little Haldon** Park on the brow of this hill, then walk a short distance away from the road for a worthwhile view of the sea near Dawlish.

③ Cross one carriageway of the A380 on the bridge, then follow directions on to the Exeter-bound carriageway of the A380. A few hundred yards along the road, turn right again across the other carriageway on to B3381, signposted Starcross.

🏢 **Starcross** Here, Isambard Kingdom Brunel tried out an astonishing engineering concept: locomotives driven by atmospheric pressure. The idea was a failure, but the pumping house survives and there is a fascinating museum which has drawings, photographs and relics of the railway. Open Mon–Fri, and Sun afternoon.

🏰 **Powderham Castle** Grand home of the Earls of Devon, this 14th-C castle has been much altered, over the years, resulting in a curious mixture of strength (four of the original towers still stand) and decoration (the music room is by Wyatt).

🦌 The deer park has a fine avenue of cedars leading up to the castle. Open Sun–Thurs, mid-May to mid-Sept.

④ Continue along the same road for about 2 miles (3 km), then turn right on to A379. Follow signposts to Exeter.

⭐ **Exeter** A bran tub of a city: dip in and beyond the busy centre (rebuilt after extensive bomb damage in 1942), discover buildings, alleyways and even underground passages from many parts of its history which goes back to Roman times. Tourist information: tel. (0392) 72434.

✝ **Exeter** The lovely Gothic cathedral offers a satisfying unbroken vista down the long, rib-vaulted nave. Amongst a wealth of interesting details, note the minstrels' gallery with its carvings of musical angels, and the much-pinnacled, 14th-C bishop's throne, which has nothing whatsoever to do with humility.

🏢 **Exeter** Down by the waterfront, the wonderfully imaginative Maritime Museum has the world's largest collection of working boats, many of which can be explored. The collection is displayed indoors (in Victorian warehouses), on the shore and afloat. A fine place for children. Open daily.

🍺 **Exeter** Two old and attractive pubs which serve good food are The White Hart in South St., and The Ship in Martin's Lane, just off Cathedral Close.

⑤ From the Exe Bridge take the Moretonhampstead road (B3212). Not far out of Exeter, turn left on to a road marked for the A30, M5 and Ide. After ½ mile (0.8 km), turn right to Ide.

⭐ **Ide** As an instant contrast to the city, this long village has a ford, a 13th-C bridge, some genuinely old cottages and a delightful fake called Tudor Cottage.

⑥ Park at the Forestry Commission Belvedere car park on left. To see Lawrence Castle (see below), walk back a short way along the road and turn right up the drive.

🏯 **Lawrence Castle** Known locally as Belvedere Tower, this 70-foot (21-m) folly was built in 1788 as a monument to Major-General Lawrence, founder of the British Empire in India. The incredible view from the top encompasses nearly the whole of Devon. Open every afternoon in summer, weekends only Oct–Apr.

✗ **Haldon Forest** A picnic site about 1 mile (1.5 km) further along this ridge-top road is

also the starting point for a variety of walks (the shortest is 2½ miles/4 km) laid out by the Forestry Commission.

⑦ *From Belvedere car park, take the little road opposite, leading down off the ridge. The road winds down into the pastoral Teign Valley. Follow signs for Trusham.*

Trusham Worth pausing here to look inside the church, which has two unusual monuments. The Staplehill family are commemorated by a painting on wood (16thC), while John and Mary Stooke are shown in two painted medallions (1697).

⑧ *In the middle of Chudleigh Knighton take a right fork. This is still the B3344; continue along it to Bovey Tracey.*

Route Two: 17 miles (27 km)
In sequence from: Bovey Tracey
Direction of travel: clockwise

---

⑨ *Drive through the town to the lower end where a road turns off right for Haytor (B3344).*

Parke Rare Breeds Farm A quarter of a mile (0.5 km) along this road is the entrance to the farm and an information centre run jointly by Dartmoor National Park and the National Trust. The farm contains rare and traditional breeds of sheep, cows, pigs and poultry in a fine setting. *Open Easter to Oct.*

There are also woodland and riverside walks accessible at all times of the year.

Haytor A grassy slope leads to the actual tor, standing at 1,490 feet (454 m).

The Dartmoor tors are composed of granite, which formed 390 million years ago, firstly as molten magma. Gradually eroded by rain and frost, their weird shapes are the moor's most characteristic feature. Haytor is one of the easiest to reach.

Haytor The Rock Inn, below Haytor in Haytor Vale, serves excellent food and has a pleasant garden.

Dartmoor This open, rolling land, dotted with prehistoric remains, all belongs to somebody. Most of it is also 'common land', which means that the commoners (usually local farmers) have the right to graze their sheep, cattle and ponies here.

Widecombe in the Moor The first view of this famous village is from the top of Widecombe Hill on the approach road.

Widecombe Fair, as celebrated in the song, is still held on the second Tuesday in September and does indeed attract 'Uncle Tom Cobleigh and all'.

● *Mills Farm, Dartmoor, with Higher White Tor rising in the background.*

Widecombe in the Moor The church, known as the 'Cathedral of the Moor', is an imposing reminder of the wealth and piety of the medieval tin miners who lived and worked in the area. Note also the 16th-C Church House with its granite pillars, and the charming village sign.

Hound Tor Only ¼ mile (0.5 km) from the road on the right hand side, this rocky viewpoint is easily accessible.

☆ **Jay's Grave** Less than 1 mile (0.5 km) from Hound Tor a little grave can be seen by the roadside. This is the grave of a young girl who hanged herself and was buried at the parish boundary in the early 19thC. There are often flowers at this lonely little mound, placed by unknown hands.

Manaton Just south of this old moorland village is Bowerman's Nose, a curious pile of rocks resembling a man in a hat.

☆ **Becky Falls** On the far side of Manaton, the Becky (or Becka) Falls tumble down over 70 feet (21 m) of granite boulders. Well worth taking the short path down to the Falls – a popular spot.

Honiton, Exmouth and Lyme

This tour amply rewards those who take the time to venture inland from the seaside holiday resorts.

Route One explores some of the tiny lanes of the south-east corner of Devon. A wise old clergyman once explained why Devonian lanes are so narrow – 'It's because the hedges are so close together' – but passing bays make overtaking possible. The views along this route are a constant source of pleasure and give the visitor a strong sense of location.

Route Two gives a taste of three of England's loveliest counties: Devon, Dorset and Somerset.

Route One: 64 miles (102.5 km)
Directions in sequence from: Seaton
Direction of travel: anticlockwise

• *An unusual view of the harbour and Cobb at Lyme Regis. The Cobb is the sea wall-cum-causeway seen curving out to the right.*

☆ **Seaton** Pink-flushed cliffs (to the west) and pebble beach are the attraction here, as well as a unique electric tramway with open, double-decker tramcars that run along the Axe valley to Colyton and back.

① *From centre, follow signs to Colyton.*

Colyton St Andrew's church, just off main square, has interesting monuments to the Pole family, depicted with their many children.

② *Leave Colyton by crossing the river (not B3161), then take left fork signposted to Honiton, climbing to Roche Forest (car park, picnic area and fine views).*

🛆 *Pass through Offwell (pausing to see enjoyable carvings in church) and turn left on to A35. Note the 19th-C Bishop's Tower on the left (built by the Bishop of Landaff to give employment to the poor) and views across the Otter valley on right.*

☆ **Honiton** Noted for its lace and pottery, the town, entered past old toll house and gates, has an impressive Georgian main street.

🎨 **Honiton** On left as you enter the main street, the Pottery (established in the 18thC) welcomes visitors to its workshops.

🎨 **Honiton** Lace-making demonstrations can be seen at the Old Lace Shop near the Pottery. Lace and embroidery on sale here, too.

③ *Leave town by A375. Take short diversion, signposted Gittisham on right near top of hill, through Beech Walk beauty spot. Then bear left to rejoin main road.*

Gittisham Common Turn right at The Hare and Hounds (casting wary glance at Rolling Stone, reputed to have been an ancient altar for human sacrifice) then down steep hill to Ottery St Mary. Extensive views to distant Dartmoor.

Ottery St Mary The church (one of the best in Devon), dates back to the 13thC, and was in part modelled on Exeter cathedral. Among many delights, the clock (inside) and the weather-vane are both around 600 years old.

🏛 **Ottery St Mary** Chequered stonework in the Court of Sovereigns is just one of the interesting features of 16th-C Cadhay manor house, 1 mile (1.5 km) north-west. *Open in summer, Tues, Wed. Thurs. 2–6.*

☘ **Woodbury Common** On B3180, commanding views of Exe estuary. Several parking places.

⚓ **Exmouth** A pleasant resort with 2 miles (3 km) of sandy beaches and foreshore, interesting docks and sweeping views from the Esplanade. *Tourist information: tel. (0395) 263744.*

🏛 **Exmouth** A la Ronde, a re-creation by two 18th-C English ladies of San Vitale, Ravenna, has a shell gallery and contents reflecting the ladies' idiosyncratic taste. *Open Mon–Sat 10–6, Sun 2–7, Apr–Oct. The house is 2 miles (3 km) north of the town on A376.*

⑤ *Leave from eastern end of Esplanade near Maer Rocks car park and take Maer Lane just after leaving sea front (ignore Budleigh Salterton signposts).*

🏛 **Littleham** Lady Nelson, deserted wife of the Trafalgar hero, lived in Exmouth and was buried in Littleham's pleasant churchyard. *Follow the lane alongside the church to join A376.*

☆ **Budleigh Salterton** Unspoilt town with an air of Edwardian tranquillity. Millais painted his *Boyhood of Raleigh* here.

🏛 **Budleigh Salterton** Fascinating little Fairlynch Museum near the sea front specializes in local and natural history, costume and lace. Frequent exhibitions. *Open summer only.*

🏛 **East Budleigh** *Leave town on A376, turn left at Rolle Arms crossroads.* One mile (1.5 km) west of East Budleigh is Hayes Barton (not on map), birthplace of Sir Walter Raleigh. Bed and Breakfast available here: you can sleep in the room where Raleigh was born.

✿ **Bicton** *Rejoin A376.* Just beyond 'Scriptural Directing Post', at crossroads, lies Bicton Park. Its 50-acre grounds include an 18th-C Italian garden, American pines, and a woodland railway. *Open daily, Apr–Sept.*

Otterton *Return to crossroads and take Otterton turning for Otterton Mill, a water-powered flour mill still working and open to visitors Easter to Oct 10.30–5.30; 2–5 rest of year. There is also a restaurant.*

⑥ *At end of village take left turn signposted Sidmouth, then right after ½ mile (0.8 km) for Peak Hill. Superb views from car park at the top.*

☆ **Sidmouth** The charm of this seaside town lies in its Regency houses, which are especially fine along the front.

114

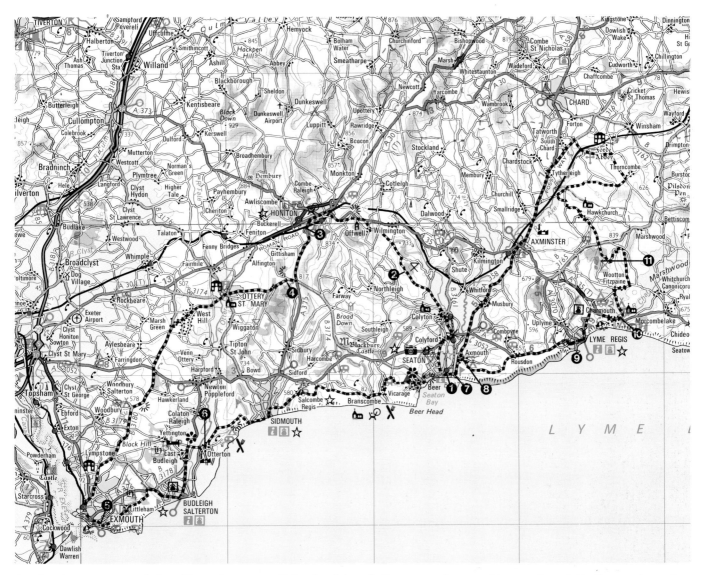

☆ **Salcombe Regis** Beyond the village, the donkey sanctuary, open daily, invites visitors to wander around and look at its 1,500 donkeys.

🏠 **Branscombe** Spread out along a valley designated an area of outstanding natural beauty, this lovely village has a part-Norman church, St Winifred's (below road on right) and a smithy (on left) said to be 18thC and still working.

🍴 **Branscombe** The Mason's Arms is a picturesque inn which dates back 700 years. Restaurant and bar meals.

✿ **Beer** Fishing village with smuggling associations. The Modelrama and Pleasure Gardens on the hillside has model and miniature railways and fine views across Lyme Bay.

Route Two: 52 miles (83 km)
Directions in sequence from: Seaton
Direction of travel: anticlockwise

---

⑦ *Leave Seaton from eastern end of sea front, crossing bridge over River Axe. B3172 runs*

parallel to the river and offers some splendid views.

⑧ *Turn right in centre of Axmouth and then right again after passing chapel.*

☆ **Lyme Regis** Shortly after entering town, take Cobb Road (car park on right) for stroll in the breeze along the Cobb harbour wall. Here the self-willed Louisa, in Jane Austen's *Persuasion*, fell 'and was taken up lifeless!' Louisa recovered but the Cobb was immortalized.

The contemporary novelist John Fowles lives in Lyme Regis and he has underlined the Cobb's, and Lyme's, place in literature by making it the central setting of his novel *The French Lieutenant's Woman*, also a successful feature film with a script by Harold Pinter. *Tourist information: tel. (029 74) 2138.*

⑨ *Leave by Charmouth road. Extensive views before turning right on to A35.*

🚗 **Charmouth** Take first right past church for pleasant beach renowned for fossils.

🏛 **Charmouth** Return to main street and turn right for Barney's Fossil and Country Life

Museum. *Open daily, Easter to September.*

⑩ *Turn left at the end of main street into lane signposted Wootton Fitzpaine.*

🏠 **Catherstone Leweston** Hidden among trees along drive to manor house is an interesting Victorian church on site of 14th-C chapel.

⑪ *In Wootton Fitzpaine turn right into Whitchurch Rd. then left following 'Fishponds' signs through pleasant wooded area.*

🏠 **Hawkchurch** Spirited carvings in the church include animals playing musical instruments, and a bird with a monkey's head.

🏛 **Forde Abbey** Cromwellian house created from 12th-C monastery, and known for its ancient tapestries. *Open Wed, Sun and Bank Holiday Mondays, 2–6, May–Sept. Visitors can pick fruit and vegetables, mid-June to early Aug, daily.*

🏭 **Axminster** The carpet factory, established in 1755, put the town on the map. *Telephone (0297) 32244 for times of factory tours* – but do not expect the brilliance of the old designs.

Purbeck

The coastal sections of these two loops are as exciting as any seaside driving in southern England. Huge, bare downs rise above the sea on Route One, with roads riding up and down. West of Weymouth, there are fascinating views down on to Chesil Beach, the extraordinary pebbly spit which has claimed the lives of so many sailors. Inland, the scenery is tamer, but full of possibilities: a visit to T. E. Lawrence's spartan cottage, or the Bovington Tank Museum; a climb up to Corfe Castle; a detour through Purbeck. Part of Route One is through an army range, perfectly safe when the gates are open: check with the number given at ⑥.

Route One: 36 miles (58 km)
In sequence from: Wareham
Direction of travel: anticlockwise

🅗 **Wareham** Driving through the main street you get an excellent impression of the town's dignified, mainly 18th-C character, but none of its violent past. It was a fortress in pre-Roman times, with great earth ramparts north, east and west; the River Frome guarded the south side. The Romans and later defenders developed the ramparts into defensive forts and walls and the remains are a strange sight in an otherwise domesticated place.

🍺 **Wareham** The popular stopping place is the quay by the bridge over the Frome with the neat group of former warehouses nearby, and views over the expansive water meadows. Downstream, the Frome flows into Poole Harbour, and makes useful yacht anchorage. The Bear Hotel is conveniently close for a drink.

⛪ **Wareham** St Mary's church has Roman, Saxon and Norman elements, and the coffin in which King Edward was laid after being murdered by his stepmother, Elfrida, at nearby Corfe Castle.

⛪ **Wareham** St Martin's-on-the-Wall has a Saxon chancel arch a thousand years old, and much from the Normans, but its most arresting feature is a fine wooden figure of T. E. Lawrence – Lawrence of Arabia, the scholarly man who successfully united and led the Arab tribes against the Turks in 1914–18. He is seen in his adopted uniform: full Arab dress.

① *After leaving Wareham on the A352 look carefully for this right fork: it comes just after crossing the railway line, marked Worgret Heath.*

🌿 **Unclassified road between A352 and B3390** Fine views soon open out right over the Frome valley. The road now runs through heathland well suited to tank training – hence Bovington Camp. Thomas Hardy spent his childhood close by at Higher Bockhampton (see page 118), which sits at the edge of a similar, neighbouring tract of heath, whose severe beauty made a deep impression on the writer.

② *What looks like a crossroads on the map is a T-junction; turn right, and in rather more than 100 yards (91 m), left.*

🏛 **Junction with unclassified road to Bovington Camp** A signpost here indicates a detour to the National Trust property of Clouds Hill at Moreton. If T. E. Lawrence's effigy in the church at Wareham aroused your curiosity, a visit to this cottage may add something to your understanding of this enigmatic figure. After the First World War he tried to live down his own legend, entering the RAF as an aircraftman under the name of Ross. Later he changed his name to T. E. Shaw, and as Private Shaw served temporarily in the tank regiment at Bovington, renting Clouds Hill. In 1935, after discharge from the services, he returned to the cottage with his secretary. The place leaves a disturbing impression: the motto over the door in Greek, 'Nothing Matters'; barest furniture; horrible aluminium wallpaper in the guest room. The record collection upstairs seems the sole sweetener of an austere existence, soon cut short by a fatal motor cycle crash. He is buried in the nearby church at Moreton; the coffin is inscribed 'To T.E.L., who should sleep among kings'.

🏛 **Bovington Camp** The Royal Armoured Corps and Royal Tank Regiment Museums contain 140 examples of tanks and armoured cars dating from 1915 to the present day; working models, conducted parties, model makers' drawings, shop, refreshments. *Open daily except for certain days – tel. (0929) 462721.*

③ *Turn left on to the B3390: pleasant driving through woods, splendid in May and June when the masses of rhododendrons are in flower. At the major crossroads turn left on to the A352 and in 2 miles (3 km) ④ turn right for Chaldon Herring. Drive considerately on these spectacular, narrow lanes.*

🅗 **Chaldon Herring** The sea is not visible from the village, but it is very close, hidden behind the downs: the local lord of the manor might claim anything of value in wrecks washed up on neighbouring beaches. *Turn left at the village green to find the pub.*

🍺 **Chaldon Herring** The Sailor's Return claims to be a 16th-C pub, and it certainly can have seen little modernization. It is a warren of tiny rooms, drinks served from a narrow counter in the passage.

〰 **West Lulworth** The front line of defence against the sea hereabouts is sharply folded, unstable Portland limestone strata. The sea broke through, attacked the softer clay beds behind, and then the chalk, which is being eroded even now. The result, an amazingly rounded cove with lovely blue water, is remarkable and beautiful even when overrun on a sunny Bank Holiday. No one should miss getting out of the car for a stroll. There is a well-signposted public footpath west along the cliff to Durdle Door, another astonishing piece of sea sculpture. *Leave West Lulworth on the B3070.*

⑤ *Fork right, signposted Whiteway Hill.*

⑥ *Fork right through the gates, entering the firing ranges. These are safe and open to*

traffic most weekends of the year, and most of August, but liable to closure without warning when firing practice takes place. *Check before departure with the Range Officer by telephoning (0929) 462721. (At weekends or during dark hours ask for the guardroom.)*

✹ **Unclassified road east of East Lulworth** This stretch of road is the most dramatic of the drive, with strategically sited stopping places for one or two cars: views inland over the ranges, and out to sea; shell craters and ruined tanks add a bizarre note.

⑦ *Turn right through the gates for a detour to Tyneham (open most weekends and most of August; to check whether firing is in progress, telephone number given at ⑥).*

➹ **Tyneham** was laid waste by artillery shells, but local pressure has resulted in re-opening. You can park the car, picnic, explore the nostalgic village remains and walk down to Worbarrow Bay and Tout (lookout point).

⑧ *A road leads right to Kimmeridge; to continue, turn sharp left (unsignposted) for Church Knowle. Beyond Kimmeridge village is a parking area with access to Kimmeridge beach, with its shale cliffs,* ≋ ledges and rock pools. This wild and lovely place (despite the BP drilling rig on the cliff) will fascinate anyone with a passing interest in marine biology. See the information board in the car park.

🏛 **Corfe Castle's** remains have a history worthy of their dramatic, haunting appearance. The Norman castle was defended gallantly for six weeks against 600 Parliamentary troops in the Civil War – by a woman, Lady Bankes. Three years later it was seized

● *Corfe Castle, guardian of Purbeck.*

through trickery and reduced to its present condition. *Open daily.*

⑨ *To return to Bournemouth, follow the B3351 to Studland and the Sandbanks ferry. The road leads through the heart of the Isle of Purbeck, a detour worth making for its own sake.* ('Isle' is more or less apt: the peninsula was formerly rather inaccessible, with the Frome to the north, Poole Harbour in the north-east and the English Channel surrounding it to the east and south; a landward approach has however always been possible from West Lulworth.)

☆ **Swanage** is the home town of two famous building families, the Mowlems and the Burts. Their wealth is responsible for some of the place's unexpectedly grand features: the town hall's facade, for instance, was designed by Christopher Wren.

≋ **Chapman's Pool,** approached through Worth Matravers, is, like Lulworth Cove, the work of erosion, its water a remarkable blue.

❢ There is a fine walk out around **St Alban's Head** from Worth Matravers: it passes cavernous quarries where local stone has been hacked out of the cliffs.

> **Route two: 36 miles (58 km)**
> Directions in sequence from:
> Warmwell crossroads
> Direction of travel: anticlockwise

⑪ *Take this inconspicuous unsignposted turning left through white gates by lodge. Later keep left, then right, at T-junction.*

➍ **Maiden Castle** A vast prehistoric fort covering 115 acres, with eight lines of defence evident in some places: hours of strolling.

⑫ *Triangular intersection of roads not indicated by map.*

➍ **Winterbourne Abbas** Nearby are the Nine Stones, possibly the remains of an ancient British temple.

➍ **Long Bredy** Here is Kingston Russell, the house where Hardy, Nelson's much-loved admiral, was born.

✹ **B3157 north-west of Abbotsbury** Here are the best views down on to Chesil Beach. Many find the sight of the 8-mile (13-km) natural spit rather disturbing – and perhaps for good reason. Even in calm weather, the undertow caused by the steepness of the bank makes landing difficult; in bad weather, the place is a death trap. During one storm in 1824 an entire sloop was carried to the crest of the bank: the crew climbed off and walked into Portland.

Chesil plays a dramatic role in Meade Falkner's *Moonfleet* (1898), a spellbinding tale of smuggling in these parts which gives as good a feel for the coast from here to St Alban's Head as anything yet written.

➍ **Abbotsbury** Ruins of a Benedictine abbey
➹ and the former monks' swannery, a lake holding swans and wildfowl. *Open daily May–Sept.*

⚓ **The Isle of Portland**, composed of limestone, resisted the erosion of the sea, and provided from its quarries building stone that Inigo Jones admired enough to incorporate in the Banqueting Hall at Whitehall. It appears in other London buildings too, including St Paul's Cathedral. In fact, the whole coast from Portland to Poole was formerly a rich quarrying resource, producing not only Portland Stone but shale, which burns much like coal, and the honey-coloured Purbeck stone.

⑬ *In Weymouth keep going east at junctions: A353 is easily picked up at sea front.*

≋ **Osmington** Early this century the cliffs to the west of the village collapsed under enormous pressure from water-saturated clay which had built up behind. The resulting mud-flow was like lava emptying from a volcano.

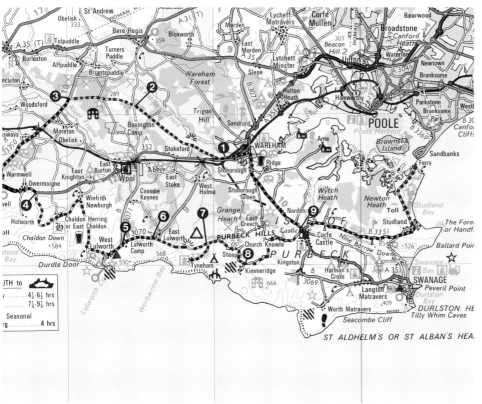

Blackmoor Vale and the Dorset Hills

Each of the four towns included in this tour has something different to offer: Shaftesbury is visited for its views; Sherborne's abbey is one of the glories of southern England; Dorchester has associations with Thomas Hardy; and Blandford Forum (its name is misleading as it has no Roman connections) has many Georgian buildings.

In between there are ancient churches, lovely manor houses and charming villages. There are also a few surprises, such as the interior of Bere Regis church and the astonishing Cerne Giant.

Route: 104 miles (167 km)
In sequence from: Shaftesbury
Direction of travel: anticlockwise

☆ **Shaftesbury** Panoramic views of the Blackmoor Vale, from this windy, hill-top town of ancient origin, put the first lap of the tour into perspective. The best look-out point is from Park Walk, beside the Abbey ruins (open daily, Easter to Oct, strictly for those with the imagination to flesh out excavations). Tourist information: tel. (0747) 2256.

☆ **Shaftesbury** At the same end of the town, Gold Hill, a steep old street with cottages and cobblestones, starred in a television commercial for a brand of brown bread.

① Leave town on B3091, then turn right on to unclassified road signposted to Stour Row and Marnhull.

☆ **Marnhull** This smart village with a handsome church was Marlott in Thomas Hardy's Tess of the d'Urbervilles.

✗ **Marnhull** Near the church, the Crown pub, offering a set-price menu (the dishes follow the tone set by the village) or bar meals, was the model for The Pure Drop in Tess.

② Leave village on Fifehead Magdalen road. At T-junction, turn left then continue on to Henstridge.

🏠 **Purse Caundle** Only minutes from the A30, yet a secret, quiet place with a 15th-C manor house visible from the main street. The house is open 2–5, Thurs, Sun and Bank Holidays, mid-Apr to end-Oct.

• Milton Abbas, model village on the site of a former market town. Even the church is designed to harmonize with the village.

☆ **Sherborne** An appealing atmosphere pervades this small, neat town of predominantly yellow-ochre stone buildings. In the main street, good quality shops include food stores selling Dorset knobs (crisp little rolls delicious with butter and cheddar or Dorset blue cheese), and new and second-hand bookshops.

✝ **Sherborne** Allow time in the abbey church to absorb not only the exquisite richness of the fan vaulting (15thC), but also the medieval carved and painted nave bosses depicting humans, animals, birds, a mermaid and a dragon. The abbey, founded in 705, also has several striking monuments. Note the pun of the horses' heads on the Horsey tomb.

Sherborne School, next to the abbey, occupies some of the old monastic buildings.

♏ **Sherborne** To the east, the town has two castles. The Old Castle (12thC) is now a ruin. The New Castle, built by Sir Walter Raleigh, has fine furniture, Old Masters, gardens laid out by Capability Brown and a 50-acre lake. Open Thurs, Sat, Sun and Bank Holiday Mon, 2–6. Easter to Sept.

🏠 **Longburton** Worth fetching the key from the address on the door, to see the painted canopied tomb in the church of St James.

③ A short distance from the church, turn right, follow signpost to Leigh (once famous for witches). At Leigh, follow signpost to

---

Chetnole. At Chetnole, take Evershot road to T-junction, and left on to A37.

An even more attractive route is from Leigh to Batcombe, but only drivers prepared to tackle an extremely steep road culminating in a T-junction should attempt the drive.

☆ **Sydling St Nicholas** A tucked-away village that has much to offer including a smithy dating from 1800 (in the main street), a church known for its gargoyles and monuments, and a flint-walled, Elizabethan tithe barn, splendid still in spite of the corrugated-iron roof.

🗿 **Cerne Abbas** The Cerne Giant, conspicuous from the road, is a vast, chalk-cut pagan fertility figure flaunting its masculinity. The Church objected strongly when it was weeded in the late 19thC, on the grounds that local morality would deteriorate.

☆ **Cerne Abbas** The village (Tudor houses, duck pond, remains of a 10th-C abbey) boasts several pubs including the ancient-looking New Inn. *M OLD BAKEHOUSE*

④ On leaving the village, turn right just past the church, and follow signposts to Piddletrenthide.

⑤ At Piddletrenthide, turn left on to B3143, then almost immediately turn right on to unclassified road if in search of a good lunchtime stopping place.

✗ **Plush** The Brace of Pheasants, a deservedly popular pub-restaurant, is favoured by the whole county: book for meals.

☆ **Dorchester** Thomas Hardy's Casterbridge has commemorated the author with a statue at Top o' Town and a reconstruction of his study in the County Museum, High West St., open Mon–Sat.

Also in High West St., Judge Jeffreys' Restaurant occupies the site where the infamous judge lodged during the Bloody Assize of 1685. The town is built mainly in grey Portland stone, but has an air of bustling activity that defies gloom, especially on Market Day, Wed.

❉ **Dorchester** Maiden Castle, the largest and most elaborate prehistoric earthworks in Britain, looks impressive from A354, just south-west of the town, but walkers will want to explore its ditches and ramparts, some of which rise to around 89 feet (27 m).

🏠 **Stinsford** Hardy's heart was buried in St Michael's churchyard, although his ashes were buried in Westminster Abbey. However, local wags used to say that the surgeon's cat ate the heart and another had to be substituted.

At nearby Higher Bockhampton (not on map, but follow signpost from A35) the thatched cottage where Hardy was born and lived for many years can be seen from the outside daily (except Tues morning), Apr–Oct. (There is a 10-minute walk from car park.) Interior seen by appointment only.

☆ **Puddletown** First, feast your eyes on the fine tombs of the Martyn family in the village church, then travel a short way down the A354 to Athelhampton, much of

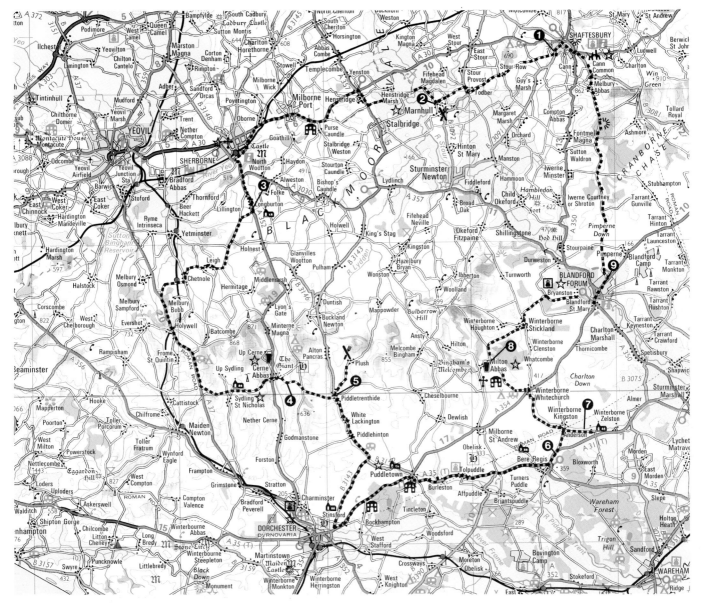

which was built by Sir William Martyn in the 15thC. *House open 2–6, Wed, Thurs, Sun and Bank Holidays, mid-Apr to mid-Oct; also Tues and Fri afternoons in Aug.*

The partly battlemented house has a superb great hall with an open timber roof, and lovely grounds divided into several gardens, each suiting a different mood.

Tolpuddle The 'martyrs' who made this village famous (in 1834 they were transported to Australia for joining a trade union) used to meet under the spreading sycamore tree that still stands, propped up but healthy, on the green.

Bere Regis At the far end of the village, just before the Royal Oak pub, turn right down lane to St Peter's church, to see an astonishing carved and painted roof – almost life-size apostles jut out from the walls and look down on the congregation.

⑥ *Returning to main road follow signs to Winterborne Kingston at two roundabouts. At village, turn right to Winterborne Tomson (not on map).*

Winterborne Tomson Just beyond the manor house at Winterborne Anderson, turn left down lane to discover a rare gem of a church. Tiny, round-ended and built of stone and flint, it was saved from dereliction around 50 years ago through funds raised from the sale of Hardy manuscripts.

⑦ *Return to Winterborne Kingston and follow signposts to Milton Abbas. Turn left into village.*

Milton Abbas In the late 18thC, Lord Milton 'moved' the old village of Milton Abbas out of sight of his grand new home. However, posterity has benefited from his ruthlessness: the 'new' village with its almost identical thatched cottages survives very much as he built it, with not a TV aerial in sight.

Milton Abbas Lord Milton's house, now a public school, is *open during spring and summer school holidays*, and the magnificent abbey church, 14th–15th C but much restored, is *open daily*.

Milton Abbas The thatched Hambro Arms pub serves real ale, and fits neatly into this 'model' village.

⑧ *Return to road at top end of village, turn left then first right to Winterborne Stickland.*

☆ **Blandford Forum** The deep-red bricks of the beautifully proportioned Georgian buildings, particularly in the Market Place, give this town a welcoming warmth. Best avoided on Saturdays when heavy traffic rattles through the centre, Blandford has a small but lively contemporary art gallery showing changing exhibitions (Hambledon Gallery, Salisbury St.,) and good bookshops.

⑨ *Leave the town on the Salisbury road, A354. While still in the built-up area, take left turn along unclassified road signposted to Shaftesbury.*

Blandford–Shaftesbury Green, gently rolling Dorset countryside gives way to spectacular views at Fontwell Down, before the road plunges down the appropriately named Zig-zag Hill back to Shaftesbury.

Ⓜ MILTON MANOR

New Forest

Take care when driving on Forest roads, especially at night, when ponies are difficult to spot. If you find an animal in trouble, contact the police, who will alert an agister (Forest wildlife warden).

The Forestry Commission, which manages the New Forest, both commercially and for the pleasure of visitors, has done more or less everything possible to accommodate the motorist (and camper) without spoiling the place's natural beauty: picnic places, tent and caravan sites proliferate.

Route One: 30 miles (48 km)
In sequence from: Lyndhurst
Direction of travel: clockwise

☆ **Lyndhurst** Chief town of the New Forest, with a long-winded, one-way system; interesting food shop, Strange's, speciality local venison. *Tourist information: tel. 042128 2269.*

🏛 **Lyndhurst** The 17th-C hall attached to Queen's House at the top of the High Street is the meeting place of the ancient Verderers' Court, which meets to administer Forest affairs.

The stirrup over the fireplace once measured the size of Foresters' dogs – those too big to pass through were considered a danger to game.

William the Conqueror took over the New Forest as a royal hunting ground – the meaning here of the word 'forest'.

⛪ **Lyndhurst** St Michael's church, next to Queen's House, is 19thC with fine stained glass by William Morris. Buried in the churchyard is Alice Hargreaves, Lewis Carroll's inspiration for Alice.

〰 **Lyndhurst** Leaving the town, notice the extensive 'lawns' left and right. Cropped short by the ponies, these expanses comprise, with heath and woodland, the main elements of the Forest's scenery – a remarkable survival of a medieval landscape into the 20thC.

🦋 **Longdown, nr Ashurst** *About 1 mile (1.5 km) on left along unclassified road, signposted Beaulieu from the A35,* is the New Forest Butterfly Farm. Fascinating world-wide collection of butterflies and the like in an indoor tropical garden; *open daily Apr–Oct.*

𝖵 **Denny Lodge** The forest road to this keeper's lodge, signposted from the B3056, provides excellent chances of seeing fallow or even roe deer.

🚶 **Beaulieu** Whatever your feelings about the razzmatazz of the stately homes business, seeing the ruins of the Cistercian abbey, founded by King John in a fit of conscience, is worthwhile.

🏛 **Beaulieu** Lord Montagu admits that Palace House, purchased in 1538 by his ancestor, the Earl of Southampton, and originally the

gatehouse to the Abbey, is undistinguished as stately homes go, but it stands in an exceptional position at the head of the Beaulieu River.

🏛 **Beaulieu** The National Motor Museum is arguably the best of its kind in the world, and superbly laid out: the complete history of motoring in a collection of more than 200 vehicles. Monorail; veteran car and bus rides; model railway; restaurant; café. *Open daily.*

① *If detouring to Exbury, be ready for the double right turn here.*

✿ **Exbury** Over 250 acres of rhododendrons and azaleas, glorious during early summer. *Open afternoons mid Apr–early June, closed Sat.*

② *For Lepe beach, continue straight on following the sign to Inchmery; car park and beach in 2 miles (3 km).*

⚓ **Lepe** Country Park and shingle beach with fine view across Solent; café.

🚢 **Bucklers Hard** In the 18thC great warships, including Nelson's Agamemnon ('Am and Eggs' to her crew) were built and launched between the two rows of pretty labourers' cottages. Despite summer crowds, an evocative place, and a popular yachtsman's port.

🏛 **Bucklers Hard** The Maritime Museum relates the village shipbuilding story. *Open daily.*

⛪ **Bucklers Hard** The little chapel, half-way up the 'street', was once a cobbler's shop, with a cellar beneath used for storing smuggled goods.

✗ **Bucklers Hard** The Master Builder's House Hotel was the home of famous shipbuilder Ⓜ Henry Adams. Relaxed public bar; buffet bar; restaurant.

⚓ **Bucklers Hard** Half-hour cruises along the Beaulieu River in summer. For departure times go to Pier Kiosk; well-signposted riverside walk from Bucklers Hard to Beaulieu.

③ *Leaving car park turn immediately left on to unsignposted minor road. At T-junction turn left, signposted East End.*

🏚 **Bucklers Hard–Lymington** At St Leonards (not on map) are the substantial remains of an extremely large medieval tithe barn.

🌿 **Bucklers Hard–Lymington** Soon after the tithe barn a lovely view to the Isle of Wight opens out, left.

④ *At signpost 'Sowley 1 mile' (Sowley not on map) turn left.*

☆ **Lymington** Still a strong sense of the 18thC in this pleasant sea-faring town – imposing Georgian houses in the High St., from the bottom end of which a cobbled alleyway

Ⓜ STAMWELL HOUSE

leads to the Town Quay. Street market on Sat; ferry to IOW.

⑤ *Follow signs for A337, towards Bourne-mouth.*

❗ **Keyhaven** At T-junction in Keyhaven village turn left for ferry to Hurst Castle (signposted) or right for a bracing walk along the shingle spit out to the Castle.

🏰 **Hurst Castle** One of Henry VIII's coastal forts; Charles I was held here briefly *en route for execution; open daily, closed Sun morning; regular ferries to Castle from Keyhaven.*

🏖 **Detour to Milford Beach:** *In Milford on Sea, take the road signposted 'Beach'. This is a steep, shingled beach with a marvellous view of the Needles. Return to the B3058 and follow the signs for Christchurch/Bournemouth.*

⑥ *In about 1 mile (1.5 km) watch carefully for this right turn after a corner: you want Downton Lane; it should (if the signpost is intact) be signposted Hordle.*

🍺 **Downton** The Royal Oak pub: home-cooked food and Pompey Royal bitter.

⑦ *Keep left at this fork, ambiguously marked 'Stopples Lane'.*

⑧ *At the next T-junction turn right, then in 100 yards (91 m) left, signposted Tiptoe and Sway.*

⑨ *At the next junction (with the B3055) turn right and in 100 yards (91 m) left for Tiptoe and Wootton.*

⑩ *Just before the junction with the B3058 (beside The Inn), turn right, signposted Brockenhurst.*

🌿 **Wootton–Brockenhurst** Sweeping views of the heath, with its lovely colouring, especially at Hinchelsea Moor picnic area.

✗ **Brockenhurst** The Rose and Crown pub serves good food, including pasta from the Italian chef.

🏛 **Brockenhurst–A35** Past Rhinefield House, the road enters Rhinefield Ornamental Drive, an 1859 plantation of magnificent tall trees, mainly conifers, with many interesting foreign species. Walks from Blackwater car park.

> **Route Two: 20 miles (32 km)**
> Directions in sequence from:
> Downton (Wiltshire)
> Direction of travel: anticlockwise

🏠 **Breamore House,** *signposted from the A338, is an Elizabethan house dating from 1583; interesting furniture; authentic Great Kitchen; carriages on display. Open afternoons Apr–Sept; closed Mon, Fri.*

⑪ *In Breamore village take minor road left signposted Woodgreen.*

⑫ *In Woodgreen turn right signposted Godshill.*

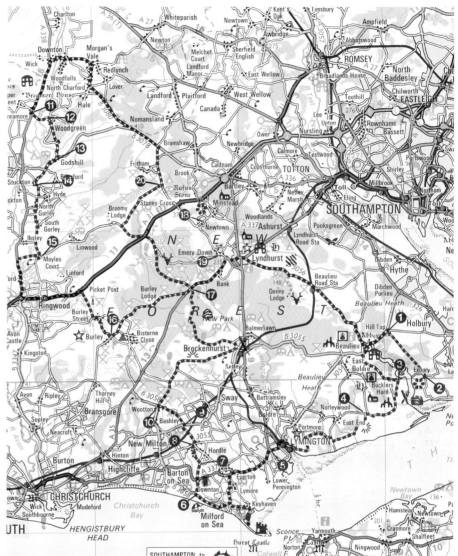

⑬ *At T-junction with B3078 turn right signposted Fordingbridge. In a third of a mile (0.5 km), turn half left down a very minor road at the corner signposted Stuckton.*

⑭ *At this unsignposted T-junction turn left. Then at the North Gorley junction keep left, signposted South Gorley.*

⑮ *Reaching Moyle's Court, follow signs for Ellingham and Ringwood.*

☆ **Burley** Popular New Forest centre; strong smuggling associations.

⑯ *After left turn by shops, continue straight ahead, along Chapel Lane, signposted 'Burley Church'.*

⑰ *Soon after joining A35, turn left on to the unclassified road marked 'Boldrewood Ornamental Drive'. This runs through woodland containing superb beeches. Look for the pollards.*

🏚 **Minstead** makes a worthwhile detour: *the simplest approach is via Lyndhurst. Its cottage-like church contains an extremely rare 17th-C triple-decker pulpit, a Norman font, intriguing galleried pews and a luxury*

family pew with its own fireplace. Conan Doyle is buried here.

✿ **Minstead** Furzey Gardens: an authentic forester's cottage, dating from 1560, surrounded by gardens. *Open daily.*

⑱ *To rejoin the route, keep left at this unmarked fork, and left again at the T-junction ½ mile (0.8 km) on, which is also unmarked. At Emery Down, turn sharp right ⑲ by The New Forest Inn, signposted Boldrewood and Linwood. Expect a superb drive through incomparable New Forest scenery; there is a deer sanctuary at the left end of Boldrewood car park. Soon rejoin marked route.*

⑲ *Having crossed the war-time airfield of Stoney Cross, turn right at the T-junction if you wish to visit the Rufus Stone (later left on to the A31, and first left again signposted Brook and Downton). The stone, a popular but rather disappointing spot, marks the place where William Rufus, second Norman king of England, is supposed to have met his death in a hunting accident. If continuing the route, turn left (unmarked).*

🍺 **Fritham** Royal Oak – simple Forest pub.

South Downs

Together, these two loops encompass almost every type of Sussex scenery. You sample the highest points of the South Downs – surprisingly lonely in parts – and the secluded villages of the Weald, typically set in woodland. There are numerous opportunities to leave the car and have a short stroll; those who stay inside all the way round really do miss the flavour of this area: there is nothing quite like a warm summer's day on the tops of the downs, with a cooling wind blowing in from the sea, whispering through the grass.

Route One: 39 miles (63 km)
Directions in sequence from: Lewes
Direction of travel: clockwise

☆ **Lewes** is a county town full of interest, standing in a hollow and sprawling up a hill alongside the River Ouse. It began life as a Saxon trading centre, gaining in prestige after the Norman Conquest with the building of the castle and of the most important Cluniac priory in England. The town still retains much of its medieval character and a wealth of architectural interest. 'Lewes Town Walk' published by East Sussex County at 50p is useful.

⚔ **Lewes** Of the Norman castle built on a high mound in the centre of the town, the keep (magnificent view over the town from the top) and the barbican remain. Close by, Barbican House is a Georgian building housing a museum of local archaeology. Castle and museum open Mon–Fri, also Sun afternoon, Apr–Oct.

🏛 **Lewes** South of the castle stands Southover Grange, an Elizabethan manor house built with Caen stone taken from ruins of the nearby St Pancras Priory (demolished in 1539 as a result of the Dissolution of the monasteries). The diarist John Evelyn (1620–1706) lived here as a boy and the Prince Regent often stayed in the 1790s. The gardens are open to the public daily. Tourist information: Lewes House, 32 High St. Tel (079 16) 71600.

① Leave Lewes by Offham Rd. At the junction with the A275, turn right towards East Grinstead.

② Turn left on to the B2116 signposted Hurstpierpoint. From this road under the Downs there are many fine views over the Weald of Sussex.

☆ **Ditchling** Use the car park so that you can stroll round this attractive village. Near the Early English cruciform church and the
🏛 village pond stands a Tudor manor house, with an interesting outside staircase, which belonged to Anne of Cleves.

③ From Ditchling village, turn left at crossroads just after village car park on to B2112. For Beacon, after 200 yards (183 m) take left fork on to unclassified road.
⚞ The Beacon is 813 feet (248 m) high; you can take a bracing walk along the South Downs Way from the car park.

④ Return to the B2112, turning left on to it and left into Clayton at junction with A273.

⛪ **Clayton** The saxon church with its perfect plain chancel arch, and above it, well preserved 11th–12th-C wall paintings, is on the left just before A273. Up above, on the downs, are two landmarks, a pair of 19th-C
✹ windmills known as 'Jack and Jill'. Note folly on right of junction.

⑤ Turn right at junction of A273 and A23 (traffic lights). The village of Pycombe was once famous for its shepherds' crooks.

● The Seven Sisters – a magnificent prospect viewed from above Cuckmere Haven.

⑥ Turn left on to A281 (Horsham road).

🏛 **Newtimber Place** A moated Jacobean house which contains Etruscan style wall paintings. Open Thurs afternoons, May–Aug.

⑦ At Woodmancote (not on map) turn right on to unclassified road, signposted Blackstone.

⑧ At the B2116 turn right and in 600 yds (549 m) turn left on to unclassified road to Twineham.

△ **Warninglid–Lindfield** The route passes through Cuckfield and then on to Lindfield, both of which manage to retain their village atmosphere, despite urban encroachment.
    Short distances to the north of this area
✿ are four very fine gardens: Nymans (off map), Sheffield Park (indicated), with the
🏛 famous Bluebell Railway, Wakehurst Place and Borde Hill (not indicated). They are all intriguingly different.

⑨ A quarter of a mile (0.5 km) after joining the B2036, turn left at the roundabout into Ardingly Rd. (signposted 'Hospital'). Follow signs for Lindfield, turning left at Hickmans Lane, then right into Lindfield High Street.

⑩ Turn left in Lindfield, just before the village pond.

⑪ From the A272 turn right for Lewes, then in 50 yards (46 m) right again, signposted Plumpton Green.

⚞ **Chailey–Plumpton** The road crosses Chailey Common Nature Reserve with tremendous views of the downs and several opportunities for parking.

Route Two: 54 miles (87 km)
Directions in sequence from: Lewes
Direction of travel: clockwise

---

⑫ Leave Lewes on the A26, Tunbridge Wells road, turning right at the top of Malling Hill on to the B2192, signposted Ringmer.

⑬ One mile (2.5 km) after the B2192 and B2124 join, turn left on to unclassified road, signposted Bentley Wildfowl and Motor Museum. This is a useful stop for children; open daily Easter–Oct; Sat, Sun, Nov–Easter; closed Dec.

⑭ After Bentley join the A22, going north for ½ mile (0.8 km), then turn right on to an unclassified road for Framfield. Go straight over the next crossroads and through Framfield, then take the B2102 in the direction of Heathfield. Keep left at the junction with the B2192.

🍺 **Blackboys** Excellent 14th-C pub with extensive garden and a wide range of food.

⑮ Take the first right outside Blackboys, down the unclassified road for Waldron and Horam.

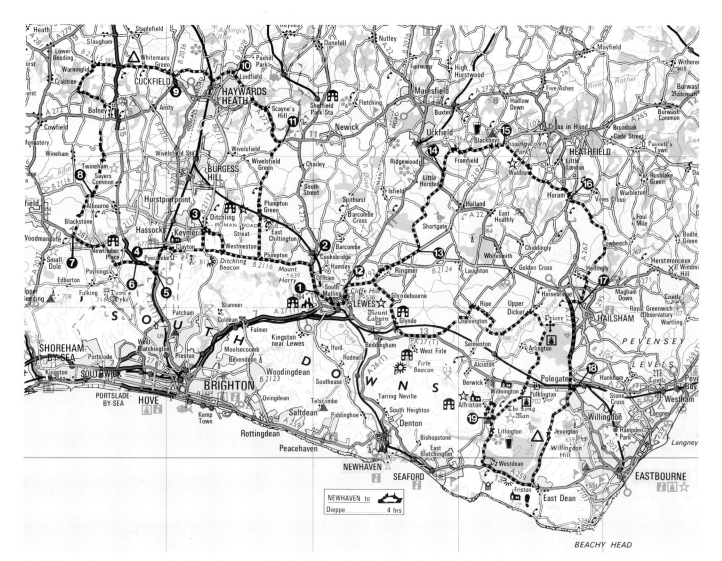

BEACHY HEAD

☆ **Waldron** A pretty, tree-shaded village which has a vineyard and a shop where you can taste the local wine.

⑯ *In Horam take the minor road on the left opposite Merrydown Wine & Cider Works for Hellingly and Hailsham. In Hailsham* ⑰ *follow through-town traffic signs to the A22 and there turn left.*

⑱ *Just after junction with A27 at Polegate, turn right at traffic lights on to minor road for Wannock (not on map).*

△ **Polegate–Friston** A beautiful, downland dry valley road leads through the tiny village of Jevington to Friston where the church, with its charming beamed roof is approached by a revolving tapsell gate. There is a fine walk on to the Seven Sisters cliffs from Crowlink car park, which is signposted from the village pond.

☆ **Friston–Exceat** (Exceat not on map) A high, downland road with superb views.

☆ **Exceat** Seven Sisters Country Park, on the southern edge of Friston Forest, encompasses 692 acres of the Cuckmere valley and part of the Seven Sisters chalk cliffs.

▯ **Litlington** Charming village with typical flint buildings. On the left is The Plough and Harrow, which serves real ale and good pub food; garden. There is an interesting nursery almost opposite.

⑲ *Just after Lullington Court, turn left, sign-posted Alfriston, then left at next junction, over narrow bridge and left at next junction to Alfriston. For Drusillas, turn right at last junction.*

☆ **Alfriston** A busy tourist village, but well worth visiting. The 17th-C Star Inn was probably a smugglers' haunt, and certainly sheltered pilgrims on their way to Canterbury. Have a look at the rather imposing church which is often called 'The Cathedral of the Downs'. Nearby stands the 14th-C rectory, The Clergy House, bought in 1896 for £10 by the National Trust – their first property. *Retrace route to Litlington road, then turn left to Wilmington.* In 600 yards (549 m) is **Wilmington**, whose church is said to be the smallest in the country. In late winter the roadsides here are a mass of snowdrops.

▣ **Wilmington Priory and the Long Man** The famous Long Man of Wilmington, a long staff in each hand, looks down from the side of Windover Hill on which he was carved, no one knows when. He is a 231-foot (70-m) figure cut in the Downs and is best viewed from the priory car park on the left near the remains of a 13th-C Benedictine priory, now an agricultural museum. *Open daily, Mar–Oct. Closed Tues and Sun mornings.*

✝ **Micheham Priory** Much restored moated 13th-C priory, with Tudor barn, gatehouse and working water mill selling flour. Lunches and teas are available and there are various exhibitions on display, including tapestries, furniture and miniature musical instruments. *Open daily, Apr–Oct.*

▥ **Firle Place** Firle Place has been the home of the Gage family since the 15thC and contains notable paintings, furniture and porcelain. *Open Sun, Mon and Wed, June–Sept. Also Thurs in Aug and Bank Hols at Easter–Aug.*

☆ **Firle Beacon** 713 feet (217 m) high with extensive views, another in the chain of warning beacons.

▥ **Glynde** Glynde Place, home of the Hampden family, is a fine Elizabethan manor with some interesting works of art inside – a charming house which still feels very much like a home. *Open Wed, Thur, June–Sept.*

The Weald and the Cinque Ports

Here are two areas in close proximity, yet strong in contrast. The hilly, enclosed countryside of the Weald remains one of the most thickly wooded areas of lowland England. It is also a region of orchards and of hop gardens: the oasts of Kent are one of the county's defining features, and in winter the poles and wirework of the hop gardens rise starkly above the hedges.

Altogether different are the levels around Winchelsea and Rye: once marshland, but now drained, they are an open, flat and sometimes mysterious landscape of sheep pasture and tillage with only the occasional up-standing feature.

Route: 80 miles (128 km)
In sequence from: Cranbrook
Direction of travel: anticlockwise

① *In Cranbrook free car park to right off St David's Bridge (the road to the mill).*

☆ **Cranbrook** opens up into an attractive, typically Wealden high street with upper storeys clad in white-painted weatherboarding or hung with decorative tiles. Walk from the church along Stone St. with its curious side alleys and jettied upper storeys towards Union Mill. The bend on Mill St. is a perfect example of an old Kentish street. *Tourist information: tel. (0580) 712538.*

✽ **Cranbrook** Union Mill is a smock mill dating from 1814, still in excellent condition. *Open Sat afternoons, Easter to Sept, and Bank Holiday Mon.*

② *Leave town on the road past Union Mill.*

③ **Sissinghurst** An optional, but strongly recommended detour; *turn right at the A262 and then first left along the lane to Sissinghurst Castle (signposted).* Arguably one of the most beautiful gardens in England, and certainly one of the most famous, Sissinghurst was created in the 1930s by Vita Sackville-West and Harold Nicolson amongst the remains of what had been one of the most splendid Elizabethan houses in Kent. Also visit the tower where Vita had her study. *Open Tues–Fri afternoons and all day Sat and Sun, Apr–Oct.*

④ *At this deflected junction, follow the signs for Tunbridge Wells (A262).*

⑤ *Turn right here, along a lane signposted to Colliers Green (not on map). Take it slowly: there are few useful signposts.*

⑥ *At this unsignposted junction turn right, then first left, following the sign for Marden.*

● *Scotney Castle, near Wadhurst, is 14th C with 17th-C additions.*

This is orchard country, and the low, squat trees, trained to easy picking height, can be seen growing in disciplined rows. Go there in mid-to-late April for blossom time.

⑦ *At this junction (signpost obscured by trees) fork right.*

⑧ *Turn left here (signpost broken – it should point the way to Curtisden Green).*

⌐ **Curtisden Green** Here the Rev. Kendon set up a mission to improve the working conditions of hop pickers during the 1880s.

⑨ *Take the left fork signposted to Cranbrook, then go immediately right at a small triangle of grass with a converted oast on your left (junction unsignposted).* Here are sweeping views of a typical Wealden valley filled with orchards and hop gardens. *At the T-junction following immediately, turn right along the A262 to enter Goudhurst.*

☆ **Goudhurst** A picture postcard hilltop village, though somewhat marred by main road traffic. It is best seen starting at the bottom end, by the duck pond.

⛪ **Goudhurst** The church, entered via a marvellous yew arch, has notable painted wood tombs of the Colepepper family: one shows father, mother and 18 children at prayer.

♟ **Goudhurst** The Star and Eagle, next to the church, is a 14th-C heavily beamed inn. If you are looking for tea and a cake try the quaint Hughenden Tea Room.

⑩ *Just before a telephone box on B2079, take the unsignposted lane to your right.*

⑪ **Bedgebury Pinetum** For another worthwhile detour *carry on along the B2079 for about ¼ mile (0.5 km) to explore this outpost of Kew Gardens.* The pinetum consists of over 200 species of conifer; *open daily.*

⑫ *Fork left here.*

⑬ **Scotney Castle Garden** *Make the difficult right turn at the junction of B2169 and the A21.* This leads to another romantic garden, with a 14th-C moated castle ruin at its centre. *Open Wed–Fri and Sat and Sun afternoons, Apr–Oct.*

⑭ *Follow the B2169 into Lamberhurst, and then turn left on to the B2100.*

⑮ *After passing the county boundary sign into East Sussex, take the first (unsignposted) right turn down a single track road; a narrow and very bendy lane.*

⑯ *After a sharp right hand bend, take a sharp left at this unsignposted T-junction. Then ignoring all right and left turns including two signposted to Wadhurst, keep going straight on for Wadhurst.*

⫰ **Wadhurst–Mayfield** Here you pass through one of the Wealden 'holloways', cut down into the soft yellow sandstone by centuries of erosion by horse, bullock and foot traffic.

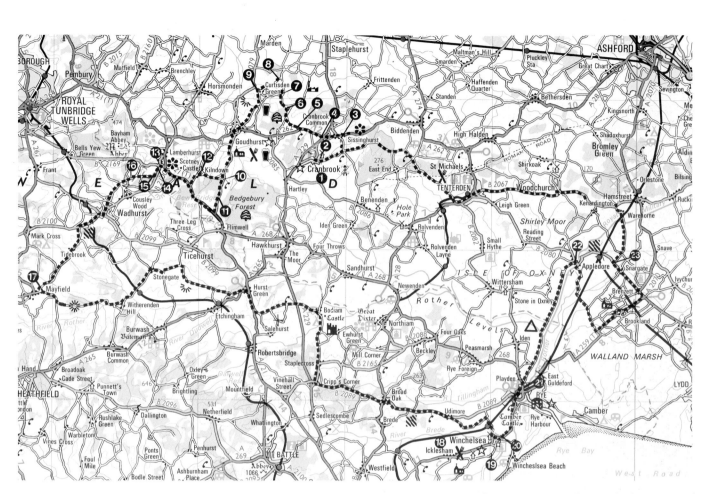

⑰ Fork left at the steep triangular green, following the signpost for Witherenden.

⚹ **Mayfield–Witherenden** A lane characteristic of many in the Weald which run along the top of ridges, with river valleys out of sight on either side. You have to stop and peer over gates to see the views.

⚹ **Stonegate–Hurst Green** Good views, or rather glimpses, over the pretty, rolling country of the Linden valley.

🏰 **Bodiam** The 14th-C castle owes much of its beauty and popularity to the fact that its moat is still in water. *Open daily Apr–Oct; Mon–Fri Nov–Mar.*

⑱ **Udimore** Turn right here along a lane marked 'Winchelsea, Narrow Road' – a warning worth heeding. Along it you will drop off the ridge into the flat-bottomed and formerly marshy valley of the River Brede. After turning right towards the level crossing you will be travelling at only a little higher than sea level. Look out for the thick-fleeced Romney Marsh sheep.

⑲ At this junction in Winchelsea climb the hill, bear right immediately after the fortified entrance gate and then turn left at a sign indicating the way to the church.

✰ **Winchelsea** Perched on its hilltop like a demure English equivalent of some Italian fortified town, Winchelsea has an atmosphere entirely of its own. The broad, straight streets are the result of a very early piece of town planning: Edward I began to rebuild here on the French 'gridiron' pattern after Old Winchelsea had been swallowed by the sea, but the town never grew to the extent planned, ironically enough since gradual silting up put paid to its prospects as a port. Today the whole place seems fast asleep.

⛪ **Winchelsea** Like the town, St Thomas's 14th-C church is only a fragment of the building first intended, but it is impressive, with striking modern stained glass and interesting wall tombs.

✗ **Winchelsea** Manna Plat in Mill St. is an inventive and reasonably priced little restaurant. Reserve in advance (lunches only on Sat and Sun).

⑳ Leave the town keeping the church on your right hand side, and follow the road through the Strand Gate and down the hill. At the bottom take a right turn to follow the A259 to Rye.

✰ **Rye** The 'Cinque Ports' were a confederation of five harbours grouped together for defence by Edward the Confessor. Originally the five were Hastings, New Romney, Hythe, Sandwich and Dover, but c. 1156 Winchelsea and Rye were also included. The ports supplied the crown with fighting ships and with skilled seamen. As at Winchelsea, the sea gradually retreated from Rye, although the town still retains a river channel that is navigable by small boats. Walk down the splendid cobbled Mermaid St.; like the church square it is lined with buildings of all periods.

🏠 **Rye** The Mermaid Inn (rebuilt much as it now stands, in 1420) is known through the novels of Russell Thorndike, who used it as a setting for his 'Dr Syn' smuggling stories; the interior is genuinely ancient.

㉑ Leaving Rye on the A268 turn right immediately after the railway bridge.

△ **Rye–Appledore** This is a causeway road, with the Royal Military Canal on the right. Planned as a strategic alternative to Martello towers in defence against Napoleon, the 23-mile (37-km) long canal was built between 1804 and 1809 at vast expense. Militarily it proved worthless.

㉒ Cross the canal and take an immediate right turn. This lane will lead you into the heart of marshland. Only the reed-filled drainage channels could qualify as 'marsh' nowadays and, sadly, field drainage is enabling farmers to put vast areas into intensive agricultural use. But to date enough of the old pastures survive to give this flat landscape a character of its own.

🏠 **Brookland** St Augustine's church has a uniquely-shaped steeple clad with wooden shingles, and a powerful sense of the past.

㉓ Half a mile north of the leaning tower of Snargate church, take a (badly signposted) right turn along a single-track causeway road to the pretty village of Warehorne.

✗ **Tenterden** Peggoty's Tea Shoppe at 122 High St. has home made cakes that are indeed what they claim to be.

Exmoor

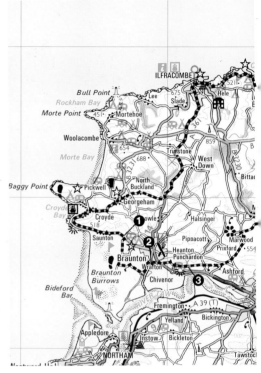

Glorious views dominate this tour which begins with a sprinkling of seaside resorts, goes westwards for the thrill of Atlantic surf, then extensively explores the beauty of Exmoor. Perhaps seen at its best in late summer, when the deep purple of the heather near the coast mixes with the bright yellow of the western gorse, the moor and its villages inspired such poets as Samuel Taylor Coleridge and Robert Southey. It is a splendid area for exploring on foot, and both routes include several opportunities for easy or strenuous walks; those who stay in the car will, however, still be rewarded by the charm and diversity of the landscape.

Route One: 55 miles (88 km)
Directions in sequence from: Lynton
Direction of travel: anticlockwise

☆ **Lynton and Lynmouth** The largest settlement in Exmoor National Park, these twin villages are connected by a cliff railway and steep Lynmouth Hill. The buildings are largely Victorian with Swiss-style architecture and some older thatched cottages.

▣ **Lynmouth** At the Exmoor National Park information centre, on the Esplanade, an interesting display concerning famous 19th-C sea rescues includes an early lifeboat. *Open Easter to Oct.*

⛴ **Lynmouth** From the harbour, motor-boat trips along the coast are best in late spring and early summer, when nesting sea birds can be seen.

✗ **Valley of Rocks** This dry valley has curious rock formations, many with associated legends. Picnic area, wild goats and spectacular cliff walk.

❢ **Lee Bay** A sheltered bay offering a nature trail and tea gardens (summer only). A beautiful toll road leads to Woody Bay.

✗ **Hunters' Inn** Heddon's Gate Hotel has panoramic views over lush Heddon Valley. In the restaurant local specialities include venison and salmon. *Open Easter to Nov.*

❧ **Knap Down** Fine views over Combe Martin and westwards along the coast.

☆ **Combe Martin** Seaside resort with several interesting buildings including the eccentric Pack of Cards Inn, built by a gambler in the 18thC, and the church of St Peter ad Vincula, which has a fine tower and painted screen.

☆ **Watermouth** Landlocked harbour with caves and 19th-C mock castle.

☆ **Ilfracombe** The main tourist resort of the area has large Victorian hotels and a picturesque harbour with hilltop mariners' chapel. *Tourist information: tel. (0271) 63001.*

▥ **Ilfracombe** Chambercombe Manor, a medieval manorial farmhouse in the south-eastern outskirts of the town, has an intriguing secret room, a vast cider press in the kitchen, and a water garden. *Open Mon–Fri, and Sun afternoon, Easter to Sept.*

☆ **Georgeham** Henry Williamson, author and

● *Double-arched packhorse bridge, Allerford.*

naturalist, lived here and is buried in the churchyard.

❚ **Georgeham** The Rock Inn serves traditional ales and good, inexpensive bar meals.

☆ **Croyde** Attractive village of thatched cottages, somewhat spoiled by holiday camps. The sandy beach is suitable for surfing and ❢ there are exhilarating walks to Baggy Point.

▣ **Croyde** The Gem Rock and Shell Museum has a collection of shells, minerals and semi-precious stones, and a shop. *Open Mar–Oct.*

❧ **Saunton Down** Lay-bys provide fine views across Saunton Sands and Braunton Burrows to Taw and Torridge estuary, Westward Ho! and Hartland Point.

① *Take first turning on right after village (signposted Braunton Burrows). Then take second unsignposted road to the left.*

❢ **Braunton Burrows** Large area of sand dunes, famous for wild flowers including orchids in early summer. Nature trail from Sandy Lane car park or board walk to Airy Point from end of toll road.

☆ **Braunton Great Field** One of two remaining medieval open fields in England. The strip cultivation pattern contrasts with grazing land of adjacent Braunton Marsh, where medieval barns and linhays (animal shelters) can be seen.

② *At Braunton, turn right at T-junction (unsignposted), continue through Wrafton and straight across A361. Then turn right after The Williams Arms.*

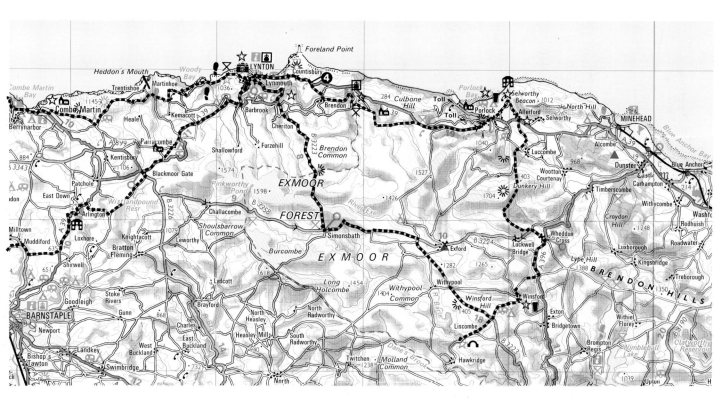

Wrafton The Williams Arms, a busy thatched inn, has several bars and a restaurant offering a wide variety of dishes.

Heanton Punchardon Fine view from the church over RAF Chivenor to Taw Estuary and Appledore.

③ *After leaving village, continue straight ahead at two crossroads, avoiding the main part of Ashford. At Guineaford, take left turning on road signposted to Marwood Church.*

Marwood The 12-acre garden at Marwood Hill has lakes, a 'bog' garden, camellias, rhododendrons and a collection of Australian plants. *Open daily.*

Arlington The Regency home of the Chichester family, Arlington Court retains the atmosphere created by its last owner, Miss Rosalie Chichester (d. 1947), an inveterate collector of small items.

The coach house contains a fine collection of horse-drawn vehicles. Extensive grounds with nature walk and lake with bird-watching hide. *Open Sun–Fri, Apr–Oct.*

Parracombe St Petrock's Church (made redundant when a new church was built nearer village centre in Victorian times) has fascinating interior, unaltered from 18thC. Closed in winter, but key obtainable in village.

> **Route Two: 45 miles (72 km)**
> Directions in sequence from: Lynton
> Direction of travel: clockwise

Countisbury Small hill-top settlement. Short walks to Foreland Point for views back to Lynton and Lynmouth, and to Iron Age fort on Wind Hill for views over East Lyn valley.

④ *On leaving village take first turning on right for Brendon. At Brendon, cross the bridge and turn left.*

Malmsmead A beauty spot with an old bridge over Badgworthy Water, Malmsmead is the centre for exploring *Lorna Doone* country. Large car park, picnic area, gift shop and riding stables.

Malmsmead The Natural History Centre has wildlife displays and organizes guided walks. *Open Wed, Thurs, May–Sept.*

Oare The small, plain church of St Mary is famous as the setting for the marriage and shooting of R. D. Blackmore's heroine, *Lorna Doone.*

Porlock Delightful village at bottom of notoriously steep Porlock Hill, which can be avoided by a toll road affording magnificent views. Worth pausing in the village to look at the medieval Doverhay Manor House (now a museum and information centre), and the 13th-C church of St Dubricius, which has interesting monuments.

Porlock The thatched Ship Inn is known for its associations with poets Coleridge and Southey. Bar meals are available.

Bossington Footpaths lead from the village to the beach and to Selworthy Woods. Good views from Bossington Hill, particularly at sunset.

Bossington Somerset Farm Park is an old manorial farmhouse with a medieval chapel of ease. Visitors see the farm at work and the farm animals, including shire horses. Displays of farm crafts. *Open Sun–Fri, afternoons only, Easter to Sept.*

Allerford Attractive village with medieval pack-horse bridge and ancient Pyle's Mill, *open daily. To reach the mill, turn left on to A39, then right on to minor road.*

Webbers Post Good views over Horners Woods. There is also a nature trail to Cloutsham and back (3 miles/5 km), through old woodland rich in wildlife including red deer.

Dunkery Hill Lay-bys afford fine views over Avill Valley to Brendon Hills and Quantocks. Short walk to summit of Dunkery Beacon, Exmoor's highest point at just over 1,700 feet (518 m), with even more extensive views including large areas of Exmoor, the Vale of Porlock and over Bristol Channel to the Welsh coast.

Winsford Charming village on River Exe with many small bridges.

Winsford At the 14th-C Royal Oak Inn excellent salads are served in the bar.

Tarr Steps From Spire Cross, a 1½-mile (2.5-km) detour (plus short walk from car park) leads to an ancient clapper bridge, said to be Britain's oldest bridge although its date is unknown. The wooded valley of the River Barle provides a beautiful setting.

Winsford Hill Extensive views from summit at Wambarrows (Bronze Age burial mounds). Much of south-east Exmoor can be seen and beyond to Blackdown Hills and Dartmoor.

Brendon Two Gates Views over open moorland eastwards and westwards.

Watersmeet At the junction of the East Lyn and Hoaroak rivers there are waterfalls, wooded gorges and a 19th-C hunting lodge, now an information centre and tea garden.

The Mendip Hills and Somerset Levels

Don't drive the south-eastern half of this circuit unless you are in the mood for exploring a succession of true country lanes, many single-track, and sometimes with scarce passing places. They need to be driven slowly, with careful navigation; your reward will be a unique introduction to the country south-east of Bath. It has a truly remote feel and is full of surprising views – a contrast to the bustle of Bath, and the tourist centres on the north-east side of the loop.

At ⑮ the pace quickens: you have straightforward, often exhilarating driving along the spine of the Mendips, then along attractive classified roads back to Bath.

Route: 70 miles (113 km)
Directions in sequence from: Bath
Direction of travel: clockwise

① *Leaving Bath on the A367 southwards, take the obvious left fork signposted Combe Hay and Wellow.*

△ **Combe Hay** is not as pretty as its name: don't bother to detour left into the village. The beautifully engineered road winds on, giving some splendid views as it snakes through the (mostly) gentle hills hereabouts: drive considerately.

② *Turn left at the T-junction and in 75 yards (69 m), right signposted 'Caution Deer Ford'. The ford is in a hundred yards or so. If the river is high, there is a narrow bridge alongside. Remember to dry your brakes by going a few yards with the pedal depressed: you will be needing them.*

③ *Fork left (signpost missing), and continue*
△ *to drive with great care. The lane is mostly well-surfaced, but there is some pitting, and cow dung may make it slippery after rain. Hoot at the frequent blind corners, and appreciate a real sense of remoteness until Norton St Philip's church tower, with its four grand little pinnacles, suddenly comes into view. It is said to have been the gift to the church of a rich clothier.*

④ *Turn left at the A366 and at a rather confusing crossroads in the village centre, turn right on to the B3110, signposted Beckington and Frome.*

Norton St Philip The village was an important trading and collecting centre for Mendip wool. Merchants would gather at The George Inn, an interesting timber-framed building dating from the 14thC. It receives the accolade of a single star in *The Good Pub Guide*: Wadsworths 6X on hand pump.

⑤ *Just out of the village watch for this right turn signposted Laverton.*

⑥ *Follow left.*

⑦ *Go straight over, bearing right, signposted Buckland Dinham.*

⑧ *Cross the A362 (no signpost), continuing straight ahead.*

⑨ *After the right bend, be ready to turn right signposted Great Elm and Mells.*

⑩ *Turn right – no signpost.*

⑪ *Turn right and in 30 yards (27 m) left signposted Leigh upon Mendip and Wells.*

Mells People idolize this pretty village, with its Elizabethan manor house and a church which brings together an astonishing amount of work by distinguished 20th-C artists, including Burne-Jones, Munnings and Lutyens. They designed memorials to members of the Horner family, who ruled here from the Middle Ages until the First World War. The Horners were farmers of land belonging to the Abbots of Glastonbury until one Jack Horner suddenly became the principal local squire in his own right at the time of the Dissolution of Glastonbury Abbey. Jack had paid good money for title to the land, but many thought he had misappropriated the deeds – that he had 'put in his thumb and pulled out a plum' – for he was indeed the subject of the nursery rhyme.

⑫ *At the next crossroads go straight across – signposted Leigh upon Mendip and Wells.*

⑬ *Soon go left, signposted Chantry.*

⑭ *Turn right, signposted Leigh upon Mendip and Wells. Route-finding is now simple: keep following signs for Wells, leaving behind the rather broken-up hills of the eastern end of the Mendip ridge.*

⑮ *Turn right, signposted Shepton Mallet and Wells.*

⑯ *Turn right and in 25 yards (23 m) left, signposted Wells.*

⚶ *Fine views open out left over the Somerset Levels, with a first sight of Glastonbury Tor, which is to haunt the route for a while.*

⑰ *If you intend to visit the cathedral, continue into the town; otherwise look carefully for the A371 on your left, signposted Shepton Mallet.*

Wells The clear spring that gave the town its name still bubbles in a pool in the Bishop's garden. Tradition claims that a church was first founded here in 704, near the springs. *Tourist information tel: 0749 72552.*

✝ **Wells** The present cathedral, famed for its modest size but great beauty, was begun about 1176. You cannot leave without taking in at least the famous Chapter House, with its fan vaulting, and the amazing west front, which Pevsner describes as 'the richest receptacle of 13th-C sculpture in England'.

Vicars' Close is reputed to be the oldest inhabited street in Europe.

Many come just to see the 14th-C clock,

BATH
Abbey, Assembly Rooms, Bath St., Pulteney Bridge, Pump Room, Roman Baths, Royal Crescent, Theatre Royal: visit these (and other) great sights of Bath, absorb its atmosphere of gracious ease, and you might reasonably conclude that the place has never been anything but an oasis of modest, sober and righteous living.

Yet the rise of this spa town to a centre for fashionable society in the 18thC owes much to a far from righteous pursuit: gambling. Georgian Society loved its gaming; when they had finished taking each other's money in London, they flocked to Bath for the summer season, and started again. Indeed Richard 'Beau' Nash, who occupied the city's unpaid post of Master of Ceremonies for more than 50 years, probably lived largely from a share of 'house' profits, just like a present-day racketeer. It is difficult to understand how otherwise he could maintain his legendary style of living: finest clothes, gilt coach-and-six, stakes at table and a live-in whore at his large house in St John's Court.

If Georgian Bath was not quite so genteel as its façade, pre-Georgian Bath had a positively seamy side. Through the Middle Ages, Tudor and later times, the public baths, fed by the thermal springs, were all but a euphemism for a brothel. Things improved slightly after 1737, when the Corporation ordered that 'no Male person over 10 should bathe without a Pair of Drawers and a Waistcoat and no Female without a Decent Shift'.

with its animated striker. It strikes each quarter hour, with the best action on the hour.

Wells – The Bishop's Palace On the moat surrounding the Palace live swans which fascinate visitors as much as the clock: if visitors refrain from feeding them, they ring a bell for food. Within the lovely palace grounds are: the palace itself (13thC); ruins of the Great Hall and a beautiful chapel. Palace and grounds *open afternoons, Thur and Sun, Easter–Oct, every day in Aug; also on Wed, May–Sept.*

Wookey Hole A detour from Wells; this commercialized complex, operated by Madame Tussaud's, the London waxworks exhibition, offers an inclusive tour (two hours) of waxworks storeroom, fairground collection, adjacent paper mill, and, of course, the caves; open every day March–Oct and 10.30–4.30 Nov–Feb (except week before Christmas).

⑱ *To leave Wells from the centre, follow signs for the A371 and Shepton Mallet.*

⑲ *At Dulcote turn right and immediately left, signposted North Wootton. Keep following signs for North Wootton.*

⚶ **North Wootton** This is Somerset's vineyard country. The local vineyard is signposted from the village; *conducted tours by appointment: tel. 0749 89359.*

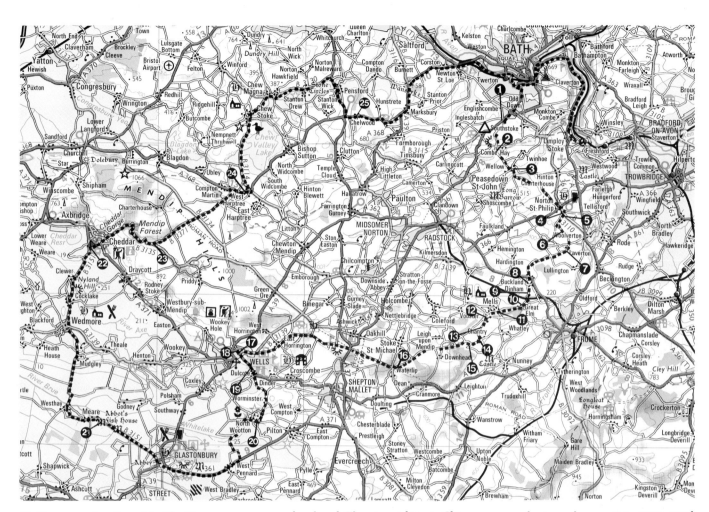

20 *At crossroads adjacent to The Crossways Inn, turn right, signposted Wells. Continue, ignoring signposts right and left, for about 250 yards (229 m) to the fork outside the village. Bear left signposted for Glastonbury and West Pennard, and keep following signs to the junction with the A361, where turn right.*

North Wootton – Glastonbury Leaving this village you are well and truly away from the Mendip plateau and into the Somerset Levels. It was formerly an impenetrable, mostly flooded area of marshland and islands, one of which Alfred used as a refuge after defeat by the Danes, and another of which was Glastonbury Tor. Many find it has a certain, bleak beauty.

Glastonbury Nowhere in England has the same blend of history, legend and mystery. One tale tells of Christ himself coming here as a child, with his uncle, Joseph of Arimethea: another of Joseph bringing the Holy Grail – the cup used at the Last Supper; and several legends link the place with King Arthur. It could well be the site of the earliest Christian shrine in the country; certainly the abbey, apparently dating from as early as the 7thC, was one of the first, and richest, in England, owning at one time an eighth of Somerset. The ruins are *open daily (from 9.00 June, July and Aug); cassette guided tour available.*

Glastonbury Tor Legends cluster here, too. The hill is topped with a tower that once

graced a chapel. The view, taking in Glastonbury, Wells and the Bristol Channel, is rightly famous.

Glastonbury 'No 3' restaurant in Magdalene St. has earned an impressive reputation locally: seriously, good food and prices to match; book early. The Rifleman's Arms in Chilkwell St. has a 'family room' for simple meals, and an interesting landlord.

Meare The curious tall building on the right is the Fish House of the Abbots of Glastonbury: a base for catching fish from the lake which was once here.

Wedmore King Alfred made a historic peace here with the Danes in 878. The church is noted for its magnificent south doorway, which will remind you of Wells.

Wedmore The George Hotel has an authentically atmospheric old bar.

21 *Follow signs for B3151 and Cheddar.*

Wedmore–Cheddar There are now repeated views of the Mendips rising up from the Levels: they scarcely top more than about a thousand feet (914 m), but they are massive. Watch closely for a fascinating view of Cheddar Gorge, too.

22 *Turn right signposted Cheddar.*

Cheddar Gorge The Mendip Hills are soluble limestone: rainwater, and under-

ground rivers have eaten away much subterranean rock over the ages, forming underground tunnels and caves. In the case of Cheddar Gorge, the network of caverns grew so much that the roof fell in, producing the spectacular canyon. The road twists along its floor, cliffs towering above. The two show caves, one with evidence of Stone Age habitation, and both with stalactites, are between them *open all year.*

23 *Fork left – signposted Bristol and Burrington Combe.*

Burrington Combe, signposted from the B3371, is a small-scale, delightful version of Cheddar Gorge, relatively unspoilt.

24 *Follow sign for Chew Valley Lake.*

Chew Valley Lake There is ample parking space beside the road here, with excellent views over the reservoir, which can provide some interesting birdwatching.

Chew Magna From the Middle Ages to the late 18thC, this was another prosperous Mendip wool village. Then new routes south from Bristol isolated the place; but the motor car has put it back on the map once again, with all its former air of prosperity, this time courtesy of week-enders and Bristol professionals. The church contains three outstanding tombs.

25 *The A368 is mostly peaceful, straightforward driving all the way back to Bath.*

Cranborne Chase

Each year thousands of people travel from far and wide to visit the two great attractions at the west end of Salisbury Plain – Longleat and Stourhead. Too many return home without making the most of this peaceful area, traversed by the A303, but largely off the beaten track.

The highlight of the circuit is perhaps the zig-zag climb up Charlton Down into Cranborne Chase, a romantic stretch of country on the Wiltshire–Dorset border.

Route: 45 miles (72 km)
Directions in sequence from: Mere
Direction of travel: anticlockwise

Mere The Old Ship is a pub-hotel with old-fashioned bars, reasonable bar food and some fine period furnishings. The building dates partly from the 16thC, and as a private house, at the time of the Civil War, was owned by Sir John Coventry – a Royalist.

That did not, however, protect him from having his nose slit after speaking out after the Restoration in the House of Commons against the King's philandering with actresses. Parliament's consequent outrage resulted in the Coventry Act – more or less the basis of MPs' right to speak openly in the House without fear of slander proceedings.

Stourhead, with its famous landscaped grounds, is simple to find 2½ miles (4 km)

north-west of Mere on the B3092. The Pleasure Grounds, centred on the lake, can be taken in by a one-mile (1.5-km) walk of continually changing 'natural' scenes, all artificially contrived. The 18th-C house has considerable furniture, paintings, and other works of art. *Gardens are open 8–7 (or dusk) daily all year, last admission 6.30. House open 2–6, Sat–Thurs, May–Sept; 2–6 on Mon, Wed, Sat and Sun, April and Oct.*

① *Turn left, signposted B3095.*

② *Turn left on to the B3081.*

③ *Having climbed up to Shaftesbury, follow the road sharply round a left bend and soon reach a roundabout where follow signs for Salisbury (A30). At the next roundabout ④ also follow signs for Salisbury, A30 and Ringwood, but be ready to turn right 100 yards (91 m) after leaving the roundabout on to B3081, signposted Ringwood and Tollard Royal.*

Shaftesbury is an old and interesting town: see page 118. *Tourist information: tel. (0747) 2256.*

④ *Turn left, signposted Zig-Zag Hill.*

△ **Shaftesbury–Tollard Royal** The B3081's ascent of these downs, by a sequence of hairpin bends, is as un-English as the grandeur of Cheddar Gorge. When you get to the top, superb views will keep you entertained all the way to Tollard Royal: one of the outstanding 'scenic routes' of the south.

Shaftesbury–Tollard Royal The extensive ridges on the slopes of the downs are known as 'lynchets': terraces dug up on the otherwise barren hillsides to allow cultivation.

Win Green The National Trust owns and conserves the summit of this hill and surrounding land: fine, airy walking along the ridge of the downs and views all round.

Cranborne Chase 'Chase' means a royal hunting ground, and this one had that status for a thousand years until hunting rights ceased in 1828. Since then most of the forest (which Thomas Hardy thought the oldest in England) has been cut down. The heart of the Chase – the Inner Chase – is an area of about 10 by 3 miles (16 by 5 km) centred on Tollard Royal. Murderous battles between keepers and poachers were notorious here, and at one time the two sides resorted to protective clothing – padded jackets and straw-lined helmets – for their encounters.

Tollard Royal King John's House is so-called because, by tradition, King John stayed here on hunting expeditions. It is a curious place, part of it certainly 13thC, and has been admirably restored.

Tollard Royal The church contains an arresting effigy of a 14th-C knight, and some early English features. A tablet commemorates General Pitt-Rivers, who lived at nearby Rushmore House (now a school) and who restored King John's House.

Tollard Royal The Larmer Grounds are another legacy of the unusual General Pitt-

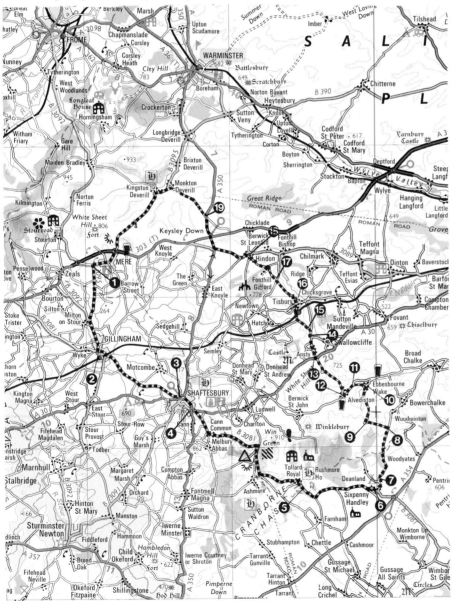

● *Looking across Stourhead's central lake, around which the pleasure grounds, dotted with follies, were laid out by Henry Hoare in the 18th C. His inspiration was European travel.*

Rivers. He laid out this corner of his estate for the pleasure of local people, and visitors – but it is no ordinary park. There is a wooden theatre, still used, and several temples in the oriental style. The 'larmer tree', an ancient wych elm, was blown down in a storm. In Saxon times and later, it was by repute a meeting place for the old Court Leet (a function of local government); and, also by tradition, for the royal hunt. *Open only for special functions.*

⑤ *Continue, ignoring side-turnings, to Sixpenny Handley.*

🚌 **Sixpenny Handley** There are 13th-C wall-paintings in the ancient church, and in the churchyard a tomb where poachers used to hide carcasses. Look for the inscribed cover.

⑥ *In Sixpenny Handley turn left signposted Deanland and Bowerchalke, and be ready to fork right ⑦ signposted Bowerchalke and Ebbesbourne Wake. Drive considerately on the narrow lanes ahead, which take you back across Cranborne Chase.*

⑧ *At the end of this fine avenue of beeches, turn left signposted Ebbesbourne Wake, and don't speed up, even though the road ahead is dead straight. At ⑨ there is a 90° right turn.*

⑩ *Turn left signposted Alvediston.*

🍺 **Ebbesbourne Wake** The Horseshoe is a down-to-earth village pub serving Wadsworths 6X. The garden looks out over the valley of the Ebble.

⑪ *Turn left signposted Shaftesbury.*

🍺 **Alvediston** Local wags corrupt the name to 'hell of a distance' – but The Crown pub should persuade you it was worth the drive.

The food is rightly popular, there is Ushers Best on hand pump, and a range of home-made country wines. Lighting and piped music are kept low.

⑫ *In Alvediston village centre turn right (inconspicuous signpost) for Ansty and Tisbury.*

⑬ *Straight on over the A30 and through Ansty, ignoring left and right turns.*

⑭ *Left, signposted Tisbury, and immediately right again.*

⑮ *Fork left signposted Wardour Old Castle.*

🏰 **Tisbury** Wardour Old Castle is a 14th-C ruin.

⑯ *In Tisbury's centre keep straight ahead, signposted Fonthill Gifford, and continue out of the village on Hindon Lane.*

🏰 **Fonthill Gifford** and neighbouring Fonthill Bishop will always be linked with the story of the dilettante William Beckford, son of a Lord Mayor of London who inherited a million pounds on coming of age. He dabbled in writing – the Gothic horror story *Vathek* is his – but entertained the public far more with his fantastic building scheme, Fonthill Abbey, on which work began in 1896. He ordered it to be half a ruined 'abbey', half a complete and habitable mansion. Its crowning glory was an enormous tower, which collapsed one night in 1825, after Beckford had sold the place and retired to Bath. Much of the Abbey was destroyed by the falling tower: the decayed remains lie in the parkland here. Subsequently, other houses were built in the park, to which there is a very grand gateway at Fonthill Bishop. Notice the lavish Victorian church.

⑰ *Go straight on, signposted Hindon.*

⑱ *Turn left in the centre of Hindon on to the B3089 signposted (A303) Mere and A303 Exeter.*

⑲ *Turn left, signposted The Deverills and Maiden Bradley.*

⑳ **The Deverills** are a series of villages along the upper River Wylye. You come on Monkton Deverill after negotiating a bold little road over the downs. At Kingston Deverill there is a charming 17th-C hall. *If visiting Longleat, take the unclassified road from here to Maiden Bradley, then turn right on to the B3092, from which the house is signposted.*

🏰 **Longleat House** has been described as a 'work of art, noble, delicate and intelligent'. The best approach is not actually from the B3092 but from the Warminster–Frome road, so be sure to view the house from that side, indeed from all four sides. Each is more or less equally important, and the building takes on a whole new dimension if you move to one side so that two façades are simultaneously in view. The grounds are some of Capability Brown's best work.

Inside the house there are fine paintings, including a Holy Family by Titian; important books; Shakespeare folios; and many other treasures including Talleyrand's desk, on which was signed the Treaty of Vienna in 1815.

And then, of course, there are the lions. *House open 10–6, Easter–Sept, rest of year 10–4; Safari Park 10–6 daily Mar–Oct.*

🚗 **Kingston Deverill–Mere** You can shorten the drive by taking the A303 but this section is worth the effort for its fine downland vistas and the wonderful panorama over Blackmoor Vale as you descend to Mere.

131

Salisbury, Stonehenge and Wilton

Salisbury's cathedral and Cathedral Close can claim to be respectively the most haunting, and the most charming examples of their kind in England; Stonehenge is the most numinous prehistoric monument in Europe; Wilton House combines literary associations with fine architecture as perhaps no other country house in Britain. Each is conveniently close to the other, and as this circuit proves, can be linked by some unforgettable country roads: you sail the tops of the downs, with astonishing views, then dive down through pretty valleys with charming settlements along their chalk streams.

Route: 45 miles (72 km)
Directions in sequence from:
Stonehenge
Direction of travel: anticlockwise

① **Stonehenge – the approach** *Coming from Amesbury on the A303, be ready to fork right on to the A34 after the dual carriageway ends – clearly signposted Stonehenge. In about 800 yards (730 m) turn right into the car park.*

ᛘ You go down some steps to a refreshment counter, bookshops and ticket booth, all turfed over at the rear, in an attempt not to spoil the site with unsightly protrusions. Here is your first hint that you are visiting not just a stone circle, but an outdoor temple, observatory, ceremonial meeting place and burial ground covering several acres. *Open 9.30–6.30 Mar 15–Oct 15; 9.30–4.30 Mar 16–Oct 14; closed Dec 24, 25, 26 and Jan 1.*

ᛘ **Stonehenge – phase one** With officialdom behind, the power of the grey stones in their simple setting starts to strike home. You will notice the sheer number of earth mounds – barrows – scattered over the surrounding downland: graves of the people who inhabited the area, and built the monument. In addition to the barrows, you should notice the vestiges of a great circular earthwork about 100 feet (30 m)

● Stone circle, outdoor temple, ceremonial meeting place and burial ground, Stonehenge is unique of its kind.

---

outside the stone circle, with an opening in the north-east marked by a stone – the Slaughter Stone. A hundred feet outside this entrance is another large stone, the Hele Stone; and inside the earthwork's inner bank is a circle of 56 holes, known as the Aubrey Holes, after the antiquarian who first observed them. These together are considered the first phase of Stonehenge.

ᛘ **Stonehenge – phases two and three** As a second phase, 82 'bluestones', brought all the way from the Preseli Hills in south-west Wales, were placed in concentric circles. The stone avenue was probably built at this time, too: it continues north-east, past the Hele Stone, then veers towards the River Avon, pointing the way the stones came from Wales. Archaeologists are certain they were loaded on boats at Milford Haven, sailed round the south coast and finally up the Avon to be disembarked nearby at Amesbury.

The third phase seems to have been the addition of the largest stones – the Sarsens – brought overland from the Marlborough Downs. The work could have been done with primitive bone tools: but you still strain to imagine the organization and discipline of the workforce.

ᛘ **Stonehenge – the theory** That, extremely simplified, is the story of Stonehenge; it spanned about eight hundred years, from around 2800 to 1400 BC; refinements may have continued another nine hundred years. What kept them at it for so long?

The most intriguing of modern theories is that the process of *continued* construction enabled the priests and rulers of those early people to time and again impress, and therefore control, their subjects. It is well known that the Slaughter Stone – Hele Stone axis is aligned with the midsummer sunrise; but archaeologists have recently worked out that most of the other features, including the Aubrey Holes, would have enabled its architects to predict, and demonstrate to credulous witnesses, a whole range of grand, sometimes frightening, phenomena such as solar and lunar eclipses. The growing complexity of the monument could well reflect the perennial rulers' need for new tricks to persuade the ruled who should remain master.

② *From Stonehenge continue west on the A344.*

ᛪ Fine rolling views soon open up over Salisbury Plain, heartland of the 'Wessex Culture' of agriculture and crafts which flourished during the Stonehenge period. There is strong evidence that these people had links with the Mediterranean, for Stonehenge is on a former trade route linking the Mediterranean and Ireland; in fact it runs through the Preseli Hills in southwest Wales from which came the smaller stones for Stonehenge.

③ *As the village of Shrewton comes to an end, turn left on to the B390, signposted 'A360 (B390)'.*

ᚥ **Shrewton–Chitterne** You now run through highly typical Salisbury Plain country: this used to be grassland, but ploughing-out and Ministry of Defence operations (witness the tank tracks) have mostly eaten it up; however, enjoy the views.

④ *Turn left signposted Codford.*

⑤ *In Codford St Mary ignore side turnings and continue straight ahead to meet the A36. Turn left and in 150 yards (137 m) turn right signposted Sherrington and Stockton.*

⑥ *Having crossed the River Wylye turn left at the T-junction signposted A303, Stockton and Wylye.*

ᛝ **Stockton** A view of the 'big house' soon opens up on the left: the original structure was put up by a wealthy Elizabethan cloth merchant, John Topp, who also endowed the Topp Almshouses in the village. A side-turning leads to the impressive Norman church and some other interesting buildings. *Continue straight ahead, under the A303, into Wylye.*

⑦ *Entering Wylye take the first right, signposted Great Wishford and go along Teapot St., soon continuing ahead into Fore St. In 200 yards (183 m) look carefully for the right turn, signposted Dinton. Immediately cross the railway line and enjoy an airy ride over the downs with more views.*

⑧ *Go through the sharp, left and right turns following the sign to Dinton.*

⑨ *Straight on down 'Steep Hollow', signposted Dinton.*

🏠 **Dinton** has several interesting houses: Philipps House, built by James Wyatt in 1813–16; Hyde's House, near the church, perhaps on the site of historian Edward Hyde's birthplace; Little Clarendon (late 15th-C) and the adjacent cottage; *Philipps House shown by appointment with the Warden, telephone Teffont 208; Little Clarendon (apply at the house).*

⑩ *Continue on St Mary's Rd. past the church, to meet the B3089, where turn left.*

⑪ *Soon after The Penruddocke Arms turn right, signposted Compton Chamberlayne. To shorten the drive continue through Barford St Martin to join the A30 to Wilton.*

🍺 **Barford St Martin** The Green Dragon is a welcoming pub with a fair range of dishes available over the bar.

⚜ **Compton Chamberlayne–Fovant** Having turned right on to the A30, watch out left for the famous regimental badges carved on the chalk down. A noticeboard explaining them is on the left of the road by three large beeches, with a side-turning where you can pull up.

⑫ *This is the first major left turn after Fovant, signposted Broad Chalke and Bowerchalke.*

⚜ **Fovant–Broad Chalke** Chiselbury Camp, out of view to the left (access on foot by track at top of hill), is a fine Iron Age hill fort, excellent for a stroll, views all round.

There is a remarkable view right after passing the quarry.

⑬ **Broad Chalke** John Aubrey, the Wiltshire antiquarian, (see under Stonehenge), lived here. Take a look at the wonderfully mellow pink-brick-and-moss north front of Reddish House, a small but grand 18th-C manor house.

⑬ *Turn left signposted Wilton opposite the large house.*

△ **Unclassified road north-west to Wilton** This can claim to be one of the best backroads of southern England: it is boldly engineered, astonishingly wide in parts for an unclassified road, and much of it is through tunnels of magnificent pollarded beeches.

⑭ *At the traffic lights in Wilton turn right and continue on the A30 to the roundabout, passing Wilton House on the right.*

⑭ **Wilton,** one-time capital of Wessex, had a great abbey whose heyday was in Saxon times, and whose eclipse was during the general destruction of the monasteries under the Tudors. The confiscated abbey and lands were given to Sir William Herbert, first Earl of Pembroke, a powerful courtier.

🏠 **Wilton House** Sir William pulled down the abbey and used its stones to build himself a mansion – the first Wilton House. The present house is much altered and rebuilt, but still shows something of the original. Famous features are the porch possibly designed by Holbein, the south and west fronts by Inigo Jones, the Double Cube Room, and, outside, the Palladian Bridge.

It is all the more splendid because of its status as a cultural hot-house. The second Earl married the sister of Sir Philip Sydney, who wrote *Arcadia* here. Shakespeare is supposed to have visited with his company; Christopher Marlowe, Edmund Spenser, Ben Jonson, Isaak Walton and many others came in their time: as a diarist wrote, 'Wilton House was like a college, there were so many learned and ingeniose persons'. *Open 11–6, Mon–Sat and Sun afternoon, Apr–Oct 14, last admission 5.15.*

🚃 **Wilton** The Royal Wilton Carpet Factory was started by the ninth Earl of Pembroke with the help of French weavers – then the acknowledged masters – poached from France, much to the displeasure of the French king. *Open daily, Mon–Fri.*

⑮ *At the roundabout take the unclassified road signposted Amesbury.*

⑯ *Turn right for a detour to Old Sarum, left to continue.*

🏛 **Old Sarum** Here a medieval town grew up
⚜ inside the earth fortifications of an Iron Age camp. Remnants of a castle and cathedral can be seen in the innermost ring. The place was the precursor of modern Salisbury, and long after its decay and de-population remained a 'Rotten Borough' – represented, until the Great Reform Bill, by two members of Parliament.

🍺 **Lower Woodford** The Wheatsheaf is a serviceable pub with a reasonably priced menu and plenty of seating space.

△ **Lower Woodford–Wilsford** The road winds along, overlooking the Avon.

🏠 **Wilsford Cum Lake** The big house on the right must be one of the best exponents in the county of the decorative chequered stonework characteristic of Wiltshire.

SALISBURY CATHEDRAL
For many, this building, wholly consistent in its Early English design, is not just beautiful architecture, but next to magic.

From whichever direction you view the spire, it seems equally impressive – though a particularly memorable approach is up St Ann's Gate. It is the highest spire in England, and while there are some on the Continent which are taller, none manage to soar quite as they should – none which point so emphatically towards heaven.

The spire rests on the great central tower. Part-way through construction, the marble pillars supporting the tower began to buckle. In a frenzy, the masons fitted two great reinforcing arches. They held, and the spire continued upwards, ton upon ton.

But the weight has pushed part of the cathedral foundations into the earth, so that today the spire leans some 29 inches (737 cm) out of the perpendicular. Atheists, and not a few believers, find it hard to understand why the whole top-heavy house of cards did not fall down long ago.
Tourist information: tel. 0722 334956.

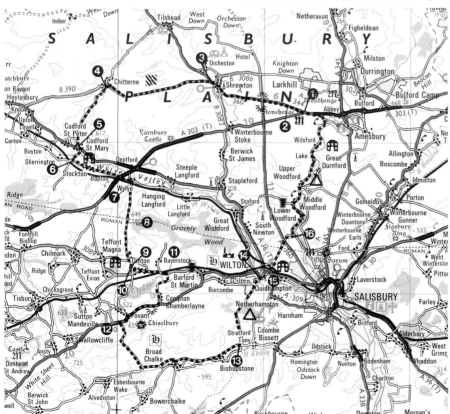

Winchester and Selborne

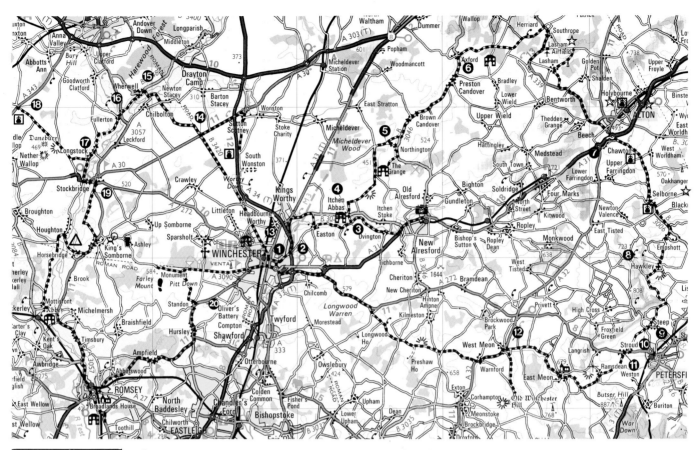

Appropriately, the ancient capital of Wessex (and in Alfred's time, of England), stands at the centre of this figure of eight. Winchester offers much to the visitor and you can gain a happy first impression of its chief glories in a short walk round the cathedral and college area. From Winchester, the two loops spread out east and west through countryside rarely lacking in character, from the lush and peaceful water meadows of the River Test to the downs and distinctive beech hangers south of Alton.

Route One: 80 miles (128 km)
In sequence from: Winchester
Direction of travel: clockwise

☆ **Winchester** *Pay and display parking next*
✝ *to the cathedral in Colebrook St.* Dominating Winchester, Alfred the Great's capital of Saxon England, is the cathedral. The longest medieval cathedral in Europe, its exterior is unimposing, but its interior is splendid, with many treasures. Look out for the spot, marked by a window and a brass tablet, where Jane Austen lies. In the next bay stands a rare black marble font.

🏛 **Winchester** A short walk takes in other essential viewing in a city rich with historic buildings of all periods from the 12thC onwards. From the cathedral's west front, walk through the beautiful close past the ancient Deanery and Pilgrims Hall and School through the 13th-C King's Gate to College Street. This leads past the house, marked by a plaque, in which Jane Austen died, to the famous Winchester College,

(founded in 1382 by Bishop Wykeham – hence Wykehamists). Then walk back on the path between the City Wall and the River Itchen to King Alfred's bronze statue in the Broadway (all signposted).

🏛 **Winchester** West of the cathedral, the Great Hall is all that remains of the 13th-C castle where Sir Walter Raleigh was sentenced to death in 1603. Here hangs the famous 'Round Table of King Arthur', dating back to the 14thC. *Open Mon–Fri, Sun in summer. Tourist information: tel. (0962) 68166.*

① *Leave town by St John's St., second left over Soke Bridge (by King Alfred's statue), and follow signs for Easton.*

② *M3 construction may force a tricky detour: turn left at the lights on to A34(T), bear right, then right on to B3047 for Abbots Worthy (not on map); turn right at Martyr Worthy (not on map) for Easton.*

🏛 **Avington** (marked on map but not named). Delightful drive through the old park and estate of Avington, with the 18th-C man-

sion and its lake on the left. *House open Sat, Sun afternoons.*

③ **Alresford** *Fork right for a detour to this*
📷 *attractive town and for the 'Watercress Line', a preserved steam railway named after the watercress beds it passes through. Open Sat and Sun, Mar–Oct.*

④ *Turn left on to B3047, then immediately right (signposted 'Veterinary Centre') and under a disused railway bridge. As you*
🌾 *bear right and uphill, wide views to the east open up.*

⑤ **The Grange** *Make a short detour south on the B3046 to visit this old house (well signposted), remodelled in Neo-Grecian*
🏛 *style in the early 19thC, with a lake. Open daily.*

⑥ **Axford** *Turn right here (signposted Herriard). Notice Moundsmere Manor*
🏛 *(unmarked, on the right), an Edwardian manor after the style of Hampton Court.*

☆ **Lasham Airfield** *Access for viewing and small parking space on right (not signposted); further on right is a collection of war planes.*

☆ **Alton** The Curtis museum in the attractive
🏛 High St., was one of the first museums of agriculture, opened in 1880. *Open Mon–Sat.* Opposite is the museum's Allen Gallery and garden (*same opening hours*).

⑦ **Chawton** *Signposted off the Liss road,*
🏛 the unassuming red brick house where Jane Austen lived (1809–17) and wrote many of her great novels, has been preserved and

● *Quintessential Hampshire – red brick cottages at Selborne nestling beneath a beech-covered 'hanger'. Up the hanger leads the zig-zag path immortalized in Gilbert White's* The Natural History of Selborne.

contains many personal relics. It gives a good idea of domestic life of the time and of Jane Austen in particular. *Open daily.*

☆ **Selborne** An attractive road leads to this charming village. On the right just past the church is The Wakes, which was in the 18thC the lifelong home of Gilbert White, vicar of Selborne and author of the much-loved *The Natural History of Selborne.* The house and grounds are now kept as a memorial to Gilbert White and his work. Upstairs is a display depicting the life of Antarctic explorer Captain Oates.

⑧ *At Hawkley bear right at Jolly Robin Forge, following signs for Priors Dean and Oakshott (not on map). The road follows Oakshott Hanger* with views eastwards of Wolmer Forest, described by White as 'a district abounding with many curious productions, both animal and vegetable'.

⑨ *Turn right in Steep (unsignposted) at T-junction of Mill Lane and Church Rd. (with Bedales School ahead.)*

⑩ *Make for Stroud – sign for Langrish.*

⑪ *Turn left off the A272 at the pub in Stroud, poorly signposted to Ramsdean; at Ramsdean bear left to Oxenbourne (not on map).*

✹ **Ramsdean–East Meon** After the intimacy of the hangers the scenery changes to grander rolling downland, with views to the south-west.

🏠 **East Meon** Attractive chalkland village with a lovely Norman church; like Winchester cathedral it has a black Tournai

marble font, one of only seven in the country. Opposite is the Court House.

⑫ **Old Winchester Hill** *Take a short detour from West Meon to see this Iron Age hill* ✹ *fort. Splendid views along the road and at the fort.*

✹ **Warnford–Winchester** This is a smooth wide road with fine views to the north.

> **Route Two: 65 miles (105 km)**
> In sequence from: Winchester
> Direction of travel: anticlockwise

⑬ *Following signs for Andover, leave town by Andover Rd. the B3420.*

⑭ **Sutton Scotney** *A short detour could be taken here to Sutton Manor Arts Centre, an* 🏠 *open-air museum of sculptures, together with a garden centre.. Open Mon–Sat, April–Oct. Signposted.*

⑮ *Turn left at T-junction in Wherwell signposted Andover. In village carry straight on, following sign for Fullerton.*

⑯ *Turn left at T-junction and shortly after turn right for Longstock.*

⑰ **Danebury** *Turn right for the majestic Iron* ✹ *Age hill fort covered with trees, with downland views to north, south and east. Sign-* ✹ *posted from road, with parking.*

⑱ **Middle Wallop** *Turn left on to A343 for the Museum of Army Flying, covering 100* 🏠 *years to the present day. Entrance poorly*

signposted on left ¼ mile (0.5 km) after museum.

⑲ *Bear right off A3057 for 'Marsh Court' on to a narrow but well-surfaced road passing school and stud farm.*

🎨 **King's Somborne** On the right is a small Arts and Crafts Centre.

🍺 **King's Somborne** The Crown is a cosy thatched village pub.

△ **River Test** The quiet road meanders through water meadows and over a series of humpback bridges in an area of great natural beauty; excellent picnic spots.

🏛 **Mottisfont Abbey** The mainly 18th-C house was converted from a 12th-C priory, and stands amid lovely parkland alongside the river. Rex Whistler decorated the trompe l'oeil drawing-room in 1939. The grounds include a comprehensive collection of old roses. *House open Wed and Sun afternoons, Apr–Sept; grounds open Sun–Thurs Apr–Sept; both closed Fri and Sat.*

🏠 **Romsey** All that remains of Romsey Abbey is the fine Norman church.

🏛 **Romsey** One mile (2.5 km) to the south of the town centre is Broadlands, family seat of the Mountbatten family. The house is full of historic associations; Mountbatten exhibition. *Open Tues–Sun, Apr–July; daily Aug–Sept.*

⑳ **Farley Mount** *Signposted from Standon.* Excellent spot to stretch your legs: woods, ! walks, views, nature reserve, monument.

The Surrey Hills and North Downs

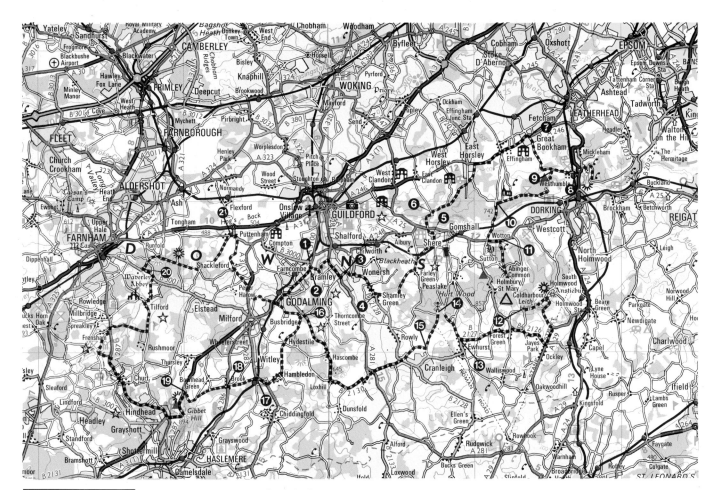

Dormitory towns and 'Tudorbethan' houses in a tame and boring landscape: that for many people means Surrey, but as this tour clearly proves, the reputation is unfair. The route passes through scenery that is at once spectacular and intimate; not large-scale, but with great variety of height and landscape. It encompasses panoramic view points, enclosed and mysterious lanes, famous beauty spots – Box Hill, the Devil's Punchbowl, Frensham Ponds – and historic houses. It explores in depth the stretch of the North Downs around Box Hill and the parallel greensand hills from Leith Hill to Hindhead which comprise most of the 'Surrey Hills'.

Route One: 75 miles (121 km)
Directions in sequence from:
Godalming
Direction of travel: clockwise

☆ **Godalming** is dominated by its Norman church, and it has attractive half-timbered 17th-C houses.

① Turn left on to the B3000 and in ½ mile (0.8 km) right (signposted) for a short detour to Losely House. This is an Eliza-
🏠 bethan manor house with paintings, furniture and 'Nonsuch' panelling. The estate's dairy produce may be familiar from the shelves of health food shops or supermarkets. Return to the A3100, turn right ② then first left, just before garage, signposted Bramley and Cranleigh. At junction with A281 turn right.

③ At Wonersh turn right (no sign).

④ Turn left, signposted Shere.

☆ **Shere** One of Surrey's prettiest villages: willows weep by its river; there are old houses, narrow streets and a charming grey stone church.

🍺 **Shere** The White Horse pub has a warm atmosphere and serves good food.

⑤ In Shere turn left at T-junction and at junction with A25 cross over, signposted East Clandon.

⑥ After steep uphill bend, turn left at top of hill (poorly signposted) for a detour to Clandon Park at West Clandon. The 18th-C
🏠 Palladian house has a rich interior which includes the Gubbay collection of Chinese porcelain birds. Open afternoons, Apr–Oct (closed Mon and Fri); restaurant.

🏠 **Hatchlands** Return to A246 turning left for East Clandon if you wish to continue the

detour to visit Hatchlands, a handsome 18th-C mansion; open Wed, Thurs, Sun afternoons, Apr–Oct.

⑦ In Great Bookham turn right off A246, signposted Polesden Lacey.

🏠 **Polesden Lacey** (signposted from road) is a Regency mansion whose heyday was the Edwardian era when it was the home of society hostess Mrs Ronald Greville. Open Sat and Sun afternoons Mar and Nov; afternoons, April–Oct, except Mon and Fri.

⑧ At the A24 turn left, following signs at roundabout for Box Hill, and turn right off the road leading past Burford Bridge Hotel. At the bottom of the zig-zag road, notice pretty Flint Cottage, from 1867 the home of writer George Meredith, and later of Max Beerbohm.

🌲 **Box Hill** is a splendid downland area with woodland and walks and majestic views
✗ southwards; named for its fine box trees.

⑨ Turn left for Ranmore (not on map), signpost difficult to spot amidst hedge.

🏠 **Ranmore** The common commands far-off views and the Victorian church with its striking octagonal tower, is a landmark for those walking the North Downs Way.

⑩ Turn left, signposted Abinger.

⑪ Turn right off A25 for Abinger Common.
🏠 On the corner note the house of the 17th-C

• *There are sweeping views across the Weald from Box Hill.*

diarist, John Evelyn; he is buried in the church just north of the A25.

△ **Abinger Common–Leith Hill** The route follows mysterious lanes under canopies of foliage so dense that on a dull day you could use your headlights.

⑫ **Leith Hill** *Bear left at the fork, following sign for Coldharbour.* Rhododendrons and unusual trees make this National Trust area (750 acres) a delight; at 965 ft (294 m) it is the highest spot in south-east England; St Paul's Cathedral and the Channel can be seen on a clear day. There are views southwards from the road, but it is best to pause and park (eg just before Coldharbour). No admission to the fine Anstiebury prehistoric camp; *turn right on to A29 for Ockley.*

⑬ *In Ewhurst turn right at sign for Peaslake, Shere, Gomshall.*

⑭ *Turn left at signpost for Winterfold (not on map); the windmill (marked on map) is not visible from the road.*

⑮ *Fork right signposted Wonersh and Guildford. At next T-junction, turn left signposted Cranleigh.*

☆ **Winkworth Arboretum** Signposted 300 yards (274 m) before, but not at, car park (on right); a hillside covered with rare trees and shrubs sloping down to a lake; teas.

Route Two: 48 miles (77 km)
Directions in sequence from:
Godalming
Direction of travel: clockwise

⑯ *Turn left off the B2130 on to Home Farm Rd. (signposted Hambledon), then immediately left again, on to Hambledon Rd.*

⑰ *Take second left off the A283, signposted Sandhills and Brook, immediately after the turning for 'British Rail Station'.*

⑱ *Continue straight over the A286 at Crossways Cottages (damaged sign is illegible).*

⑲ *An attractive wooded lane runs alongside Forestry Commission land, with a tricky and dangerous exit on to the A3 (fast traffic is just leaving a dual carriageway section).*

☆ **Gibbet Hill** Views to north-west over the famous Devil's Punchbowl, a large depression to the north of the road.

☆ **Hindhead** is likely to have heavy traffic at weekends.

☆ **Frensham Pond** *Turn left at the signpost for 'Frensham Pond Hotel', and right at the Hotel,* to skirt this expansive and picturesque pond.

☆ **Frensham Little Pond** *Turn right at signpost for this pond,* perhaps even more attractive than its neighbour. Parking on

right amidst delightful woods. Drive slowly over this surprisingly poorly-surfaced road.

☆ **Tilford** is a picturesque village. *Turn right at the Green, by the attractive Barley Mow pub, and follow sign for Elstead, Milford, Godalming, over bridge.*

☆ **Waverley Abbey** The ruins of England's earliest Cistercian house (13thC) and Park (where Jonathan Swift worked as secretary to William Temple) are closed to the public; but both can be glimpsed from the entrance to Waverley Abbey House, just over the bridge on the left. Stella's Cottage, home of Esther Johnson (associated with Swift) can be seen further on to the north of the road.

⑳ *From Waverley Abbey House take the turning northwards opposite, signposted Aldershot and Guildford, then right up Botany Hill and follow signs for Puttenham;* from the top are panoramic views.

㉑ *Turn right on B3000, then right again after 100 yards (91 m) signposted Shackleford.*

☆ **Guildford** Make a detour to Surrey's county town to see the High Street studded with historic buildings, notably the Jacobean Archbishop Abbot's hospital (with 17th-C oak carvings, stained glass windows and pictures) and 17th-C town hall; view from the top of the remains of the Norman castle's keep; modern cathedral (finished 1964); rowing boats for hire on the Wey. *Tourist information: tel. (0483) 67314.*

Vale of White Horse

The mysterious figure of the White Horse, cut into the chalk hillside, not only gives its name to the vale it overlooks but also symbolizes this area's ancient history.

Starting in an important Saxon town, the route goes across the Vale to the Ridge Way, one of the oldest roads in Europe. Walks along this historic track high up on the Downs lead to the White Horse itself and the ramparts of a hill fort occupied around two thousand years ago. The tour also includes a Bronze Age burial site likely to intrigue even those not normally moved by mounds and barrows, and some charming villages of medieval origin.

Route: 60 miles (96 km)
In sequence from: Abingdon
Direction of travel: anticlockwise

☆ **Abingdon** For 900 years an important town where the Rivers Ock and Thames meet. Its abbey, one of the richest in Britain, owned more of Berkshire than anyone except the king. The 17th-C County Hall towers over the market-place, where huge fairs were held until 1968. There are public gardens, riverside walks, an open-air swimming pool, golf and tennis. Boats for hourly hire near the 500-year-old bridge spanning the Thames. *Tourist information: tel. (0235) 22711.*

⚒ **Abingdon** The abbey buildings, Thames St., include interesting 12th–14th-C remains. *Open afternoons in summer; closed Mon, Oct–Mar.*

⛪ **Abingdon** St Helen's church, majestic with its tall spire and five aisles, is a most unusual shape, being wider than it is long (due to gradual expansion over four centuries in the only possible direction).

Picturesque almshouses and 17th–18th-C cottages nearby contrast with its grandeur.

🏛 **Abingdon** The old Gaol, an imposing riverside building constructed by Napoleonic prisoners of war, was used for a time by a corn merchant until its recent conversion to a leisure centre.

🏛 **Marcham** The manor house is now a college owned by the National Federation of Women's Institutes.

☆ **Garford** Just before the turning to the village, the route crosses the River Ock. The line of the Downs soon comes into view to the south.

⛪ **Charney Bassett** The church's Norman door has a frieze of fierce faces, and a chancel doorway carving – possibly Saxon – shows two dragons biting a man.

☆ **Goosey** 'Goose Island' has a huge village green where cattle were kept until a generation ago. Stray animals were put in an enclosure on the site of the Pound Inn.

✺ **Kingston Lisle** The Blowing Stone sits under an old oak tree by some cottages. It is a 3-foot (1-m) high, perforated sandstone sarsen; blowing into the top hole can produce a trumpet-like sound which can be heard a couple of miles away. Many legends exist, one being that King Alfred used it to summon his troops to battle.

☆ **Ridge Way** An ancient track that once stretched from the Dorset coast to East Anglia. Here you can walk in the footsteps of Bronze Age and Iron Age man, of the Romans who buried their dead on Whitehorse Hill, and the Saxons who called it a 'herepath', meaning war road. Today The Ridgeway is a signposted long-distance footpath.

♏ **Whitehorse Hill** A ½-hour walk to the west along the Ridgeway leads to the oldest hill figure in the country – a vast white horse carved in the chalk. Its origins remain a mystery; some experts believe it is Iron Age, others say it is Saxon. Particularly baffling: why is this the only hill figure to face right?

♏ **Uffington Castle** Eight acres surrounded by bank and ditch, on the hillside above the horse. Pottery finds show it was occupied around 300 BC; splendid views.

✺ **Lambourn Downs** Spread out along the road is an extraordinary Bronze Age cemetery. Although traditionally called Seven Barrows, there are more than 35 here, with examples of almost every shape.

☆ **Lambourn** This is racehorse country and training gallops have replaced the sheep that grazed here for centuries. The River Lambourn rises in pools near the village and flows 12 miles (19 km) south-east to Newbury. The route follows it for almost half that distance. *Turn left in Newbury St.*

☆ **Eastbury** Picture-postcard cottages along either side of the river. In the church, a window dedicated to the memory of poet Edward Thomas (1878–1917), and his wife Helen, was engraved by Laurence Whistler.

☆ **East Garston** Thatch and tile roofs, timber-framed and brick-infilled cottages, make this another attractive riverside village. There is no West Garston; the name comes from 'Esgar's tun' – Esgar being a Lambourn tenant at the time of Domesday.

☆ **Great Shefford** The name comes from 'sheep ford', a reminder of how important sheep once were here (Lambourn meant 'river for dipping lambs'). Today large areas of the down have been made arable.

☆ **Hungerford** A 4-mile (6.5 km) detour leads to this busy market town which has unusual customs. A constable for the Manor, who is elected annually, summons his court by

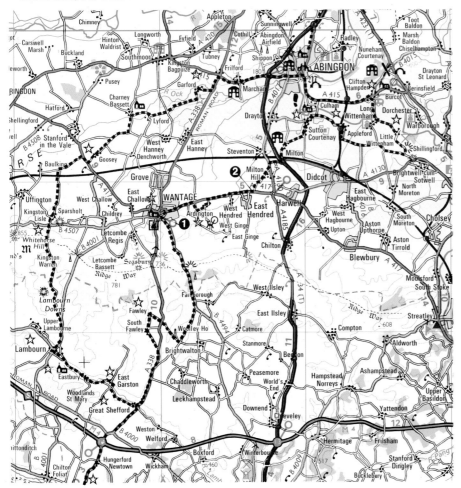

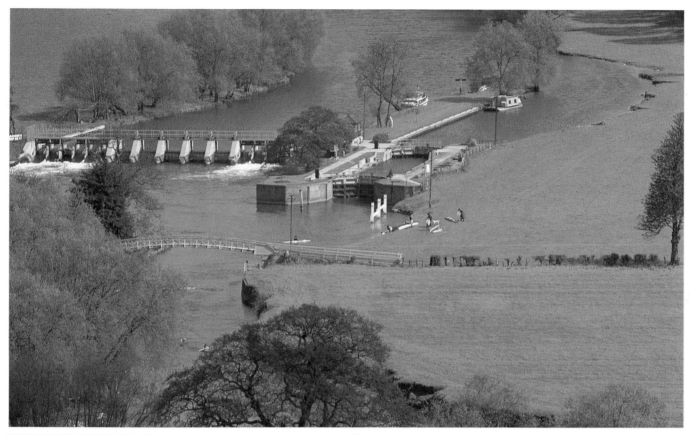

● *Day's Lock, Little Wittenham.*

horn; the Town Clerk reads the Ancient Customs granted by John of Gaunt, and two tithing men – who distribute oranges to young and old – have the right to kiss the lady of every house they visit.

Hungerford has much Georgian architecture and several antique shops.

☆ **Fawley** The village where Thomas Hardy's grandmother lived was the model for Marygreen in *Jude the Obscure*. Hardy also gave Jude the surname Fawley. This detour adds about 4 miles (6.5 km) to the tour.

᙭ **Ridgeway** Park just beyond 'Hill 1:10' sign. Walk east for ten minutes to the monument to the local landowner, Lord Wantage, which overlooks the land he owned.

① *On entering Wantage, turn left at T-junction for town car park.*

☆ **Wantage** An important Saxon town where Alfred the Great was born in 849. Today all roads lead to his market-place statue.

There are many 17th–18th-C buildings of warm local red brick with blue-glazed bricks for decoration. In the large medieval cruciform church, look for the oldest brass in England behind the north-east pillar of the tower.

▣ **Wantage** The Vale and Downland Museum, Church St., has purpose-built galleries explaining the surrounding land and landscape, and man's life here from prehistoric times. Especially interesting exhibit on how enclosures created unemployed land-

less labourers as well as the hedges-and-fields landscape. *Open Tues–Sat.*

☆ **Ardington** This estate village, built by Lord Wantage in the 1860s, has undergone a planned revival recently. New craft businesses welcoming visitors include a pottery, a picture-framer, a leather worker, jeweller, cane-chair maker, printer, a mason and furniture-makers. *Open daily.*

② *Take turning to left (signposted to Steventon). At junction with A4130, turn left again then follow signs to Milton.*

▦ **Milton** The Manor (17thC with Georgian wings) is as demure as a dolls' house from the outside. Inside, the Strawberry Hill Gothic Library is quite a surprise. *Open afternoons only, Sat, Sun and Bank Holiday Mon, Easter to late Oct.*

☆ **Sutton Courtenay** Follow signs to car park to explore rich architectural scene and Thames meadows on foot. Eric Arthur Blair (George Orwell) and former Prime Minister H. H. Asquith are buried in the shadow of All Saints' 12th-C tower.

From the church turn right and continue to end of street where path follows mill-stream to weir and Sutton Pools. A 35-minute circular walk is well worthwhile; look out for kingfishers and grebes.

☆ **Sutton Courtenay** The Sinodun Hills, crowned by the Wittenham Clumps, come into view just beyond the village. *To reach this well-known landmark above the Thames take second turning to right after Appleford (signposted Brightwell), then the second turning to left (no signpost) to car park.*

᙭ **Wittenham Clumps** Best views (as far as the Chilterns) are from the more northerly hill, while the one nearer car park has earthworks of an Iron Age hill fort.

☆ **Little Wittenham** Park by church for a stroll to Day's Lock, a bustling place on summer weekends. (Footpath continues to Dorchester's famous Abbey Church.)

✗ **Clifton Hampden** The 14th-C Barley Mow Inn (just before bridge) was described by Jerome K. Jerome in *Three Men in a Boat*: 'It is . . . the quaintest, most old-world inn up the river. Its low-pitched gables and thatched roof and latticed windows give it quite a storybook appearance, while inside it is even still more once-upon-a-timeyfied.' All still true, but today cordon bleu meals are served in the bar, restaurant or garden.

☆ **Clifton Hampden** It takes six arches to span the Thames here, but the bridge has only one lane. In 1844 Sir Gilbert Scott restored the 12th–14th-C church and designed the manor house, on a cliff above the river.

OXFORD
With its wealth of splendid buildings, its museums and churches, its bookshops, covered market and historic pubs, Oxford, which is 7 miles (11 km) north of Abingdon, demands at least one whole day to itself. Of the 35 colleges, Christ Church, Magdalen and New College should not be missed; nor should the Radcliffe Camera, the Bodleian Library, the Sheldonian Theatre or the Ashmolean. *Tourist information: (0865) 726871.*

Chilterns and Thames Valley

● *Henley: the handsome bridge and ever-popular Angel Hotel.*

Between London and Oxford the gentle landscape is interrupted by the long arc of the Chiltern Hills, stretching from the Thames valley into Hertfordshire. Avoiding the suburban outposts of High Wycombe, Marlow and Reading, this tour explores this area of outstanding natural beauty, where innumerable winding combes – some still cloaked with the famous Chiltern beech woods – lead from bare downland ridges to secluded villages.

Several large houses and churches deserve attention along the routes, but plenty of time should be reserved for West Wycombe, one of the strangest places in Britain.

Route One: 30 miles (48 km)
Directions in sequence from:
Henley-on-Thames
Direction of travel: clockwise

☆ **Henley-on-Thames** By far the most handsome of the old Thames Valley towns, Henley is best seen first from the stately river bridge of 1789, which is flanked by a pub on one side and by a grand hotel and church on the other. The centre of the town is immensely rich in half-timbered and Georgian buildings. *Tourist information: tel. (0491) 576982.*

🍺 **Henley-on-Thames** For the connoisseurs of beer, Henley is a place of pilgrimage. Brakspear's ambrosial Henley Ales, brewed in New St., can be consumed in no fewer than 16 hostelries in the town, including The Angel on the bridge, and The Three Tuns in the Market Place. When available, try the dark, wine-like Old Ale.

① *Leave town along the road that climbs the hill beyond the market-place, signposted to Peppard.*

🏛 **Greys Court** Perched on a knoll overlooking a lovely combe, this Jacobean manor house ✿ is worth visiting for its garden, set amongst the ruins of a 14th-C fortified house. *Open afternoons only, Apr–Sept. House: Mon, Wed, Fri. Garden: Mon–Sat.*

☆ **Shepherd's Green** Small but typical Chilterns 'green' village, with thatched or pantiled houses nestling around a triangle of rough grass, and a plain but pleasant pub, The Green Tree.

☆ **Stoke Row** Amid the suburban blandness of Stoke Row the Maharajah's Well comes as a delightful surprise. The oriental-style well cover, complete with golden elephant, was donated to the village in 1864 by the Maharajah of Benares. Note also the tiny hexagonal 'pepper-pot' cottage nearby.

☆ **Checkendon** Pretty village with lovingly restored brick and timber cottages. Worth 🏛 looking inside the church to see the medieval frescoes.

② *At Cane End go straight ahead at crossroads and then turn left immediately along A4074.*

☆ **Mapledurham** Perfect example of a small Thames Valley village; attractive flint and brick houses, with no hint of 20th-C infilling to destroy its architectural unity.

🏛 **Mapledurham** Fine plaster ceilings may lure visitors inside 16th-C Mapledurham House, but it is perhaps more impressive from the outside. The best view is from the churchyard, through rusty ornamental gates. There is also a working watermill nearby. *Open afternoons only, Sat, Sun and Bank Holiday Mon, Easter Sun to Sept.*

☆ **Goring and Streatley** Twin villages on either side of the Thames, linked by a wooden bridge.

🍺 **Streatley** For arguably the best armchair ⚶ view of the Thames anywhere, visit the public bar of The Swan Hotel.

☆ **Goring** Access to the riverside is by the slip road alongside the fine old mill. The locks are to the right, but the most attractive ⚑ walk, with good views of the weir and the church (set virtually at the water's edge), runs in the other direction.

③ *Go back through the village to the railway bridge, then turn left along B4009. After ½ mile (0.8 km) turn right and then left almost immediately, following signs for Ipsden.*

☆ **Ipsden** On entering the village note the fine brick and tile barn on the left, and on the right the small corn store raised on staddle stones to keep the rats out.

④ *At T-junction at end of village turn left, then turn right almost immediately at the crossroads.*

☆ **Nettlebed** The short, narrow main street is lined with brick and timber houses and old coaching inns. *Just past junction with B481 take unsignposted turning to left.*

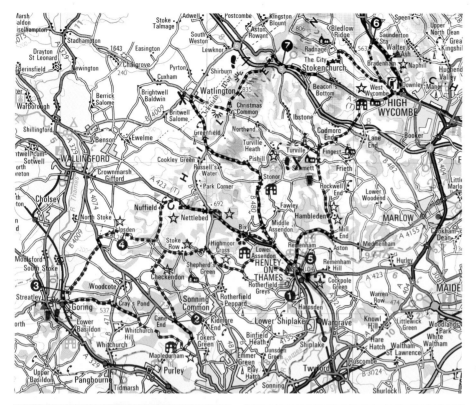

● 'Pepper-pot' cottage, Stoke Row.

Nettlebed To the left of the road a well-preserved 18th-C bottle kiln, incongruously surrounded by modern houses, is all that remains of a once thriving brick and pottery industry. *Ignoring the first turning to the right, take the unsignposted right fork almost immediately after it.*

☆ **Crocker End** (not on map) A particularly perfect example of a Chilterns 'green' village, larger than Shepherd's Green, with its cottages dotted randomly about.

Route Two: 40 miles (64 km)
Directions in sequence from:
Henley-on-Thames
Direction of travel: anticlockwise

⑤ *Leave Henley on the A4155.*

☆ **Hamble Brook Valley** One of the prettiest valleys in the Chilterns accessible by car. It is also one of the few with a stream flowing through it.

☆ **Hambleden** *After village name sign, turn right.* Attractive, carefully preserved settlement of flint, brick and timber cottages grouped around a small square next to the churchyard. *To return to the valley road, take lane leading off west side of the village square, past the church tower.*

Skirmett In spite of some rather tacky suburban appendages of recent years, Skirmett is still graced by the presence of a pub that has retained the atmosphere of an untouched village 'local'. Known in the area simply as 'Lil's', after its former proprietor of long standing, The Old Crown has soggy old armchairs in its low-ceilinged saloon, a staircase in a cupboard and no bar – the beer is served from a brick-floored cellar at the back.

☆ **Turville** An irresistibly picturesque village, much used by film makers.

✗ **Turville** The Bull and Butcher serves Brakspear's ales, good inventive quiches, and a traditional roast on Sundays.

Turville A signposted footpath leads up a steep hill to the windmill (not open to the public). The glorious view makes the short climb worthwhile.

Turville The church has an impressively massive 14th-C tower. Amongst several other interesting features are two wooden screens decorating the north aisle, erected *c.* 1737 to create a separate seating area for the Lord of the Manor, and a beautiful, semicircular stained glass window, designed by John Piper.

Fingest The church has an unusual saddleback roof on its roughcast Norman tower.

☆ **West Wycombe** Unspoiled village of 16th–18th-C houses, saved from demolition by the National Trust in 1929.

West Wycombe West Wycombe Park, the 18th-C Palladian mansion to the west of the village, was built by the notorious Sir Francis Dashwood. Its extensive grounds include a lake constructed in the shape of a swan. *Open afternoons only, Mon–Fri, June–Aug. Also open Sun afternoon in Aug.*

West Wycombe The natural caves were extended manually in the 1750s and may have been used for meetings of Dashwood's Hell Fire Club. *Open early Mar to Oct afternoons, except June to mid-Sept, 11–6.*

West Wycombe The gold ball perched on top of the tower of St Lawrence's church can seat eight people, and was used for distinctly un-religious purposes by Dashwood and his eminent friends.

Next to the church stands the sinister Mausoleum, with its single tomb.

☆ **Bradenham** *Turn off the A4010* to see this village where church and manor stand imposingly at the head of a long green.

The village is preserved against change by the National Trust, who recently made the controversial decision to allow an underground NATO command bunker to be built under the wooded hill nearby.

⑥ *Take left turning signposted to Saunderton Bottom. At junction about 2 miles (3 km) further on take the road signposted to Radnage.*

Radnage *Turn right and right again* to reach the secluded church with its squat tower, Saxon font and 15th-C timber roof.

⑦ *At the motorway junction, follow the sign indicating the A40 to Oxford, then take first turning left, signposted to Christmas Common.*

Cowleaze Wood Signposted footpaths (starting a short distance south of car park and picnic area) lead out on to the escarpment spurs of Bald Hill and Shirburn Hill. The views from both hills are inconceivable from the road.

Watlington Hill National Trust viewpoint. On the lower slopes, note the dark clumps of yew, indigenous to these hills.

✗ **Watlington** At The Tea Shop, 43 High St., the cakes would tempt a fasting saint.

Stonor Park Characterful old house which has evolved over many centuries, and is set in lovely parkland. *Open Wed, Thurs and Sun afternoons, Apr–Sept.*

Local Tours: **Wales**

Eight one- or two-day drives

Pembrokeshire

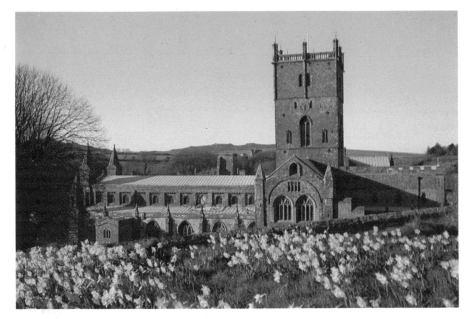

The Pembrokeshire Coast National Park is the only predominantly coastal national park in Britain, and is one of the few places where the old county name officially survives. Although the coastal path is one of the wonders of the world for walkers, a tour from north to south of the peninsula is a worthwhile expedition. The landscape is immensely varied: there are wild moors, deep wooded valleys, tidal estuaries and rolling farmland. This tour gives a taste of all these, plus several splendid castles. But the highlight will be the drive through the Preseli Hills, source of some of the stones that were used to build Stonehenge.

Route One: 72 miles (116 km)
In sequence from: Haverfordwest
Direction of travel: clockwise

☆ **Haverfordwest** Old county town and main shopping centre for Pembrokeshire. Several Georgian buildings and the Old Quay with its warehouses reflect the town's rise in importance as a port in the 18thC. *Tourist information: tel. (0437) 66141.*

🏰 **Haverfordwest** The imposing Norman castle, in ruins, dominates the main shopping streets. It houses the Castle Museum (local history) and Art Gallery. *Open Mon–Sat.*

⛪ **Haverfordwest** St Mary's church (13th–15thC) is one of the finest churches in Wales. Look out for the carved bench-end showing St Michael and the dragon.

🏺 **Simpson Cross** The Pembrokeshire Pottery and craft shop is on the left as you enter the village. *Open June–Sept.*

🌄 **Newgale** From the top of the hill above the beach there are magnificent views of the St David's Peninsula cliffs and St Brides Bay.

☆ **Solva** A bustling village with a miniature harbour reminiscent of Cornwall.

✝ **St David's** One of Britain's smallest cities, St David's is renowned for its magnificent cathedral. Built in the 12thC, it was restored and added to at intervals right up to the

19thC. Note the grotesque misericords in the choir stalls.

m   The ruins of the 13th–14th-C Bishop's Palace are near the cathedral.

① *Leave St David's on the Fishguard road (A487). Just outside the city, turn left for Whitesand, then right on to minor road to Llanrhain and Trevine.*

🛶 **Porth-gain** A short detour (*turn left at Llanrhain crossroads*) leads to the remains of a small industrial complex – stone quarry, slate quarry, harbour, brickworks, stone-crushing plant, storage hoppers, lime kiln.

🛶 **Granston** The Tregwynt Woollen Mill specializes in traditional Welsh fabrics, which are on sale in the mill shop.

🌄 **Garn Fawr** From the highest point on the minor road to Strumble Head, there are magnificent views northwards towards the coast and over a landscape of rocks, stone walls and Welsh smallholdings.

☆ **Fishguard** In reality there are three settlements. Fishguard town is the main shopping area; Goodwick, the modern port village, is located near the harbour; and Lower Town, where Dylan Thomas's *Under Milk Wood* was filmed, is a picture-postcard village located in a deep, sheltered creek.

② *Take Cardigan road from Fishguard Sq., then turn right on to B4313 to Llanychaer. Just beyond village, take left turning sign-*

● *St David's Cathedral, the fourth great church to be built on this site.*

---

posted Cwm Gwaun. At Pontfaen, turn left towards Dinas and Newport. At top of hill, turn left for mountain road to Dinas.

🌄 **Dinas** Before reaching the village, stop at the National Park viewpoint for splendid views over coast, including Dinas Island. *Turn right on to A487 in Dinas.*

☆ **Newport** Small holiday resort with a castle (now a private residence), a medieval church and an ancient street pattern. Popular bathing beaches at Traeth Mawr and Parrog.

③ *At east end of Newport (opposite bus garage) turn right on to minor road signposted to Cwm Gwaun and Cilgwyn.*

🏺 **Cilgwyn** At the Cilgwyn Bridge Candles Workshop, hand-dipped candles are made using traditional techniques. *Continue along minor road, following Maenclochog signs.*

🌄 **Tafarn-y-bwlch** Just before the minor road joins B4329, stop at lay-by for magnificent sweeping views of the Preseli Hills.

🌄 **Bwlch-y-gwynt** At the road's highest point there are impressive views to the north, where the upland landscape is dominated by the ancient volcano, Carningli. A short walk along the track to the right of the road leads to the summit of Foel Eryr, a National Park viewing point.

🛶 **Woodstock** Wallis Woollen Mill (*turn right off B4329 and follow signs*) specializes in traditional Welsh fabrics which are on sale in the mill shop.

🏛 **Scolton** The manor house is now a museum of local history, social life and archaeology. *Open Tues–Sun, July–Sept.*

Route Two: 52 miles (83 km)
In sequence from: Haverfordwest
Direction of travel: clockwise

---

④ *At large Salutation Sq. roundabout pass A40 (Carmarthen) exit and take minor road signposted Uzmaston. After ¼ mile (0.5 km) take left turning to The Rhos. At T-junction (unsignposted) turn right. In The Rhos turn right (signposted to Art Gallery and Picton Castle Grounds).*

🏛 **Picton Castle** The castle is not open to the public, but a gallery devoted to the works of Graham Sutherland, lovely gardens and a craft shop make this a deservedly popular place. *Open Tues–Sun and Bank Holiday Mon, Apr–Sept.*

⚓ **Picton Ferry** A beautiful picnic spot, with views across the estuary and the Cleddau Wildfowl Refuge, can be reached by continuing down the road beyond Picton Castle. *Return to The Rhos, turn right and continue to A40.*

⑤ *At Canaston Bridge take right turning (sign-*

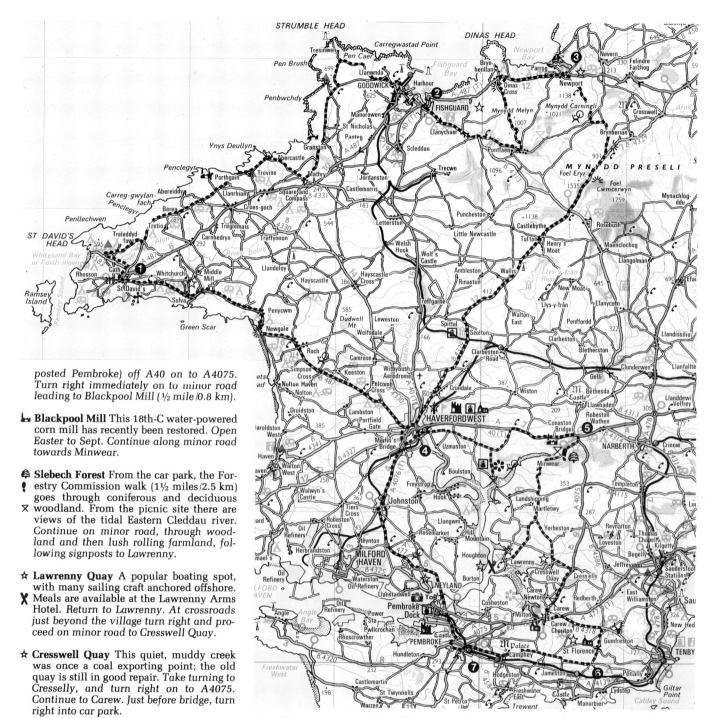

posted Pembroke) off A40 on to A4075. Turn right immediately on to minor road leading to Blackpool Mill (½ mile /0.8 km).

⅃ Blackpool Mill This 18th-C water-powered corn mill has recently been restored. Open Easter to Sept. Continue along minor road towards Minwear.

🌿 Slebech Forest From the car park, the Forestry Commission walk (1½ miles/2.5 km) goes through coniferous and deciduous woodland. From the picnic site there are views of the tidal Eastern Cleddau river. Continue on minor road, through woodland and then lush rolling farmland, following signposts to Lawrenny.

☆ Lawrenny Quay A popular boating spot, with many sailing craft anchored offshore. Meals are available at the Lawrenny Arms Hotel. Return to Lawrenny. At crossroads just beyond the village turn right and proceed on minor road to Cresswell Quay.

☆ Cresswell Quay This quiet, muddy creek was once a coal exporting point; the old quay is still in good repair. Take turning to Cresselly, and turn right on to A4075. Continue to Carew. Just before bridge, turn right into car park.

Ⅲ Carew There is much to see here including a 13th-C castle (with one façade modified in Tudor times), an elaborately decorated, 11th-C Celtic cross, a French tidal mill and a medieval walled garden; good for picnics. Open Easter to Sept.

🏚 Carew Cheriton From Carew, continue over crossroads. Worth pausing to look inside the impressive 14th–15th-C church.

⊻ Manor House Wildlife and Leisure Park Old manor house with gardens, wild animals, exotic birds, falconry displays and a model railway. Open Easter to Oct. From the car park, take adjacent road to St Florence.

☆ St Florence An attractive village, centred on the raised churchyard and battlemented church. Note the 'Flemish' chimney on a cottage next to the churchyard.

⑥ Take Manorbier road out of the village. Climb hill and take right turn towards Lamphey and Pembroke along the Ridgeway.

Ⅲ Lamphey In the village, turn right to Lamphey Palace (near Court Hotel). A ruined, medieval bishop's palace with Great Hall. Open Mon–Sat and Sun afternoon.

⑦ On entering Pembroke, turn left and follow one-way traffic system.

🏰 Pembroke Beneath the walls of the old town, the Gypsy Wagon Museum is open daily in summer. Car park nearby.

🏰 Pembroke The Norman castle is one of the finest in Wales. The main attraction is the Great Keep. Turn left shortly after passing the castle and follow signs to Pembroke Dock and Cleddau Bridge.

🌉 Cleddau Bridge From the toll bridge there are fine views of Milford Haven harbour. In summer there are river trips up the estuary from Hobbs Point (Pembroke Dock).

☆ Neyland On the way to this old railway terminus and 19th-C 'planned town', there is an interesting pottery at Honeyborough Green, open Mon–Fri.

145

Brecon Beacons and Black Mountains

Route One takes in some of the most spectacular scenery in the Brecon Beacons National Park. There are grand views of the Old Red Sandstone range that dominates the area, and to contrast with the steep, barren mountainsides there are wooded valleys renowned for their waterfalls and caves.

Route Two offers some of the best views of the long, whale-backed ridges of the Black Mountains. Driving into the heart of this range is tricky; most of the valleys are dead ends and the narrow, single-track roads become congested in summer. However, out of season it is worth taking the B4423 up the Vale of Ewyas to see Llanthony Priory.

Route One: 50 miles (80 km)
Directions in sequence from: Brecon
Direction of travel: anticlockwise

☆ **Brecon** The main centre for the National Park has a confusing one-way system. There are several handsome buildings in
✝ the centre, but the 13th-C Priory of St John the Evangelist, which was given cathedral status in 1923, lies on the western edge of the town. Inside, note the unusual stone cresset for candles.

Tues and Fri are market days, when many of the pubs stay open for extended hours.
⚲ There is a craft market in the Market Hall on the first Sat of each month. *Tourist information: tel. (0874) 2485.*

▣ **Brecon** The Brecknock Museum has excellent local history displays and includes a reconstructed assize court. *Open Mon–Sat.*

① *Go over bridge, following signs for Mynydd Illtyd. Thereafter, follow signs to the Mountain Centre.*

☆ **The Mountain Centre** Built in 1966, the centre (open daily) provides information,
✗ picnic facilities, a cafeteria, slide shows
❗ and guided walks. Take the opportunity to buy a leaflet on Ystradfellte waterfalls (see **Porth yr Ogof** below), as none are available on site.
⚶ Twyn y Gaer, the site of an Iron Age hill fort, can be reached on foot (about 1¼ hours) from the centre. From the top of the
⚶ hill there are good views of the Brecon Beacons.

② *At junction with A4215 turn left, then turn sharp right on the bend, following signs to Heol Senni. Before reaching village, take second turning on left near the bottom of the hill, signposted to Ystradfellte. The small sign is often overgrown in summer.*

At the top of the hairpin bends, pause for
⚶ *a magnificent view back across the Upper Senni Valley.*

⚶ **Maen Llia** (not on map) Just over the pass and visible from the road is a large standing stone, 13 feet (4 m) high and 8 feet (2.5 m) wide. Standing stones dating from the early Bronze Age are common locally, but their function remains a puzzle. This one may have marked the pass which was later used by the Romans.

According to local folklore, standing stones come alive on Midsummer's Eve and roam the countryside. Anyone who sees them is fated to an early grave.

③ *Either continue straight on to Penderyn, or fork right for detour to Ystradfellte and Porth yr Ogof. The narrow roads around Ystradfellte are often congested in summer.*

④ *Near the brow of the hill, turn right on to unsignposted lane immediately before forestry plantation. Drive down narrow lane to car park on right; be prepared to reverse to make room for oncoming traffic.*

▨ **Porth yr Ogof** (not on map) Here the River Mellte goes underground for nearly 1 mile (1.5 km) and has worn away the limestone into a cave system. Look down on the entrance from the easily accessible viewpoint (only experienced cavers should venture inside).

☆ **Porth yr Ogof** The area is famous for its
❗ spectacular waterfalls, accessible on foot only. Details of walks are given in the National Park leaflet; wear sensible shoes as wet limestone is slippery.

● *The River Usk at Crickhowell.*

⚶ **Penderyn** *Turn right immediately after the village sign and follow narrow road to the crest of the hill.* The church here is usually locked, but the graveyard is fascinating and
⚶ there is a good view of the surrounding countryside. *Return to village and take left turning signposted to Cwm Cadlan.*

▣ **Garwnant Forest Centre** Displays and information about the role of the Forestry Commission. *Open daily in summer; Sat and Sun afternoons only in winter.*

✗ **Nant-ddu** Detour for excellent home-cooked food and real ale at Nant-ddu Lodge.

⑤ *At Cefn-coed-y-cymmer turn left before the main Heads of the Valley road. Follow signs for Vaynor, Pontsticill and Talybont.*

☆ **Pontsarn** (not on map) *After 1¾ miles (2.75 km) park opposite the Pontsarn pub, near the top of the hill.* Walk down the bank and under the road on to the fine stone viaduct (1866), which stands 90 feet (27 m) above the Taf Fechan River.

⚶ **Vaynor** Follow the signpost to the church, to see the grave of infamous ironmaster Crawshay Bailey. Inscribed 'God Forgive Me', the huge granite slab was reputedly donated by locals who wanted to ensure that their old master and persecutor stayed underground.
⚶ From the church there are views down the valley, back to Pontsarn viaduct.

⑥ *At Pontsticill, either make a sharp left turn signposted to Talybont, or turn right just past a derelict chapel for a detour to Pant, terminus of the Mountain Railway. Turn right at end of dam.*

🚂 **Pant** (not on map) The narrow gauge Brecon Mountain Railway runs to Pontsticill (1¾ miles/2.75 km) but tickets must be bought and journeys started in Pant. The planned extension to Torpantau will include the highest railway tunnel in Britain. Trains run frequently in summer. *For details, telephone (0685) 4854.*

⚶ **Torpantau** Look left for an impressive view of the three main peaks of the Brecon Beacons, with their flat tops and steep northern scarp slopes. Pen y Fan is the highest at 2,906 feet (886 m); Corn Du and Cribyn are slightly lower.

☆ **Blaen-y-glyn** (not on map) At the bottom of the steep hill, park on right and walk along the forest path for about 400 yards (365 m)
⚶ to see a pretty waterfall and fine views.

➤ **Talybont Reservoir** Newport's water supply and a nature reserve for wildfowl.

☆ **Talbont** Starting point for pleasant walks
❗ along the canal towpath. The village is
❗ renowned for its pubs: The Star offers at least ten different real ales and bar meals; The White Hart, dating from the 14thC, serves Felin Foel (real ale) on draught.

✗ **Llanfrynach** Worth making a short detour to The White Swan for its excellent food.

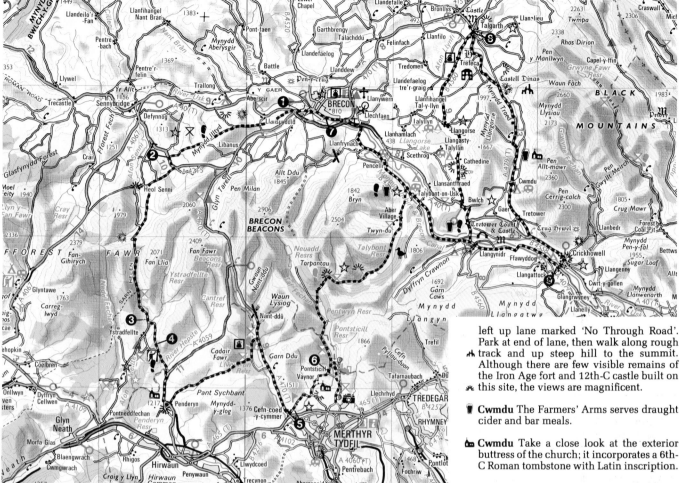

Route Two: 50 miles (80 km)
Directions in sequence from: Brecon
Direction of travel: clockwise

⑦ *Leave Brecon on A40, then turn right on to B4558.*

▯ **Cwm Crawnon** (not on map) Known locally as Upper Llangynidr. The Coach and Horses, by the canal, serves real ale and bar meals.

❗ **Cwm Crawnon** There are attractive walks beside the canal. Head towards Brecon and within half a mile (0.8 km) there are five locks, which change the water level by 48 feet (15 m).

⌒ **Coed-yr-ynys** (not on map) The six-arch bridge over the River Usk dates from the 17thC and has a 7 foot (2 m) width restriction.

☆ **Bwlch** The name means 'pass' or 'gap' in Welsh. Over the crest of the hill look out for the war memorial on the right which marks the turning on to B4560, signposted to Talgarth.

✹ **Cathedine** Good views to the right of Mynydd Troed and Mynydd Llangorse, an out-

lying spur of the Black Mountains. Llangorse Lake, to the left, is the largest natural stretch of water in South Wales.

☆ **Llangorse** Access to the lake is limited. Follow signs through campsite and caravan park. Rowing boats and windsurfing boards may be hired.

🏠 **Trefecca** The village is tiny; be careful not to miss it. *Turn right in village to Coleg Trefecca*, built in the 1750s to house the self-sufficient community founded by Howell Harris (1714–73), one of the leaders of the Welsh Methodist movement. *No admittance to the building* (now a theological college), but the early neo-Gothic exterior is worth seeing, and there is also a peaceful memorial chapel and small museum.

☆ **Talgarth** Former stronghold of temperance and Welsh Methodism.

⑧ *In Talgarth, turn sharp right, then bear left beyond the bridge, following signs to Crickhowell. Alternatively, turn left on to A479, for short detour to Bronllys Castle.*

♜ **Bronllys** The tall round tower is all that survives of this 13th-C castle, but there is a good view from the top. *Open daily.*

✹ **Castell Dinas** Just past telephone box, turn

left up lane marked 'No Through Road'. Park at end of lane, then walk along rough track and up steep hill to the summit. Although there are few visible remains of the Iron Age fort and 12th-C castle built on this site, the views are magnificent.

▯ **Cwmdu** The Farmers' Arms serves draught cider and bar meals.

🏠 **Cwmdu** Take a close look at the exterior buttress of the church; it incorporates a 6th-C Roman tombstone with Latin inscription.

♜ **Tretower** *Turn right at end of village, following signs to Tretower Court and Castle. Bear left past church and park on cobbled pavements beside 17th-C barn.* The medieval fortified manor house has been justly described as one of the most beautiful houses of its kind in the country, even though it is completely devoid of furniture or furnishings. Sensitive restoration has preserved its original atmosphere.

In the field next to the house the cylindrical tower and castle walls date from Norman times. *Open Mon–Sat and Sun afternoon.*

✹ **Gwern-Vale** (not on map) The outline of a Neolithic burial chamber can be seen beside the road.

☆ **Crickhowell** This interesting little town with its ruined 13th-C castle, 14th-C church and well-preserved 19th-C buildings is best explored on foot. Leaflets are available from The Cheese Press in the square, which also serves coffee and homemade food.

✹ **Crickhowell** From the town there are excellent views of the Black Mountains and, in the foreground (to the north), the flat-topped Table Mountain. Crug Hywel, an Iron Age fort on the summit of Table Mountain, gave the town its name.

⑨ *Go over narrow bridge then turn right, following signs to Llangynidr. Return to Brecon along B4558, which follows the route of the canal.*

Mid-Wales

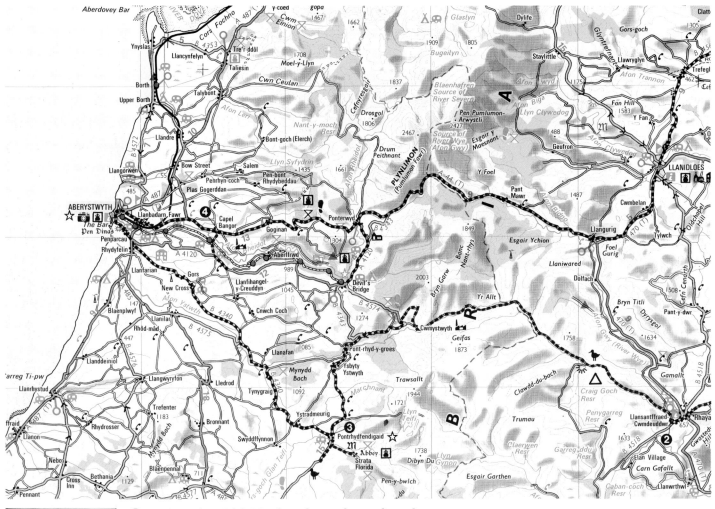

Starting in the Welsh Marches, the rural area along the border with England that for centuries was controlled by the Marcher lords, the route turns westwards across the centre of the country. The remote, wooded valleys in this part of Wales were particularly favoured by the Cistercian order of monks who built several abbeys here, notably Strata Florida. Today, these valleys are one of the last strongholds of the kite, an increasingly rare bird in Britain.

However, there is more here than tranquil countryside and abbey ruins: the route takes in several interesting towns, silver and lead mines, and a hydro-electric power station.

Route: 120 miles (193 km)
In sequence from: Newtown
Direction of travel: clockwise

☆ **Newtown** The town was once a centre for handloom weavers. Displays and exhibits describing their lifestyle can be seen at the Textile Museum, Commercial St., *open afternoons only, Apr–Oct.*

☆ **Newtown to Bwlch-y-sarnau** The winding road out of Newtown gradually climbs into the hills. Initially the landscape, dotted with black and white cottages, resembles Shropshire across the border, but as the road veers south-west the open moors and typically Welsh stone houses reappear.

① *On a sharp left-hand bend take the lane to the right, but with care! There is a signpost marked Bwlch-y-sarnau, meaning road of the pass. After 4 miles (6·5 km) fork right, go over crossroads, then after a further 3 miles (5 km) turn left for a short detour to Abbeycwmhir.*

☆ **Abbeycwmhir** This small village with its unusual church, pub, and huge, privately owned manor house, takes its name from the Cistercian abbey which is now completely ruined (parts of the walls are visible from the road). Founded in 1143 in a secluded spot, the abbey has had a chequered history: it was attacked by Henry III in 1231, and in 1401 Owain Glyndwr virtually destroyed it as he suspected that the monks were aiding the English.

Abbeycwmhir The church was built in 1866 in the Gothic style and has a tower

reminiscent of those found in Normandy. Inside there are some fine stained-glass windows.

✗ **Coed Sarnau** About 2 miles (3 km) from Abbeycwmhir, there is an excellent Forestry Commission picnic site.

☆ **Rhayader** Situated in a loop of the River Wye, the town has lost its castle and its waterfall, but still has several old pubs which are well patronized by those who come here for pony trekking, fishing and walking in the Elan Valley and surrounding area.

② *Leave Rhayader on the B4518. On the outskirts of the town turn right on to Aberystwyth Mountain Road (signposted).*

△ **Aberystwyth Mountain Road** A lovely stretch of road through the hills, with views of the Elan Valley reservoirs and river gorges. Buzzards fly overhead and there is the chance of seeing a kite – a large hawk similar in size to the buzzard but easily distinguished by its forked tail. In summer, wheatears flit across the road and sandpipers can be seen beside the lakes.

Cwmystwyth The remains of a derelict lead mine are visible from the road. Mining for lead, silver and zinc has been carried out in this region for centuries, and in medieval times the local monks were active in organ-

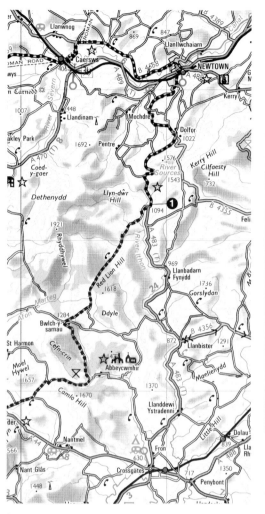

● *Aberystwyth's dignified seafront sweeps round to the old university buildings and the ruined castle gatehouse on the headland.*

izing the extraction of these valuable metals. Gold is still mined on a small scale not far south from here.

☆ **Pontrhydfendigaid** Literally 'The bridge near the ford of the Blessed Virgin'. The village is comparatively large for this region and stands on the River Teifi. *In the middle of the village turn left along road signposted to Strata Florida.*

♔ **Strata Florida** The abbey, one of the largest in Wales, was founded by the Cistercians in 1164, who held great lands here.

The Norman arch at the west end of the abbey church is the most prominent remnant of the original buildings. There are some interesting tiled pavements, and also 12th- and 13th-C undisturbed graves in the cemetery behind the east end of the ruins. These graves illustrate the normal method of burial at that time. Flat slabs of stone were used to make a box which was sunk into the ground and covered at ground level with another stone slab. A sculptured cross stood at the head.

Monks were not the only ones to be laid to rest here; important lay people and princes sought the privilege of burial within the Abbey grounds.

There is a small exhibition at the entrance to the site. *Abbey and museum open Mon–Sat and Sun afternoon.*

✦ **Tregaron** A short detour south leads to the

great bog of Tregaron through which the River Teifi flows. The name Strata Florida, meaning 'Plain of Flowers', derives from this area which is now a National Nature Reserve.

③ *Return to Pontrhydfendigaid, then turn left on to B4340, signposted to Aberystwyth.*

☆ **Aberystwyth** Serving three functions – commercial centre for mid-Wales, university town and tourist resort – Aberystwyth has several large stores, restaurants, pubs and hotels: in fact, for Wales, quite a town. *Tourist information: tel. (0970) 612125.*

🚠 **Aberystwyth** The cliff railway goes just up to the headland, but the Vale of Rheidol narrow gauge steam railway, which has its terminus in Alexandra Rd., runs 12 miles (19 km) inland to Devil's Bridge, a wooded gorge with waterfalls and three bridges. *Open Easter to early Oct.*

🏛 **Aberystwyth** The Ceredigion Museum (Terrace Rd.) is worth a visit for its folk collection and reconstructed, mid-19th-C cottage interior. *Open Mon–Sat.*

④ *At Capel Bangor turn right for a 3-mile (5-km) detour to the Vale of Rheidol hydro-electric power station.*

⛏ **Rheidol Power Station** Visitors are taken on a fascinating guided tour around the

station and can also see the fish farm run by the Central Electricity Generating Board where brown and rainbow trout are reared for stocking lakes owned by the Board. The power station is set in beautiful surroundings and there is the chance of seeing a variety of birds. *Open Easter to Oct. Return to Capel Bangor.*

🏛 **Nantyrarian** The Forestry Commission visitor centre has an exhibition on the life and natural history of the area, and a picnic site. The centre is also the starting point for two trails (1½ miles/2.5 km or 5 miles/8 km) through the Rheidol Forest.

⛏ **Llywernog** The silver mines here are the site of a mining museum which has a small exhibition, a shop, and a mining trail showing some of the underground workings. The entrance to the site is clearly marked to the left of the road. *Open Easter to Oct.*

☆ **Llanidloes** A historic and pleasant town at the union of the Severn and Clywedog rivers. The late-16th-C half-timbered market hall is the only surviving example of this type of building in Wales. The arcaded ground floor was the market place. The upper storey, which at various times served as court house and meeting house for religious groups, now houses a museum of local history. *Open May–Sept.*

⛪ **Llanidloes** The parish church has a 15th-C hammer beam roof, complete with carved angels.

☆ **Caersws** This was an important Roman garrison town with a fort guarding the crossroads.

Cadair Idris and Lake Efyrnwy

The dominating feature of the first part of this tour is the great mass of Cadair Idris, a mountain, indeed a mountain area, almost as popular as Snowdon and equally impressive. Opinions differ as to whether Idris was a warrior, king or poet, but his reputation must have been gigantic.

The second part of the tour – a loop round Lake Efyrnwy– begins at Dinas Mawddwy. From the Dyfi valley, the narrow road rises thrillingly over the highest pass in Wales, then winds its way round the lake, set in lovely wooded countryside, before returning to the A470. If weather conditions are at all doubtful, ignore this loop.

Route: 82 miles (132 km)
In sequence from: Machynlleth
Direction of travel: clockwise

☆ **Machynlleth** A market town (market day Wed) in the Dovey valley. The town centre is dominated by the large clock tower, donated by the Marquis of Londonderry in 1872.

The tourist information centre (tel. (0654) 2401) is housed in the 16th-C Owain Glyndwr Institute; it is thought that a previous house on this site was where the Welsh parliament of Owain Glyndwr met in 1404, free of English domination.

▣ **Llwyngwern** The Centre of Alternative Technology was established in 1974 on the site of an old slate quarry. The dedicated group who run the centre have created a fascinating series of working exhibits illustrating possible alternatives to the accepted ways of producing energy and food with their harmful effects on our health and environment.

Many of the houses on the site incorporate the techniques advocated, including solar, wind and water power, and food is grown without the use of artificial fertilizers. *Open daily for tours around the site.*

⚗ **Corris** At the Corris Craft Centre the central restaurant and information section is surrounded by workshops leased to local craftsmen who can be seen at work; jewellery, candle-making and picture framing are just some of the trades operating here. *Open daily.*

☀ **Corris Uchaf** From the road running up the Corris valley there are fine views of Cadair Idris with its great grey ridge.

☆ **Minffordd** (not on map) One of the routes up Cadair Idris starts from here and has been popular since Victorian times, when tired climbers could relax in the refreshment hut which Richard Pugh, a guide from Dolgellau, built at the top in 1830.

⚓ Many arctic alpine plants have their southern limit in this region. In summer, ✦ pied flycatchers, wood warblers, redstarts and many other woodland birds can be seen amongst the trees.

☆ **Tal-y-llyn** This little lake in the shadow of Cadair Idris is surrounded by trees. Fishing permits are available from The Tal-y-llyn ✗ Hotel, which looks out over the lake and is a pleasant place for a meal.

⛴ **Abergynolwyn** The inland terminus of the Talyllyn narrow gauge railway, which has been carrying passengers up the valley from Tywyn on the coast for over 100 years.

In the village turn right up the steep hill. Care is needed on this narrow road.

♏ **Castell y Bere** *At the crossroads, turn right.* The castle ruins, in a fine setting at the top of a wooded hill, are an easy walk from the car park.

Built in 1230 by Llewelyn ap Iorwerth, Prince of Wales, Castell y Bere marked a high point in Welsh independence from England. However, it was captured by Edward I in 1283.

☆ **Llanfihangel-y-pennant** The village, which lies a short way beyond Castell y Bere, was the home of Mary Jones. Born in 1784, she is famous for having walked barefoot across the hills to Bala, 25 miles (40 km) away, to buy a Bible from the Reverend Thomas Charles. Her long walk stimulated the formation of the Bible Society.

✦ **Craig-yr-Aderyn** *Return to the crossroads then carry straight on.* The huge rock which stands out ahead is known as Bird Rock. This spectacular hill has a sheer drop of 200 feet (61 m) on its north-west face, with a further several hundred feet of steep scree to its base. It is the only known inland nesting site for a colony of cormorants, whose predecessors may have selected the site centuries ago when the sea came up the valley. Today, the West Wales Naturalists' Trust protects the 20 to 30 pairs nesting here.

☆ **Llanegryn** This small village is typical of the few that are found in this sparsely populated area. It is worth pausing to look 🏛 inside the church, which has a beautifully carved rood screen, thought to have been brought from Cymmer Abbey, near Dolgellau, when it was disbanded in 1537.

☆ **Fairbourne** A popular seaside resort with ⛱ sandy beaches, safe bathing and fine views 🚂 of Barmouth and the Cambrian Coast Railway's wooden viaduct across the Mawddach Estuary.

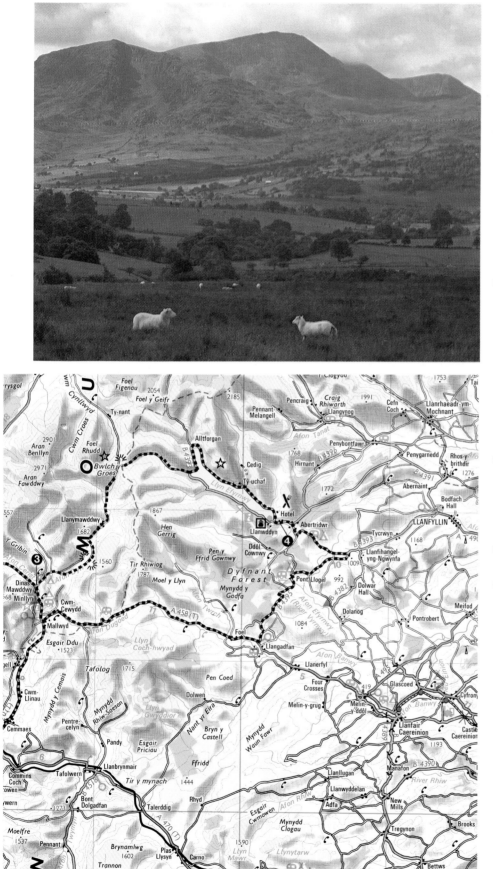

● At 2,928 feet (892 m), Cadair Idris is 431 feet (131 m) lower than Snowdon.

Fairbourne Running along beside the sea, the miniature narrow-gauge railway uses both steam and diesel locomotives. The 4-mile (6.5-km) round trip lasts 1 hour. *Trains run daily, Easter to Sept.*

① *Half a mile (0.8 km) beyond Arthog there is a sharp U-turn to the right, signposted to Cregennen. Drivers wishing to avoid this steep, narrow, gated road should take the A493 to Dolgellau, picking up the route at the Cross Foxes Hotel, on the A470, to the east of the town.*

☆ **Llyn Cregennen** A memorable spot: the great mass of Cadair Idris forms a backdrop to the little lake which is surrounded by National Trust land.

Ty Nant The pony track that goes up Cadair Idris from here is still in use. The trek takes a full day.

Llyn Gwernan The hotel by the little lake provides fishing permits, and is a delightful place for a drink.
    Further down the road the Tal-y-Waen farm trail is popular with children.

☆ **Dolgellau** The old county town of Meirionydd has, for at least 100 years, been the centre for exploring Cadair Idris, but there are also excellent short walks in the area. *Tourist information: tel. (0341) 422888.*

② *Take the A470 out of Dolgellau (passing the Cross Foxes Hotel).*

Dolgellau to Dinas-Mawddwy Great rounded hills rise up on all sides of this magnificent road as it crosses the Bwlch Oerddrws pass.

③ *Turn left on to unclassified road signposted to Dinas-Mawddwy.*

Dinas-Mawddwy The road leading out of the village and up the valley becomes extremely steep with spectacular views.

☆ **Bwlch y Groes** At nearly 1,800 feet (549 m), this is the highest point that can be reached by car in the whole of Wales. The view extends for miles across open moorland.
    Fork right at junction, for Lake Efyrnwy.

☆ **Lake Efyrnwy** This man-made lake, 5 miles (8 km) long, supplies Liverpool with water. Built in 1880, it can provide 45 million gallons a day. The lake is part of a vast nature reserve, and many woodland and water birds can be seen here.
    The old village of Llanwddyn now lies beneath the water, but a new village has grown up beyond the dam. The visitor centre in the old chapel has an exhibition illustrating the natural and social history of the Efyrnwy estate.

Lake Efyrnwy High up on the hill overlooking the reservoir, the Lake Efyrnwy Hotel serves meals to non-residents.

④ *Leave Lake Efyrnwy on B4393, and follow route back to Machynlleth.*

151

Bala and Harlech

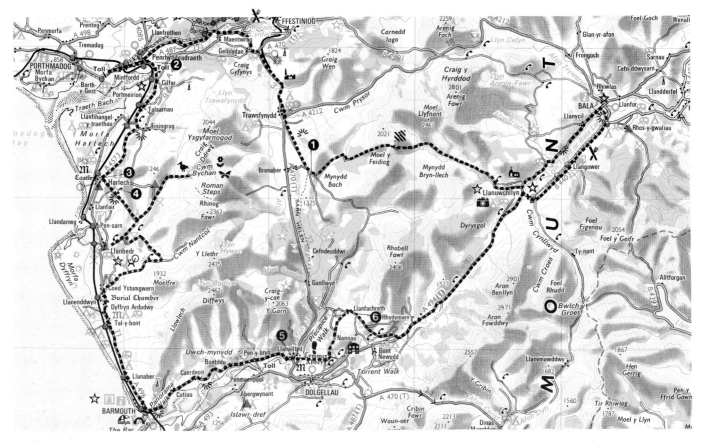

Snowdonia National Park includes not only the area around Snowdon itself, but also a large tract of land to the south, through which this tour winds its way. Between Bala and the coast lies some of the Park's loveliest scenery: secluded, wooded valleys and great stretches of high hill country. Along the route ancient Stone Age sites, the remains of a Roman fort and a medieval castle contrast strongly with the stark modernity of Trawsfynydd nuclear power station and the Italian-style village at Portmeirion.

Some of the roads on this tour are not only narrow and steep, but gated as well – please shut gates after you.

Route: 85 miles (136 km)
Directions in sequence from: Bala
Direction of travel: anticlockwise

☆ **Bala** This pleasant country town, situated at the end of the largest natural lake in Wales, has a busy, friendly air. In the past it was an important centre on the route to England from the west and many ancient trackways converge here. *Tourist information: tel. (0678) 520367.*

✹ **Bala** From the large car park at the end of the lake, there is a fine view across the water to the mountains beyond. There is canoeing, sailing and fishing for a variety of species at this end of the lake. The famous gwyniad, unique to Bala, is rarely caught by rod and line. It is a fish similar to the herring in appearance and origin.

✹ **Bala Lake** Along the lakeside road there are several large lay-bys where drivers can pause to take in the view.

🚌 *Beyond the end of Bala Lake and before*

reaching Llanuwchllyn, take the road to the right, signposted Trawsfynydd. Note the very large chapel, originally built in 1746 but restored and enlarged in 1810 and 1871. It is the oldest surviving Nonconformist chapel in Wales and is a symbol of the life of this area over the last two centuries.

☆ **Bala Lake** From the lake, the old road winds up through the hills, initially amongst low oak woods, then out on to higher open ground, passing the occasional isolated farm, then leaving even these behind.

This high country with only the sheep, views of far distant peaks and dry-stone walls, is an unchanging world, only newly planted forests breaking the old patterns. The many gates across the road mark the boundaries of the various sheep walks over these hills.

〰 **The Harlech Dome** This is the name given by geologists to the whole of this area of great arched rocks, 20,000 feet (6,096 m) thick. Frost, wind and rain have worn them away over millions of years, exposing the hard and craggy rocks below.

Foel Boeth rises above the forest of Coed-y-Brenin (wood of the king). Old copper mining spoil heaps can also be seen around here.

① *At the point where Trawsfynydd is sign-posted to the left, continue on the higher*
✹ *road. There is a fine view of the nuclear power station (see below) and its lake from the brow of the hill before the road drops down to the A470.*

🚠 **Trawsfynydd** Designed by Sir Basil Spence, the power station stands at the far end of the lake. The first to be built inland, it was opened in 1965 and is the only fresh-water cooled nuclear power station in Britain. There are public viewing areas and guided tours can be arranged.

✹ **Trawsfynydd** Across the A470 from the power station lies the site of the Roman fort, Tomen-y-mur, the most remote outpost of the Roman Empire in Britain. Built in 78AD, it is unique in having had an amphitheatre attached to it – a possible morale boost for the troops stationed at this fort on the outer fringes of the Empire. A Norman castle mound stands on the site of the old west gate. Only the outlines remain of the fort and its amphitheatre.

✗ **Maentwrog** Lying in the beautiful Vale of Ffestiniog below the 19th-C mansion of Tan-y-bwlch, the Oakley Arms Hotel is a convenient place to stop for a meal.

☆ **Portmeirion** *Passing through Penrhyndeu-draeth, turn left to Portmeirion. This unique, Italianate village was created by architect Sir Clough Williams-Ellis, who died in 1978. Lying on a wooded promon-*

● Harlech – granite, narrow streets – and castle with its bloodstained notoriety.

tory beside the broad estuary of the River Dwyryd, the village has many curious features and is a cheerful antidote to the rather plain-faced architecture of most Welsh villages. Portmeirion has been the location of several films. *Open Easter to Oct.*

② *Returning to Penrhyndeudraeth, take the road to the right signposted Harlech Toll Road. This road crosses the river on a narrow toll bridge. Proceed to Talsarnau. Just beyond the village take the B4573 to Harlech.*

➳ **Talsarnau–Harlech** From this road there are fine views of Harlech castle, looking much as it does in the picture painted by Turner around 200 years ago.

♜ **Harlech** The 13th-C castle, built by Edward I as part of his grand plan to subdue the Welsh, stands on a high rock and dominates the small town set on the side of a steep hill. Six hundred years ago the sea came right up to the base of the castle (hence the watergate), but today it is more than ½ mile (0.8 km) away.
The castle has been the scene of much fighting. In 1294 it withstood a determined siege by Madoc ap Llywelyn; in the early part of the 15thC it was the main base of Owain Glyndwr's rising against the English; and in the Civil War of 1642 it was held by the Royalists until the very end. *Open daily but closed Sun morning in winter).*

③ *Turn sharply up the hill by Barclay's Bank in the main street. Those who do not wish to go up this narrow and very steep road should take the main road southwards to Barmouth.*
At the top of the hill there are mag-
➳ nificent views of the coast to the south, and of the Lleyn Peninsula to the north. Inland lie the Rhinogs, a part of Snowdonia noted for its rough and broken landscape.

④ *On reaching crossroads go straight ahead. At the next T-junction turn left to Cwm Bychan, a lovely wooded valley.*

🐦 **Cwm Bychan** In the summer, pied flycatchers and redstarts can be seen in the valley, and the surrounding area. Lake Cwm
🌸 Bychan is also noted for its wild flowers
🦋 and butterflies. Near the far end of the lake are the wrongly named Roman Steps. These rock slabs, set in the hillside to form a long series of steps, are part of a medieval track that went from Harlech to Bala. *Return down the same road to continue on to Llanbedr.*

☆ **Llanbedr** The Royal Aircraft Establishment have an airfield here for test flying. Close by the aerodrome a road runs down to Shell Island (it is only an 'island' at high tide). As its name implies, this sandy stretch of coast is well known for its sea shells; around 200 varieties have been found here.

🎡 **Llanbedr** The Maes Atre Tourist Centre just outside the town has craft workshops, a model village and a children's adventure playground.

☆ **Barmouth** A sunny, mainly Victorian seaside town on the Mawddach estuary. The Cambrian Coast Railway runs between the
🚂 long sandy beach and the centre of the town, then crosses the estuary on a wooden
⌒ viaduct. (At present the viaduct is undergoing repairs, having been attacked by unexpected vandals – Toredo boring worms.)
➳ Wordsworth sang the praises of the view from the viaduct's footpath.

➳ **Caerdeon** Fine view of the Mawddach Estuary with the mass of Cadair Idris behind.

⑤ *At Llanelltyd, turn towards Dolgellau, then just over the new bridge turn left to Cymmer Abbey.*

O Llanelltyd Ruined walls are all that remain of a Cistercian monastery founded in 1209. In its time it wielded great influence over this part of Wales.
From the Abbey, take the road signposted to Llanfachreth.

🏚 **Nannau** The 18th-C house seen from the road at Nannau was once the home of the

Vaughan family, who were responsible for planting a great number of trees locally.
The house, one of the best in Wales, has been converted into self-catering apartments, but non-residents can drink (and eat) in the public bar.

❗ **Nannau** The 'Precipice Walk' (safe and easy in spite of its name) starts in the forestry parking area near the big house.

⑥ *Pass through Llanfachreth (the road is lined with huge cedar trees). At crossroads beside telephone box, carry straight on. Go downhill and across the next crossroads; the narrow road eventually joins the A494.*

☆ **Llanuwchllyn** Before the water level fell, Bala Lake came right up to this village.
The narrow gauge Bala Lake Railway runs between Llanuwchllyn and Bala, along the south-eastern side of the lake.
🚃 The 5-mile (8-km) round trip takes about 30 mins. *Open daily, Apr–Sept; weekends only mid–Feb to Apr and in Oct.*

✗ **Bala Lake** The Bala Lake Hotel, restaurant and golf course is open to non-residents.

Lleyn and Snowdon

Apart from one group of high hills which includes the twin peaks known as The Rivals, the Lleyn Peninsula is restfully pastoral, with small farms and grass-covered stone walls dividing the fields.

The second part of the tour, from the old slate-exporting town of Porthmadog back to historic Caernarfon, could scarcely be more dramatic. The road goes through the lovely Aberglaslyn Pass, along Nantgwynant with its splendid views of Snowdon, to the glowering Pass of Llanberis. At Llanberis itself there is the opportunity to ascend Wales's highest mountain in comfort – by train.

attack from Ireland. No high walls are left but the layout can still be seen from the stone foundations and there is a small exhibition of excavated relics. *Open Mon–Sat and Sun afternoon.*

① *At Caeathro, turn right to Bontnewydd (new bridge). Cross the A487 and follow signposts to Saron and Llandwrog. Turn right for a short detour to Dinas Dinlle.*

☆ **Dinas Dinlle** The name stems from the pre-Roman hillfort (dinas means fort in Welsh). From the airfield on the flat, marshy ground beyond the village pleasure flights can be taken over Snowdonia and Anglesey.

Further down the road, Fort Belan is an old defensive fort at the entrance to the Menai Straits. It houses a maritime museum and a pottery, and the owner arranges a ceremonial firing of cannon on request.

☆ **Clynnog-fawr** From the village the peaks known as Yr Eifl (The Rivals) can be seen to the south-west. Those who take to the hills on foot will see views of the Lleyn, Anglesey and the mountains of Snowdonia.

☆ **Nefyn and Morfa Nefyn** Renowned in the past for the number of men they sent to sea, these small towns are now quiet resorts.

From the large car park at the entrance to the golf club at Morfa Nefyn there is a pleasant walk to Porth Dinllaen, which nestles in a sandy cove.

The Ty Coch Inn lies almost on the shore but is sheltered from the westerly gales by the headland. Inland, at the crossroads where the A497 meets the B4412, the Bryncynan Inn specializes in seafood dishes.

Morfa Nefyn-Aberdaron The B4117 gradually becomes more undulating and there

● *Heart of Snowdonia – Llanberis pass.*

Route: 106 miles (170.5 km)
In sequence from: Caernarfon
Direction of travel: anticlockwise

☆ **Caernarfon** The administrative capital of Gwynedd is dominated by its huge, late 13th-C castle.

The yachting quay is a relaxing place to watch the world go by. *Tourist information: tel. (0286) 2232.*

♏ **Caernarfon** The castle was designed to be the main fortification of the ring built by Edward I to subdue the Welsh (Conwy, Harlech, Flint and Beaumaris are some of the others in this circle around Snowdon).

The first English Prince of Wales (later Edward II) had his title conferred at an investiture held here, and both Edward VIII (later the Duke of Windsor) and Prince Charles followed in this tradition. Within the castle there is a display of investiture items, and an excellent Royal Welsh Fusiliers regimental museum. *Open daily (but closed Sun morning in winter).*

♏ **Caernarfon** *Leave on the A4085, signposted to Porthmadog.* Just outside the town lies the Segontium Roman Fort, built to defend this part of the shore against

are many little side roads leading down to rocky coves, such as Porth Ysglaig, Porth Colmon, and Porthor, each with its own individual character.

☆ **Aberdaron** Picturesque resort with a good
🏖 beach. For a fine view of Bardsey Island at
🦅 the tip of the peninsula, take the narrow road to Uwchmynydd and Mynydd Mawr.
📷 Bardsey Island can be reached by boat from Aberdaron, by arrangement.

🦅 **Y Rhiw** Coming over the brow of the hill
🦅 there is a panoramic view of Porth Neigwl
🏖 or Hell's Mouth, 4 miles (6.5 km) of beach where big breakers come rolling in from the south-west. Access to this popular surfing spot is from the far end (signposted).

☆ **Abersoch** Once a small fishing village, it is now a smart sailing centre with several
🏖 hotels and a fine beach.

☆ **Pwllheli** The largest town on the Lleyn. In summer the sheltered harbour is crowded with yachts, but in winter it is a good place
🦅 for bird-watching.

🏛 **Llanystumdwy** Lloyd George lived in this idyllic village which is reached along a minor road signposted from the bypass
🏛 (A497). A small museum houses items devoted to the memory of one of the most famous prime ministers of this century. *Open Easter to Sept (except Sat and Sun mornings).* There is also a pleasant riverside
! walk much favoured by Lloyd George.

☆ **Criccieth** A delightful, south-facing sea-
🏖 side town with good swimming in clean,
🦅 clear water, and fine views of the Cardigan Bay coastline and the hills inland. Queues form at Cadwalader's home-made icecream shop near the beach.

m **Criccieth** The 13th-C ruined castle on the hill was a Welsh fortification which Edward I adapted as part of his plan to encircle the area.

☆ **Porthmadog** A great attraction here is the Ffestiniog steam railway, which runs across the Glaslyn Estuary and through the wooded hills of Snowdonia to Blaenau Ffestiniog, a distance of 15 miles (24 km).

🏛 **Porthmadog** The Maritime Museum by the harbour reflects the town's slate-exporting history. Visitors can board the old sailing ketch moored alongside. *Open May–Sept.*

🏺 **Porthmadog** The local pottery (near the main car park) has guided tours and offers visitors the chance to try their hand at 'throwing' a pot. *Open Mon–Fri, Easter to Oct. Also open Sat and Sun in high season.*

☆ **Tremadog** Attractive 19th-C architecture.

☆ **Glaslyn Estuary** In the early 19thC William Maddocks reclaimed this area by building the causeway which now carries the Ffestiniog Railway and the toll road across the estuary. The low-lying meadows to the
🦅 right of the road are good for bird-watching.

At one time the sea ran up the estuary almost as far as Beddgelert, as can be seen from the name of the little village of Nant-mor (which means 'stream of the sea').

☆ **Pass of Aberglaslyn** One of the most beautiful passes in Wales. At the point where the River Glaslyn rushes through a narrow gorge lined with pines, there is no parking, but cars can be left further up the road. Walk back either down the track of the old Welsh Highland Railway or by the river.

☆ **Beddgelert** A picturesque village lying at the junction of the Glaslyn and Colwyn rivers. A short riverside walk leads to the grave of Gelert, faithful hound of Prince Llewellyn. According to legend, Gelert saved the prince's baby son from an attack by a wolf. When the prince returned from hunting he saw blood on the dog, leaped to the wrong conclusion and killed him. In remorse the prince built a small cairn here. Cynics say the whole story was invented by an 18th-C innkeeper, to attract visitors to the village.

☆ **Nantgwynant** The road rises steeply up the pass, beside Llyn Dinas and Llyn Gwynant. At the lay-by near the top there are fine
🦅 views of Snowdon and nearby peaks.

☆ **Pen-y-Pass** The starting point for two of the main walking routes up Snowdon – the Miner's Track and the Pyg Track.

Pen-y-Pass lies at the head of the Llanberis Pass, a dramatic valley scooped out by slow-moving glaciers about ten to twenty thousands years ago. The road, which runs between towering cliffs of dark rock, is at its most impressive on a wild, wet day.

⛏ **Llanberis** The terraces and workings of the huge Dinorwic slate quarry, which once employed over 3,000 men, can be clearly seen from the road. The slate has a lovely purple tinge to it. Under the mountain of slate now lies the Dinorwic hydro-electric power station, recently completed. The entrance can be seen at the bottom of the terraces where an arched tunnel goes into the mountain.

📷 **Llanberis** The Snowdon Mountain Railway takes passengers to the summit of the highest mountain in Wales (3,559 feet/1,085 m). On a clear day the views are unrivalled; half a day should be allowed for the trip. A ride on Llanberis Lake Railway, which runs alongside Llyn Padarn, takes less time.

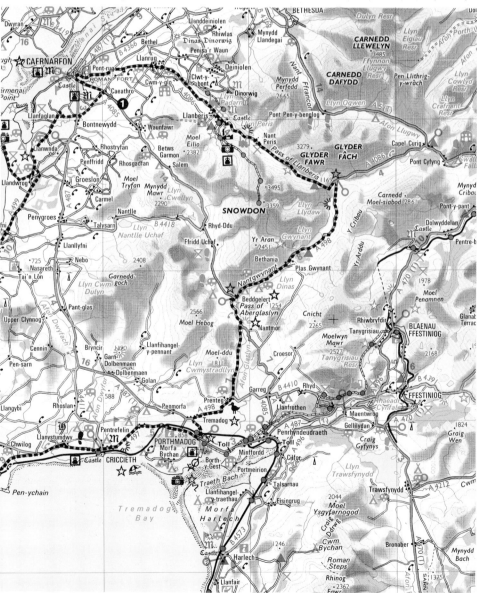

Blaenau Ffestiniog and the Conwy Valley

This tour includes one of the most beautiful roads in the whole country, the B5113 from Colwyn Bay to Pentrefoelas. From this ancient thoroughfare there are panoramic views in all directions: to the coast in the north; to the rugged eastern edge of the Carneddau range in the west; across the rolling Denbigh moors to the east; and south to the hills guarding the wild area of the Migneint.

The second half of the tour has interesting contrasts (Blaenau Ffestiniog is a slate-mining town, Betws-y-coed is situated in lovely wooded countryside) and culminates in a drive down the Conwy Valley to Conwy and its castle.

Route: 80 miles (128 km)
In sequence from: Llandudno
Direction of travel: clockwise

● *The River Llugwy rippling through Fairy Glen Ravine near Betwys-y-Coed; other attractions nearby are the beautiful Swallow and Conwy Falls.*

☆ **Llandudno** Planned solely as a holiday resort in the mid-19thC, the town has many fine examples of Victorian architecture and wrought-iron work and a pier built in 1879. *Town trail guide available from tourist office, Chapel St., tel. (0492) 76413.*

🏨 **Llandudno** Gogarth Abbey Hotel incorporates the house where Lewis Carroll stayed for summer holidays and wrote parts of *Alice in Wonderland.*

🏛 **Llandudno** The excellent Doll Museum (Masonic St.) has more than 1,000 well-dressed dolls, as well as old toys, prams, cradles and a delightful model railway. *Open Mon–Sat and Sun afternoon, Easter to Sept.*

🏛 **Llandudno** The Mostyn Art Gallery (Vaughan St.) specializes in contemporary art and often exhibits work by artists living in Wales. *Open Tues–Sat during exhibitions.*

☆ **Llandudno** The town was built beside the massive headland of Great Orme (Norse for sea-monster) whose summit can be reached by a steep road, or by tramcar or cablecar.

🐾 **Llandudno** The Marine Drive is a toll road with an anticlockwise one-way system (entrance beyond pier gates). On this 4-mile (6.5-km) drive around the Great Orme headland there are views of cliffs, coast, Anglesey and the Conwy Estuary. There is also the chance of seeing wild goats, ravens, falcons and several rare plants.

① *At end of Marine Drive return down tree-lined avenue to the promenade. Drive round the bay and over the Little Orme towards Colwyn Bay.*

🐾 **Colwyn Bay** *On entering the town take B5113 signposted to Llanrwst.* The Welsh Mountain Zoo, clearly signposted to the right at the crossroads, has an interesting collection of animals, including chimpan-

zees and sea-lions. On summer afternoons there are free-flying falconry displays. *Open daily.*

☆ **Colwyn Bay–Pentrefoelas** B5113 is the old high road to Llanrwst and the south. Initially it goes through pastures criss-crossed with hedges, but note how the hedges are gradually replaced by dry-stone walls as the road rises and enters more remote regions.

🐾 **Colwyn Bay–Pentrefoelas** From here there are good views of the Conwy estuary, the Great Orme and Llandudno.

🐾 **Colwyn Bay–Pentrefoelas** At the crossroads there are views of the Carneddau hills to the west and the expanse of the Denbigh moors to the east. (The River Conwy runs down a geological fault-line dividing the rugged Ordovician rocks of Snowdonia from the younger Silurian rocks of the Denbigh moors. This is the explanation for the difference in scenery on either side of the road.) The Welsh sheep seen in this area are bred to withstand the harsh winter climate, and the Welsh black cattle are equally hardy.

🐾 **Colwyn Bay–Pentrefoelas** From the lay-by there are fine views across the valley above Betws-y-coed to Gwydir Forest and the Llugwy valley.

✗ **Pentrefoelas** At the junction of B5113 and A5, The Voelas Arms Hotel serves bar meals.

② *Turn left for 23-mile (37-km) detour to Llyn Brenig, or continue straight across A5 to Cerrigydrudion (see below).*

🌸 **Pentrefoelas–Llyn Brenig** *From the A5, turn left almost immediately on to A543.* This road crosses the wild grouse moors of Mynydd Hiraethog. An area famous for its natural beauty, it is dotted with the remains of Stone Age settlements and has been home to many Welsh poets. There are views of distant lakes, and the brooding Clocaenog Forest.

☆ **Llyn Brenig** Huge man-made reservoir completed in 1977 and used to control the level of the waters of the River Dee. Fly fishing permits are available, and there are nature and archaeological trails, picnic sites in the woods (take fly repellent), a children's adventure course and playground, and an interpretative centre at the southern end of the reservoir.

☆ **Cerrigydrudion** Old staging-post village on Thomas Telford's London to Holyhead road (A5). In the early 19thC horse-drawn coaches took 30 hours to complete the journey on fine days.

🍴 **Rhydlydan** The Geeler Arms, standing back from the main road, serves bar meals.

③ *Turn left off A5 on to unclassified road and drive past Geeler Arms. After 1 mile (1.5 km) turn left at T-junction.*

☆ **Ysbyty Ifan** The River Conwy runs through the centre of this picturesque, typically Welsh village with its slate-roofed stone cottages. Sadly, no remains have survived of the 12th-C hospice which gave the village its name (Ysbyty means hospital in Welsh). The hospital cared for travellers passing to and from the holy island of Bardsey at the tip of the Lleyn Peninsula.

Migneint This area of bogs and moorland to the left of the B4407 is famous for its rare plants and, in summer, for its upland birds.

The source of the River Conwy is at Llyn Conwy, just to the right of the road.

Blaenau Ffestiniog Once a flourishing slate-quarrying town, it is now known for its show caverns and as the terminus of the narrow gauge Ffestiniog steam railway.

Blaenau Ffestiniog At the Llechwedd Slate Caverns, just north of the town, a battery-operated electric train takes visitors 400 feet (122 m) underground into the heart of the slate mine. Guides explain the methods used by the miners, and the conditions in which they worked 100 years ago can be clearly seen. On the surface there are craft workshops. *Open Apr–Oct.*

Dolwyddelan In 1247 the castle was the birthplace of Llewelyn, the last Welsh Prince of Wales. It was built in the 12thC to guard the packhorse route down the Lledr valley and to withstand the repeated English invasions.

Betws-y-coed The name, meaning 'chapel in the woods', refers to the old church of St Mary (near the station) which contains a fine effigy of a 14th-C Welsh prince.

Although the village is crowded in summer, there are numerous opportunities for peaceful walks, either beside the river or further afield, perhaps to the lovely Swallow Falls (2½ miles/4 km), which are approached through ancient woods. *Details of walks from the tourist office opposite Royal Oak hotel.*

In the village itself there are shops, hotels, cafés, a small railway museum and several distinguished bridges, including Thomas Telford's Waterloo Bridge (1815).

Betws-y-coed Anyone intrigued by architectural oddities should make a 2-mile (3-km) detour to the west, along the A5, to see The Ugly House, built in the 16thC.

Llanrwst *On entering this old market town, take the road to right, to Gwydir Castle.* The 'castle' – a restored 16th–19C house with a 14th-C hall – has an interesting garden: different areas were planted to commemorate historical events. *Open Easter to Oct.*

Llanrwst *From Gwydir Castle, go over narrow, arched bridge* (designed by Inigo Jones in 1636). In the centre of the town, the church of St Grwst (15thC) and the Gwydir Chapel (17thC) are both worth a visit: the latter, possibly designed by Inigo Jones, contains the enormous stone coffin of Llewelyn the Great, the Welsh prince who died in 1240.

Llanrwst Near Inigo Jones's bridge, Tu Hwnt i'r Bont is a 15th-C courthouse, now a café.

④ *Take B5106 back over bridge and travel up the valley to Trefriw.*

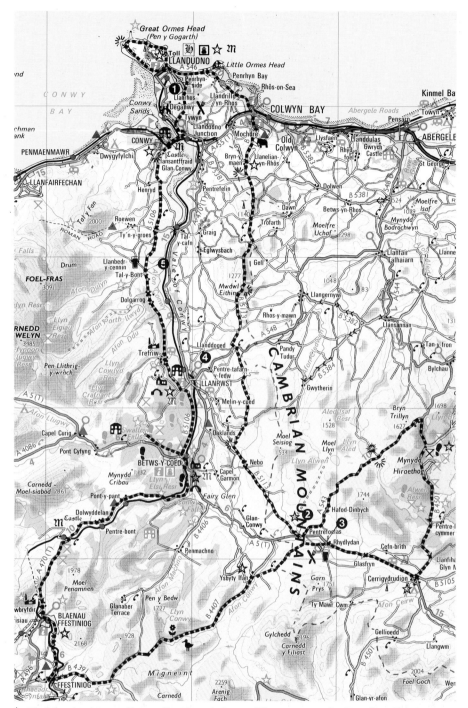

Trefriw At the woollen mills, the whole process of making traditional Welsh cloth can be seen free of charge, Mon–Fri. The shop (*open daily*) sells all kinds of woollen goods including tweed made at the mill.

⑤ *At Tal-y-Bont turn left on to unclassified road which goes up hill to Llanbedr-y-Cennin.*

Llanbedr-y-Cennin Dating from the 13thC, the Olde Bull Inn has fine views of the valley and a cosy atmosphere.

Conwy Walled town famous for its 13th-C castle. One of a series built to subdue the Welsh, it is still more or less intact and is considered one of the finest in the country.

There are superb views from the ramparts. *Open daily (but closed Sun morning in winter).*

Conwy On the quay, visitors can squeeze into the smallest house in Britain; *open Easter to Oct.*

Conwy Plas Mawr (easily identified by its crow-stepped gables) is a fine example of an Elizabethan mansion. Entrance in the High St.; *open daily.*

Conwy *Leave town on the A55, which goes across New Bridge.* From here, two interesting engineering feats can be seen: Telford's suspension bridge (1826) and Stephenson's railway bridge (1848).

Anglesey and the Menai Strait

Although Anglesey is well known for its air of timeless tranquillity, there is excitement to be found here too. The tour begins by crossing Telford's famous suspension bridge across the Menai Strait, and soon leads to Plas Newydd with its breathtaking views across to Snowdonia. Further down the coast, the walk from the headland to South Stack lighthouse is a memorable experience, while at the end of the tour Beaumaris Castle is not to be missed.

In between there are fascinating prehistoric sites, small resorts, fine beaches, and some notable opportunities for bird-watching.

Route: 98 miles (157.5 km)
Directions in sequence from: Bangor
Direction of travel: clockwise

☆ **Bangor** University city with a 12th-C
✝ cathedral restored by Sir Gilbert Scott in the 19thC. Next to it, the Bishop's Garden has a selection of plants mentioned in the Bible.

⌒ **Telford Suspension Bridge** This elegant bridge (579 ft/176 m between towers) was built in 1826 by Thomas Telford, to carry the London to Holyhead road over the Menai Strait. A masterpiece of engineering,

it was designed to allow a fully rigged sailing ship to pass beneath at high tide.
⚜ From the bridge, there are fine views of the Strait and Stephenson's railway bridge.

⚜ **Menai Bridge** This lay-by is a convenient place to stop and gaze at the bridges and the small chapel on the island in the middle of the Strait.

Stephenson's Britannia Bridge was built in 1850 and was originally of tubular construction. After a serious fire in 1970, it was rebuilt using the original pillars but with a road deck over the railway line, to give a second road-crossing on to the island.

Note the strong tidal current running between the bridges.

☆ **Llanfairpwllgwyngyllgogerychwyrn-drobwllllantysiliogogogoch** The village with possibly the longest name in the world, meaning 'St Mary's church in a hollow by the white hazel close to the rapid whirlpool by the red cave of St Tysilio'. The place is usually called 'Llanfair PG' – the full name is a joke to humour visitors.

Near the village, on the A5, the Anglesey column (1816) commemorates the first marquess. At the Battle of Waterloo, where he was the Duke of Wellington's second-in-command, he lost a leg. Subsequently he became the first person to have an artificial leg fitted; this famous limb can still be seen at Plas Newydd (see below). It is worth climbing the 115 wooden steps to the balcony at the top for a panoramic view of Snowdonia and Anglesey.

Turning from the A5 on to the A4080, note the 18th-C toll house with the original scale of charges still printed on the wall.

🏠 **Plas Newydd** Although it is now a National Trust property, the Marquess of Anglesey still lives in this beautiful 18th-C house which stands on the site of a much older building. The famous Rex Whistler mural in the dining-room is one of the notable features of the house. From the grounds,
⚜ there are magnificent views across the Strait to Snowdonia. *Open Sun–Fri, late Apr to early Nov, afternoons only. Telephone (0248) 714795 for exact times.*

🐦 **Brynsiencyn** *Take the lane that carries on straight ahead when the A4080 curves around the Groeslon Inn. This narrow lane leads down to the shore and then runs along its edge. It is an excellent place for bird-watching, using the car as a hide. Many waders, ducks and shore birds come close to the road when all is quiet.*
🍺 Further down the road the Mermaid Inn, situated almost opposite Caernarfon Castle, serves bar meals.

☆ **Newborough** This ancient village lies on the edge of the vast Newborough Warren nature reserve.
Turn left at the crossroads in the centre of the village and drive to the beach. This
✕ is a fine place for a picnic. On one side
⚜ there are views of Snowdonia and the Lleyn Peninsula, and on the other side there is the rocky Llanddwyn Island (another peninsula), which has a 19th-C lighthouse
⚑ and a nature trail. The beach is a good place to look for seashells.

✕ **Malltraeth** The Forestry Commission has provided some excellent picnic sites overlooking Malltraeth Sands – a remote and unspoilt estuary.

The road runs by a series of pools, where
🐦 many rare species of birds can be seen.

The artist Charles Tunnicliffe – famous for his bird paintings – lived here for many years.

☆ **Aberffraw** In the 10thC this little town was the capital of the kingdom of Gwynedd.
🐚 The secluded beach can be reached across high sand dunes.

● *Telford's Suspension Bridge gracefully spanning the Menai Strait.*

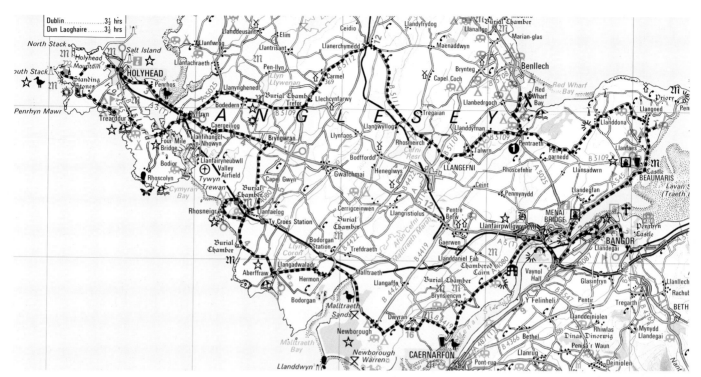

• *Ruined 12thC Norman chapel, Din Lligwy.*

ⅿ **Porth Trecastell** A sandy cove close to the road. Nearby, on the grassy headland, there is a large megalithic burial chamber.

☆ **Rhosneigr** A popular seaside village with several cafés and some fine sandy beaches and rocky coves close by.

   To the north of the village, the Valley Airfield is where RAF pilots come to learn about low-level mountain flying. Many of the latest fighter planes can be seen (and, unfortunately, heard) around here. You may also see the yellow rescue helicopter, which is called out almost daily on rescue missions at sea or in the mountains.

☆ **Four Mile Bridge** *Go over the bridge (B4545) to Holy Island.* Just beyond the bridge, a narrow lane leads to Rhoscolyn
⚓ Bay, one of the best beaches on Anglesey.
❗ There are beautiful cliff-top walks across
🦋 the grassy heath. In summer the butterflies are marvellous to see.

☆ **Trearddur Bay** Small resort with a famous
⚓ golf course and safe bathing at several fairly sheltered sandy coves and beaches.

☆ **South Stack** From the top of the magnifi-
🦋 cent cliffs (where the remains of 4th-C hut circles can be seen) there are 360 steps down to the narrow bridge which crosses the gorge on to the lighthouse islet. A good
🐦 head for heights is needed. The folded and ancient rocks are a nesting place for puffins, choughs and many other sea birds.

☆ **Holyhead** The best view of the ships and ferries coming in and out of the harbour is from the breakwater. Built in 1873, it has a promenade right along its 1½-mile (2.5-km) length. *Tourist information: tel. (0407) 2622.*

🐦 **Holyhead** The Penrhos Nature Reserve and Sanctuary (entrance close to the modern Rio Tinto aluminium smelting plant) is run by ex-policeman Ken Williams and is well

worth visiting. Here injured birds are looked after until they are well enough to be released. *Open daily.*

☆ **Bodedern–Pentraeth** Inland, Anglesey is interlaced with small lanes, running between hedge-lined fields or rough pastureland. The trees all lean away from the force of the westerly gales that sweep in from the Irish Sea in winter.

   Llyn Alaw and the Cefni Reservoir are two of the larger lakes, but there are many
🦋 smaller ones on the island. Standing stones, tumuli, and burial chambers abound, an indication that two to three thousand years ago Anglesey was quite well populated. It was also the centre of the old Druidic religion until the Romans attacked, destroying this corner of Celtic resistance.

① *At Pentraeth, turn left on to the A5025 for 4-mile (6.5-km) detour to Red Wharf Bay.*

⚓ **Red Wharf Bay** At low tide this beautiful spot has 10 square miles (25.5 sq. km) of sand.
✗ The Ship Inn provides excellent bar meals, and the Min-y-Don Hotel is also popular.

🦋 **Llanddona** There are good views of Red Wharf Bay from the unclassified road leading to this small, scattered village, famous for its witches.

ⅿ **Penmon** Although the priory was founded here in the 6thC, the church dates from the 12thC and has a fine Norman nave and transept. Close by there is a massive 16th-C dovecote and a holy well. Near the dovecote, a lane leads down to Penmon Point.
🦋 The spectacular views of Puffin Island and the Great Orme across the bay are well worth the small fee.

☆ **Beaumaris** For many years the administrative capital of Anglesey, Beaumaris has a 17th-C courthouse (close to the castle; *open May–Oct*) and a gaol built in 1829. The
🖼 latter has displays which throw light on the way criminals were treated in the mid-19thC. *Open late May to Sept.*

ⅿ **Beaumaris** The castle was the last of the great fortifications put up by Edward I to subdue the Welsh. It is considered to be the finest example of medieval defensive architecture in Europe, although it never saw any major battles. *Open daily (but closed Sun morning in winter).*

🍺 **Beaumaris** The Olde Bull's Head pub was built in 1617. Situated conveniently close to the castle (in Castle St.) it offers bar meals, an interesting selection of sandwiches and real ale.

🦋 **Menai Bridge–Bangor** *Return to the mainland across the new road deck above the London to Holyhead railway. Fine views of Plas Newydd and the suspension bridge.*

Local Tours:Midlands, East Anglia and Northern England

The Lower Wye and the Forest of Dean

The Wye Valley is one of the loveliest areas in Britain. The high ground on either side of the river offers views which are often fine and occasionally almost theatrically dramatic – witness the famous double bend at Symond's Yat. Several towns owe their charm to the Wye, but the valley's most romantic spot is undoubtedly Tintern Abbey, which even the crowds and coaches cannot spoil.

Although the Forest of Dean is geographically close to the Wye, its unique atmosphere created by the close-knit, fiercely independent community of foresters and miners (there are iron and coal mines in the Forest) can still be felt.

Route One: 50 miles (80 km)
In sequence from: Monmouth
Direction of travel: clockwise

☆ **Monmouth** Charming and restful county town, where the River Monnow flows into the Wye. In Agincourt Sq., the 18th-C Shire Hall is fronted by a statue of Henry V, who was born in Monmouth in 1387. Another statue commemorates Charles Rolls, co-founder of Rolls-Royce. *Tourist information: tel. (0600) 3899.*

⌒ **Monmouth** Thirteenth century Monnow Bridge, with its two-storeyed fortified gatehouse, is the only one of its kind in Britain.

🏛 **Monmouth** Nelson's fighting sword is the prize exhibit at the Nelson Museum, Priory St. This and other mementoes of the admiral were collected by Charles Rolls' mother, Lady Llangattock. *Open Mon–Sat and Sun afternoon.*

① *Drive north through town (signposted Ross) to roundabout at Dixton. Return south for ½ mile (0.8 km) along A40, then turn first left at traffic lights, to reach A4136.*

☆ **The Kymin** Steep 1½-mile (2.5-km) drive up to the pavilion built in the 18thC by the Kymin Club, whose upper-class members met here once a week in summer. They also erected a temple commemorating the Battle of the Nile in 1798. The view to the west

---

• *The Wye Valley – beloved of salmon fishermen and connoisseurs of landscape.*

⚘ was praised by Nelson when he breakfasted here in 1802.

☆ **The Buck Stone** Once a rocking-stone, it is now cemented in place, having been rolled down to the road below by some touring actors in 1885. To reach the Stone, park in lay-by on left and walk short distance up steep path (not signposted).

✲ **Staunton** After leaving village, note standing stone on left, immediately before fork.

⚘ **Symonds Yat** The exceptional view of the River Wye, snaking its way through a thickly wooded gorge, attracts too many admirers in high summer. Out of season it is magnificent. 'Yat' is an old local term for gateway, and Symond was a High Sheriff of Herefordshire in the 17thC.

𝗆 **Goodrich** The 12th–14thC castle has been described as the noblest ruin in Herefordshire, its moat hewn like a precipice out of solid rock. *Open daily (but closed Sun morning in winter).*

▦ **Goodrich** Buried under the church altar is Jonathan Swift's grandfather, Thomas, who was responsible for the village's whimsical, Y-shaped vicarage.

⚑ **Goodrich** The remains of the 14th-C Flanesford Priory can be seen to the left, immediately before bridge.

▦ **Walford** Hill Court, a monumental mansion of 1700, is approached by an impressive avenue of elms, said to have been planted by philanthropist John Kyrle, the 'Man of Ross', in the 18thC. *The house is not open to the public, but visitors can go up the avenue to the Garden Centre.*
  Note the picturesque black-and-white Old Hall opposite.

☆ **Ross-on-Wye** In the centre of this delightfully situated town, the 17th-C stone market house stands on rows of open arches. Nearby, St Mary's church (mostly 13th and 14thC) has some good 15th-C glass and a monument to John Kyrle (1637–1724) who lived in Ross and became its most famous benefactor. Outside the church, the plague cross records the 315 deaths here in 1637.

▦ **Forest of Dean** The old court room of the Restoration-style Speech House, now an inn, is the meeting place for the ancient Verderers' Court, which meets to administer Forest affairs. The arboretum behind the inn has 300-year-old holly trees.

⚘ **Forest of Dean** Superb views to the east, across the forest.

🚂 **Parkend** The track to the left of the road belongs to the Dean Forest Railway; steam trains run every Sun, June–Sept, from the Norchard Steam Centre on B4234 near Lydney, about 3 miles (5 km) to the south.

⚒ **Clearwell** At the ancient iron mines, eight caverns house geological samples and mining equipment. *Open Easter to Sept (closed Mon, except in July and Aug).*

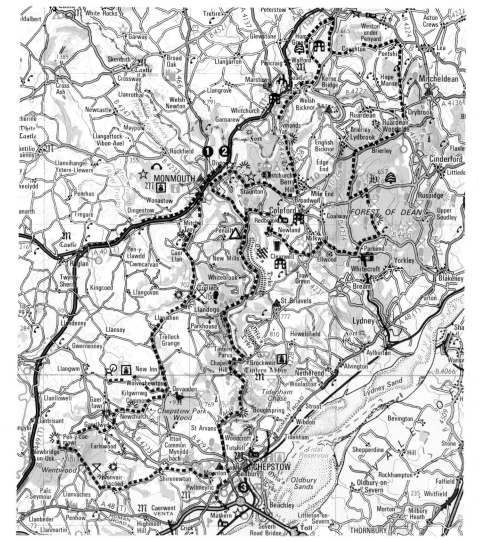

High St. Continue down Middle St. to car park in Bridge St.

ɱ **Chepstow** The impressive castle, stretched out along the cliff top, was one of the first Norman fortifications to be built in stone instead of wood. *Open daily (but closed Sun morning in winter).*

ɦ **Chepstow** St Mary's church has much Norman work, including a splendid, richly moulded arch now in the west doorway.

☆ **Mathern** A 2-mile (3-km) detour *(take Newport exit at Mounton roundabout)* leads to
ɦ this old village, with its 15th-C church.

⊼ **Wentwood** The reservoir has a pleasant picnic site with good views. For a more
❊ impressive panorama, climb Gray Hill, opposite. There are tumuli and a Neolithic
❊ stone circle on the east side of the hill.

❊ **Pen-y-cae-mawr** (Short detour.) On the descent there are fine views to the west.

❊ **Gaerllwyd** Neolithic tomb in semi-wrecked condition. The huge broken capstone has five supporting stones *in situ*. Tucked behind hedge along B4235, it is visible from the road.

❊ **Newchurch** From the road, there are superb views right across to the Bristol Channel.

🐦 **Devauden** Beaufort Aviaries (entrance on the green next to the pub) have rare pheasants, tropical birds and peacocks. *Open daily.*

▣ **Wolvesnewton** A 3½-mile (5.5-km) detour leads to the Model Farm. Built at the end of the 18thC, it has a unique, cross-shaped
⚘ barn, housing a Folk Collection and Craft Centre. *Open Sat–Mon, Easter to June; daily, June–Sept; Sun afternoon only, Oct–Nov.* To reach the farm, go up signposted lane on left, ¾ mile (1 km) past Wolvesnewton church.

❊ **Trelleck** Harold's Stones – three mysterious, aligned standing stones – are signposted (for pedestrians) on right, just before left bend into village. Named after King Harold, they date from Neolithic times.

❊ **Beacon Hill** On a clear day this short detour leads to an exhilarating view of the Black Mountains and Brecon Beacons to the west.
⊼ Popular picnic spot with excellent forest
❗ walks. Best views are from the road.

❊ **Lydart** Fine views of mountains to the west, and of Monmouth to the north, enfolded in its circle of hills.

ɱ **Raglan Castle** A detour to Raglan Castle (8 miles/13 km) south-west on the A40) should not be missed if time allows.

Raglan stands on the site of a Norman keep but the present building dates from the 15th–16thC, when military castles were developing into Tudor palaces. The detached, hexagonal, five-storeyed tower or keep, which is surrounded by a moat, is the most interesting part of the defences. Inside the castle, the grand staircase, niches and fireplaces show the transition taking place. *Open daily (but closed Sun morning in winter).*

🏰 **Clearwell Castle** England's first neo-Gothic mansion, built in the mid-18thC, was badly damaged by fire in the 1920s but has been restored in recent years. Attractions include a Hornby model train layout. *Open Tues–Fri, Sun, Easter to Oct.*

🍺 **Clearwell** The Wyndam Arms, dating from the 14thC, serves real ale and delicious light lunches.

ɦ **Newland** All Saints church has been called the 'Cathedral of the Forest'. The 13th–14thC tower has five elaborate pinnacles. Inside there are grand effigies and a 15th-C monument to the Forest's Free Miners who had the right to claim ownership of a pit if they had worked in the mines for more than a year and a day.

🏰 **Newland** A row of attractive almshouses lies to the south of the church.

Route Two: 45 miles (72 km)
In sequence from: Monmouth
Direction of travel: clockwise

② *Leave Monmouth as for Route One, but keep on A466 after crossing bridge at traffic lights.*

△ **Wye Valley** The road follows the meandering course of the Wye through a variety of river valley landscapes perhaps unequalled in Britain. The scenery is not large in scale, but its special quality has been celebrated by writers and painters alike.

▣ **Tintern** The old railway serving local industries (iron, wireworks, paper mills) is no longer in use, but the station has been preserved as a small museum.

ɱ **Tintern** The splendidly-sited abbey was founded by the Cistercians in 1131, but most of the extensive and elegant ruins date from the 13th–14thC, when it was almost entirely rebuilt. The spirit of the place, celebrated by Wordsworth in his famous poem, still shines undimmed through the tourist industry surrounding it. *Open Mon–Sat and Sun afternoon.*

❊ **Wynd Cliff** The rewards of a bracing climb up 365 steps, many of them hewn out of the cliff-face, are panoramic views over the Severn. Poorly signposted car park off road to right, opposite unsignposted picnic area on left immediately before 'bend in the road' sign.

③ *On entering Chepstow turn left. Go through the old West or Welsh Town Gate to the*

The Cotswolds

The Cotswolds are part of a limestone belt that crosses England from Dorset to Humberside and is especially prominent between Bath and Chipping Campden. The tour begins on the gentle side of the Cotswolds, where the land rises gradually, and crosses to the steep western escarpment with its wooded combes. Note how the limestone appears everywhere – on ploughed fields, in dry-stone walls, but best of all in the vernacular architecture that gives a simple but dignified unity to the entire area.

Sheep have been the other major influence on Cotswold life – and this is evident all along the route.

Route One: 48 miles (77 km)
In sequence from: Bourton
Direction of travel: anticlockwise

☆ **Bourton-on-the-Water** A wealth of natural and man-made attractions in main Cotswold tourist centre. River Windrush, spanned by five graceful bridges, flows crystal-clear between shops and impressive houses. Use car park.

▣ **Bourton-on-the Water** The Motor Museum in an old mill, houses a superb display of vintage cars and related collectors' items. Upstairs, the Village Life Collection includes a re-creation of a Victorian shop. *Open Mar–Nov.*

🐦 **Bourton-on-the-Water** Birdland has a unique collection of rare species, including humming birds; penguins are a speciality here too. *Open daily.*

▣ **Bourton-on-the-Water** The Model Railway layout covers more than 400 square feet (37 sq. m); visitors operate the trains with push-buttons. *Open daily Apr–Sept; rest of year weekends, Bank Holidays and school holidays only.*

🚶 **Guiting Power** The church, down the lane from the village green, has Norman doorways, nave and priest's door.

① *At crossroads beyond the village turn left to Roel Gate for descent from Cotswold escarpment.*

● *Guiting Power, North Cotswolds: 'Guiting' derives from the Old English, 'God's forest'.*

🚶 **Guiting Power–Winchcombe** Splendid view of Winchcombe and Severn vale with Malvern Hills in distance. This road was an old salt way from Worcestershire.

☆ **Winchcombe** The King of Mercia founded an Abbey here in the 8thC and this was the 'county town' of Mercia until the Norman invasion. It retains a prosperous look and much traditional Cotswold architecture.

🏰 **Winchcombe** Elizabeth I, Anne Boleyn and Charles I all spent time in historic, and less than tranquil, Sudeley Castle. Catherine Parr (widow of Henry VIII) died here; her tomb, designed centuries later by Victorian architect Gilbert White, is in the chapel. Excellent collection of paintings, furniture and toys. Delightful grounds with Elizabethan garden. *Open Apr–Oct.*

▣ **Winchcombe** The tourist information office *(tel. (0242) 602925)*, folk history museum and Simms' Museum of Police Memorabilia are all in the Town Hall. *Open Mon–Sat, Mar–Sept.*

✗ **Winchcombe** Home-cooked food, a friendly, old-world atmosphere and a garden are to be found at the White Lion Inn, North St.

⛰ **Belas Knap** Neolithic burial mound 1,000 feet (304 m) above sea level. From roadside, follow yellow arrows for 1 mile (1.5 km) to reach this well-preserved long barrow.
A short way along the road from Belas
🚶 Knap there are fine views to the west. Note how the road follows the contour of the hill alongside Humblebee Woods.

☆ **Compton Abdale** Charming village lying in a steep fold of the hills. At the crossroads, note the stream tumbling into an old stone
🚶 trough. St Oswald's church, high on a cliff, has a Perpendicular tower bedecked with strange gargoyles.

② *Follow signs for Roman Villa, and descend into the valley of the River Coln, which rises in hills near Sevenhampton. The route follows the river for almost 10 miles (16 km).*

🏛 **Chedworth Roman Villa** Well-preserved remains show how elegantly some Romans lived. There are three beautiful mosaic floors and the best surviving example of a bath suite with choice of Turkish or Swed-
▣ ish-style baths. The museum shows smaller finds. *Open Tues–Sun and Bank Holiday Mon, Mar–Oct; Wed–Sun, Feb, Nov to Dec.*

🚶 **Chedworth–Fossebridge** *On leaving villa follow sign marked Yanworth (good views south over Coln Valley to Chedworth Woods) but turn right before village. The valley soon begins to open out, the hills becoming less steep as the road approaches Fossebridge.*

☆ **Fossebridge** One of the Romans' most perfect roads, the Foss Way, crosses the River Colne here, on its direct route from Exeter to Lincoln.

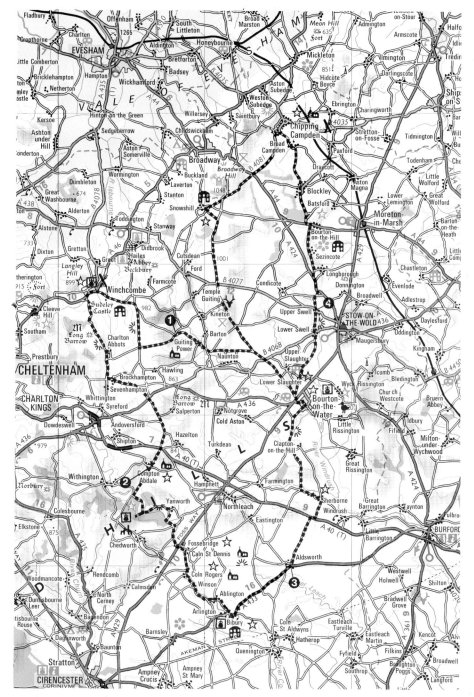

Sherborne to Bourton-on-the-Water Views across the Windrush valley to Little Rissington's disused airfield, now a medical centre for us forces.

☆ **Lower Slaughter** This classic Cotswold village beside the River Eye (babbling to the Windrush under clapper bridges) is almost too good to be true; inhabitants sitting in the sun outside their houses look like actors on a film set. The name comes from 'sloe-tree' which abounds locally. *Turn right, then left, then right again through village, then follow signpost to Lower Swell.*

> **Route Two: 32 miles (51 km)**
> In sequence from: Bourton
> Direction of travel: anticlockwise

Lower Swell Just beyond the village, there are views across the valley to Stow-on-the-Wold, once renowned for its sheep fairs.

④ *At junction with B4077 turn left (signposted Tewkesbury), then right (signposted Longborough). At T-junction, turn right then immediately left (signposted Stow). At next T-junction turn left, then take turning to right (signposted Sezincote) beyond pub.*

🏛 **Sezincote** An astonishing mansion (remodelled 1805) combining Hindu and Muslim architecture, with equally impressive gardens combining classic English landscape design with concepts brought back from India. *Open afternoons only: house, Thurs, Fri, May–July, Sept; garden, Thurs, Fri, Bank Holiday Mon, Jan–Nov.*

☆ **Chipping Campden** The English historian G. M. Trevelyan called the High Street 'the most beautiful village street in England'. Campden's former wealth – it was the centre of the wool trade from the 13th–17th C – can be seen in its splendid houses and inns, but most of all in its church.

The Cotswold Games were held annually on nearby Dover's Hill from 1612 to 1852 – a sort of English Olympics, famous for sports such as shin-kicking. The Games, revived in 1963, take place on the first Friday after the Spring Bank Holiday.

✗ **Chipping Campden** The Badger Inn serves excellent home-cooked food.

🏛 **Snowshill Manor** An eccentric collector of model ships and telescopes, bicycles and sedan chairs, Samurai armour and old farm implements, toys and clocks and much more, left his collection and this charming manor house to the National Trust. His own quarters, in a converted outhouse, underline his unusual way of life. *Open Wed–Sun and Bank Holiday Mon, May–Sept; Sat, Sun and Bank Holiday Mon, Apr and Oct.*

☆ **Snowshill** Soon after leaving the village the route crosses exposed, treeless uplands, illustrating why the Cotswolds are sometimes described as 'bleak'.

Ⴤ **Cotswold Farm Park** The most complete collection of rare British farm animals, including Old Gloucester cattle (their milk is used to make Double Gloucester cheese). *Open late Apr to Sept.*

🏛 **Coln St Dennis** The Norman church has a marvellous central tower overlooking Coln water meadows.

☆ **Coln Rogers** Named after Roger of Gloucester who gave 'Colne in the Hills' to the monks of Gloucester in 1150. Fine church with Saxon nave and chancel, unusual in this area.

☆ **Bibury** One of the prettiest Cotswold villages, much visited for its row of picture-postcard stone cottages where 17thC woollen weavers lived, drying their cloth beside the Coln. Village houses and 'wool church' display a wealth of architectural detail. Parking space may be short in summer.

☆ **Bibury** The Trout Farm, which has 40 rearing ponds covering eight acres, supplies a quarter of a million trout to our fishing waters annually. Visitors may feed and purchase fish. *Open daily.*

🏛 **Bibury** In a 17th-C corn mill, the Cotswold Country Museum is *open daily Mar–Oct, weekends only Nov–Feb.*

③ *At Aldsworth, turn left into village, then immediately right, signposted Bourton-on-the-Water.*

☆ **Sherborne** The 4,000-acre Sherborne estate, on the River Windrush, belonged to the Dutton family from 1551 to 1982, when it was bequeathed to the National Trust. The most famous member of the family was 'Crump' Dutton, gambler and hunchback.

The Upper Wye

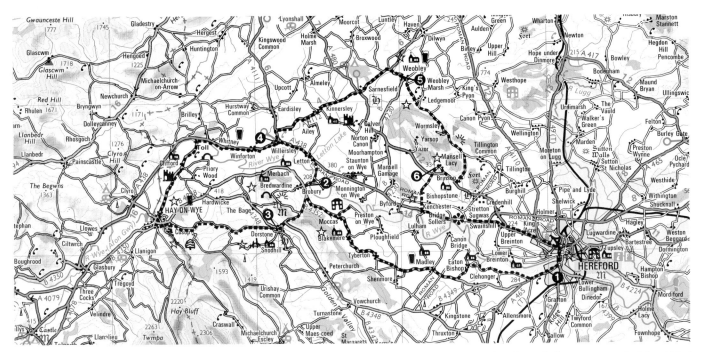

Cascading down from its source in mid-Wales, the River Wye loops eastwards into England along a valley that quickly tames it into huge meanders – a transformation that is one of the main pleasures of this tour.

Starting in Hereford, the route follows the Wye through lush water-meadows surrounded by wooded hills, before climbing to wind-swept heights reached along steep and narrow (but well-maintained) roads. Along the way there are remarkably unspoiled half-timbered villages, several Norman churches and a small town with an outsize reputation for second-hand bookshops.

Route: 59 miles (95 km)
In sequence from: Hereford
Direction of travel: clockwise

☆ **Hereford** Although the city dates back to Saxon times, there was much rebuilding in the 18thC. However, several buildings have survived from earlier days, notably the cathedral with its splendid Norman nave (and rare, medieval map of the world); the half-timbered, 17th-C Old House in High Town; and 14th-C All Saints church, easily recognized by its crooked spire. *Tourist information: tel. (0432) 268430.*

① *Leave Hereford on A465 (signposted to Abergavenny). After about 2 miles (3 km) turn right, signposted Belmont Abbey.*

⌂ **Belmont Abbey** (not on map) The Roman Catholic church (formerly a cathedral) was built in 1850. Worth going inside to see the excellent Victorian architecture. *Continue along Ruckall Rd., which becomes a pretty, undulating lane.*

⌂ **Eaton Bishop** The Norman church is well worth a visit for its fine, 14th-C stained glass windows, chiefly browns, yellows and greens. *Continue along the deep-set lane. At T-junction turn right on to B4352.*

⌂ **Madley** Down a lane to the left of the straggling main street, the exceptionally

large church (built to accommodate travelling pilgrims) has what is claimed to be the second largest font in England.

▮ **Madley** The impressive python skin tacked to a ceiling beam in the lounge of the Red Lion, was brought back from Africa by one of the pub's customers.

☆ **Moccas** A 6th-C Celtic saint established a monastery here after seeing a white sow with piglets (an old religious sign of good fortune); hence the village name, which is Welsh for 'pig's marshy meadow'. The monastery has gone but the small Norman church is worth seeing.

▥ **Moccas** Turn right to Moccas Court, a Georgian mansion designed by Adam and set in a park laid out by Capability Brown. The main feature of the house is a circular room that has never had a fire lit in it for fear of damaging the 200-year-old French wallpaper. *Open Thurs afternoons only, Apr–Sept.*

☆ **Bredwardine** Francis Kilvert, the famous Victorian diarist, was vicar here from 1877 until his death two years later. (He died from peritonitis ten days after returning from honeymoon.) His grave in the church-yard is identified by its white marble cross, to the left of the giant yew under which the Kilvert Society have placed a seat.

⌂ **Bredwardine** Monuments inside the

church include one to a knight killed defending Henry V at Agincourt. Just past the church, there are glorious views from the 18th-C brick bridge.

② *Anyone wishing to shorten the tour should cross the bridge and continue to junction with A438. One mile (1.5 km) beyond Letton's Norman church (with its 800-year-old iron door-hinges) turn right on to A4111 and right again almost immediately on to A4112 (signposted to Leominster). Continue to Kinnersley (see below).*

For the complete tour, return towards Moccas on B4352 for ½ mile (0.8 km), then take turning to right, signposted to Dorstone, along a narrow, steep lane (1:4, but with passing places). Turn right for short detour to Arthur's Stone.

⋔ **Arthur's Stone** This Bronze Age burial chamber (reached along a rather bumpy lane) consists of a huge slab of sandstone some 20 feet (6 m) long and nearly as wide, perched on stone uprights. Superb views over the Wye Valley nearly 1,000 feet (304 m) below.

☆ **Dorstone** Approached down a steep hill (again 1:4) the village retains its basic Norman layout: the castle (now in ruins), inn and church all stand around the tri-angular green (once the market place).

Dorstone stands at the head of the lovely Golden Valley, which lies in the shadow of the Black Mountains of Wales. Anyone planning a separate expedition here should take a look at the interesting Norman churches at Peterchurch and Abbey Dore.

⌂ **Dorstone** In St Faith's church (much restored in Victorian times) an ancient tomb recess is thought to commemorate Richard de Brito, one of the four knights who murdered Thomas à Becket in Canterbury Cathedral (1170) and who lived here after serving 15 years in exile in Palestine.

③ *To return to the Wye Valley, go past the church, then bear left on to unclassified* road (signposted to Mynydd Brith) which rises to over 980 feet (299 m) before dropping to Cusop (short detour to left).

☆ **Cusop** The yew trees in the churchyard are reputed to be those mentioned in the Domesday Book.

Nearby, the Martyr's Grave commemorates a Methodist preacher who was stoned to death by a mob he was trying to convert.

☆ **Hay-on-Wye** On the border of England and Wales, this pleasant market town had been burned down at least five times by the Middle Ages.

The ruined Norman castle was replaced by a 17th-C mansion, now owned by the man whose second-hand bookshops brought fame to the town; Hay is still a Mecca for book lovers.

Two fine stone buildings grace the end of Market St. – the Cheese Market (two storeys) and the single storey Butter Market. At the foot of the steep slope below them is a rather splendid Victorian clock tower.

Hay-on-Wye The town has several pubs and hotels including the Swan and the Three Tuns (which is on the B4350).

Clifford The castle was sacked by Owen Glendower in 1402. The ruins tower 150 feet (46 m) above the Wye and are best approached along a footpath leading off to the left at the point where the castle comes into view.

In the village, a steep road to the right leads to the parish church which contains a medieval wooden effigy of a priest.

Whitney Toll Bridge The bridge has crossed the Wye on giant wooden pillars since the 1790s. Strangely, an Act of Parliament that freed it from taxes has never been revoked. Toll charges are very low.

Whitney The windows of the Boat Inn jut out almost over the river.

④ At T-junction in Willersley, turn left on to A4111, then right on to A4112.

Kinnersley St James's church, with its massive tower and interesting interior, fronts the Elizabethan castle (not open to public).

Sarnesfield In the churchyard (on a left-hand bend) the tomb of Herefordshire's famous builder of black-and-white houses, John Abel, is engraved with the epitaph he wrote for himself. Weathering has made it hard to read, but there is a transcript inside the church.

☆ **Weobley** Perhaps the greatest concentration of half-timbered houses and inns in Herefordshire. A pocket borough until 1832, Weobley was famous for its ale and its witches, but is now an opulent backwater. In 1943 fire destroyed many buildings, providing surprisingly open views at the old borough's centre.

Weobley The church, with its tall, 14th-C steeple, contains a life-size statue in white marble to Col. John Birch, promoted from travelling trader to cavalry commander by Cromwell. (However, after the Civil War, Birch became a Royalist.)

Weobley There is a good choice of old pubs, including the Red Lion, the Royal Oak and The Throne (formerly The Unicorn), where Charles I stayed in 1645.

⑤ At the top of the central square, turn left at The Salutation and then sharp right on to minor road signposted to Wormsley.

☆ **Weobley–Brinsop** The road climbs out of the lush valley towards the tree-clad summits of a chain of hills overlooking the Wye. From the golf course there are splendid views to the left. Go over the crest of the Ravens' Causeway and turn right at junction, to Brinsop.

Brinsop The tiny church spans the centuries, from a Norman tympanum of St George and the dragon to modern stained glass in memory of the poet Wordsworth, whose family had connections hereabouts.

☆ **Mansell Lacy** Worth making the short detour along the minor road to the right, to see the village's spirited half-timbering, especially the former shop and post office which has a dovecot in the gable.

⑥ Follow lane back to A480. At crossroads go straight ahead to Bishopstone.

☆ **Bishopstone** A short detour to the left at the crossroads leads to Kenchester, where archaeologists are still finding remains of the Roman fortress-town known as Magnis. Return to crossroads.

✿ **Bridge Sollers** The Weir, a National Trust garden on the right just beyond the village, is particularly splendid in spring. There are magnificent views up-river. Open afternoons only: Sun–Fri, Apr to early May; Wed and Bank Holiday Mon, early May to Oct.

● Hereford landscape; distant Brecon Beacons.

The Malverns

● *The footpath running from end-to-end of the Malvern Hills makes an easy 9-mile (14.5-km) walk. It offers some spectacular views, and, in the right conditions, almost incredible sightings: for example, the Mendips (south) and the Wrekin (north).*

The sharp ridge of the Malvern Hills cuts up from the Severn plain, separating the flat brown soil of Worcestershire from the rolling red sandstone of Herefordshire. Rainwater which collects in the granite fissures and issues from the hillside is so pure that patients came from far and wide to take the 'cure'.

Today, the hills themselves are the main attraction, and this tour is designed to show their beauty and grandeur from all angles. Route One goes round them in a complete circle, while Route Two climbs up to within walking distance of the Worcestershire Beacon, the hills' highest point.

Route One: 50 miles (80 km)
In sequence from: Great Malvern
Direction of travel: anticlockwise

☆ **Great Malvern** Hillside town, famous for the purity of its spring water. Developed as a spa in Victorian times, it now makes its living from high technology, education (Malvern College public school lies to the south of the town), and special products such as the Morgan sports car. *Tourist information: tel. (068 45) 2700.*

⛪ **Great Malvern** Priory church, founded in 1085, still has its original Norman arches, although most of the structure is 15th-C Perpendicular. A beautiful building, like a small cathedral, it is softly lit by daylight filtered through rare and lovely medieval stained glass.

🏛 **Great Malvern** Abbey Gateway (in town centre), originally the gatehouse of the Benedictine Priory, is now the home of the Malvern Museum. Water-cure exhibits are most entertaining. *Open Mar–Oct.*

☆ **Great Malvern** The Festival Theatre (formerly the Assembly Rooms) opened in 1885. During the Malvern festivals of 1929–39 Shaw was playwright-in-residence.

☆ **Great Malvern** The handsome, listed railway station (1860) is worth a visit for its painted, cast-iron column capitals, each one a unique arrangement of leaves and fruit.

☆ **Leigh Sinton** This is a hops-and-fruit village. Stop at The Somers Arms for local ales and cider, or at Norbury's farm shop for apples.

⚘ **Storridge** On the way to this village astride the low pass through the foothills, look left for an impressive view of the northern end of the Malvern Hills.

🏠 **Storridge** A 1-mile (1.5-km) detour along a narrow lane to the right (signposted Birchwood) leads to Sir Edward Elgar's summer cottage, Birchwood Lodge, now a farmhouse. *No admittance*, but the cottage (on right) is visible from the lane.

⚘ **Stony Cross–Bosbury** B4220 goes through red-soiled farmlands and wire-railed hopyards. From the road there are glimpses of the western slopes of the Malverns.

☆ **Bosbury** Pretty village deep in hop country. Near the church, the remains of a 13th-C palace – once the country seat of the Bishops of Hereford – serve as a hop store.

⛪ **Bosbury** The mainly Norman church has a 15th-C screen with fine fan tracery and interesting tombs. The massive, unbuttressed, separate tower, was a fortified refuge during border raids by the marauding Welsh.

🍺 **Bosbury** The Bell Inn, a well-kept, timber-framed pub among timber-framed houses, serves good bar meals.

☆ **Ledbury** Old market town with many architectural styles along both sides of the wide main street. The Market House, *c.*1655, is a fine example of chevron timber-framing. John Masefield, Poet Laureate from 1930 to 1937, was born in Ledbury, at Knapp House.

⛪ **Ledbury** The parish church of St Michael and All Angels has a 13th-C detached tower surmounted by an 18th-C spire. The parents of Elizabeth Barrett Browning are buried here and she grew up at nearby Hope End.

☆ **Ledbury** Church Lane is a notable medieval street, often used as a film location – even the loos are listed. Along the narrow, cobbled roadway, the Old Grammar School (1480–1520) is now a heritage centre. Various buildings show the evolution of timber-frame construction.

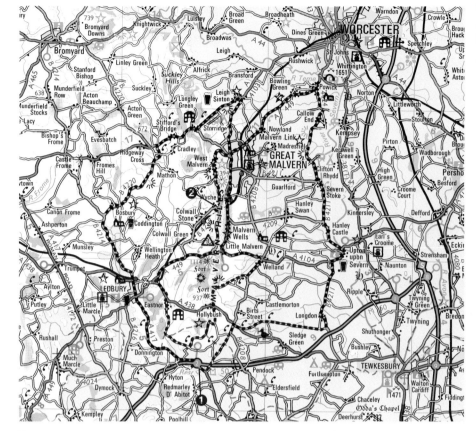

Route Two: 27 miles (43 km)
In sequence from: Great Malvern
Direction of travel: clockwise

☆ **Malvern Wells** As the original centre of the Malvern water cure, the village began to be developed as a resort during the 18thC. Elgar lived at 86 Wells Road.

☆ **Malvern Wells** *For the Holy Well take turning to right off A449 (Holy Well Rd.).* Water from this spring has been bottled for sale since 1622. The building around the fountain, where the public may drink, is in cottage *ornée* style, 1843. *Continue along minor road which rejoins A449.*

Little Malvern All that remains of the Benedictine priory established here in the 12thC, is the church and the guest hall, now part of Little Malvern Court. *House open May–Sept by appointment only, telephone (068 45) 4580.*

Little Malvern Sir Edward Elgar (1857–1934) is buried in the churchyard of St Wulstan's Roman Catholic church.

Castlemorton Common Fine mid-range view of the hills. *After crossing common on minor road which leads towards the hills, bear left along the foot of the hill. Cross A438, then take first turning to right.*

☆ **Whiteleaved Oak** (not on map) Pretty, isolated hamlet at the summit of this minor pass through the hills. *Continue for 2 miles (3 km), then turn right.*

Eastnor Early 19th-C crenellated castle containing paintings, tapestries, carved furniture and armour.

British Camp Also known as the Herefordshire Beacon, this superb example of an Iron Age hill fort has earthwork ramparts that are visible for miles. The path to the summit (1,114 feet/340 m) starts near the large car park alongside A449.

△ **Jubilee Drive** B4232, a lovely contour road along the western face of the hills, was constructed in 1887; fine views.

Worcestershire Beacon On a clear day the view from the summit (1,395 feet/425 m) extends across at least 12 counties. There are paths to the top from the various car parks along the B4232.

② *Return to Great Malvern either by the short route through Wyche Cutting or along the contour road through West Malvern and North Malvern.*

WORCESTER
A city that merits at least half a day to itself. Priority should be given to the cathedral, with its fine monuments, crypt and cloisters. Walk down the High St., past the eye-catching 18th-C Guildhall (which houses the tourist office) to the Royal Worcester Porcelain Works (Severn St.) for factory tours, showroom, seconds shop, and museum.

Ledbury The Feathers Hotel, a 16th-C coaching inn, is a quiet place for a drink or afternoon tea in oak-beamed ambiance.

① *Turn left along minor road signposted to 'The Malverns'. At junction with A438 turn right, following signs to the Waterfowl Sanctuary.*

Birtsmorton The Waterfowl Sanctuary has more than 800 birds belonging to around 80 species. *Open daily.*

☆ **Upton upon Severn** Former port, now a residential town and pleasure-boat haven. There are good riverside walks.

Upton upon Severn The heritage centre within the old lantern-topped church tower, known as the Pepperpot, has local history displays.

Upton upon Severn At The Anchor Inn (1601), Cavalier bridge-defenders sought boozy comfort at the expense of duty and allowed Cromwell's men to surprise them. Ale (called Jolly Roger) is still brewed round the back.

☆ **Upton upon Severn** Cromwells, across the road from the Pepperpot, sells luxury chocolates hand-made on the premises.

☆ **Upton-Powick** Five miles (8 km) from Upton, pause for a stroll across the undulating common land known as the Old Hills (on left of road). From here there are fine views of the whole Malvern range, with tree-tufted May Hill beyond.

∩ **Powick** The old bridge over the River Teme (alongside the modern bridge carrying the

● *The church at Little Malvern.*

A449) was the site of the first skirmish of the Civil Wars in 1642. The last battle of the wars (1651) was fought on the nearby river meadows.

Powick At the base of the tower of St Peter's church there are shot marks made by Cromwell's guns in 1651.

☆ **Powick–Great Malvern** While travelling along the A449 glance at the skies above the hills; sometimes the cloud effects are remarkable.

Shakespeare Country

S tratford-upon-Avon, where Shakespeare was born in 1564, is a honeypot that draws visitors from all over the world, but this ancient market town is only part of the story. The surrounding countryside that he knew so well and which is certain to have inspired him, is explored in this tour: the leafy lanes of England's heartland lead to unspoiled, half-timbered villages, stately homes set in spacious parkland and historic towns such as Warwick.

Other points of interest along the route include Edge Hill, site of the first major battle in the Civil War, which began less than thirty years after Shakespeare's death.

Route One: 42 miles (67 km)
Directions in sequence from:
Stratford-upon-Avon
Direction of travel: anticlockwise

☆ **Stratford-upon-Avon** In summer, this national shrine is overcrowded by mid-morning, so arrive as early as possible. The Bard dominates the scene of course, but newer attractions, from boat trips to brass rubbing, compete for attention.

In spite of all the tourists, Stratford has kept its dignity. The genuine Tudor buildings set the tone; the world-famous Royal Shakespeare Company performs in a rather plain theatre built in the 1930s, and even Marks & Spencer's has a classical facade. *Tourist information: tel. (0789) 293127.*

🏠 **Stratford** Pilgrims have flocked to picture-postcard Henley St. for three centuries to see the house where Shakespeare was born. *Open daily (but closed Sun morning in winter).*

🍷 **Stratford** The Black Swan, known to all as the Dirty Duck, is beside the river and the theatre. It offers an unfussy menu of typically English fare.

🏛 **Stratford** The World of Shakespeare (on Waterside) presents a colourful audio-visual pageant of English life in 1575. *Open daily.*

🏛 **Stratford** The Motor Museum in Shakespeare St. has elegant and exotic cars from the 1920s; some were built specially for Indian Maharajahs. *Open daily.*

🏠 **Charlecote** Superb parkland (where Shakespeare is said to have been caught poaching) surrounds a red brick Elizabethan house which has an enchanting gatehouse and some astonishing Victorian interior decoration. *For opening times, telephone (0789) 840277.*

☆ **Barford** Delightful village with tree-lined streets and an intriguing mixture of architectural styles.

Turn right on to B4462 for Warwick.

🏰 **Warwick** England's liveliest, if not finest, medieval castle, dominates the town. Madame Tussaud's have done it proud, opening the private apartments and populating them with waxen monarchs and nobles. Children usually prefer the dungeon and torture chamber. Allow plenty of time. *Open daily.*

🏠 **Warwick** Lord Leycester's Hospital, a well-preserved group of half-timbered buildings, has been a home for war veterans since 1571. Visitors see the Great Hall, dining hall and Guildhall (now a museum). *Open Mon–Sat.*

🏛 **Warwick** The Doll Museum in Castle St. has antique dolls and period toys from all

---

• *To complete Stratford's appeal is the chance of a river trip on the Avon, or the Stratford Canal.*

over the world. *Open daily, Mar–Oct; Sat, Sun only, Nov–Feb.*

☆ **Royal Leamington Spa** A short detour east leads to this youthful spa town which has smart Regency and Victorian terraces, flower beds galore and chic shops.

⛪ **Claverdon** Dedicated Royal Family followers come to see alabaster tomb of Thomas Spencer, ancestor of the Princess of Wales.

☆ **Henley-in-Arden** In the main street, a remarkable number of 15th–17thC oak-framed buildings have survived, including inns where Dr Johnson dined and a 15th-C Guildhall *(open to the public when the caretaker is at home).*

Do not miss Henley's renowned Tudor Dairy ice-cream.

⛪ **Wootton Wawen** St Peter's, the oldest church in Warwickshire, dates back to King Canute's time, with examples of Saxon, Norman, Early English, Decorated and Perpendicular styles.

🍴 **Wootton Wawen** The Bull's Head is a 14th-C coaching inn with oak beams and open fires. Extensive bar and restaurant menu.

① *Leave village on B4089. After about 1 mile (1.5 km) turn left across narrow bridge over River Alne, then turn right to Aston Cantlow.*

☆ **Aston Cantlow** Worth pausing in this attractive village to look inside the 13th-C
⛪ church where Shakespeare's parents were married. Do not be put off by the chicken-wire around the door; it is there to keep out birds not visitors.

🏭 **Great Alne** The working water mill is no longer open to visitors, but stone-ground flour is on sale Mon–Fri.

☆ **Alcester** In the middle of this friendly market town, Malt Mill Lane, with its overhanging upper storeys and brick cobbles, has recently been superbly renovated.

🏠 **Alcester** A 2-mile (3-km) detour north of the town leads to Coughton Court. The wives of several of the men involved in the Gunpowder Plot awaited the outcome in this Elizabethan house, which also has Jacobean associations and relics. One of the most touching exhibits is the chemise worn by Mary, Queen of Scots, at her execution. *Open afternoons, Wed–Sun and Bank Holiday Mon, May–Sept. For other times, telephone (0789) 762435.*

🏠 **Alcester** At Ragley Hall, the epitome of Palladian elegance, the present Marquess of Hertford has had the courage to commission a family portrait in the form of a vast mural. The house, 2 miles (3 km) south-west of the town, *is open afternoons only, Tues–Thurs, Sat, Sun and Bank Holiday Mon, Apr–Sept.*

🍴 **Wixford** The Fish Inn, which boasts that 'Shakespeare probably drank here', is a

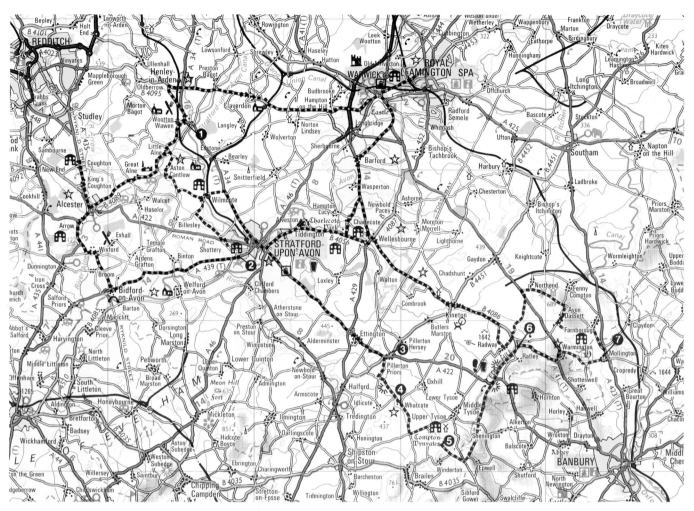

popular riverside pub. The menu includes several fish dishes and authentic West African curry.

☆ **Bidford-on-Avon** The Falcon Inn, where Shakespeare ended a pub crawl, is now an antique shop. Note also the 15th-C bridge and the wood carvings in St Laurence's church.

② *About 1 mile (1.5 km) from Stratford, turn left along road signposted to Shottery.*

🏠 **Shottery** Anne Hathaway's Cottage is virtually unchanged since young Will wooed his wife here. Worth waiting in the queue in high season. *Open daily (but closed Sun morning in winter). Follow signposts to Wilmcote.*

🏠 **Wilmcote** The home of Mary Arden, Shakespeare's mother, gives insight into the life of a wealthy Tudor farmer and his family. *Open daily (but closed Sun morning in winter). Continue on minor road to Pathlow, then take A34 back to Stratford.*

Route Two: 40 miles (64 km)
Directions in sequence from:
Stratford-upon-Avon
Direction of travel: anticlockwise

③ *Soon after entering Pillerton Priors turn right along B4451 (signposted to Halford),* then almost immediately turn left down single track lane.

☆ **Pillerton Priors–Whatcote** A high road with splendid views on all sides.

☆ **Whatcote** A lonely Saxon village.

④ *Turn right opposite the Royal Oak pub on to narrow road, signposted to Brailes. At crossroads turn left towards Tysoe, then at 'Give Way' sign, turn right (hairpin bend).*

🏠 **Compton Wynyates** Sadly, this Tudor manor house is no longer open.

⑤ *Follow signs for Epwell, then Edge Hill. (The road follows an ancient ridgeway with sweeping views.) At junction with A422, turn right, then left to Edge Hill.*

❗ **Edge Hill** There are walks through the beechwoods overlooking Radway village and the site of the first major battle of the Civil War in 1642. View to Welsh border.

🍺 **Edge Hill** The Castle Inn with its eerie, mock-Gothic tower, offers Hook Norton real ale and a grand view.

🏠 **Edge Hill** Upton House, 1 mile (1.5 km) south-west on A422, is a 17th-C National Trust property.

⑥ *For Warmington, turn right on to B4086, left on to A41, then right again.*

☆ **Warmington** A dream village, complete with village green, a pond and cottages in local Hornton stone. Victims of the Battle of Edge Hill are buried in the churchyard.

⑦ *Beyond Mollington, turn left on to A423 Coventry road, then take the second turning on left to Farnborough.*

🏠 **Farnborough Hall** Although the Hall is famous for its terrace walk – a splendidly successful example of 18th-C landscape gardening, now threatened by a motorway – the house has fine Rococo plasterwork, well worth examining in detail. *Open afternoons only, Wed, Sat and Bank Holiday Mon, Apr–Sept.*

Radway The battleground village that may have inspired novelist Henry Fielding, who wrote *Tom Jones* while staying at Radway Grange.

Kineton At the Kineton Gallery, a popular craft centre, attractions include a collection of spinning wheels from all over the world.

☆ **Kineton–Wellesbourne** A once-famous, now slightly sullied drive through Compton Verney Park and over the Foss Way.

☆ **Wellesbourne** A combination of 18th-C brick, timbered and thatched cottages, becoming rather urbanized now. *Take care through the traffic scheme and look out for a sudden right turn to Stratford.*

Cambridge, Ely and the Fens

Starting in Cambridge, with its feast of architectural treasures, Route One moves out across the flat landscape of the fens. After the richness of the city this is plain fare, but it is as refreshing as a green salad: dykes, ditches and windmills give the area a distinctive character and there are frequent opportunities to see its abundant waterfowl. Then, with perfect timing, Ely cathedral comes into view. The exterior is one of the sights of East Anglia and the interior is a masterpiece of medieval design.

Route Two visits some of the well-known villages on the other side of Cambridge, including Grantchester.

Route One: 42 miles (67 km)
in sequence from: Cambridge
Direction of travel: anticlockwise

① *Leave Cambridge on A1303.*

🏠 **Anglesey Abbey** Mainly Tudor hall incorporating 13th-C crypt of the old Augustinian abbey. The 18th-C-style gardens, laid out between 1926 and 1966, are highly imaginative; do not miss the Emperor's Walk, a long avenue lined with statues. *House and garden open afternoons only, Wed–Sun, mid-Apr to mid-Oct. Garden also open Mon and Tues afternoons, mid-Apr to early Oct.*

☆ **Lode** The B1102 follows a line of 'shore' or 'coastal' villages built on the firm chalk shores of the fens, each with its own 'lode' (or satellite port-village) set at the head of an artificial cut from the River Cam. This village, actually called Lode, is worth a quick detour for its houses of thatch and Cambridge white brick.

⛪ **Swaffham Prior** Two fine churches share a single churchyard. St Mary's has an octagonal tower; the church of St Cyriac is derelict but interesting.

🪟 **Swaffham Prior** Note the windmill to the left of B1102.

✦ **Devil's Ditch** This ancient earthwork, which crosses the road directly beneath a row of pylons, was probably dug in early Saxon times, to protect local inhabitants against attack from the south-west.

● *Ely Cathedral, with its Octagon and soaring west tower, seems to dwarf the modest fenland market town which lies huddled at its feet.*

Linear dykes or ditches are a characteristic feature of fen landscape, spanning open terrain between natural barriers such as woodland, marsh or river.

☆ **Reach** The main port for Cambridge in medieval times. Driving through the fens, notice the dark, fibrous peat which forms the basis for the area's vegetation.

☆ **Upware** The 'Upware Republic', a group of Cambridge undergraduates including Samuel Butler, used to meet here in the 1850s in a pub that has since burned down.
✗ For riverside picnic site, turn left at telephone box into cul-de-sac.

✦ **Wicken Fen** The oldest nature reserve in Britain (owned by the National Trust), and one of the few areas of the Great Fens of East Anglia to remain undrained. It comprises a series of different fenland habitats – ranging from open water, through sedge fields, fen carr or scrub, to fen woodland as the water table falls – each with its own flora and fauna. Look out for the only surviving example of the typical fenland windpump. Poorly signposted from A1123.

🪟 **Downfield** The windmill is conspicuous from the A1123.

♨ **Isleham** A 7-mile (11-km) detour leads to a barn-like Norman chapel, once part of a Benedictine priory.

☆ **Soham–Stuntney** The A142 follows a causeway built over the flooded fenlands by Hervey, first Bishop of Ely. Fine views of Ely cathedral ahead.

☆ **Ely** Until the 17thC, when the fens were drained, Ely was an island. Pilgrims made their way to the great cathedral across the causeways or in boats, their oars disturbing the eels which gave the city its name.

Today, several roads converge here, but it has remained a quiet place. Historic buildings near the cathedral include the Bishop's Palace and the Ely Porta, the gateway to the old abbey (now part of the King's School). *Tourist information: tel. (0353) 3311.*

✝ **Ely** The cathedral is one of England's most splendid medieval churches. On entering, the initial impact of the view down the uninterrupted Norman nave is breathtaking in its simplicity, but the cathedral's special glory is its 14th-C Octagon, a unique, eight-sided tower and lantern.

Children will be kept happily occupied walking the maze under the west tower; the path is the same length as the height of the tower.

🦆 **Welney** A 10-mile (16-km) detour north from Ely will reward wildfowl enthusiasts. Eight hundred acres of the Ouse Washes comprise one of the most important nature reserves in Europe, where a wide variety of birds, including widgeon and godwits, can be viewed from hides or from an observatory. *Open Aug–May. To reach Welney, leave Ely on the B1411 via Pymore, soon joining the A1101, which crosses the Old Bedford River just before Welney.*

▣ **Stretham** To the south-east of the village the Stretham Engine, built in 1831 to pump water out of the fens into the higher river, is preserved intact as a miniature museum. Visitors see the boilerhouse, engine house and scoop wheel. Situated at the riverside,
✗ this is an attractive place for a picnic. *Open daily.*

⚕ **Denny Abbey** The refectory and ruined chapel are all that remain of the abbey, founded in the 12thC. *Open Apr–Sept.*

☆ **Landbeach** Modern Marina Park with boating lake, heated swimming pool and bird-watching area. Other amenities include a camping site, café, shops and bars. *Open in summer.*

Route Two: 44 miles (70.5 km)
in sequence from: Cambridge
Direction of travel: anticlockwise

② *Leave Cambridge along Queen's Rd., then turn left on to A1303.*

🏠 **Madingley** The large Tudor mansion set in a great park belongs to the University. No admittance to the house, but the grounds are open to the public.

⛪ **Bourn** The tiled maze on the floor beneath the church tower is much older than the maze at Ely. (Church mazes were fairly common in Europe, but rare in England.) *Church key obtainable from the vicarage or*

Post Office. Nearby, the Elizabethan manor house is now a private clinic.

Caxton The windmill to the right of the road leading into the village is the oldest in the country; car park signposted on right.

Wimpole Hall The 18th-C mansion is surrounded by a landscaped park of national importance (Capability Brown and Repton worked here).
The Home Farm has rare breeds of livestock.
Park open all year. House and garden open afternoons only, Apr–Oct, closed Fri. Home Farm open daily (except Fri) late Apr to Sept; early Apr and Oct, Sat, Sun and Easter Mon only.

Grantchester Celebrated in poetry by Byron, Tennyson and Rupert Brooke, this popular riverside village retains its charm and its Orchard tea gardens.

Trumpington Worth looking inside the church to see England's second oldest brass, depicting Sir Roger de Trumpington who died in 1289.

Duxford The Imperial War Museum at Duxford Airfield (off A505, just west of M11) has an impressive display of military and civil aircraft, including the Concorde prototype, artillery, missiles and a midget submarine. *Open mid-Mar to early Nov.*

Pampisford The church has Norman carvings over the door. Close by there is an attractive row of thatched cottages with old water pumps.

Linton A 5-mile (8-km) detour leads to Linton Zoo and gardens (on right of B1052). This wildlife breeding centre has an interesting assortment of animals, including bears, leopards and binturongs (bear cats from south-east Asia). *Open daily.*

Wandlebury Prehistoric monuments are scarce in Cambridgeshire, but the outer bank of an Iron Age hill fort can be seen here (the inner bank was destroyed by 18th-C landscaping). The surrounding footpaths are much used at weekends by Cambridge families exercising their dogs.

CAMBRIDGE
A car is an encumbrance in this ancient city of winding streets, so aim to park it as soon as possible. Queen's Rd., parallel to the river to the west of the city, has free parking but spaces are snapped up early. The multi-storey car park in Gonville Pl. is the next choice; if full, try the car parks in Park St. or Lion Yard. Failing that, go to the tourist office in Wheeler St. (behind the Guildhall) and ask advice.

Forgetting the parking problem, it is almost as though the medieval founders of the university planned the city's layout with tourism in mind: most of the important buildings lie in a convenient line along King's Parade, Trinity and St John's.

Days could be spent here absorbing the atmosphere of each historic college, wandering through old courts and flower-filled college gardens, browsing in book shops and museums, or drifting along the River Cam in a punt. But for those in a hurry, priority should be given to (from south to north) Queens' College (15th-C Cloister Court and Hall decorated by William Morris); King's College Chapel (outstanding fan-vaulting and Tudor ornamentation); Trinity College (go through the grand gateway to the Great Court); and St John's (three courts leading to Bridge of Sighs). If time permits, return south along The Backs to the Fitzwilliam Museum.

Tourist information: tel. (0223) 358977.

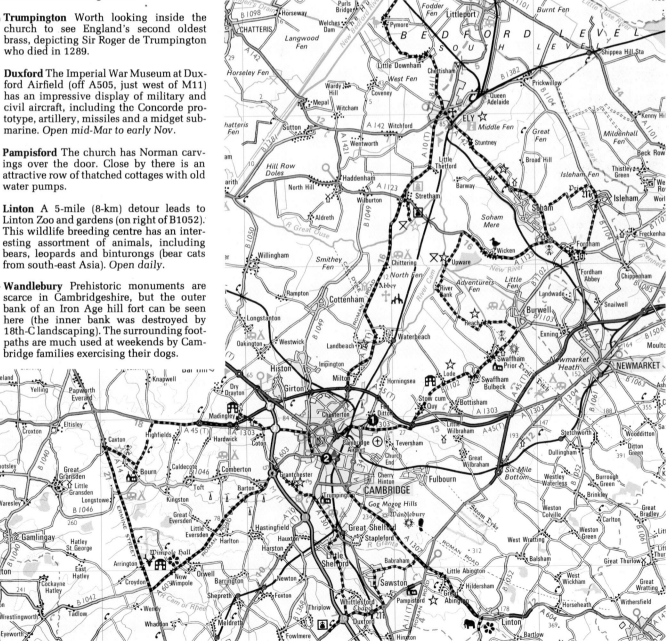

Constable Country

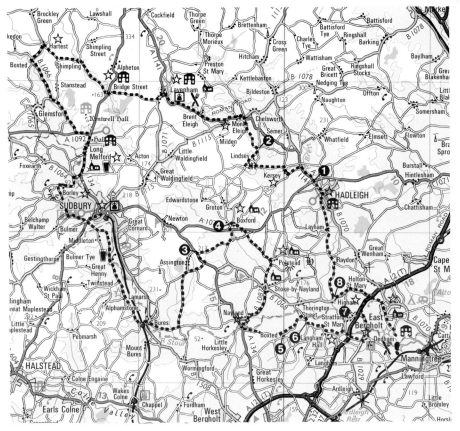

The Vale of Dedham, immortalized by the artist John Constable (1776–1837), epitomizes the ideal English landscape in many people's minds. Ironically, modern farming methods have altered the look of East Anglia, but the Vale is still lovely, and many of the places Constable painted can still be recognized.

Elsewhere on this tour, the upland landscape of central Suffolk can sometimes seem like one vast wheatfield with occasional interruptions. However, these 'interruptions' include Kersey, Long Melford and Lavenham: outstanding survivals from the Middle Ages.

Route: 73 miles (117 km)
In sequence from: Hadleigh
Direction of travel: anticlockwise

☆ **Hadleigh** Delightful old market town, notable for its long High Street of low, leaning buildings. Church St. (just off High St.) has 15th-C town hall (formerly the Cloth Hall), 14th C church and the remains of a deanery in close proximity.

① *At deflected junction on the new Hadleigh bypass take the Lavenham road (A1141). Pass mill on right, then take left turning to Kersey (unsignposted).*

☆ **Kersey** Walk down the steep village street to the watersplash early in the morning, and it may seem that the medieval occupants of the old houses have yet to rise and throw open their casements. Recent renovation has given some of the houses a 'film set' quality, but the village is justifiably famous.

② *Turn left and left again for Monks Eleigh.*

☆ **Monks Eleigh** A triangular, cottage-lined green rises, exactly as it should do, to the church. If the scene seems familiar, this is because it was once used on railway posters, although the railway (*now closed*) never came nearer than Lavenham.

☆ **Lavenham** Arguably the most perfect and unforgettable township of timber-framed buildings left in England.

🏠 **Lavenham** The Guildhall, dominating the market place, dates from 1529. Today it houses a museum which includes a useful exhibition on the medieval cloth trade. *Open daily late Apr to early Nov; weekends only in early Apr and late Nov.*

⛪ **Lavenham** The church (15th–16thC) is magnificent from the outside, with a massive, unfinished tower. Inside, the proportions are not quite as good as at the remarkable churches of Long Melford or Stoke-by-Nayland (see below).

✗ **Lavenham** The Old Tea Shop, opposite the church, does a traditional English tea with home-made cakes. Rather more sophisti-

cated cake-making may be enjoyed at the Bank House Tea Shop, 95 High St.

☆ **Bridge Street** Before reaching the main
🏠 road note the splendid moated Hall to the left. *Go over A134, turning right then immediately left, then right to Shimpling.*

☆ **Hartest** In East Anglian terms, the road leading down into this pretty village is positively Alpine. Hartest has grown up around a large green; church and pub stand together at the southern end.

☆ **Long Melford** The High Street running southwards from the splendid green, is broad and very long indeed. To park, turn left at The Black Lion pub.

⛪ **Long Melford** The fine Perpendicular church has the spaciousness and height of a small cathedral, and the Lady Chapel, with its separate entrance, is an unusual and lovely additional feature.

🏠 **Long Melford** Melford Hall is a mellow, mid-16thC red-brick house with distinctive pepper-pot turrets, massive yews in the garden and an octagonal gazebo. *Open afternoons only, Wed, Thurs, Sun and Bank Holiday Mon, Apr–Sept.*

🏠 **Long Melford** More romantic than its neighbour, moated Kentwell Hall (*c.*1564) is approached along a glorious avenue of lime trees. It is gradually being restored to something of its former splendour. *Open afternoons only, Wed, Thurs and Sun, early Apr to late June; Wed–Sun, late July to Sept. Also open Bank Holidays.*

🍺 **Long Melford** The Crown Inn serves Adnams excellent Southwold bitter.

☆ **Borley** Notorious Borley Rectory, 'the most haunted house in England', was built in 1863 and destroyed by fire in 1939. Both the builder and his son died in the Blue Room; messages appeared on walls, disembodied voices were heard, bells were rung and, since the fire, a ghostly nun is said to have appeared on the site and in the churchyard. All in all, an ideal place for a picnic.

Beyond Borley, sweeping, sky-filled views of East Anglia at its best can be seen from the road.

☆ **Sudbury** A short detour leads to this old silk-weaving town, with its three churches (St Peter's is the best) and splendid Corn Exchange (1841) in the south-eastern corner of the market-place.

The house where Thomas Gainsborough was born (46 Gainsborough St.) is now,
🖼 appropriately, an art gallery. *Open Tues–Sat; Sun and Bank Holiday Mon, afternoons only.*

🍺 **Henny Street** Tiny village (not on map) with an unpretentious little pub, The Mill, right next to the river.

③ *Look out for the first unsignposted, single track road to the right off A134.*

☆ **Boxford** A village of great charm. Most of the old timber-framed houses are still plastered over in the traditional Suffolk manner. The River Box, which gives the village its name, runs through the centre.

● *Watermill on the Essex–Suffolk border: mills like this provided the important service of fulling to cloth towns such as Dedham: newly woven material was soaked in water, then beaten to give it density and strength.*

🏠 **Boxford** St Mary's church has an imposing, crumbling, 15th-C stone porch on the south side, and a rare 14th-C wooden north porch. The decorated, lead-capped spirelet on the tower is unusual, and the interior of the church is elegant, airy and plain.

④ *Return to the main road. Turn left, then take first turning to the right, signposted to Polstead.*

☆ **Polstead** From the duck pond, a pretty, steep little street of thatched and tiled cottages rises to a triangular green.

🏠 **Polstead** St Mary's church has Norman nave arcades built of brick which give the interior of the church an individual appearance. From the churchyard there is a good

🌼 view of Stoke-by-Nayland's magnificent church tower.

📖 In 1827, the notorious murder of Maria Marten took place in a red barn (long since demolished) not far from St Mary's.

🏠 **Stoke-by-Nayland** The church is one of the most memorable and ethereally lovely Perpendicular churches in East Anglia. Constable often painted it – not surprisingly, since its tall tower of faded pink brick is strikingly prominent from the valley floor.

Inside, the clerestory seems to float on piers of light golden stone and the tall, narrow tower arch suggests an entry to Heaven better than many a sermon. Note also the beautifully carved oak doors in the porch.

☆ **Nayland** *At the 'Give Way' sign turn left to enter the square.* This is another highly individual little cloth-making township of plastered and openly half-timbered houses,

some with oversailing upper storeys. Walk up Fen St. for a delightful juxtaposition of cottages and stream, with a plank foot-bridge to each front door. The church has a (not very good) painting of Christ by Constable.

⑤ *Ignore the sign to Boxted School and take the next turning on the left signposted to Higham. After 2 miles (3 km) take turning right (before bridge), signposted Boxted Cross, then follow signs for Langham.*

⑥ *Immediately after a white building (water works) turn left along a black-surfaced, unsignposted road. Turn right at T-junction after ¼ mile (0.5 km), then at next junction, fork left. At second T-junction turn right.*

☆ **Langham** A private drive which is also a public footpath leads to the church and Church Farm, the subjects of Constable's painting *The Glebe Farm*. Walk past the farm and look back to see it from the artist's viewpoint.

☆ **Dedham** The near-perfect centre has changed only superficially since Constable's time, and possesses another grand (if rather austere) Perpendicular church, whose tower is a feature of many of the artist's paintings. In *The Cornfield* he moved it about ¾ mile (1 km) to the east and reduced it in size in order to improve his composition.

The Vale of Dedham was referred to as 'Constable Country' not only within his lifetime, but within his hearing, as he was travelling by coach to London.

Tourist information: tel. (0206) 323447.

✗ **Dedham** The Marlborough Head inn, in the

village centre, serves first-rate bar food.

❗ **Dedham** Flatford Mill can be reached by car (see below) or on foot (½-hour walk) across the water meadows – the very stuff of Constable's landscapes. The footpath begins at the eastern end of the village street: go along the drive to Dedham Hall and turn right before the first buildings.

⑦ *Turn left at the church (note its bold flint and stone exterior) to join the A12 (follow Ipswich signposts). After about ¾ mile (1 km) turn right.*

☆ **East Bergholt** This is the village where Constable was born and lived. Of the surrounding countryside he said: 'These scenes made me a painter.'

🏠 The church has a tower that was never completed and its bells hang upside down in a timber frame in the churchyard.

🏛 **Flatford Mill** *Follow the one-way system to the car park. From here there is a short walk to the waterside.* Willy Lott's cottage is much as it appears in *The Haywain*, but beyond it the fields have been transformed into a gigantic gravel quarry. The mill is now a field centre, and is not open to the public.

For a pleasant saunter along the old tow path, cross the footbridge next to the shop and tea room.

⑧ *At Higham take unsignposted turning to right before reaching centre of village. (As the road goes down the hill, note the delightful, tiny oval cottage on the left.) After about 2 miles (3 km) take turning left signposted to Shelley, then follow signposts back to Hadleigh.*

The Suffolk Coast

● *The beautifully preserved post mill at Saxtead Green. A post mill is one which pivots around a central post so that the sails can catch the wind no matter which direction it blows.*

Flat but not dull, sometimes pleasantly melancholy, eastern Suffolk rarely sets out to charm, but usually ends up captivating the visitor. Between Ipswich and Lowestoft, major and minor rivers wind their unpredictable way towards the sea, passing through marshlands and estuaries haunted only by birds and by those who pursue them with binoculars. The coast, with its long, lonely beaches, is undisturbed by modern seaside razzmatazz; even on sunny days the wind blows, making mind-clearing walks seem a better idea than bathing.

Route: 90 miles (144 km)
in sequence from: Aldeburgh
Direction of travel: clockwise

☆ **Aldeburgh** The town, situated between
🛥 estuary and marsh, way out on the east coast, seems a little cut off from the rest of the country, but this is part of its appeal. The High Street boasts a comfortable little cinema which shows an interesting selection of films, and a fish and chip shop justly famed for the freshness of its fish (straight off the boats) and for its smoked salmon. The sea front with its quaint look-out towers is quickly reached through any of the alleyways between the shops and houses. *Tourist information: tel. (072 885) 3637.*

🏛 **Aldeburgh** The Tudor Moot Hall, near the beach, is indicative of the town's importance in earlier times. The chimneys were added in the 19thC.

☆ **Snape** *Go over the bridge and turn left.* The former Maltings, now converted into a con-

cert hall, is the main venue for the annual Aldeburgh Festival, started by Benjamin
📷 Britten in 1948. Boat trips and craft shops
🛍 are other attractions here.

✗ **Snape** A short distance along the Iken road
❗ look out for signposted entrance to a picnic site. From here footpaths lead along the broad, reed-filled Alde Estuary, with the tower of the ruined church at Iken standing romantically across the water.

☆ **Orford** Once a flourishing port, Orford is now cut off from the sea by a shingle spit. The upper end of the village feels distinctly 'inland', so it comes as a surprise to see sailing boats moored at the bottom of the main street.

𝕞 **Orford** Standing in massive silhouette at the upper end of the village, the castle keep dates from 1165. *Open Mon–Sat and Sun afternoon.*

✗ **Orford** The Butley Orford Oysterage is a small, simply furnished restaurant highly recommended for its fish dishes.

☆ **Hollesley** A 2-mile (3-km) detour leads to Shingle Street where Martello towers stand guard against Napoleon's return.

☆ **Shottisham** An attractive, unpretentious village, centred round the pub.

☆ **Woodbridge** A well-kept town with several interesting buildings including an old tide
🏛 mill (by the estuary) and an Elizabethan Shire Hall in the centre. Good book shops in the main, traffic-free shopping street.

🍺 **Woodbridge** Ye Olde Bell and Steelyard, New St., serves locally brewed Adnams beer. Note the 'steelyard' apparatus next door, once used for weighing cartloads.

① *Leave town on B1483. Go over traffic lights, then take second turning to the right, signposted to Lower Ufford.*

☆ **Ufford** *At the post office, turn left and then follow the road to the right. At the end of*
🏰 *the cul-de-sac on right,* the Church of the Assumption has possibly the tallest font cover in Britain, 18 feet (5.5 m) high and superbly ornamented.

② *At T-junction beside pylon turn left across A12 and then turn right immediately.*

③ *At Wickham Market turn right to enter the market square. Continue on B1483, then turn left along B1078. After a short distance fork right and go over the stream.*

☆ **Wickham Market–Easton** The road follows the valley of the River Deben, which inspired Britten to write his Spring Symphony.

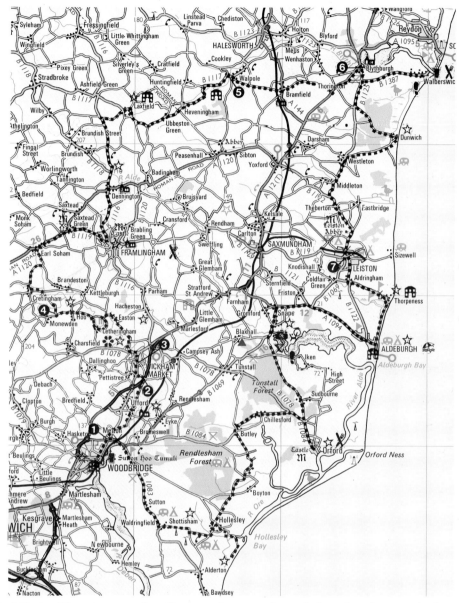

☆ **Dennington** Immediately north of the village, where the farmers have retained some hedges and pastures and a good number of mature hedgerow oaks, it is possible to see what Suffolk looked like before the onslaught of the 'barley barons'. Compare this with the empty expanses which begin 1 mile (1.5 km) further north.

☆ **Laxfield** This remote and pretty village with its fine church tower, has a half-timbered guildhall – a sign of its past importance.

🏛 **Heveningham Hall** The best Palladian building in Suffolk is closed for restoration (re-opening 1986), but can be glimpsed from the B1117.

⑤ *At Walpole, go over the bridge, turn right and then immediately left for Bramfield.*

🏚 **Bramfield** The thatched church has an unusual, round, detached bell-tower, a beautiful rood screen and a fine but chilling 17th-C tomb.

🏚 **Blythburgh** For many, Holy Trinity church will be the high point of the tour. In this weathered, faded great building it is easier to project oneself into the realities of the Middle Ages than in any other East Anglian church. Perhaps it is the combined effect of light and spaciousness, or the roof bearing an array of stiff-winged angels, or the heaving floor of pale pink brick, or the situation above the marshy estuary of the Blyth. Whatever the reason, the atmosphere is memorable.

⑥ *Continue along the lane past the church, and cross the A12 on to the B1125. For 2-mile (3-km) detour to Walberswick, turn left on to B1387.*

☆ **Walberswick** The ruined church, the ancient bar at The Bell Hotel, Mary's restaurant (scrumptious sea food dishes) and two walks highly recommended for bird-watching, all make a trip here worthwhile. One walk runs along the shore from the end of B1387. The other goes across Westwood Marshes to a ruined windmill: return along B1387, then fork left along 'By-road'. Car park on right has a board showing routes.

☆ **Dunwich** Whereas Orford was cut off from the sea, Dunwich – once the capital of East Anglia – was swallowed by it. From 1326, when a violent storm demolished three of the town's nine churches, Dunwich was gradually washed away and is now a rather desolate village.

𝔪 **Leiston Abbey** A signposted track off B1125 leads to the largest set of monastic ruins in Suffolk. *Open daily.*

⑦ *Take the Aldeburgh road through the town, then turn left along B1353 to Thorpeness.*

☆ **Thorpeness** In the years preceding World War II, eccentric entrepreneur Stuart Ogilvie planned Thorpeness as a self-catering holiday village for those who wanted 'to experience life as it was lived when England was Merrie England'. With its neo-Tudor buildings and fantastical House in the Clouds (a disguised water-tower) the place is so weird that it has to be explored.

☆ **Easton** There are several well-preserved houses here, and a pub which is almost too picturesque to be true. On leaving the village note on right the longest 'crinkle-crankle' or ribbon wall in the world.

❀ **Letheringham** The gardens adjoining weather-boarded Letheringham Mill are worth a visit. *Open afternoons only; Sun, Apr–Sept; Wed and Bank Holiday Mon, June–Sept.*

④ *Turn right from Cretingham (not signposted). After 1 mile (0.8 km) turn left at junction.*

☆ **Cretingham** The rather suburban, eastern approach may give the impression that all is lost here, but stop on the bridge and look back for a picture-postcard view of the church and old cottages.

𝔪 **Saxtead** The post mill, in excellent state of repair, stands on the edge of a large green. *Open Mon–Sat, Apr–Sept.*

☆ **Framlingham** A delightful small town with a three-sided market-place on a slope beneath the church.

🏚 **Framlingham** The church of St Michael is a Perpendicular building, distinguished by its unusually spacious chancel which contains four magnificent 16th-C tombs. One is dedicated to Henry Fitzroy, bastard son of Henry VIII. The tomb of the Duke of Norfolk, to the right of the altar, is among the finest of its type surviving in Europe, with all figures still intact.

𝔪 **Framlingham** The 12th–13thC castle is the most splendid fortified ruin in Suffolk. The chimneys reflect the Tudor inhabitants' desire for a touch of comfort. *Open daily (but closed on Sun morning in winter).*

✗ **Framlingham** The Crown and Anchor, Church St., serves good pub lunches or more elaborate evening meals.

🏚 **Dennington** Among many treasures to be found inside the church are a set of wonderfully carved benches, two parclose screens and an alabastar tomb, all 15th-C.

The Shropshire Highlands

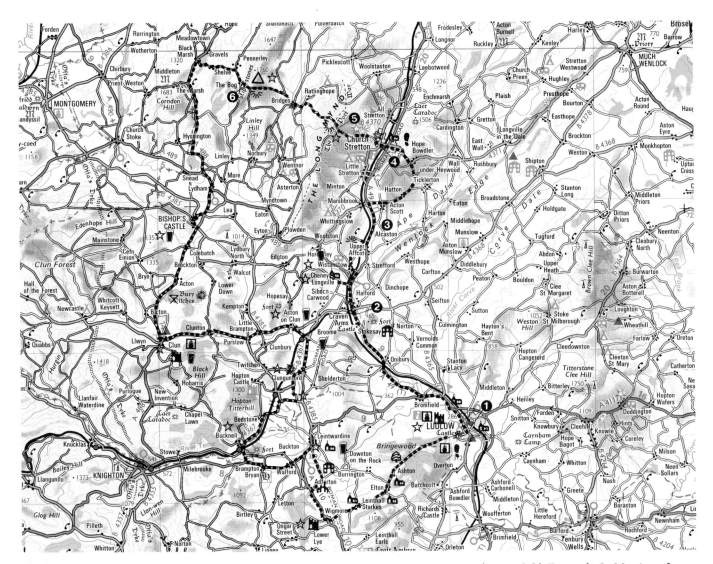

South-west Shropshire is a sparsely populated haven dominated by high hills and moorland ridges, but also includes gentle valleys, dreaming villages and many castles built by Marcher lords to hold back the Welsh.

Although it is one of the highlights of the tour, the road across the Long Mynd should not be attempted in poor weather, and an alternative route has been suggested. Conversely, those who have time to spare on a clear day should drive a few miles east from Ludlow along the A4117 for stupendous views into Wales.

Route: 75 miles (121 km)
Directions in sequence from: Ludlow
Direction of travel: anticlockwise

☆ **Ludlow** Eight centuries of building styles line narrow medieval streets within the town walls. The centre is a jackdaw's nest of hidden treasures well explained in local guidebooks. Plenty of small shops and locally produced food ranging from crusty bread and cakes to venison, pheasant and other game, which are sometimes on the menus of the town's many restaurants and pubs. *Tourist information: tel. (0584) 3857.*

🏰 **Ludlow** The Norman castle, where Prince Arthur – Henry VIII's elder brother – died on honeymoon with Catherine of Aragon, became an Elizabethan palace known as 'the Windsor of the West'. *Open daily in summer.*

Instruments of torture found in the castle are on show in Ludlow museum, in the Butter Cross. *Open Easter to Sept.*

🏛 **Ludlow** St Lawrence's, the largest parish church in Shropshire, has a tall tower (136 feet/41 m), superb stained glass, masterly woodcarving and painted Tudor tombs.

① *Follow Shrewsbury signposts along one-way traffic system. One mile (1.5 m) north of the town join A49 and continue to Bromfield.*

🏛 **Bromfield** To reach St Mary's, a former Benedictine priory, turn on to A4113 for a few yards, then turn left again. Park by half-timbered priory gatehouse. Inside the church there is a naïve folk-art chancel ceiling of angels and clouds. *Return to A49.*

🏰 **Stokesay Castle** A fortified manor-house built by a wealthy Ludlow wool merchant in the 13thC, Stokesay is possibly the best-preserved example of its kind in England. In Tudor times the half-timbered gatehouse was added. *Open Mar–Nov (closed Tues, Mar–Oct; Mon and Tues in Nov).*

② *Go through Craven Arms then take second turning on left for detour to Cheney Longville.*

☆ **Cheney Longville** The village was recently made a conservation area because of its medieval street layout. *Return to A49. Turn left and then right almost immediately under a railway bridge.*

☆ **Wistanstow** This Saxon village on the old Roman road has a comfortable inn, The Plough, which has its own brewery. A short distance further on, Holy Trinity church dates partly from the 12thC. *Continue along the straight road that later turns abruptly back to join the A49.*

● *Stokesay Castle, fortified manor house, one of the earliest of its kind in Britain.*

Wistanstow–Acton Scott The view straight ahead is dominated by the southern end of heavily wooded Wenlock Edge. The stone tower topping it is Flounders' Folly, built in the 19thC to mark the boundaries of four estates. *At junction with A49 turn left. After about 1 mile (1.5 km) turn right at signpost to Acton Scott.*

③ *Continue through Acton Scott. After about 1 mile (1.5 km)· take first turning to left (unsignposted). At T-junction turn left to Hope Bowdler and Church Stretton.*

☆ **Church Stretton** This small spa town, built by the Victorians on the site of a much older settlement, has a Norman church, sparkling air, pure water and plenty of opportunities for hill walking. Cardingmill Valley (clearly signposted from crossroads at town centre) is a National Trust property and one of the best places for walks.

④ *At central crossroads take Burway road (1:5 gradient and cattle grid) to the steep uplands of the Long Mynd. If weather is doubtful, ignore this part of the tour and head south through Little Stretton; turn right at A49 and again at A489 and drive up the Onny valley (wonderful view of the Long Mynd to the right) to **Bishop's Castle** (see below).*

☆ **The Long Mynd** Vast National Trust-owned, ancient plateau (1,695 feet/517 m) where grouse whirr and sheep roam free through heather and whinberry bushes. The single-track road has plenty of passing places. Pause at car park on left for magnificent views.

⑤ *Where road divides, fork right to Ratlinghope. Descend to valley and fork right to Bridges. Just beyond the Horseshoes pub turn right then left (an obviously more important road), then almost immediately turn sharp right (signposted to Squilver) over cattle grid.*

☆ **Stiperstones** Third highest hill in Shropshire (1,732 feet/528 m), with its craggy crest resembling the back of a prehistoric monster. The road goes across desolate moorland with enormous views. From the car park on right a path leads to the Devil's Chair, where Old Nick is supposed to sit exulting during thunderstorms.

⑥ *Beyond the summit, take right turning signposted to Shelve. Go past Stiperstones Field Centre, then turn right on to straight road signposted to Gravels and Minsterley. After ½ mile (0.8 km) turn left to Shelve. At T-junction turn left on to A488.*

☆ **Bishop's Castle** All that remains of the Norman castle (built by a Bishop of Hereford) are some stones in the car park of the Castle Hotel. Next to the Town Hall, the half-timbered 16th-C House on Crutches has a projecting upper storey supported on two stout wooden posts.

Bishop's Castle The Three Tuns has been brewing its own beer for centuries.

Bury Ditches From the car park and picnic area to the left of the road, paths lead up the hill to the enormous Iron Age fort.

☆ **Clun** Go downhill (past lane leading to the ruined 12th-C castle) into the tiny square where the museum contains an outstanding collection of flint tools and weapons. *Open afternoons only, Tues, Sat and Bank Holidays, Easter to Oct.*

Clun Sir Walter Scott stayed at The Buffalo inn while writing *The Betrothed*. The Sun serves real ale and bar meals.

☆ **Aston on Clun** On the left, the tall tree decked with flags (or their remains) is the Arbor Tree, decorated every 29 May since 1786 to celebrate the wedding of the local squire.

The Kangaroo Inn was named soon after Captain Cook discovered Australia. Note the unusual circular house next door.

Broome The pub's name – The Engine and Tender – hints at the hamlet's origin; it grew up around the railway station when the line was constructed between Craven Arms and Swansea.

☆ **Clungunford** One of the four villages (the other three are Clunton, Clunbury and Clun) described by A. E. Housman in *A Shropshire Lad* as 'the quietest places under the sun'. The churchyard contains an excavated Bronze Age barrow. *Continue on B4367 (take care on bends). At point where road bends to right, go straight ahead on minor road to Beckjay.*

☆ **Beckjay** (not on map) The thatched cottage dates from 1296.

☆ **Bucknell** Looming over the village to the south east is Coxall Knoll, reputedly the site of the final battle between the British chief Caratacus and the Romans. *Go over Lingen bridge and turn left on to A4113.*

Brampton Bryan Scene of a Civil War siege, when Lady Brilliana Harley defended the castle while her husband was away serving Parliament. As wealthy Earls of Oxford, the family later gave their names to London's Oxford St. and Harley St. The castle remains were incorporated into the Hall and are best viewed from the grounds of the church.

☆ **Leintwardine** The Roman town of Bravonium. The chancel of St Mary Magdalene's church is noticeably higher than the nave because part of an old Roman wall lies beneath it.

The Lion, at the bottom of the long main street, is a famous fishing inn.

Leintwardine–Wigmore The line of the river bridge points southwards to a narrow Roman road. One mile (1.5 km) along it is half-timbered Paytoe Hall (*not open to the public*). The remains of Wigmore Abbey, with its handsome gatehouse, can be seen ½ mile (0.8 km) further on.

☆ **Wigmore** The remains of the 12th–14thC castle (*not open to the public*) can be seen from the approach road. The village itself, though peaceful now, was vibrant in medieval times when royalty came to visit.

Opposite the church, on the other side of A4110, an unclassified and unsignposted road leads past The Compasses inn and through the heart of Mortimer Forest.

Mortimer Forest (not on map) The road weaves past Norman churches at Leinthall Starkes, Elton and Aston. On the right after a long climb are car parks with access to paths. The road rolls over Maryknoll and down through conifers, with an exhibition centre and forest trail marked on the right.

Whitcliffe (not on map) The view from a small lay-by on the left sums up Shropshire hill country. Below lies Ludlow in its fertile plain. To the left are the Stretton Hills; the wooded slopes to their right are outliers of Wenlock Edge; while the county's highest hills, the Clees, can be seen straight ahead.

The Leicestershire Uplands

This tour weaves in and out of three counties: Lincolnshire, Northamptonshire and Leicestershire. It also goes through the rural district of Rutland, the smallest county in England until 1974, when in spite of protestations it was absorbed by Leicestershire.

The main reason for exploring the region must be the great wealth of beautiful towns and villages built in the local stone. Its colour ranges from grey to a brilliant orange-brown; since most villages had their own quarry, the difference in the colour of building materials used in neighbouring settlements can be quite startling.

> **Route: 82 miles (132 km)**
> In sequence from: Stamford
> Direction of travel: clockwise

☆ **Stamford** One of England's finest old towns, Stamford is built almost entirely of limestone and retains a strongly medieval atmosphere in spite of all the traffic. It has several ancient churches, monastic remains, almshouses, and some remnants of the colleges which made the town an important rival to Oxford during the 14thC.

There is restricted-period parking in Broad St., near the town centre, but spaces here are quickly filled. Pay car parks are situated in North St. (to the north of the centre) and Wharf Rd. (by the river). *Tourist information: tel. (0780) 64444.*

Stamford St Mary's church, with its elegant, unforgettable Early English tower and 'broach' spire (a typical feature of local churches), is best seen from the bridge over the River Welland at the bottom of St Mary's Hill.

Stamford A Victorian brewery, complete with steam engine, has been re-opened as a museum (All Saints St.). *Open Wed–Sun and Bank Holiday Mon, Apr–Sept.*

Stamford The George Hotel, St Martin's St., is one of the country's best-known old inns. The Georgian front disguises a 16th-C core of enormous character, and there is a 450-year-old mulberry tree in the garden.

① *Go over the bridge and along St Martin's St., then leave town on B1081. For short detour to Burghley House, turn left on to B4113 (just outside the town) and look out for signpost.*

Burghley House Burghley is often cited as the finest Elizabethan house in the country. The exterior is indeed magnificent, but the State Rooms, with their wall paintings, Old Masters, tapestries, elaborate silver fireplaces and carved woodwork by Grinling Gibbons, are almost overwhelmingly grand. The Heaven Room is particularly flamboyant.

After looking round the house, go for a refreshing stroll round the deer park, laid out by Capability Brown. *Open Mon–Sat and Sun afternoon, Apr to early Oct.*

● *Ashby Castle, Ashby-de-la-Zouche, like Oakham and Rockingham Castles, a Leicestershire stronghold well worth a visit.*

☆ **Easton on the Hill** Go straight over the A43 and along the High St. Turn right at the war memorial. A large village of some character; the stone here is noticeably more golden than at Stamford. *Return to the A43 by continuing along High St. bearing left.*

☆ **Collyweston** Much of the village lies to the south of the main road and repays exploration on foot. Collyweston is famous for its stone tiles, which grace roofs here and in neighbouring villages. The tiles have a beautiful texture and attract lichens and mosses as they age.

🌲 **Rockingham Forest** Here the road enters what was once a much more extensive forest, which was used as a royal hunting ground. Wild deer can still be seen occasionally.

☆ **King's Cliffe** In the valley of the limpid Willow Brook, this lovely village has 17th-C almshouses and many pleasing domestic buildings.

☆ **Apethorpe** The Old Hall and its park add to the beauty of the village. Worth looking inside the church to see the huge 17th-C monument, with its life-size figures of Charity, Justice, Wisdom and Piety.

☆ **Woodnewton** Many of the cottages are set at right angles to the street, an arrangement to be found throughout villages in this part of England.

🏰 **Fotheringhay** Mary, Queen of Scots, was beheaded here in 1587. All that remains of the castle where she was imprisoned is a grassed-over mound next to the River Nene (follow signposted footpath from Castle Farm).

Fotheringhay The church is a glorious fragment of a 15th-C collegiate church. The loss of its chancel only serves to emphasize the extraordinary grace of the octagonal lantern which rises above the tower.

② *Just beyond Tansor church take a right turning (signposted to Cotterstock and Oundle), then keep straight on.*

☆ **Oundle** The High St. has several superb stone buildings dating from the Middle Ages onwards. Note in particular The Talbot Inn (1626) and The White Lion (1641), now a private house.

The town is also the home of a well-known public school, whose buildings stand close to the church.

③ *Beyond the market-place, turn right at the war memorial. After about 2 miles (3 km) turn left at signpost to Glapthorn and go through village. At unsignposted T-junction, turn left.*

🏛 **Deene Park** From the A43, there is a good view of this mainly 16th-C house. The Earl of Cardigan, who led the Charge of the Light Brigade, lived here. *Open afternoons only: Sun and Bank Holiday Mon, June–Aug.*

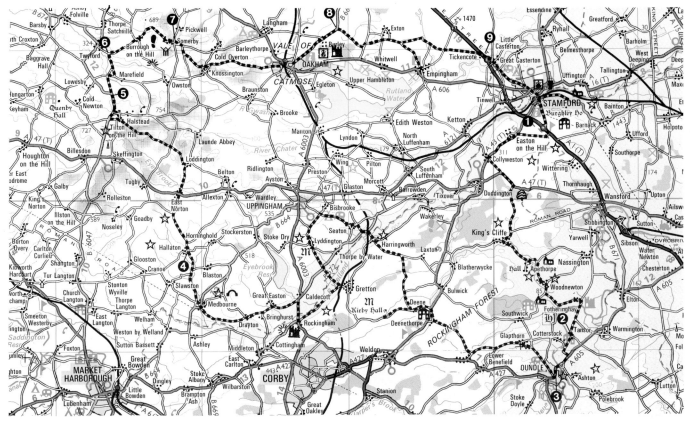

ʍ **Kirby Hall** A 2-mile (3-km) detour leads to this romantic and imposing ruin of an Elizabethan house, probably altered by Inigo Jones. *Open daily (but closed Sun morning in winter).*

☆ **Harringworth** The Welland Viaduct was built in the late 19thC. One of the longest railway viaducts in the country, it has 82 arches and is still in use.

☆ **Lyddington** In contrast to Stamford and Oundle, most of the buildings in the long and almost completely unspoiled main street of this lovely village are made of ironstone. In places, veins of a type of low-grade iron ore can be seen running across the stone, which in direct sunlight varies in colour from bright orange to a deep orange-brown.

In spite of its beauty, ironstone has not always been highly regarded.

ʍ **Lyddington** The Bede House, next to the church, is an interesting fragment of the palace of the Bishops of Lincoln, dating mainly from the 14thC. *Open Mon–Sat and Sun afternoon, Apr–Sept.*

☆ **Rockingham** Only a stone's throw from industrial Corby, this pristine village is overlooked by its castle, which was converted from fortification to stately home in the 16thC. The combination of Norman masonry and Elizabethan interior has produced a building of great character. Charles Dickens, who often visited the castle, used it as his model for Chesney Wold in *Bleak House.*

From the formal garden with its fantastically shaped yew hedges, there is a fine view over the Welland valley. *Open afternoons only, Sun, Bank Holiday Mon,*

Thurs, Easter to Sept. Also open Tues afternoon in Aug.

☆ **Medbourne** Completely surrounded by disused railways, the village owes its partly 'red brick' Victorian appearance to the importation of brick for building along these railway routes.

⌒ **Medbourne** *Turn right and then left at the church for Hallaton. At the ford, note the medieval packhorse bridge.*

④ *At Hallaton, turn left along Medbourne Rd. (at the end of a row of Council houses and by a garage sign). At the next junction go straight on to the village centre.*

☆ **Hallaton** Pleasant, compact village with a pretty green and an interesting mixture of building materials. Note how some cottages have ironstone lower storeys and brick upper storeys which were added on later.

The best view of the village is from the church porch. *Leave on East Norton road, signposted from the green at the centre.*

☆ **Hallaton–Tilton on the Hill** As the road climbs the Leicestershire hills – famous fox-hunting country – note how the hedges often resemble long, low woven baskets. The craft of hedge-laying is vigorously alive in Leicestershire.

☆ **Tilton on the Hill** True to its name, this is one of the highest villages in Leicestershire. *At the crossroads by the church turn left to the junction with B6047, then turn right.*

⑤ *Where the B6047 veers to the left, carry straight on down gated road signposted to Marefield. At junction, turn right over cattle grid, then fork left along Twyford road. (On*

right, note the red and blue brick viaduct, long since disused.)

⑥ *At the T-junction, turn right to Burrough on the Hill.*

ʍ **Burrough on the Hill** *Just beyond the village, take rather difficult right turn into car park for Burrough Hill country park. Pleasant walks with long views over the surrounding country.*

⑦ *Go through Somerby, then turn right at T-junction. Follow road around bend then turn right to Knossington.*

☆ **Oakham** Main town of the old county of Rutland. The best part of the town lies between the market place and the church, whose spire dominates the Vale of Catmose.

There is unrestricted parking in the market-place, except on market days (Wed and Sat); restricted-period parking in side streets.

▥ **Oakham** The castle remains include a 12th-C hall decorated with horseshoes donated by peers of the realm when they entered the castle for the first time. *Open daily (but closed Sun and Mon mornings).*

▣ **Oakham** The Rutland County Museum has an outstanding collection of rural life exhibits. There is also a Victorian shop and a large collection of Anglo-Saxon jewellery. *Open Tues–Sat all year; Sun afternoon, Apr–Oct.*

⑧ *At water tower turn right along lane signposted to Exton and Stamford.*

⑨ *After underpass, turn right at T-junction and follow signposts to Stamford – B1081.*

181

Norwich and the Norfolk Coast

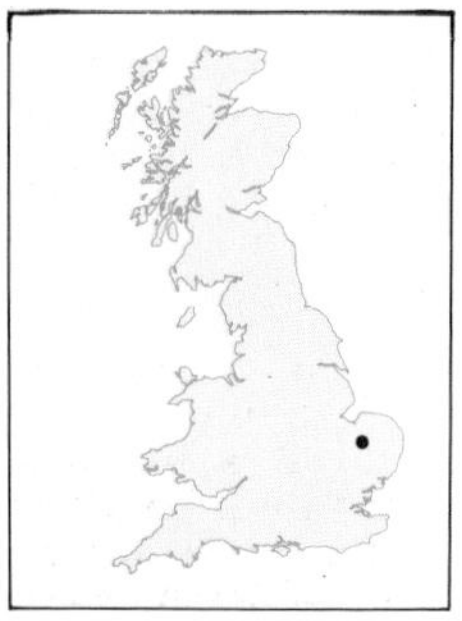

At least three subtly different types of landscape are explored on this tour. To the north-west of Norwich, the farmlands are open and sweeping or enclosed by hedges and woodlands. South-east of the city, the Yare and Bure rivers wind through flat marshland which blends almost imperceptibly into the Norfolk Broads, one of the most popular sailing areas in the country. Although the Broads are notoriously difficult to see from the road, you may catch tantalizing glimpses of sails moving between fields.

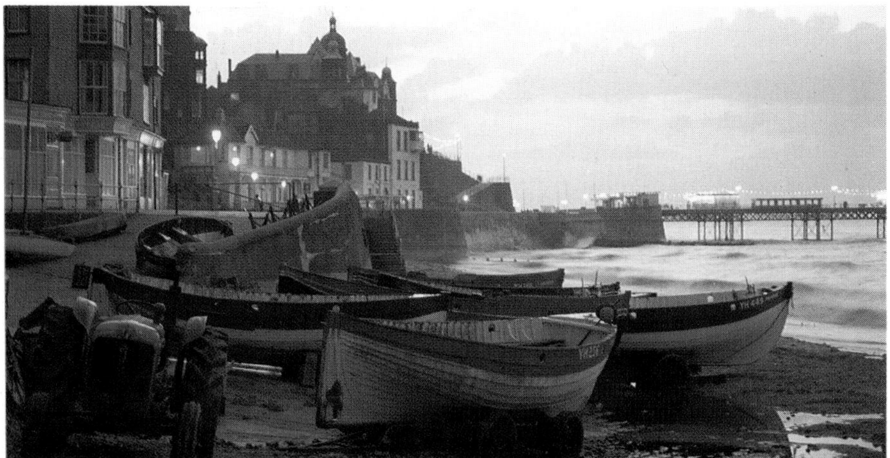

• *The front at Cromer, a fashionable resort in Edwardian times, and still one of the most charming East Anglian seaside towns.*

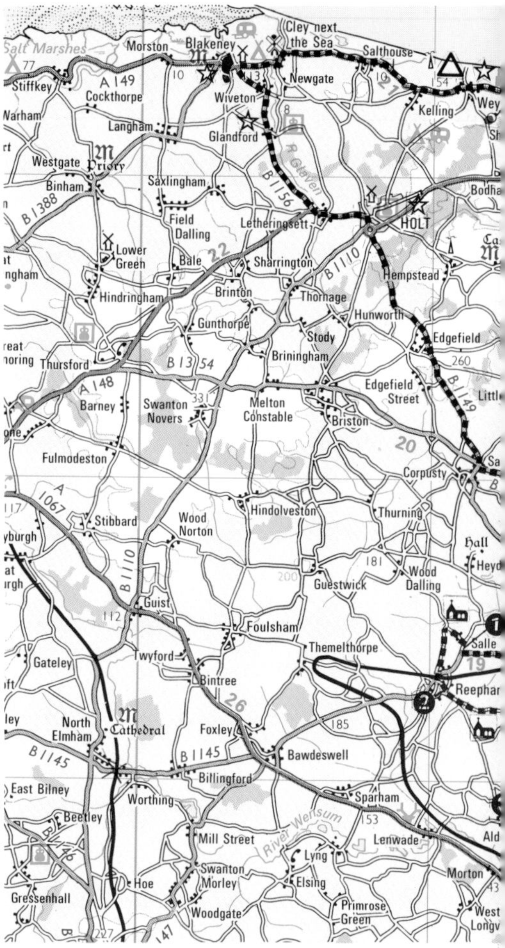

Route: 112 miles (180 km)
In sequence from: Aylsham
Direction of travel: anticlockwise

☆ **Aylsham** Pleasant little town with some good Georgian-fronted buildings in the market-place. Most of the houses are roofed with local, blue-glazed pantiles. Humphrey Repton, the great landscape gardener, is buried in the churchyard.

Cawston *On entering the village, fork left down New St., then go over crossroads.* The 14th–15thC church of St Agnes possesses a glorious hammer-beam angel roof and a rood screen with painted figures in unusually good repair.

① *At a triangular junction, turn right for Salle (not signposted).*

Salle The church, almost isolated amongst the fields, is one of the grandest in Norfolk. Compared with Cawston, the nave is wider and possesses more elegant piers. The engineering of the roof is also more daring although the result is not quite so lovely.

☆ **Reepham** Dominated by its 18th-C orange-brown brickwork, this small town has two churches, intriguingly joined together.

Reepham The Old Brewery House, in the market place, is a pub of great character. Bar meals are available.

② *Leave Reepham on the Norwich Road, then take the second turning on left, signposted to Haveringland.*

Booton (not on map) St Michael's church, essential viewing for anyone with a taste for the more ostentatious flowerings of Gothic Revival architecture, has twin towers that have no equal, a massively tall tower arch, and bulky angels resembling ship's figureheads.

St Michael's was designed by its rector, Whitwell Elwin, an amateur architect.

③ *Go through Swannington, then take left fork, signposted to Felthorpe. At crossroads go straight ahead, then turn left on to Norwich road at T-junction.*

☆ **Norwich** *Go straight across first roundabout. At second roundabout follow signs for city centre. At third roundabout turn left. At fourth roundabout turn right.* The cathedral and the castle are the obvious attractions, but reserve time to explore one of the largest open-air markets in Britain (the fish stalls sell samphire in season), and to stroll down medieval Elm Hill, Tombland and Bridewell Alley. *For details and directions, go to the Tourist Office (14 Tombland, opposite the cathedral). Tel. (0603) 666071.*

✝ **Norwich** The Cathedral is on a rather smaller scale than most, with Norman nave arcades and an exquisite 15th–16thC roof. There are enjoyable carved bosses in the cloisters, and The Close has a rich collection of domestic architecture.

Norwich The vast Norman keep of Norwich Castle houses an extensive museum and the best single collection of works by the Norwich school of painters. Of particular interest are the paintings of John Sell Cotman (1782–1842), one of England's most original and under-estimated watercolourists. *Open Mon–Sat and Sun afternoon.*

④ *Leave Norwich on A146, signposted to Lowestoft, then turn left to Kirby Bedon.*

Rockland St Mary Beyond the village the road descends to the level of the flat marshy meadows of the Yare valley. Look out for the ruins of a small castle on private land, to the left as you enter Claxton.

⑤ *At Hales, turn left on to B1136, then immediately turn left again at crossroads, along single track road signposted to Heckingham. Follow signs for Reedham Ferry.*

Heckingham (not on map) Turn left off route to see the prettily situated church which has a thatched roof, an elaborate Norman doorway and an octagonal flint and brick tower. *Three hundred yards (274 m) beyond church, turn left along 'By-Road'.*

☆ **Reedham Ferry** Ring the bell to call the ferryman, who will take you and your vehicle across 200 yards (183 m) of water. *Daily service;* there is a small charge.

☆ **Halvergate** New 'suburbs' have encroached, but it is still possible to identify the character of the old village.

! **Halvergate** Just beyond the village a well-defined track leads out across Halvergate

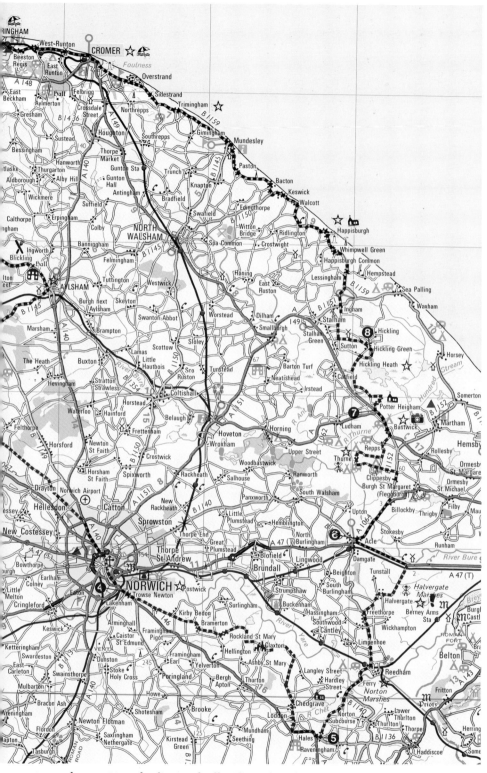

Potter Heigham The 14th-C thatched church has a stone sculpture of a pagan god (the Old Man of the Woods) set incongruously into a niche above the porch. *Follow the unsignposted lane to the left of the church. At the T-junction turn right.*

☆ **Hickling Heath** *Take right turning (signposted Hickling Broad) to the boatyard and mooring area.* Two hundred yards (183 m) further on a house-lined track leads to a cluster of old thatched boathouses, some with reed walls, and one of the best views of the water from dry land.

⑧ *Turn right (signposted to Sea Palling). Just beyond the post office turn left along unsignposted lane. At T-junction, turn left.*

☆ **Happisburgh** Note the use of pebbles from the beach on houses in the village street.

Happisburgh Perched on the cliffs, the church is a landmark for sailors.

☆ **Trimingham** Opposite the church, the side-road has a sign saying 'No Highway Beyond Barrier'. This was the old main road until the sea washed away the cliff from underneath it. One house stands perilously close to where the tarmac juts out into space.

☆ **Cromer** The oldest part of this small resort lies between the church and the sea. Do not miss narrow Jetty St. with its bow-fronts. Cromer's famous crabs can be bought direct from fisherman J. Lee at 15, New St.

☆ **Sheringham** Another pleasant, small resort with good bathing. Fishing boats are moored in a small inlet on the shingle strand.

☆ **Sheringham–Blakeney** The loveliest stretch of the Norfolk coast: rolling farmlands slope down to salt marshes cut off from the sea by a long shingle strand. 'Hides' are provided for bird-watchers.
Along the way, stop off at Cley next the Sea to look at the handsome windmill. In the main street, Cley Smoke House sells home-cured, oak-smoked fish.

☆ **Blakeney** In spite of its popularity, this little port has retained most of its character. Park beside the quay, then walk up the delightful High St.

Blakeney A footpath which begins to the east of the quay goes across the salt marshes along the top of a dyke.

☆ **Glandford** From the main street, a road marked 'Unsuitable for Motors' leads to an attractive ford with a footbridge over the river, here adapted into a mill race.

☆ **Holt** Tidy town rebuilt after a fire in 1708.

Blickling Hall The first view of this splendid Jacobean house at the end of its drive is breathtaking, and the interior – particularly the elaborate plasterwork ceiling in the Long Gallery – does not disappoint. *Open Tues, Wed, Fri–Sun and Bank Holiday Mon, Apr–Oct. Afternoons only on Sun and in Apr and Oct.*

✗ **Blickling** The Buckinghamshire Arms Hotel serves excellent meals; restaurant open evenings and Sun lunch only. Uses fresh local produce.

---

marshes, past two derelict windmills. The former marshland, stretching away eastwards to the horizon, is used for rough grazing but much of it is now threatened with conversion to arable use.

⑥ *In the centre of Acle, turn right on to Caistor road (A1064).*

☆ **Thurne** An untidy little village with two windmills and a busy mooring inlet off the River Thurne used by Broads boat people.

Look out for the occasional 'quanting' boat, carrying cut reeds for thatching.

☆ **Bastwick** *Turn left along A149 (no signpost), then left again after ½ mile (0.8 km).* In summer, boats can be hired just beyond Potter Heigham bridge.

⑦ *Take turning to right (signposted Yarmouth) and go over main road. At T-junction turn right along road misleadingly marked 'No Through Road, Church Only'.*

The White Peak

The Peak District National Park is divided into two regions: the Dark Peak to the north (see following tour) and the White Peak, a limestone plateau intersected by deep gorges and narrow dales, bounded on the western side by the long line of the Gritstone Edge.

Apart from offering some of the best scenery in Britain, the White Peak has old mills, ancient stone circles and stately homes. (Chatsworth, the 'Palace of the Peak', lies just off the route to the north-east of Haddon Hall, and deserves at least half a day to itself.) Inevitably, visitor numbers are high, yet there is still an air of timelessness.

Route One: 58 miles (93 km)
Directions in sequence from: Leek
Direction of travel: clockwise

☆ **Leek** The silk industry gave the town prominence 200 years ago, and still flourishes here. There are many old mills and cobbled back streets. St Edward's church (founded 1042) has a Saxon cross in its churchyard. *Tourist information: tel. (0538) 384195.*

▣ **Leek** Brindley Water Mill, Mill St., is a preserved, operational corn mill. Upstairs, a museum commemorates James Brindley, 18th-C canal engineer. *Open afternoons only, Sat, Sun and Bank Holiday Mon, Easter to Oct. Also Mon, Tues and Thurs afternoons in July, Aug.*

☆ **Hulme End** Terminus of the old Leek and Manifold narrow-gauge railway. The track has gone but the old railway buildings and the Light Railway Hotel survive.

☆ **Hartington** This compact village, huddled around its green, has a duckpond, a 14th-C church, and a Stilton cheese factory with a shop. Walking sticks and shepherds' crooks are a local speciality.

☆ **Hartington–Middleton** Limestone country at its best. The route follows sheer-sided, dry valleys, crosses ancient bridges over rivers which flow one week but are gone the next, and passes old lime kilns, lead mines and industrial remains now reclaimed by nature.

ᛗ **Arbor Low** A 2-mile (3-km) detour leads to this late Stone Age or early Bronze Age stone circle, the 'Stonehenge of the north'. An impressive sight, even though the stones are lying down.

☆ **Middleton** The village guards the entrance to glorious Bradford Dale, which can be glimpsed to the right of the road.

🚹 **Youlgreave** All Saints church has a unique Norman font. In June, the village's well-dressing ceremony draws large numbers of visitors.

🌿 **Youlgreave** On leaving village, look left to see Conksbury's medieval packhorse bridge, Raper Lodge and the end of Lathkill Dale, the most hidden and picturesque of all the Derbyshire dales.

① *At junction with B5056, turn left for short detour to Haddon Hall, or right and then left almost immediately on to unclassified road to Stanton in Peak.*

🏚 **Haddon Hall** Magnificent 14th–15thC fortified manor house, renowned for its medieval tapestries and furniture. *Open Tues–Sat, Apr–Sept.*

🌿 **Stanton in Peak** Just beyond the village, there are distant views to the right over the White Peak, Derbyshire and Staffordshire. Stanton Moor, to the left, has standing stones, 70 Neolithic barrows and a stone circle called the Nine Ladies.

🚹 **Birchover** The chapel has a memorial to Joan Weaste, burned as a heretic in the 1550s, during the reign of Bloody Mary.

☆ **Winster** In the main street (which has been virtually untouched for 250 years) the Market Hall (15th–17thC) houses a National Trust information centre and shop.

② *Go through Wensley on B5057, then turn right at signpost to Oker and Snitterton. At junction with A6, turn right to Matlock Bath.*

☆ **Matlock Bath** Clinging to the side of the Derwent gorge, the town became famous for its medicinal springs in the 17thC. Boat trips on the river and canal are the best way to see the surrounding scenery; the Heights of Abraham can be reached by cable car from the riverside. There are show caves, model village, and museum of lead mining (in *The Pavilion, which also houses the tourist office (tel. (0629) 55082)*).

♈ **Matlock Bath** Riber Castle (built by Victorian hosiery manufacturer John Smedley) is now a ruin, but the grounds are a wildlife park for endangered European species. *Open daily.*

③ *Leave Matlock Bath on A6, then turn right on to B5036, and right again on to A5012, past water mill and lodge.*

🍃 **Via Gellia** Famous for its trees, this valley was named after the local Gell family.

④ *Turn left at Hopton signpost. Go over crossroads, then turn right on to B5035. (After about 2 miles (3 km) there are extensive views over the Vale of Trent and the White Peak.)*

🚹 **Kniveton** Worth pausing to see the tiny ancient church and massive churchyard yew tree.

☆ **Ashbourne** One of the best small Georgian towns in England, Ashbourne is famous for its Shrovetide football game, its mineral water and its gingerbread. St Oswald's church with its fine spire should not be missed. The Green Man and Black's Head pub serves real ale.

⑤ *Leave town on A515, then turn left to Thorpe. Follow signposts to Dove Dale car park between Thorpe and Ilam.*

☆ **Dove Dale** The most famous dale, an essential stop for exploration on foot. Memorable

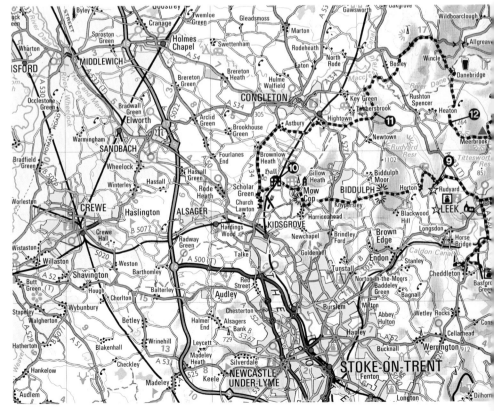

sights include towering pillars of stone, gorges, hidden caves and natural arches.

✗ The Izaak Walton Hotel, near Ilam, is recommended for its food.

⑥ *Turn right at the cross in Ilam, wind through village, then turn left down road signposted to Castern and Throwley.*
One mile (1.5 km) from Ilam bear sharp right before Rushley Farm. After short distance, route passes through Throwley Hall farmyard. Turn left after first barn. Close yard gates behind you.

⑦ *At T-junction in Calton, turn right then right again at fork. At Waterhouses, take left turning by Old Crown pub, signposted to Cauldon Lowe and Cheadle.*

▯ **Cauldon** The Yew Tree Inn's drab exterior disguises an Aladdin's cave of working polyphons, pianolas, pennyfarthings, and assorted curiosities including a pair of Queen Victoria's stockings. Real ale, bar meals and table skittles (local pub game).

▣ **Froghall Wharf** An industrial archaeologist's paradise, deep in the secluded Churnett Valley. There are horse-drawn narrow boat trips (2 pm, Thurs and Sun) along the Caldon canal.

⑧ *At Ipstones, turn left and follow 'Leisure Drive' signs towards Cheddleton.*

▣ **Basford Bridge** The old railway station is now the North Staffordshire Steam Railway

● *Hartington: Stilton and walking sticks.*

Centre and museum. *Open afternoons only, Sun–Fri, May–Sept; Sun and Bank Holidays only rest of year.*

▙ **Cheddleton** Unique flint mill, with two massive water wheels, operates every Sat and Sun afternoon. *To reach mill, turn left along A520 towards Wetley Rocks.*

> **Route Two: 40 miles (64 km)**
> Directions in sequence from: Leek
> Direction of travel: clockwise

☆ **Rudyard** Kipling was named after this compact village at the foot of the reservoir.

⑨ *Turn right at mini-roundabout in Rudyard. Bear left uphill, then turn left at signpost to Horton. Turn right at Horton Hall, then follow signposts to Lask Edge.*

✹ **Lask Edge** (not on map) Panoramic views extend across nine counties.

🛡 **Mow Cop** Climb up the hill to the mid-18th-C mock ruin for immense views from the fringe of the Gritstone Edge.

⑩ *Turn left out of car park at Mow Cop, then turn right down steep Top Station Rd. Go over level crossing, turn left then right over canal, then turn right again down Stonechair Lane. At A34, turn right (or left for detour to pub).*

✗ **Scholar Green** A 1-mile (1.5-km) detour leads to The Bleeding Wolf inn (excellent bar meals and Robinsons Ales).

🏠 **Little Moreton Hall** One of the most perfect black-and-white half-timbered manor houses in Britain. *Open afternoons only: Mon, Wed–Sun, Apr–Sept; weekends only in Mar and Oct.*

✹ **Hightown** *Go over traffic lights, then bear right at Coach and Horses pub. About 2 miles (3 km) along the road, the Bridestones Neolithic burial chamber (on left) is accessible by footpath.*

⑪ *Bear left and follow road around the edge of The Cloud (extensive views from the top), then turn sharp right.*

▯ **Danebridge** The Ship Inn, dating from medieval times, is Cheshire's oldest pub.

⑫ *Follow road around the edge of Swythamley Hall estate; bear left at telephone box, then turn left at junction by copse. Follow Meerbrook signposts. (Spectacular view ahead of the Roaches and Hen Cloud.) Turn left in Meerbrook in front of Three Horse Shoes pub. Close gates across road.*

✹ **Roach End** (not on map) Good place to stop and gaze across Cheshire (to the west) and Staffordshire (to the south).

✗ **Morridge Edge** (not on map) The Mermaid Inn is renowned for the quality of its food and beer. From the lay-by near the pub, there are unrivalled views.

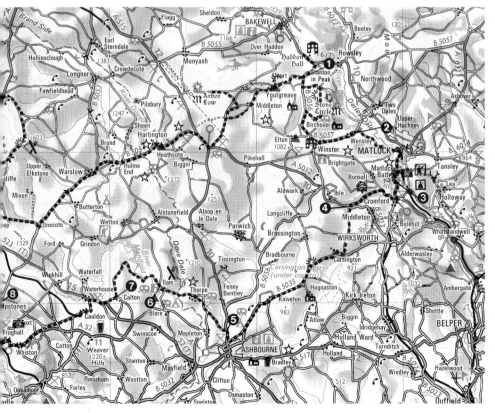

The Lincolnshire Wolds

● *Arable country near Louth, on the E side of the Wolds. Modern intensive production methods give huge yields from this rich soil.*

Acounty of contrasts, Lincolnshire divides into three distinct regions: Kesteven, to the south-west, is attractively wooded; Holland, to the south-east, is the reclaimed fenland area famous for its bulb fields; while Lindsey, in the north, is dominated by the rolling Wolds.

Starting in Woodhall Spa, the little resort that grew up around its medicinal spring, this tour does a figure of eight through some of the Wolds' loveliest scenery. This is Tennyson country: the old Poet Laureate was born in Somersby, went to school in Louth, and derived much of his inspiration from the Lincolnshire landscape.

Route: 96 miles (154.5 km)
In sequence from: Woodhall Spa
Direction of travel: clockwise (at start)

☆ **Woodhall Spa** Small Victorian resort attractively set amid pine and birch woods and farmland. The mineral spring is closed but the rheumatism treatment centre is still in use. *Tourist information: (0526) 52461.*

☆ **Woodhall Spa** Near the championship golf course, the tall Tower on the Moor is thought to date from the 15thC.

☆ **Woodhall Spa** *To leave town, go through Jubilee Park then turn right at crossroads along route signposted to Old Woodhall. The Wellington Monument, to the left, is said to face Waterloo. Close by, Waterloo Wood was grown from acorns planted after the battle (1815).*

① *Join B1191 then turn left for Horncastle (in sight down the hill).*

☆ **Horncastle** The Romans named it Banovallum (the walled place on the River Bain) and traces of the old walls can still be seen around the town, incorporated into various buildings including the public library.

⛪ **Horncastle** St Mary's church has a brass to Sir Lionel Dymoke (1519). As King's Champion he defended the monarch against challengers. His descendant at nearby Scrivelsby Court still holds the title.

② *Leave town centre on A153 (signposted to Louth). After ¾ mile (1 km) turn right at signpost to Fulletby.*

③ *Turn right at T-junction in Fulletby (signposted to Belchford) then turn left and right again, towards Tetford.*

⚘ **Fulletby** Just beyond the village there is a good view over 'Tennyson Valley'.

④ *On reaching Tetford take turning to left, signposted to Ruckland.*

⚘ **Tetford–Ruckland** The road rises to one of the highest parts of the Wolds with fine views all around of unspoiled country.

⑤ *Just beyond Ruckland turn right. At junction with A16, turn right to Burwell. Pass through village, then take turning to left and follow signs to Muckton.*

✗ **Little Cawthorpe** Turn right past the duckpond to charming old pub called The Splash (good bar meals). *Carry on across the ford; if flooded, do a U-turn and go round the village to rejoin the road on the other side of the ford.*

☆ **Louth** This busy, rambling market town with its confusing one-way system is dominated by the impressive tower and spire (295 feet/90 m) of St James's church. Dating mainly from the 15thC, the church has numerous stone carvings of animals, birds and humans; look out too for the Louth Imp.

Well-preserved 17th–18thC houses can be seen in Westgate and Upgate in the town centre.

⑥ *Leave town on A157, then turn right on to A631. Just past South Elkington turn right on to minor road signposted to North Elkington.*

☆ **Binbrook** Just south of this neat Wolds village lie old wartime airfields; to the north the massive, operational RAF base is all too conspicuous. Turn left along B1203 to Tealby.

☆ **Tealby** Tennyson's grandfather lived in this lovely village and the poet spent much time here, at Bayons Manor (demolished 1964). There is, of course, a 'Tennyson Walk' around the village, starting at the church.

⑦ *Turn left on to A631. At North Willingham, turn right on to unclassified road to Hain-*

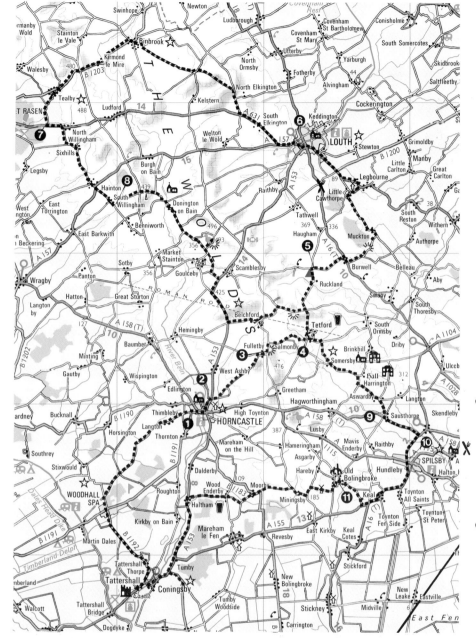

ton. Pass through village, then go over A157 to South Willingham.

⑧ *At South Willingham, turn left up hill (passing television mast) and continue on to Donington on Bain.*

🏠 **Donington on Bain** Tiny parish church where newly-married couples were pelted with hassocks – until one injured a vicar. *Continue straight on to Stenigot (not on map).*

☀ **Stenigot** Half a mile (0.8 km) beyond village turn left along Louth road to the top of Red Hill. Fine views make this detour worthwhile. *Return down hill and turn left.*

☆ **Belchford** The long-distance walk known as the Viking Way goes through the village on its journey from Leicestershire to the Humber. *Keep left through village. After 1 mile (1.5 km), turn right at T-junction.*

☀ **Belchford–Tetford** For a short distance the route goes along the old Bluestone Heath road which runs north–south across the Wolds. Not far from the T-junction there is
☀ a viewpoint with a map of the surrounding countryside. On a fine day it is possible (with binoculars) to see Lincoln Cathedral, more than 20 miles (32 km) to the west. *Continue to crossroads, then turn right and go down the hill to Tetford.*

🍺 **Tetford** Turn left into the village, continuing past the church to The White Hart Inn, on right. Tennyson once supped at this 16th-C inn, and Dr Johnson is reputed to have drunk here. The old settle where both great men sat is preserved in the bar.
Next door, the cabinet-maker's workshop is open to the public.
At T-junction turn left, then turn first right at signpost to Somersby.

☆ **Somersby** In 1809, Tennyson was born at

🏠 the Old Rectory (the central house of the three opposite the church where his father was rector). The castellated house next door is thought to have been designed by Vanbrugh.
🏠 The church has a memorial to the poet. *Follow signposts to Bag Enderby.*

🏠 **Harrington** Turn left at T-junction to reach the mellow Hall, with its Elizabethan porch the same height as the house. In the fine grounds, the terrace was the 'high Hall garden' of Tennyson's *Maud. Open afternoons only, mid-week and some Suns, Apr–Oct.*

⑨ *At Sausthorpe, turn left on to A158. Before reaching Partney, turn right to Spilsby.*

☆ **Spilsby** A statue in the market square commemorates the Arctic explorer Sir John Franklin, born in Spilsby.

🏠 **Spilsby** Worth looking inside St James's church to see the fine 14th–16th-C tombs of the Willoughby family.

✗ **Spilsby** In the town centre an old grocery has been converted into a restaurant where well-known painters display their works and top musicians play chamber music.
The restaurant is opposite Moden's Bakery, where you can buy traditional Lincolnshire plum bread.

⑩ *Leave Spilsby on the A16. After about 2 miles (3 km), fork right on to A155, then almost immediately turn right at signpost to Old Bolingbroke.*

🏚 **Old Bolingbroke** Opposite the tiny post office a short lane leads to the remains of the famous castle where Henry IV was born in 1367. *Return to post office and turn right (signposted to Hagnaby).*

⑪ *Turn left at T-junction, then take first turning to the right up the hill to the white tower of an old windmill. At junction, turn left to Miningsby.*
Just beyond Miningsby, turn left at signpost pointing to the wonderfully named village of Claxby Pluckacre. Two cattle gates lie ahead (remember to shut them).

🍺 **Haltham** Turn left on to the A153 to reach the only pub in England to be called The Marmion Arms. This 16th-C hostelry was named after the Duke of Marmion, another King's Champion.

☆ **Coningsby** *Before reaching village, turn left along B1192 for a short detour to the* RAF *station where the operational Battle of Britain aeroplanes are usually kept. Flight times on notice board on perimeter fence.*

☆ **Coningsby** The clock on the 15th-C church tower has only one hand (minute hands were not used until the 17thC). However, because the clock face is so massive, it is possible to tell the time to within five minutes.

🏰 **Tattershall Castle** (*Short detour along A153.*) The huge, red brick, five-storeyed keep (all that remains of the 15th-C castle) is an outstanding example of a fortified manor house. *Open Mon–Sat and Sun afternoon.*

187

The Dark Peak

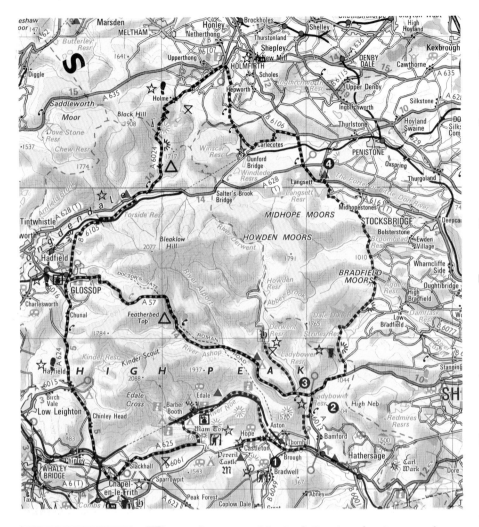

The northern part of the Peak District takes its name from the dark grey gritstone which forms wild, bleak moorlands with steep valleys or cloughs, edged by dramatic outcrops of weather-worn rocks. Dominated by the massive bulk of Kinder Scout – at 2,088 feet (636 m) the highest point in the National Park – the area is immensely impressive, both above and below ground.

Anyone wishing to visit more than one of the caverns near Castleton may not have time to do the complete tour, but the short cut back to Glossop along the A57 goes over the Snake Pass, one of the most spectacular roads in the Pennines.

Route: 64 miles (102.5 km)
In sequence from: Glossop
Direction of travel: anticlockwise

☆ **Glossop** This busy town on the edge of Greater Manchester is a popular starting point for hikes into the Peak District, particularly along the Doctor's Gate, a Roman and medieval track behind the town which climbs up to Bleaklow and the Snake Pass. The track was named after Dr John Talbot, vicar of Glossop in the 16thC.

▣ **Glossop** The Dinting Railway Museum (off A57, 1 mile/1.5 km to the west of the town) has a fine collection of main line steam locomotives and related displays. *Train rides (lasting ten minutes) every Sun from Apr–Oct. Museum open daily.*

☆ **Hayfield** Worth leaving the A624 (Hayfield bypass) to spend a little time in this old textile town which is well served by pubs. and cafés, and has a pleasant centre.

Hayfield is the traditional starting point for the ascent of Kinder Scout; close by, Kinder Downfall (where the River Kinder flows over the edge of the crags), often freezes up in winter.

For the less energetic, the Sett Valley trail (along the route of the old railway line to New Mills) offers 2 miles (3 km) of easy, level walking. Information centre at start of trail with bicycles for hire.

☆ **Chapel-en-le-Frith** The town grew up around a tiny chapel built 'en le frith' or in the forest in the 13thC. In 1648, after the Battle of Preston, 1,500 Scots soldiers were imprisoned in the chapel for 16 days. Tragically, 40 of them did not survive the ordeal

in Derbyshire's 'Black Hole'. The present church, which stands on the site of the old chapel, dates from the 18thC.

Chapel has a number of pleasant old inns, including The Packhorse, in the town centre. The market place, which is 776 feet (237 m) above sea level, has a 17th-C market cross and stocks.

☆ **Mam Tor** The 'shivering mountain' is a ridge of shales so unstable that over the centuries the road across it has moved constantly. Recent movement has proved so violent that the main A625 road has now been closed, leaving traffic to find its way down the steep Winnats Pass or by a circuitous route through Edale.

✗ **Mam Tor** From the car park and picnic area, just past the junction with the Edale road, a short walk leads to the site of a Roman fort on the summit of Mam Tor (a magnificent viewpoint).

Two fascinating show caves, the Blue John Mine and Treak Cliff Cavern, lie directly ahead and are *open daily in summer*. The former is one of the deepest caverns in England (240 steps); the latter has stalactites and stalagmites as well as visible deposits of the Blue John stone.

⚒ **Edale** From the approach road, there are superb views along this remote valley.

Edale village, the starting point of the 250-mile (402-km) Pennine Way, has two pubs, both offering bar meals. (Use car park at entrance to village.)

▣ The National Park information centre has excellent local history, wildlife and farming displays.

☆ **Castleton** A short detour from the Hope Valley road leads to Castleton, a large village worth visiting for its dramatically sited, ruined castle (*c.* 1086) – the model for Sir Walter Scott's *Peveril of the Peak* – and its show caves. There are also several craft shops, cafés and pubs.

▣ **Castleton** Spectacular Peak Cavern has a gigantic entrance known as the Devil's Hole, where rope-makers lived and worked until fairly recently. Although their cottages have gone, the old rope-walk can still be seen. *Open Easter to mid-Sept.*

▣ **Castleton** At Speedwell Cavern (just beyond the village) visitors travel by boat along an illuminated underground canal built by 18th-C lead miners. *Open daily.*

① *Return to route and follow signposts to Thornhill. From the village follow signposts to Ladybower along a superb, winding road, mainly through woods. At the junction with A6013, turn left for Ladybower.*

☆ **Ladybower Reservoir** Between 1935 and 1943, two Peak District valleys were flooded to make this vast reservoir, and two entire villages – Derwent and Ashopton – were drowned. Although the old packhorse bridge at Derwent was moved to Slippery Stones higher up the valley, most of the buildings were left standing and their remains emerged in times of drought. Finally, the old church had to be demolished to prevent people from attempting to reach it across dangerous mud. Nevertheless, local people still claim they can some-

● *Dark Peak country.*

times hear the sound of tolling bells coming from the churchyard.

② *Turn left at junction with A57. After about 1 mile (1.5 km) turn right for 2-mile (3-km) detour to Derwent Dams.*

☆ **Derwent Dams** These two huge dams, which were built between 1901 and 1916 to create the Howden and Derwent reservoirs, were where the World War II 'dam busters' practised with dummies of Barnes Wallis's skidding bomb before their famous raid on Germany.

✕ There is now an attractive picnic area and visitor centre below Derwent Reservoir, at Fairholme, where bicycles may be hired during the summer months. On Sundays and Bank Holidays the road to the top of the reservoirs is closed to motor traffic (*except for a minibus service which operates from the car park*). The scheme, which means pedestrians and cyclists have the quiet road along the wooded edge of the reservoir all to themselves, has recently won a major tourist award.

③ *Return to the A57. To continue along the route, turn left then left again after about 2 miles (3 km) on to the unclassified road signposted to Strines.*

Alternatively, those wishing to return to Glossop at this point should turn right on to the A57, for the Snake Pass. The road ascends through a beautiful wooded gorge almost Alpine in character and goes past the famous Snake Inn before reaching the desolate moorland summit.

☆ **Strines–Langsett** This beautiful, switch-back road passes the old Strines Inn (real ale, bar meals). There are superb views all along across several reservoirs and down towards the outskirts of Sheffield. Several steep hills and winding bends require care-ful driving. *Follow signs to Midhopestones. Before village, fork left to Langsett.*

④ *At Langsett, turn left. At crossroads by The Flouch Inn, keep on A616. Soon after cross-ing railway line turn left on to B6106, then left again to Saltcotes.*

☆ **Winscar Reservoir** The reservoir in its bleak valley seems even more cut off from the rest of the world now that the railway no longer comes to Dunford Bridge.

☆ **Holmfirth** This little Pennine town, for-merly a busy textile manufacturing com-munity, is now known to millions as the setting for the television series *Last of the Summer Wine*. The cobbled streets with their grey stone cottages and mills have a splendid backcloth of green hills. There are shops, a tourist information centre, a choice of cafés and pubs, and a fine 18th-C church.

☆ **Holme** Still in *Last of the Summer Wine* country, the village has great charm.

Just before the centre of the village, a road to the right leads to Digley Reservoir, a superbly situated man-made lake which ✕ has a car park and picnic area.

On the other side of the A6024, Brownhill and Ramsden Reservoirs are only accessible ❗ on foot. However, it is a pleasant walk, and the reservoirs can be reached in about 15 minutes.

Although this part of the Peak District lies in Yorkshire, the landscape around all three of Holme's reservoirs is more like the Scottish highlands.

✙ **Holme Moss** The high moorland pass over △ Holme Moss, with its television mast, offers some of the finest views in the Peak District: back across the Holme Valley and into West Yorkshire on the ascent; down into Long-dendale and the Woodhead Pass beyond the summit. The road is one of the highest in the Pennines and is often the first to be closed in bad weather.

☆ **Longdendale** In spite of man's interference in the form of reservoirs, trunk road and the now derelict railway, the valley has a bleak beauty. From the B6105, which leads back ✙ to Glossop, there are interesting views across industrial Tameside to Greater Man-chester.

189

The Forest of Bowland

Nothing could be further from the stereotyped image of Lancashire as a county of mills and cloth caps than the wild and often breathtakingly lovely Forest of Bowland. ('Forest' is used here in its medieval sense of an area preserved as a royal hunting ground.)

Bowland has something of the epic quality and grandeur of the Scottish Highlands; two passes included on this tour cross the great moorland ridges of the central massif and are as impressive as any in England. But the forest is also surrounded by wooded valleys and pastoral country of great beauty, with a number of unspoiled villages.

Route: 69 miles (110.5 km)
In sequence from: Clitheroe
Direction of travel: clockwise

● *Access to the wildest parts of the Forest of Bowland is restricted, but a locally available leaflet gives details.*

☆ **Clitheroe** One of England's oldest market towns (its charter dates back to 1147), Clitheroe is dominated by its castle. Perched on a limestone rock at the end of the main street, it has the smallest surviving Norman keep in England, and now contains a museum exhibiting local and Civil War relics (*open Tues, Thurs, Sat and Sun, Apr–Sept*). There are magnificent views of the Bowland Fells from the castle. *Tourist information: tel. (0200) 25566.*

① *Take the B6243 Longridge road out of Clitheroe, but soon after crossing the River Ribble, fork right along the unclassified road signposted to Bashall Eaves, Whitewell and the Trough of Bowland.*

🏰 **Browsholme Hall** Although this beautiful house (pronounced 'Broozem') dates from 1507, the fine red sandstone front was added in 1604. The Hall has been the home of the Parker family for many centuries, the most famous member being Thomas Lister Parker (1779–1858), a great patron of the arts, who enlarged the house in time for a

visit from his friend the Prince Regent in the early years of the 19thC. Turner sketched the house on one of his frequent visits to the area.

Members of the Parker family show the public round the Hall from 2–5 on Sat in June, July, Aug. For other times, telephone (025 486) 330.

☆ **Whitewell** Superbly situated in a wooded gorge of the River Hodder, this little village provides another excellent vantage point for viewing the Bowland Fells.

The church, which stands close to the river, contains a large Flemish tapestry on loan from the Parker family.

From Whitewell follow the Lancaster road.

☆ **Dunsop Bridge** A moorland village on the very edge of the wild country of Bowland. There is a fine walk along the banks of the River Dunsop into Whitendale and Middle Knot.

The Forest of Bowland is said to have been one of the last places in Britain where

herds of wild deer and packs of wolves roamed. There were also herds of bubali – wild, hornless cattle which were pure white except for a black tip to their noses. The remnants of these cattle survived in nearby Gisburne Park well into the last century and were included in James Ward's famous painting of Gordale Scar in the Tate Gallery, London.

☆ **Trough of Bowland** This steep and narrow pass follows a moorland clough or valley to squeeze a way through the fells. Beyond the summit, the lovely heather moor (one of the finest grouse moors in the north) is part of the great Abbeystead estate. Soon the infant River Wyre is reached, and the road enters a wooded stretch; the attractive beckside glades provide plenty of picnic places.

🌿 **Lee–Quernmore** About 2 miles (3 km) from Lee, stop at the car park on the crest of the fell to ascend the little stone tower. From here the view extends right across to Blackpool Tower to the south-west, and Morecambe to the north-east. It is even possible to see beyond the Arnside and Barrow peninsulas to the great hills of the Lake District.

Continue along the same road, then turn right at the crossoads towards Caton.

☆ **Quernmore** Pronounced 'Quarmer', its name undoubtedly refers to the underlying moorland gritstone used for making millstones. The village, in what is now a peaceful valley, was once in a lawless wilderness: in the reign of Edward III, the 'men and freeholders' in the Forest of Quernmore were fined 520 marks, a considerable sum in the currency of the time, for their trespasses. The Quernmore Forest was the last of the ancient Lancashire hunting forests to be disforested in 1811.

⛪ **Quernmore** The church, built by the Garnett family in 1860, has a stained-glass window with an interesting history. The Garnetts sent a window to the English Church at Cannes in the south of France, but the ship carrying it was wrecked on the voyage and a replacement window had to be sent. Eventually the cargo of the wrecked ship was salvaged by a Greek merchant and auctioned at Marseilles, whereupon Mr Garnett bought back the window for his own church at Quernmore.

Continue on the Caton road. Bear right into Caton as road swings left towards Lancaster.

☆ **Caton and Brookhouse** Pleasant villages in Lonsdale, close to the famous river bend known as the Crook of Lune, which was painted by Turner. There is now a picnic site nearby. The parish church, in Brookhouse, has a 500-year-old tower.

🏰 **Hornby** A stone village, with a romantic, almost fairy tale castle superbly positioned above the River Wenning. The subject of another Turner painting and engraving, the castle dates from the 13thC, but was almost entirely rebuilt in the Gothic style in Victorian times.

⛪ **Hornby** The church, with its unusual octagonal tower, is well worth a visit. There is the massive base of a Saxon cross in the churchyard, and several fragments of Saxon crosses inside the church, including one that has carvings of two figures under a tree with loaves and fishes at their feet.

Return to the B6480 by following the signposts to Wray and Bentham.

☆ **Wennington–Low Bentham** Note the list of tolls high on the wall of the toll-house (now a nursery) on the left side of the road.

☆ **Low and High Bentham** These twin villages 1 mile (1.5 km) apart, both have unspoiled main streets.

🍺 Low Bentham has an agreeable pub, The Punch Bowl.

✼ **High Bentham–Clapham** From the road there are superb views across to Ingleborough (2,376 feet/724 m) in the north and back across the Bowland Fells. The wide area of unenclosed land in the foreground is called Clapham Common.

☆ **Clapham** A photogenic Yorkshire Dales village with a tree-lined stream, Clapham Beck, running through the centre. Cottages (mainly 18th-C) line the twin main streets on either side of the stream, which is ∩ crossed by a number of bridges, including an old packhorse bridge. The medieval 🏰 church, much restored in Regency times, is well worth a visit.

⚓ **Clapham** Ingleborough Hall, now an Outdoor Education Centre, was the home of Reginald Farrer (1880–1920), the remarkable botanist and explorer who brought back many rare plants from the Far East, including several rhododendrons and the beautiful Farrer's gentian.

🏚 **Clapham** Ingleborough Cave, about 1 mile (1.5 km) from the village, is one of Yorkshire's glittering prizes. A passage around 800 yards (731.5 m) long links chambers filled with gleaming stalactites and stalagmites, fringed pools and weirdly shaped rocks. A leaflet explaining how to reach the cave (on foot, but mainly over level ground) is available from the information centre in the village.

② *From the centre of the village, return down the main street, continuing across Clapham bypass (A65) on the Slaidburn road.*

☆ **Bowland Knotts** The road from Clapham (single track with passing places) soon leaves outlying farms behind and ascends to the top of Bowland Knotts – 'knott' is a northern word for peak or summit.

✼ At a large, black, outcropping rock near the summit there is a small lay-by offering a very fine view in both directions: northwards across the limestone country of the Yorkshire Dales, with Ingleborough the dominant feature in the foreground, and the Wenning and Ribble valleys immediately below; southwards back into the heart of Bowland, with Stocks Reservoir and forestry plantations below.

✕ **Stocks Reservoir** The Forestry Commission picnic site at Cocklet Hill is a convenient place to stop and explore Gisburn Forest and the edge of Stocks Reservoir. The name Stocks comes from the hamlet of Stocks-in-Bowland which was drowned when the 344-acre reservoir was built. Only the

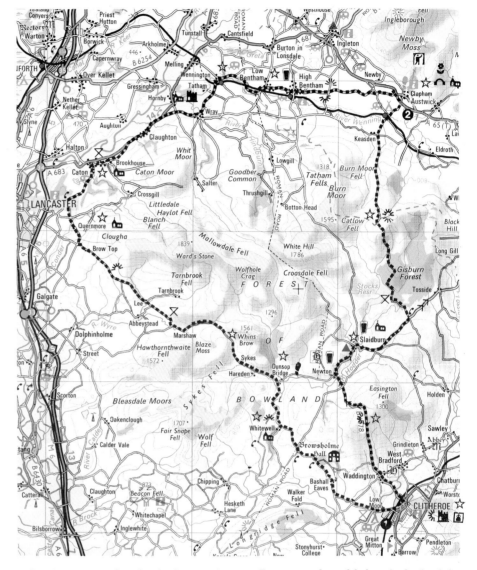

church was saved and rebuilt near the roadside, but a little green hillock close to the hamlet could not be flattened and survives as an island bird sanctuary in the middle of the reservoir.

☆ **Slaidburn** The 'capital' of Bowland, Slaidburn lies in a shallow bowl of the fells just below the meeting point of the River Hodder and Croasdale Beck. The village itself is unspoiled and full of character. It has numerous shops and cafés and an old grammar school dating from 1717.

🏰 **Slaidburn** The 15th-C church has a canopied, high-decker pulpit and a splendid rood screen, both dating from the 17thC.

🍺 **Slaidburn** The Hark to Bounty Inn (named after a hound called Bounty that used to bark when his master went in for a drink, leaving him outside) has a panelled room in which the old Forest Court was held.

🏚 **Newton in Bowland** The Friends' Meeting House dates from 1767, and is one of many that were built in the area after 1652, when George Fox, founder of the Society of Friends, had his famous vision on Pendle Hill, near Clitheroe. The vision inspired

Fox to preach, and led to the birth of the Quaker movement.

🍺 **Newton in Bowland** Forest deer-keepers used to live in the cottage that is now The Parkers Arms Hotel, an attractive pub with a garden.

☆ **Waddington Fell** The B6478 to Waddington and Clitheroe climbs to over 1,000 feet (304 m) and is a dramatically beautiful ✼ road. There are fine views of the Bowland Fells and across Clitheroe to the massive form of Pendle Hill, said to have been frequented by witches.

Just past the summit, The Moorcock Inn takes its name from the ubiquitous red grouse of the fells.

🏚 **Waddington** This pretty village, which has gardens laid out on each side of a stream, once sheltered an English king. In 1464, after the battle of Hexham, Henry VI fled from his enemies and took shelter with the Waddington family at the Old Hall, which can still be seen in the centre of the village. Unfortunately the King's hiding place was discovered by his enemies: as they arrived he escaped through a window, only to be captured in Clitheroe Wood.

The South Pennines

Gritstone dominates the South Pennines. It has created a wild, open landscape of moorland and sheep pasture, criss-crossed by dry-stone walls and dotted with farms.

The same dark stone was used to build the terraced cottages that were erected near the textile mills during the Industrial Revolution.

Today, many of the mills are silent, but towns such as Hebden Bridge and Todmorden have retained much of their nineteenth century character. Other settlements originated as communities of hand-weavers, whose lives were ruined by the coming of the factories.

Route One: 56 miles (90 km)
In sequence from: Hebden Bridge
Direction of travel: anticlockwise

☆ **Hebden Bridge** The capital of the South Pennines, this busy market town has grown around the Tudor bridge across Hebden Water. Its streets are built in steep terraces along the hillsides, connected by stepped alleyways, and back doors are often a floor higher than front doors. The whole effect is reminiscent of a Cornish or Mediterranean fishing village. *Tourist information: tel. (0422) 843831.*

☆ **Hebden Bridge** Hardcastle Crags (*follow signs on left of A6033 after ½ mile /0.8 km*) are a combination of rocks, woodland and steep Pennine valleys. A useful place to make for if you are in search of picnic areas and woodland walks.

🚗 **Hebden Bridge** A former mill houses a collection of early Austin and Morris cars (including the famous bull-nosed Morris), motor cycles and bicycles. *Open daily in summer, Sat and Sun afternoons rest of year.*

To reach the mill, take right turning off A6033 1 mile (1.5 km) from town, and follow signs to 'Automobilia'.

🚂 **Oxenhope** The Worth Valley Railway featured in such films as *The Railway Children* and *Yanks. Frequent steam train service to Haworth and Keighley; daily in July and Aug; Sun only rest of the year.*

🏛 **Oxenhope** The museum has more than a dozen locomotives from America, Sweden and Britain, including the Victorian 0-6-0 locomotive used in *The Railway Children.*
✗ There is also a picnic site beside the museum, which is open *when trains are running.*

☆ **Haworth** Famous for its Brontë connections, this bleak village has a cobbled main street unaltered since the days when Charlotte, Anne and Emily were writing their novels.

🏛 **Haworth** At the Parsonage, where the Brontës lived, their possessions are touchingly displayed. Even the furniture adds to the sadness of the story: visitors see the couch where Emily died, and the table round which the three sisters and their brother took their endless 'walks'. *Open daily.*

🍺 **Haworth** The Black Bull was where the notorious and unfortunate Branwell Brontë drank himself to an early grave.

① *At the top of the village, turn left on to Stanbury and Colne road, bear left at first fork signposted Penistone Hill Country Park.*

🏇 **Penistone Hill Country Park** An area of open moorland dedicated to recreation. There are parking places, picnic areas and superb views. Excellent starting point for walks to the Brontë Falls (much loved by Emily) and Top Withens (the supposed inspiration for *Wuthering Heights*).

② *Continue along road past Penistone Hill; turn right over reservoir dam to road junction, then left to Stanbury village.*

☆ **Stanbury** Typical Pennine village with 17th–18th-C cottages and farmhouses, and two pleasant inns. *Continue directly ahead down to Ponden.*

🏚 **Ponden** The 17th-C Hall, considered by many to be the original of Thrushcross Grange in *Wuthering Heights*, is now a craft centre. Nearby, Ponden Mill sells locally made textiles.

③ *Continue to next junction before taking sharp right turn to Oldfield and Oakworth. Soon after Golden Fleece pub in Oakworth, turn left and follow road signposted to Sutton and Laycock. Go past cemetery, then turn left to Gooseye.*

☆ **Gooseye** This curiously named little mill hamlet crowds into a narrow gill. One of the old mill buildings is now a restaurant and club, and The Turkey Inn is celebrated for the production of its own excellent Gooseye ale.

④ *Continue up extremely steep, winding road to junction. Turn sharp right into Laycock. At Keighley, go straight ahead at traffic island and left at traffic lights along main street to next set of traffic lights. Watch out for Cliffe Castle car park sign on left.*

🏛 **Cliffe Castle** Built by a Victorian wool magnate, this ornate mansion is now a natural history museum. *Open Tues–Sun.*

Return to main road, turn left to traffic island, then right along Bradford main road to East Riddlesden.

🏛 **East Riddlesden Hall** Fine Jacobean house with strong Civil War associations and great atmosphere. Virtually unaltered, it has fine ceilings and fireplaces, rare rose windows and, inevitably, a ghost.

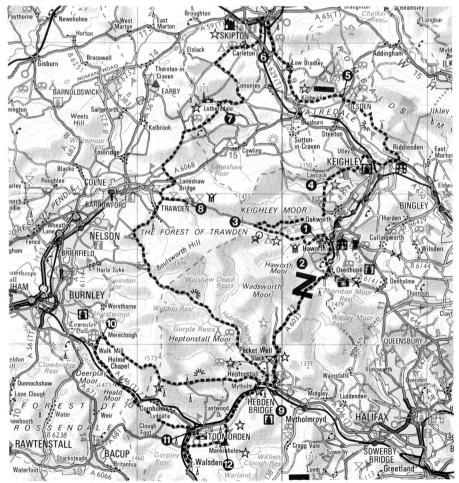

The tithe barn, predating the house, has a collection of vintage farm vehicles. Its cruck-style roof dates from monastic times and is one of the finest examples in the north of England. *Open Wed–Sun and Bank Holidays, July–Aug; Wed–Sun afternoons, Sept–Oct.*

Go up Granby Lane opposite the Hall. At junction, turn left. From this road there are views across Airedale, Keighley and into Worth valley.

⑤ *At Silsden, turn right into main street; when road bends left keep straight on following Farnhill signs.*

☆ **Kildwick** The hall, a fine 17th-C house with gabled facade and mullioned windows, is now a high-class restaurant.
At top of village bear right, following signs to Bradley. At junction with A6033 bear right to Skipton.

☆ **Skipton** Large, bustling market town with fully roofed medieval castle at the top of the High St. *The castle is open daily.*

⑥ *Leave town on Keighley road (A629), then take third road right past bus station, signposted to Carleton. From Carleton follow Earby road uphill to junction, then turn left. Take right turning at second junction, signposted to Lothersdale.*

☆ **Lothersdale** Beautiful, isolated valley which has more of the character of the Yorkshire Dales than the Pennine valleys. The village has a mill *(open in summer)* with a huge waterwheel, and a pleasant pub, Webster's. Afternoon teas are served at the post office.

⑦ *Follow signs to Colne, turning left on outskirts of town to Laneshaw Bridge beside The Emmot Arms. Cross A6068 and follow Wycoller signs to village car park.*

☙ **Wycoller Village and Country Park** Wycoller is a medieval weavers' settlement which gradually sank into decay after the Industrial Revolution, becoming practically a deserted village. With its picturesque packhorse bridges and ruined hall, it is now the focal point of a country park.
Cars are not allowed in the village, and visitors must walk about ¼ mile (0.5 km) from the car park; exceptions are made for the disabled.

⑧ *Follow Trawden signs from Wycoller road end; turn left in Trawden, soon bearing right to follow Hebden Bridge signs over narrow moorland road via Widdop.*

☙ **Trawden–Hebden Bridge** The splendid views from this road are of a wild, desolate landscape reminiscent of the Scottish highlands. The White Cross inn has real ale and good food.

> **Route Two: 27 miles (43 km)**
> In sequence from: Hebden Bridge
> Direction of travel: anticlockwise

⑨ *Leave town on A646; follow signs around turning circle up hill to Heptonstall.*

☆ **Heptonstall** Hilltop village (originally a

● *Heptonstall, once a focal point for weavers.*

handweavers' settlement) with a ruined church, an octagonal Methodist chapel (built 1764 and still in use) and a Tudor cloth hall.

☙ **Heptonstall–Burnley** Fine views along the entire length of this road which for much of its length follows The Long Causeway, a major trade route in medieval times.

☆ **Mount Cross** An extraordinary, medieval wayside cross which reveals strong Viking influence in its design, and dates back to the period of Viking settlement in the south Pennines. *To reach the cross, turn left at Shore/Stone Cross sign. A quarter of a mile (0.5 km) along lane, park and walk along track on left. Cross is in field on left.*

⑩ *At Mereclough, turn left at T-junction and go down to Holme. For Towneley Hall, turn right on to A646. At major road junction keep right towards Burnley. Turn into Country Park soon after junction.*

▣ **Towneley Hall** Substantial art gallery and regional museum.

☙ **Cliviger Gorge** Superb views throughout the length of this steep Pennine pass.

☆ **Todmorden** The fine, neo-classical Town Hall dominates the scene, but the most charming building is the post office, a Jacobean house.
As at Hebden Bridge, cottages and farmhouses cling to the hillsides often at fantastic angles; considerable driving skill is required to negotiate the steep lanes.

⑪ *Leave town on the Rochdale road (A6033). Just past Walsden post office, turn left to Lumbutts and Mankinholes, then bear right after ½ mile (0.8 km) to Lumbutts.*

☙ **Lumbutts** This tiny village has an extraordinary relic of the textile industry: a tall water mill, which once held three waterwheels, fed by water syphoned up from nearby dams.

☆ **Mankinholes,** half a mile (0.8 km) from Lumbutts, has several fine 17th- and 18th-C houses and cottages.

⑫ *From Mankinholes, go down wooded road, turning sharp left at junction to join A646, 3 miles (5 km) from Hebden Bridge.*

The Yorkshire Wolds

The Romans and Vikings probably knew more about the Yorkshire Wolds than most Britons do today. Holiday-makers pass them by in their haste to reach the better-known Dales and Moors, which is why there is hardly a better place for a peaceful tour of discovery along uncrowded roads that link unspoilt villages (their pure Danish names – Thorngumbald, Wetwang, Kirby Grindalythe – might make you think you are in another country).

The loneliness of the high Wolds is balanced by the first part of the tour which takes in down-to-earth Great Driffield, the seaside resort of Hornsea, and Beverley.

> **Route: 88 miles (141 km)**
> In sequence from: Great Driffield
> Direction of travel: clockwise

☆ **Great Driffield** Its prefix belies this small, unspoilt, red-brick market town, although it is said to have been the capital of an ancient kingdom.

⛪ **Great Driffield** The parish church with its soaring 15th-C tower has some fine 12th-C features including its font. In the porch, note the medieval aristocrats portrayed in the windows.

🍺 **Great Driffield** The Bell Hotel in the main street retains its old coaching inn atmosphere and offers an enticing lunch buffet.

① *Leaving town on B1249, go over railway crossing and follow an old canal (now frequented by anglers).*

🌳 **Wansford** The strange, gnarled tree on the right on entering village is 300 years old and hollow. There was once a competition to see how many people could fit inside it.

⛪ **North Frodingham** The imposing old church has Saxon origins.

☆ **Beeford** Apparently slumbering beside the

A165, it is known as far away as China for its fine pedigree pig exports.

𝗆 **Skipsea** On left of B1249, at entrance to the tiny resort of Skipsea, an impressive earthwork is all that is left of an important feudal fort demolished 600 years ago.

☆ **Atwick** Just before entering the village, the road passes over a remarkable, unseen engineering feat. Beneath lies the biggest natural gas storage in Europe – seven huge holes holding the equivalent of 400 gasometers.

☆ **Hornsea** The sea-front of this small resort with its sandy, shingly beach packed with groynes, looks like a Victorian lithograph.

🏺 **Hornsea** The famous, prettily laid out pottery on the south side of the town is visited as much for its leisure park as for its tours round the factory. *Telephone (04012) 2161 for times of tours.*

🦢 **Hornsea Mere** Formed by the melting of Ice Age glaciers, this vast lake is both a pleasure boat centre and a nature reserve with many waterfowl. *Guided tours every Sat and Mon at 1.30, but visitors may walk round the lake unescorted.*

Look for signpost and narrow entrance to Mere near town centre.

② *On leaving Hornsea Mere follow short one-*

● *Vale of Pickering – gentle lowland separating Wolds and North York Moors.*

way system and turn left along B1244.

③ *Turn left along B1243 and continue through pretty village and scenic route via hamlet of Rise to A165 at South Skirlaugh. Turn left into main road, then right almost immediately into Benningholme Lane. After 1 mile (1.5 km) take road signposted to Arnold at T-junction. Almost at once turn left along road signposted to Wawne.*

🚶 **Meaux** Directly across the road at the T-junction is the site of Meaux Abbey. All that can be seen today are the gravestones of two of the monks, a pile of masonry and some mounds on the land belonging to Abbey Farm.

④ *Turn right at T-junction, following sign to Beverley. At A1035, turn left.*

☆ **Beverley** A pleasant market town with many fine Georgian buildings, visited mainly for its exceptional minster. Narrow streets and busy traffic (especially since the nearby Humber Bridge was opened) make this a place to explore on foot. *Tourist information: tel. (0482) 867430.*

⛪ **Beverley** The minster, one of Britain's most splendid Gothic churches, is as big as a cathedral. Allow time to enjoy the magnificent workmanship of the stone and wood carving, particularly on the canopy of the Percy tomb, and the 68 misericords (the largest collection in England).

⛪ **Beverley** St Mary's church (mainly 14th–15thC) is outshone by the minster but deserves attention. In the north choir aisle, beside a doorway, look out for the carved stone rabbit said to be the inspiration for the White Rabbit in *Alice in Wonderland*.

🍺 **Beverley** The old White Horse Inn (better known as 'Nellie's', after a former landlady) serves good lunches. This traditional, pre-plastic era pub is near the bus station.

☆ **Beverley** Drive through the last of the old walled town's five original gates, North Bar, and along a street of fine town houses, once the homes of rich woollen clothmakers, to join B1248.

☆ **Cherry Burton** Turn left into village. An old granary (belonging to a country mansion visible on right a short distance further on) houses an interesting antique shop.

🍴 **Cherry Burton** The old Bay Horse pub has a reputation for English and French food.

⑤ *Take right fork just beyond the pub and follow signs to Etton.*

☆ **Etton** Almost every village round here has a pond and Etton is no exception.

⑥ *Turn right in centre of village then left at signpost to 'Pasture School'. After ½ mile (0.8 km) take left turning at T-junction, signposted Malton, along B1248.*

☆ **Lund** A typical Scandinavian name but this

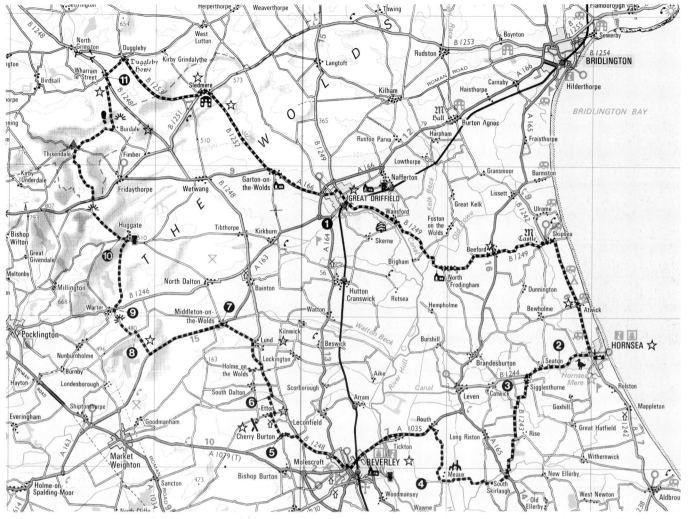

rambling, charming place won a best kept village award and is pure 'Yorkshire'. From centre of the village follow signposts to Middleton.

⑦ *Turn left in centre of Middleton-on-the-Wolds, along A163. After 3½ miles (5.5 km) take right turn signposted Warter.*

☆ **Kiplingcotes** About 250 yards (229 m) after taking the turn for Warter, look out for a sign marked 'Winning Post', which marks the end of the course of the oldest race in Britain. Every March the famous Kiplingcotes Derby is staged here.

⑧ *Continue to T-junction, turning left before going right shortly, at signpost to Warter.*

⚘ **Warter** The view over the little hamlet in its lovely valley is one of the prettiest in the Wolds, now rising all round. The place itself is owned by the Guinness Trust but, strangely, lacks a pub.

⑨ *Turn right on entering village, then left almost immediately, at sign for Huggate.*

🍺 **Huggate** An unspoiled hamlet of farms and cottages with an old inn, The Wolds, where roast beef and Yorkshire pudding is nearly always on the menu.

⑩ *Take Millington road, then turn right after*

a ¼ mile (0.5 km), for Fridaythorpe road. After nearly 2 miles (3 km) look out for broken signpost and two large bell-shaped stone objects. Turn right.

⚘ **Huggate–Burdale** This is the heart of the Wolds. The narrow, open road crosses one of the loneliest, highest points with barely a house in sight. Vast fields – some are 150 acres or more – stretch everywhere.

☆ **Burdale** Nothing to see but a defunct railway bridge and a pond said to have been used in the Iron Age. *Turn sharp left beside pond and go up steep hill.*

⚘ **Wolds Way** At the top of the hill there are superb views across the Wolds. This is also a good starting point for a walk along part of the Wolds Way national footpath.

☆ **Wharram Percy** A small sign on left marks the car park for those visiting one of the most mystic villages in England. Deserted 500 years ago, only the church stands above ground but the outlines of houses are clearly visible and the atmosphere is eerie.

The steep walk down from the car park can be slippery in wet weather.

⑪ *Just before Wharram le Street turn right at signpost for Duggleby. At Duggleby, turn right on to B1253 and follow signs for Sledmere.*

☆ **Sledmere** Turn left into the village but stop after 100 yards (91 m) at one of Britain's most fascinating World War I memorials. It is covered in stone carvings depicting local men working on the farm and fighting in the Waggoners Corps. Oddly, it was carved by an Italian.

🏠 **Sledmere** This neat, pretty village is estate owned and dominated by Sledmere House, a fine Georgian building, restored after a fire earlier this century.

Famous for its furniture, its ceilings, its Turkish Room and its long library, the house was built by Sir Christopher Sykes, a great 18th-C agriculturalist responsible for making vast areas of bare Wolds into good farming land. His son, Sir Tatton ('Old Tatters') was an extraordinary character, larger than life. *Open 1.30–5.30, Tues–Thurs, Sat, Sun, May–Sept. Telephone (0377) 86208 for opening times from Easter to May.*

☆ **Sledmere** Two miles (3 km) from the village it is impossible to miss seeing a massive monument to the Sykes of Sledmere House – just one of many in the area.

⛪ **Garton-on-the-Wolds** Standing beside one of several old Roman roads in this area, the parish church has a particularly impressive Norman tower and a fine west doorway.

Return along A166 to Great Driffield.

The Dales

● *Classic Dales landscape: rugged tops, with limestone outcrops, but a lush, green pastoral valley floor.*

grammar school remains in use as a primary school.

✗ Burnsall The Red Lion pub, by the river serves real ale and is noted for its food.

☆ Linton Tiny village dominated by a gracious, 18th-C almshouse (thought to have been designed by Vanbrugh) and well worth the slight detour from the route.

☆ Grassington The capital of Upper Wharfedale has a fine cobbled square and many 17th- and 18th-C cottages and houses built around narrow courts or 'folds'.

In the mornings, queues form outside the bakers' shops, drawn by the smell of freshly made pies and other Yorkshire specialities.

▣ Grassington In the Upper Wharfedale Museum (in the Square) old farming equipment and domestic relics throw light on life in the Dales in the pre-mechanical era. *Open 2–4.30 Apr–Oct, weekends only during winter months.*

☆ Grassington A five-minute walk from the village leads to Linton Falls, which tumble impressively over limestone crags.

⛪ The Norman church is a further five minutes' walk away.

▥ Stump Cross Caverns Remarkable limestone caves containing well-lit stalagmites and stalactites. Recent excavations have uncovered remains of prehistoric animals including bears, hyaenas and wolverine. There are many items of archaeological importance on display in the visitor centre. *Open daily Apr–Oct, weekends only in winter.*

☆ Pateley Bridge This unspoiled small town at the top of Nidderdale is a useful centre for riverside walks. From the ruined church of St Mary (follow signs to 'Panorama Walk') there are extensive views.

③ *Return along B6265 across river, then take right turning (by garage) signposted to Lofthouse.*

⚙ Wath The 35-foot (11-m) high waterwheel at Foster Beck Mill was constructed in 1904 and powered a textile mill producing heavy yarn. It now forms a central feature of a popular pub and restaurant.

☆ Gouthwaite Reservoir The hamlet of Gouthwaite, and Gouthwaite Hall, were drowned to enable this beautiful reservoir to be constructed in the 1890s. Today it is also a wildfowl nature reserve, which can be seen from the road. It is especially interesting in winter when it is visited by migrant geese.

☆ Ramsgill An attractive village with a green which still boasts a horse trough.

✗ Ramsgill The Yorke Arms offers traditional English dishes at lunchtime.

④ *Continue to Lofthouse, then turn into first lane on left, signposted to How Stean.*

The Yorkshire Dales take their individual names from the rivers that flow along valleys carved out by glaciers.

This tour of the eastern Dales begins in Wharfedale, where the lovely landscape can be seen magnificently from the road. On the way to Nidderdale, gritstone gives way to limestone: at Stump Cross Caverns there is an opportunity to explore the underground beauty of limestone caves, while High Stean Gorge reveals what the wind can do to limestone. But for many, the high point of the tour will be the ruins of one of England's greatest monasteries: Fountains Abbey.

Route: 80 miles (128 km)
Directions in sequence from: Ilkley
Direction of travel: clockwise

☆ Ilkley Originally an important Roman fortress-town, Ilkley became a popular health resort in the 18thC because of its moorland springs. The Museum, in a Tudor manor house near the church, tells the town's story. *Open Tues–Sun. Tourist information: tel. (0943) 602319.*

☆ Ilkley Immortalized by a Victorian music-hall ballad, the moor is a fine place for a bracing walk. White Wells, a restored 18th-C bath-house, is only ½ mile (0.8 km) from town centre *(follow signposts to 'Moor').*

① *Take road over the river to Middleton and Langbar.*

✹ Beamsley Beacon A short walk from the road leads to the summit, and superb views across Wharfe valley. Beamsley was part of a chain of sites across northern England where fires were lit to announce the arrival of the Spanish Armada.

② *Continue down to Beamsley, turn right at junction then left on to A59.*

† Bolton Abbey These Augustinian priory ruins in a beautiful setting were painted by Turner and Landseer, and described by Wordsworth and Ruskin. The nave of the church escaped destruction and is still in use as the parish church.

There are two car parks, riverside and woodland walks (1½ miles/2.5 km to Strid Woods, where the river presses through a narrow gorge) and nature trails.

△ **Bolton Abbey** The Grassington road is one of the most beautiful in England; fine views across Wharfedale all along.

✗ Barden Tower A 17th-C priest's house attached to a former hunting lodge of the Clifford family, lords of Skipton, is now an excellent restaurant which also serves afternoon teas. The studios of Dales artist Mark Thompson are also open to the public.

☆ Burnsall This grey-stone village, lying in a great bowl of hills, has a village green on the riverside. The church has Viking hogback gravestones, and the attractive 17th-C

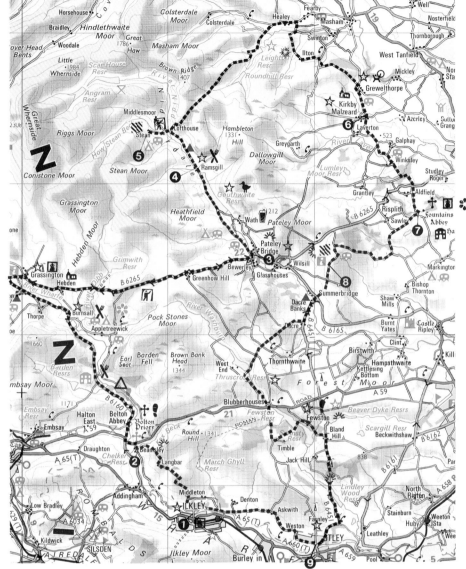

† Fountains Abbey Acknowledged to be one of the finest monastic ruins in Western Europe, this magnificent Cistercian abbey (founded 1132) lies on the sheltered banks of the little River Skell. Its wealth came from the growth of the wool trade; wool from the Yorkshire Dales was exported through the medieval port of York to the growing city-states of Renaissance Italy. The great cellarium with its elegant arches – one of the glories of Fountains – was where much of this wool was stored.

A model of the original abbey, with many recent archaeological finds, can be seen in the museum close to the Abbey. *Abbey and museum open daily.*

↟ Fountains Hall Built with stones taken from nearby Fountains Abbey after the Dissolution, this is a fine example of Jacobean–Renaissance architecture.

✿ Studley Royal A ten-minute walk from Fountains Abbey leads to an estate which, in terms of 18th-C formal and landscape gardens, is almost as important as the Abbey itself. Artificial canals and a lake reflecting temples and towers form a rare example of the neo-classical garden, while the deer park above the valley is more typically English parkland, with views across to Ripon Cathedral. *Open daily.*

⑦ *From Fountains Abbey car park, turn right on to the Harrogate road, then bear right at junction. Keep straight on avoiding right turns to Sawley. After climbing steep hill, take right turning, signposted to Brimham Rocks. Turn left at junction. Brimham Rocks car park is on the right.*

⧠ Brimham Rocks On a headland above Nidderdale, a group of gritstone rocks have been carved by the wind into weird and often astonishing shapes. Paths wander between the rocks, and there are fine views.

⑧ *From the car park, turn right and follow lane downhill. At crossroads, go straight across on to B6451, signed Otley. After 1½ miles (2.5 km) take right turn signposted to Greenhow. At crossroads keep straight on to Thrushcross Reservoir.*

☆ Thrushcross Reservoir Thrushcross was built in the 1960s when the upper Washburn valley was flooded, covering the village of West End.

☆ Fewston and Swinsty Reservoirs The second and third of the chain of reservoirs that forms Washburndale's little lakeland. There are good views of the reservoirs from the dam bridge, and a pleasant walk (about 3 miles/5 km) around Swinsty Reservoir.

⧫ Lindley Wood Reservoir There are fine views from the steep switchback road leading from the woodland picnic site at Norwood down to the reservoir.

☆ Otley This bustling market town (market day Fri) has managed to preserve its ancient courts and alleyways, old shops and inns. South of the town there are extensive views of Wharfedale from Chevin Hill.

⑨ *Go back across the river, then take first turning on left to Ilkley via Weston and Askwith.*

⧠ How Stean Gorge A narrow gorge, where the limestone has been carved into strange and fantastic shapes, has been made safe with handrails to facilitate pedestrian access. The path winds thrillingly above foaming torrents, underneath overhanging crags and across footbridges. There is even a small cave which can be explored with the aid of a torch, but it is muddy underfoot.

⑤ *Return to Lofthouse, taking the steep road left through the village, signposted to Masham. At Healey, turn right, following the Ilton signposts. The road goes through a steeply wooded gorge and over a bridge; turn left at next junction, then go along lane through woods signposted to Druids' Wood. There is a short walk from the car park to the Druids' Temple.*

⧫ Druids' Temple A miniature Stonehenge in the middle of a Yorkshire forest is an eerie sight. It was built c.1820 by William Danby, local squire and owner of Swinton Hall, as a means of creating employment. A plan near the car park outlines local walks.

☆ Grewelthorpe An agreeable village with a long green and large pond, several 18th- and early 19th-C cottages and two unspoiled pubs.

Nearby, Hackfall Woods beside the River Ure were a major tourist attraction in Victorian times. Today, the sham castle and grottos overlooking a steep wooded gorge are overgrown but still accessible by riverside footpath.

⧫ Grewelthorpe The Grewelthorpe Weavers' shop in the village has fine fabrics made on hand looms, and a selection of clothes made from their own fabrics.

☆ Kirkby Malzeard Situated at the crossing of many ancient trackways, lanes and paths, the town has a market charter which dates from 1307, and a medieval market cross restored in the 19thC. The church is particularly fine, with a great deal of Norman work, and a 13th-C priest's doorway.

⑥ *Leave by lane signposted to Galphay and Grantley. At the fork, keep on the Grantley road to the right, but turn left shortly along lane signposted to Winksley. Continue through village; at T-junction turn left up narrow road, cross B6265, then follow signposts to Aldfield and Fountains Abbey.*

The North Yorkshire Moors

The name conjures up a vision of a wilderness bare of everything except ghostly monks (one-time inhabitants of the great abbeys at Whitby and Rievaulx). Yet below the high, heather-clad moors lie attractive stone hamlets, large forestry plantations and, to the south, the plain of Rye Dale.

The tour begins at Pickering, the terminus of the old Yorkshire Moors Railway. Those who take a ride on one of the lovingly preserved steam trains could arrange to be met at Grosmont by drivers doing the complete route suggested below. From the train there is a good view of the mighty, space-age domes of the Fylingdales early warning system.

Route: 100 miles (161 km)
In sequence from: Pickering
Direction of travel: anticlockwise

• *Busy Whitby harbour, where cobles – the characteristic fishing vessel of NE England – can be seen.*

☆ **Pickering** Pleasantly old-fashioned market town, threatened by a modern housing-estate sprawl. There is a colourful market every Mon in the main street. *Tourist information: tel. (0751) 73791.*

Pickering The Beck Isle Museum, beside the river, has interesting displays illustrating rural life in Yorkshire over the last 200 years. *Open Easter to mid-Oct.*

Pickering Not much remains of the Norman castle where Richard II was held prisoner, but it is worth walking up the steps at the top for the splendid view.

Pickering The medieval wall paintings in St Peter's church were hidden for centuries and are now the town's star attraction.

Pickering Steam train enthusiasts can travel from here to Grosmont (about 1 hour) on the North Yorkshire Moors Railway, *open Apr–Oct.* The railway was built by George Stephenson in 1836.

☆ **Thornton Dale** Known as the 'prettiest village in Yorkshire', Thornton Dale's old stone houses beside the Beck are most attractive, but may be almost obscured by sightseers in high summer.

① *In the centre of the village take road signposted to Whitby, up the hill. After about 1 mile (1.5 km) turn right into forested area.*

☆ **Low Dalby** This small village marks the beginning of the Forest Drive, a toll road through Forestry Commission plantations. *Follow signs carefully, leaving by Langdale End exit.*

Hackness Set in a broad and lovely dale, this former estate village on the River Derwent has a church which merits a visit. Dating in part from the 11thC, it contains inscribed fragments of an even earlier cross.

② *Leave village on road signposted to Silpho. Beyond the village, fork left and, shortly after, turn left at crossroads. Just before Harwood Dale turn left, then left again after about ½ mile (0.8 km) on to A171. Leave main road at turning to Robin Hood's Bay.*

Fylingthorpe From the approach road to the village there are fine views of the moors and the steeply shelving coastline. The village itself was a popular resort in Victorian times.

☆ **Robin Hood's Bay** This famous old smugglers' haunt is an unspoilt warren of narrow streets and alleys. Be warned, however, that the village can only be reached on foot, down a steep hill; cars must be left in the car park at the top of the cliffs (some of the highest in Britain).

③ **Whitby** *Follow 'Town Centre' signs to the harbour/car park (beside bus station).*

Whitby The ruined abbey dominates not only the town but religious history, for it was here in 664 that the Synod of Whitby agreed when Easter should be celebrated.

☆ **Whitby** In the alleys overlooking the harbour there are several interesting antique shops. Whitby jet jewellery, made popular by Queen Victoria when she was in mourning, can still be found here.

Whitby A flight of donkey steps leads from the harbour to St Mary's, an extraordinary church with a roof built like a ship's hull and a surprising Georgian interior well worth investigating.

☆ **Whitby** *To reach the sandy beaches and the promenade follow the one-way system leading up the 'Khyber Pass'. Park beside the garden overlooking the sea.*

The garden contains a statue of Captain Cook, who first went to sea in Whitby-built ships, and the huge jaw-bones of a whale.

④ *To leave town, drive along the front on the cliff top, then follow Scarborough/Teeside signs round a slightly complex traffic system. At T-junction, turn right on to A171.*

Grosmont The terminus of the North Yorkshire Moors Railway (see **Pickering**, above).

⑤ *On entering Egton, take left fork for Egton Bridge, down a steep hill.*

☆ **Egton Bridge** A tiny village renowned for its vast, Victorian, Catholic church and for its annual gooseberry fair. Villagers claim that the world's biggest gooseberry was grown and shown here.

Just past the church turn right for Glaisdale, then turn left at T-junction at the top of the hill.

Glaisdale Just before entering the village there is a pretty picnic spot beside an old stone bridge over the River Esk.

☆ **Lealholm** The stepping stones across the river – just one of the attractions of this delightful Esk Dale village – provide the name of the antique shop which has a large collection of second-hand books. *Turn left in village along the road to Danby.*

☆ **Danby** The Moors Centre at the edge of the village supplies information on the North Yorkshire Moors National Park.

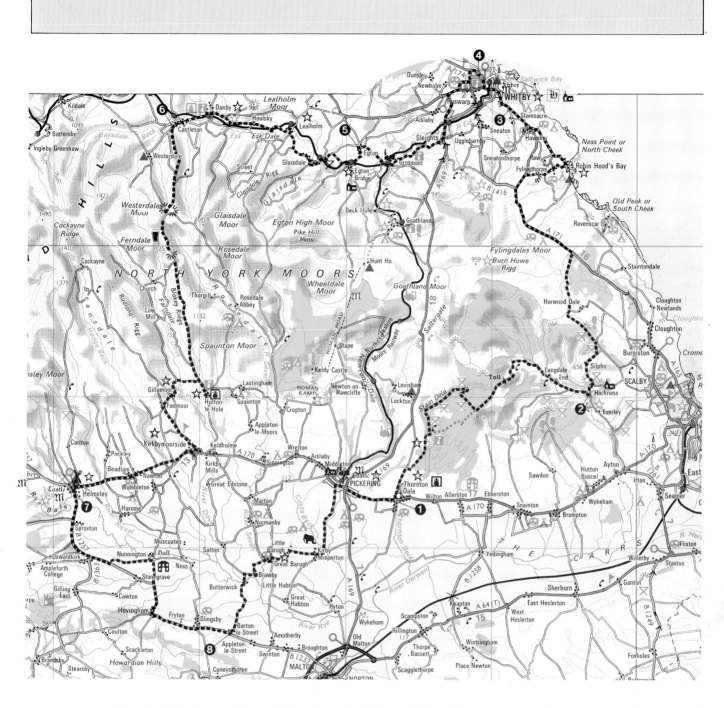

⑥ *On leaving Castleton, fork left along road signposted to Rosedale.*

🌾 **Castleton** to **Hutton-le-Hole** The road crosses wild moorland with magnificent views on either side. After about 4 miles (6.5 km) a cross dating from Celtic times marks one of the Moor's highest points.

🍺 A little further on, the isolated Lion Inn serves bar meals, and just beyond the pub the view stretches out for about 30 miles.

☆ **Hutton-le-Hole** This remarkably pretty village has strong Quaker associations, but is best known today for its Ryedale Folk Museum. Indoors there are lots of country life exhibits; in the Folk Park several old houses and shops have been reconstructed. *Open Apr–Oct.*

On leaving the village turn back along route for a short distance, then turn left to Gillamoor.

☆ **Gillamoor** Mr Frimble's Country Store is a surprise in this tiny village. It sells fashion-able, locally-made clothes, and a better than average selection of souvenirs.

☆ **Kirkbymoorside** Gay with stalls on market days, this friendly town has several fine old inns. *At the roundabout at the bottom of the main street, take the Helmsley road (A170).*

☆ **Helmsley** Delightful old market town built in warm stone. The ruined castle, which dates from the 12thC, is *open Mon–Sat and Sun afternoon.*

A worthwhile detour about 3 miles (5 km) west along B1257 leads to Rievaulx Abbey, another 12th-C ruin, *open daily (but closed Sun morning in winter).* Surrounded by hills, these substantial remains look superb from the Rievaulx Terrace; *open Apr–Oct.*

✗ **Helmsley** The Spanish owner of The Feversham Arms has produced an unusual menu that puts Yorkshire specialities side by side with exotic dishes from his native country. He also offers an amazing choice of sherries.

⑦ *Leave town on A170 signposted to Thirsk. Fork left on to B1257, signposted to Malton, then left again on unclassified road to Nunnington Hall.*

🏠 **Nunnington Hall** Large 16th–17thC manor house built on the banks of the River Rye. It has fine panelling and a beautifully carved chimneypiece, but is best known for its collection of miniature rooms. *Open 2–6, Tues–Thurs, Sat, Sun and Bank Holiday Mon, Apr–Oct.*

On leaving, turn left and return to B1257.

⑧ *At Barton-le-Street turn left to Brawby.*

🐘 **Kirby Misperton** At the Flamingo Park Zoo more than 1,000 animals and birds can be seen in natural surroundings from ground level or monorail. There are all sorts of extra diversions including Britain's biggest looping rollercoaster. *Open Apr–Sept.*

Windermere, Eskdale and Coniston Water

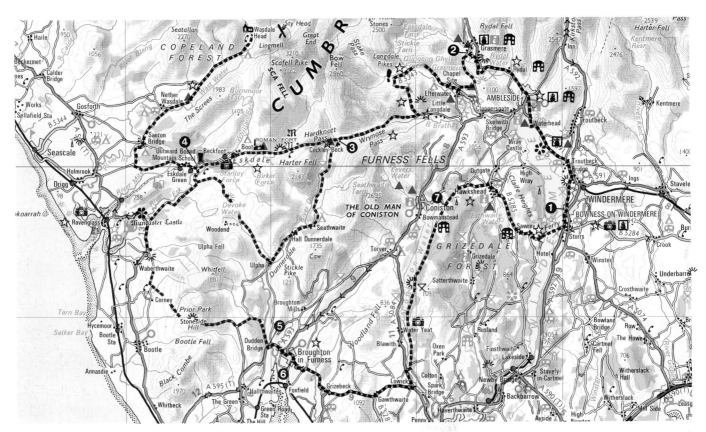

Starting in Windermere, the tour takes to the heights over mountain passes where roads are narrow and twisting and are often closed in winter because of snow and ice. On summer days those who make an early start will not only avoid most of the traffic, but will enjoy the pleasure of morning light on dramatic scenery.

For the energetic, there are opportunities for water sports and walks throughout the tour. For those whose love of landscape has been inspired by books, there are literary shrines to suit all ages: Wordsworth, Ruskin and Beatrix Potter all had houses in the area.

> **Route: 68 miles (109 km)**
> In sequence from: Windermere
> Direction of travel: anticlockwise

☆ **Bowness-on-Windermere** Bustling lakeside town with numerous hotels, shops and restaurants. From the pier, steamers ply to both ends of Windermere: Lakeside to the south, Waterhead to the north. Motor boats and rowing boats can be hired and there are motor-launch trips round the lake.

① *From the lakeside promenade take the road past 15th-C St Martin's Church, then fork left (the road is signposted to Keswick).*

🏠 **Bowness-on-Windermere** The Steamboat museum (*open Mon–Sat and Sun afternoon, Apr–Oct*) displays vintage craft and offers trips on the lake. Nearby, a car park with picnic area gives access to the lake shore.

⛰ **Hammarbank Viewpoint** Park here to take in extensive views across Windermere to the central mountains. *At mini roundabout turn left (signposted to Keswick).*

🏠 **Brockhole** The National Park Centre has exhibitions, films, a cafeteria, a lakeshore ❀ walk and flower and shrub gardens.

☆ **Ambleside** This popular centre has hotels, cafés, shops, a Dolls' House Museum (Kirkstone Rd.) and an interesting mural in the church of St Mary. A ½-mile (0·8-km) walk leads to Stock Ghyll waterfalls.

🏠 **Ambleside** The road passes photogenic Bridge House, a tiny 17th-C cottage on a bridge over Stock Ghyll.

🏠 **Rydal** Rydal Mount, Wordsworth's home from 1813 to 1850, has portraits and many of the poet's personal possessions. *Open daily, except from mid-Jan to end Feb.* By the church, Dora's Field (named after Wordsworth's daughter) is carpeted with daffodils in spring.

☆ **Rydal** To the left, Loughrigg Fell rises steeply from the far shore of Rydal Water. (*Park at White Moss Common just beyond the lake.*)

⛰ **Rydal–Grasmere** The road runs on through a wood. At a sharp bend Grasmere comes into view – when unruffled by the wind, the lake reflects the surrounding mountains. Silver Howe lies across the lake; ahead, Helm Crag is surmounted by the Lion and the Lamb – rocks with animal-like silhouettes.

🏠 **Grasmere** Before the turn into the village, a road to the right leads to Dove Cottage (Wordsworth lived here from 1799 to 1808) 🖼 and the Wordsworth Museum; *both open Mar–Oct. Tourist information: tel. (09665) 245.*

② *On leaving village, fork left at signpost to Langdales. The narrow, twisting road leads to Red Bank, a short steep hill (1:4). At top where road divides take the right turn signposted to Langdales.*

Descend into Great Langdale on open road over Elterwater Common with fine ⛰ *view of Wetherlam (2,502 feet/763 m) and to the valley head. Sharp left bend near bottom of descent signposted to Colwith; at Elterwater crossroads in the valley bottom, turn right (signposted to Great Langdale).*

☆ **Langdale** Spectacular valley with the Langdale Pikes standing prominently ahead, their rocky outline against the sky. From the large National Trust car park at the New Dungeon Ghyll Hotel, walkers can explore ❗ the Pikes: the path climbs steeply beside rushing waterfalls.

☆ **Langdale** The road takes a sharp left turn out of the valley head, then climbs a steep hill with tight bends to Blea Tarn. All around there is splendid mountain scenery. Just beyond the road's summit there is a small car park; walk from here to the edge of Blea Tarn (about ¼ mile/0.5 km) for a ⛰ classic view of the Langdale Pikes.

• *Esthwaite Water is skirted by the route between Windermere and Coniston Water.*

☆ **Little Langdale** *Descend to the head of Little Langdale on a steep narrow road across a boulder-strewn and juniper-scattered mountainside. In the valley bottom turn sharp right, signposted Wrynose.*

☆ **Wrynose Pass** A long and sometimes extremely steep climb to the summit (1,281 feet/390.5 m) along a narrow road with unprotected drop into the valley on the left.
    The carved Three Shires Stone at the summit marks the former meeting place of Westmorland, Cumberland and Lancashire.

③ *At Cockley Beck, turn right over bridge for Hardknott Pass (1,290 feet/393 m).*

☆ **Hardknott Pass** Narrow and steep (1:3 in places), with severe bends, this is certainly the Lake District's most exciting road. However, there is a less taxing alternative route that is also interesting: *go straight on at Cockley Bridge, through beautiful Duddon valley. At Ulpha, turn right up steep twisting hill signposted to Eskdale. Cross Birker Moor (superb views) and rejoin route at George IV Inn (see* **Eskdale** *below).*

ɱ **Hardknott Pass** Hardknott Castle (on the descent) is a partly reconstructed Roman
ᴪ fort in a magnificent situation with views across the upper Esk to England's highest mountains, Scafell Pike and Scafell.

☆ **Eskdale** There is only one road down this beautiful dale with its pink granite buildings, its walks, woods and rocky cliffs.
ʮ   At Boot, a working water mill can be visited. Close by, at Dalegarth, narrow-
⛟ gauge railway enthusiasts can take a train down the valley to Ravenglass and back.
    Also near Dalegarth, Stanley Force waterfall (reached along a rocky path through a deep wooded gorge) is a fascinating sight after heavy rain. *Follow valley road to*
🍺 *junction at George IV Inn (meals available).*

☆ **Wasdale** A detour along the most dramatic valley in the Lake District, to Wasdale Head and back, adds 19 miles (30.5 km) to the tour. *At George IV Inn turn right, then go through the scattered hamlet of Eskdale Green to Wasdale.*

☆ **Wasdale** The pastoral nature of the first few miles gives no warning of what is to come. Wastwater, the deepest lake in England, is dark and foreboding. Beside the lake the road is an open, narrow, undulating strip of tarmac, while across the water the great awe-inspiring fans of scree drop from black crags directly into the lake. High mountains stand about the valley head, Scafell Pike and Scafell to the right, and the conical peak of Great Gable in the centre.

✗ **Wasdale Head** Meals are served to non-residents at the Wasdale Head Inn (famous for its associations with early rock climbers) at the end of the public road.
🛐   Close by, St Olaf's church (16th-C) is one of the smallest churches in England.

④ *At George IV Inn take road signposted to Ulpha and Broughton. After ½ mile*

(0.8 km) *turn right, and take the narrow and twisting road running beside the River Esk to junction with A595.*

☆ **Ravenglass** A short (5-mile/8-km)
✿ detour takes in Muncaster Castle (*open Tues–Sun afternoons mid-Apr to Sept, and well-known for its rhododendrons and azaleas*) and Ravenglass village, where Roman remains have been found. This is also the
⛟ starting point for the narrow-gauge railway. *Return to junction where detour began, and turn right on to Barrow road (continuation of A595).*

ᴪ **Corney Fell** *After about 1 mile (1.5 km), turn left along 'scenic route'.* The road goes over rolling moorland with Black Coombe stretching out into the sea on the right.

⑤ *Rejoin the A595; turn left over the bridge and follow signs into Broughton.*

☆ **Broughton in Furness** An attractive little town with a spacious market square and several interesting 18th–19thC buildings.

⑥ *Follow A595 up to Grizebeck (note slate quarrying on the right). At beginning of descent keep left, signposted Lancaster, and at next crossroads turn left, signposted Torver and Coniston. This is a curving minor road which goes past Lowick church.*
    Cross A5084 and take road marked 'Nibthwaite and East of Lake', which then turns north to run beside the River Crake to Nibthwaite (not on map).

⛴ **Coniston Water** The steam boat *Gondola*, originally launched in 1859 and now beautifully restored, takes passengers from Parkamoor pier near the south end of the lake to Coniston village and back.

✗ **Coniston Water** The road, running close to the lake, has parking and picnic places and easy access to the shingly shore. There are
ᴪ dramatic views across to Coniston Old Man (2,635 feet/803 m); Peel Island, in the foreground, featured in Arthur Ransome's *Swallows and Amazons* as Wild Cat Island.

🏛 **Coniston Water** Brantwood, home of art critic John Ruskin, 1872–1900, has paintings and memorabilia. *Open daily in summer; Wed–Sun in winter.*

⑦ *Near the head of the lake where the road divides, take right turning to Hawkshead. No cars allowed in the village, but there is a car park off the bypass.*

☆ **Hawkshead** The village where Wordsworth went to school has quaint buildings, cobbled passages and narrow alleys, and there are several inns, cafés and gift shops.
    Leave the village by road signposted 'Windermere by Ferry'.

🏛 **Hawkshead–Windermere** Hill Top, behind the Tower Bank Arms in Near Sawrey village, was the home of Beatrix Potter. In high season there can be a long wait to see inside this small cottage which contains some of the artist's original drawings. *Open Apr–Oct.*

☆ **Windermere Ferry** The ferry service operates daily, every 20 minutes until 9 in winter and 10 in summer, and the crossing takes seven minutes. There may be queues, particularly around 5 on summer afternoons. The ferry takes ten cars so time of waiting can be calculated.
    On disembarking, drive to the top of the ferry road, then take left turning to Bowness-on-Windermere.

Caldbeck, Buttermere and Derwent Water

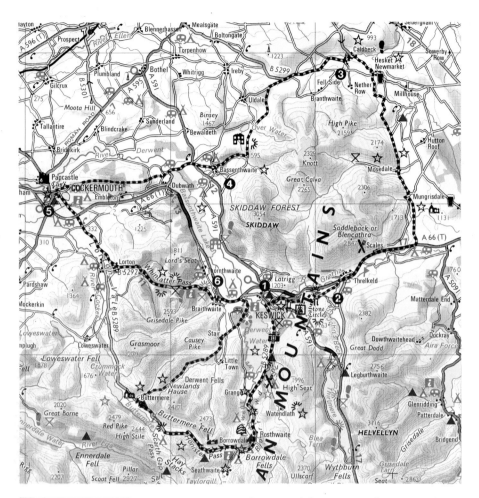

E ver since it was 'discovered' by nineteenth-century travellers, the Lake District has attracted more than its fair share of tourists. Many are content to follow the main roads that link the better-known sights, but this tour explores further afield to give a taste of every aspect of the area: waterfalls cascading down mountainsides; forests; high bare peaks; tranquil lakes; and, in the valleys, cultivated fields contrasting with the untamed landscape of the great passes.

Although scenery is the main theme, the tour includes the small towns of Keswick and Cockermouth, and the Bronze Age Castlerigg Stone Circle.

Route: 64 miles (102.5 km)
In sequence from: Keswick
Direction of travel: anticlockwise

☆ **Keswick** The principal town in the northern Lake District has crowded, narrow streets, a Moot Hall (restored 1813) in the market-place, a theatre and a museum containing manuscripts and relics of literary luminaries who lived in the area (open Mon–Sat, Apr–Oct). Tourist information: tel. (0596) 72645.

① Leave town by Penrith road and immediately after junction with Windermere road take minor road to right signposted Castlerigg Stone Circle.

ᛗ **Keswick** About 1 mile (1.5 km) from the town, a short walk across a field leads to Castlerigg Stone Circle, over 3,000 years old and the best example of prehistoric standing stones in the north of England. From here there is a magnificent mountain panorama, with Helvellyn to the south, and Skiddaw and Blencathra to the north.

② Continue on minor road, taking right turn at two T-junctions, then turn right again on to A66.

✗ **Scales** At the top of a long hill the White Horse Inn serves good bar meals, and is the most popular starting point for climbers ascending Blencathra.

Continue on A66 for about 4 miles (6.5 km). At crossroads, turn left to Mungrisdale.

☆ **Mungrisdale** This tranquil village lying close under the hills has a tiny, whitewashed church (1756) with a three-decker pulpit.

🍺 **Mungrisdale** The Mill Inn is picturesquely set beside the River Glenderamackin.

☆ **Mosedale** At the Friends' Meeting House (1702), coffee and cakes are served from May to September. A short detour can be made into the Caldew Valley (cul-de-sac) which has fine picnic places beside a rocky river. At the end of the road there are old mines and spoil heaps; the area was exceptionally rich in minerals, and specimens can still be found here.

☆ **Mosedale** Beyond the village the road runs over unfenced common with the steep boulder-strewn slopes of Carrock Fell on the left; some of the boulders are huge and appear precariously balanced.

☆ **Hesket Newmarket** The village has many 18th-C houses set about a green, and a useful pub, The Old Crown.

☆ **Caldbeck** John Peel, the fox-hunting enthusiast immortalized in a well-known song, was born in this charming village in 1776. His grave can be seen in the churchyard. There are also craft shops, tea places and, of course, The John Peel Inn.

❗ **Caldbeck** Over the bridge a small car park is the starting point for a 1-mile (1.5 km) walk to the Howk, a limestone gorge.

③ Leave village on B5299 signposted Uldale and Bassenthwaite, then fork left after 3 miles (5 km) on to minor road (signposted to Keswick) and left again at turning to Orthwaite and Mirkholme.

🏛 **Caldbeck–Bassenthwaite** At Orthwaite (not on map), the 17th-C Hall, well seen from the road, declares its antiquity in its mullioned windows and architectural detail.

The spectacular Dash Falls are glimpsed in the distance to the left. Beyond Orthwaite Hall, take next turning to the right to Bassenthwaite.

☆ **Bassenthwaite** Huge new farm buildings dominate the village, but a few old houses survive; note, near The Sun Inn, a stone over a cottage door which reads 'This house done by John Grave 1736'.

④ Go through village then turn right on to A591. At crossroads near The Castle Inn, turn left to Bassenthwaite Lake.

☆ **Bassenthwaite Lake** The only lake in the Lake District (the others are 'meres', 'waters' or 'tarns').

Cross Ouse Bridge over the outflow, take right turning (signposted Cockermouth), then go right again at turning marked Golf Course and Higham Hall, along a quiet and elevated road to Cockermouth.

☆ **Cockermouth** The wide, tree-lined main street has several old and interesting buildings, including the house where Wordsworth was born in 1770. House open Mon–Wed, Fri, Sat, and Sun afternoon, Apr–Oct.

Fletcher Christian, mutineer on the Bounty, was also born in the town, in 1764.

🏰 **Cockermouth** The partly ruined castle, which dates from the 12thC, is still lived in (only occasionally open to the public).

⑤ Leave town on B5292 signposted to Lorton and Buttermere. Before Lorton when road

• *Boating on Derwent Water has not always been mainly for pleasure. The lake was once a significant commercial thoroughfare, with cargo boats carrying ore from mines around the valley for smelting at Keswick.*

divides take left fork signposted to Braithwaite and Keswick.

☆ **Whinlatter Pass** Near the foot of the pass Spout Force waterfall may be reached by a marked rough track (½ mile/0.8 km).

At the summit, there is a Forestry Commission's Visitor Centre.

The pass has extensive forest on both
✗ sides with marked walks; on the descent a
✹ picnic site affords a fine view over Bassenthwaite Lake to Skiddaw.

⑥ *Turn right in Braithwaite and look for signs to Newlands.*

☆ **Newlands Hause** Approached along the pastoral Newlands valley, the pass across Newlands Hause has hairpin bends.

Keskadale Oaks, on slopes to the right, are remnants of ancient forest cover. There is a steep final climb to 1,092 feet (333 m).

☆ **Buttermere** A grand backdrop, provided by the towering peaks of High Crag, High Stile and Red Pike, makes this modest lake (it is only 1¼ miles/2 km long) one of the loveliest in the Lake District.

Tiny Buttermere village has a fittingly
⌂ tiny Victorian church which stands in a splendid position.

✹ **Buttermere** *Take the Keswick via Honister road,* which runs well above the lake giving extensive views. Ahead, with an exceptionally steep side silhouetted against the sky, is Fleetwith Pike. Rowing boats for hire at Gatesgarth Farm (end of lake).

☆ **Honister Pass** A twisting road, narrow in places, steep near the summit (1,174 feet/358 m), runs between boulder-strewn mountainsides; Fleetwith Pike is on the right and Dalehead on the left.
⌂ At the top of the pass, Honister slate quarries have been in operation for more than 200 years.

The descent into Borrowdale is gentle at first, across open moorland, but the final drop into the hamlet of Seatoller is steep.

☆ **Seatoller** The National Park Dalehead Centre provides information about Borrowdale and mountain expeditions.

A diversion can be made to Seathwaite
☆ (1 mile/1.5 km), the wettest inhabited place in England.

🏠 **Borrowdale** With its steep mountainsides, bare crags, clear river and abundant trees, Borrowdale contains the essence of the Lake District. The extensive oak woodlands are protected as they are of international importance and in them the red squirrel can still be seen.

☆ **Borrowdale** Beyond Rosthwaite the road twists close to the river through the narrow pass called the Jaws of Borrowdale.

There is a car park among the silver birches at Quay Foot. From here, a short walk is signposted to the Bowder Stone, a huge, precariously balanced rock; there is a wooden staircase to its summit.

☆ **Borrowdale** Pause for tea (there is a choice of places) at picturesque Grange, where an arched, 17th-C bridge spans the wide river. In summer parking may be difficult.

✗ **Borrowdale** A little further down the valley the Borrowdale Hotel serves excellent meals, while the Lodore Swiss Hotel provides a more luxurious setting, with matching prices. Behind the latter, the Lodore Falls are an impressive sight after heavy rainfall.

☆ **Derwent Water** With its indented shoreline and wooded islands, Derwent Water is considered by many to be the most beautiful of the English lakes.

Across the water, the ridge of Maiden
✹ Moor and Catbells rises above Brandlehow Woods, the first property acquired by the National Trust in the Lake District. (The Trust now owns a quarter of the National Park.)
📷 A frequent public launch service calls at various points around the lake.

☆ **Watendlath** A detour can be made to Watendlath, 3 miles (5 km) along a narrow, twisting, sometimes congested road. The rewards include Ashness Bridge, one of the most photographed places in the Lake District, and Surprise View – a splendid view
✹ trict, and Surprise View – a splendid view over Derwent Water from the edge of a vertical cliff.

Watendlath itself is an artists' hamlet, cradled in the fells.

✗ **Derwent Water–Keswick** Calf Close Bay is an excellent place for a picnic. The car park is in Great Wood to the right of the road.

Teesdale

● *High Force waterfall near Newbiggin, Teesdale.*

S urrounded by fells and moors with a distinctly wild look about them, the lush green finger of Teesdale lies in sheltered serenity beside the placid river. The calm is deceptive, however, for along this route are two of England's most impressive waterfalls, the aptly named High Force and Cauldron Snout.

There are other surprises on this tour. In the very English town of Barnard Castle, a French château houses works of art, and further along the route a tiny moorland village has been turned into a cowboy town.

> **Route: 80 miles (128 km)**
> In sequence from: Barnard Castle
> Direction of travel: clockwise

☆ **Barnard Castle** Chief town of Teesdale, with fine broad streets and intriguing narrow alleys. Dickens stayed here when he was doing research into the Yorkshire schools (for *Nicholas Nickleby*) in 1838, and would still feel at home. *Tourist information: tel. (0833) 38481.*

♏ **Barnard Castle** The ruins of the Norman castle dominate the town. *Open daily.*

▣ **Barnard Castle** The Bowes Museum, built in the style of a château, houses exceptionally fine works of European art. The large collection of Spanish paintings, including works by El Greco and Goya, is particularly important. Other pleasures include porcelain, tapestries and a children's room which has toys and dolls' houses. *Open Mon–Sat and Sun afternoon.*

✗ **Barnard Castle** Oliver Cromwell was entertained at 15th-C Blagraves House on The Bank; today this fine gabled house is a restaurant specializing in *haute cuisine* and traditional northern dishes.

☆ **Barnard Castle** The Tea Cozy café in the town centre serves a wide choice of teas. Upstairs, the pine furniture workshop is worth a visit.

① *Leave town across Tees bridge, then turn right for Cotherstone.*

☆ **Cotherstone** Call in at the Post Office – for cheese! Here you can buy one of England's rarest varieties named after the village and made on local farms.

☆ **Romaldkirk** An exceptionally pretty, well-preserved stone village with several village greens (which still have their stocks and old pumps). The 12th–15thC church of St Romald has interesting features, and the Rose and Crown is a fine 18th-C inn with a good reputation for food and comfort.

☆ **Mickleton** On entering the village, look out for signs of feudal strip farming still visible to the right of the road.

☆ **Middleton-in-Teesdale** This Victorian-looking village is a popular base for exploring the dale on foot. There is also angling on the River Tees. *Tourist information: tel. (0833) 40806.*

☆ **High Force** Park beside the High Force pub and follow the steep path opposite, which leads through woods to one of the most impressive waterfalls in England. Here the River Tees drops 70 feet (21 m) over a cliff.

☆ **Langdon Beck** Cauldron Snout, another spectacular waterfall, is reached by turning left at the inn. After 2½ miles (4 km), park and walk 1 mile (1.5 km) to where the river roars angrily down a ravine.

This detour should not be attempted in wet weather, when the path becomes dan-

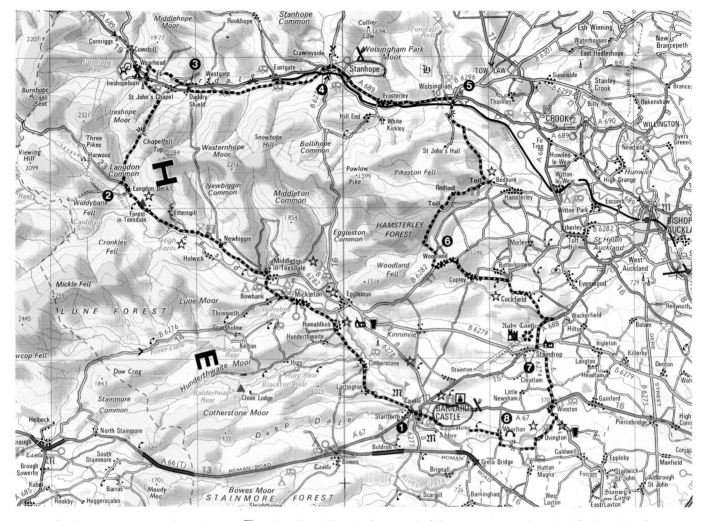

gerously slippery. Even in good weather it is not recommended for anyone unused to difficult walking conditions. Allow several hours for the expedition.

② *Just past Langdon Common turn right at signpost to St John's Chapel. (This is a lovely road with splendid views across the fells.) After just under 4 miles (6.5 km) turn left to Ireshopeburn.*

✿ **Ireshopeburn** A local weaver makes and sells his wares in the corner house on the left side of the street.

✗ **Ireshopeburn** Turn right in the village for the Rancho del Rio restaurant. 'Cowboys' and 'Indians' from all over the north-east flock here for regular 'shoot-outs' and Country and Western evenings. Try the ranch-house specials on the menu.

③ *At Daddry Shield, take right turning (signposted Brotherlee) beside 'tidy village' sign, then turn left. The road follows the River Wear, with fine views. After 3 miles (5 km) watch out for heavy lorries serving the unsightly cement works.*

✗ **Stanhope** The Horsley Arms (just outside the town) is a stately home of a hotel which nevertheless serves light meals at the bar.

④ *Turn left on to B6278, then after ¼ mile (0.5 km) turn right on to A689.*

🄗 **Wolsingham** John Wesley preached here and the three stone steps from which he mounted his horse are still outside the surgery, in the centre of the village.

⑤ *Take unclassified road (signposted Bedburn) across River Wear and up a steep hill (panoramic views at top), then fork left.*

☆ **Bedburn** Turn right for Forest Drive through Hamsterley Forest (signposted), a pretty mixture of woods and pastures (small charge).

⑥ *At the end of the Forest Drive, turn right on to turning point, then take left turning up narrow road. At the top of the hill, turn right at T-junction. At second T-junction, turn left on to B6282 and continue into Woodland village.*

☆ **Cockfield** The village is well named: the king-sized bathing huts on the common at the far end are chicken houses and pigeon lofts. Cockfield is the pigeon fanciers' capital of County Durham.

Just beyond the huts turn right at fork.

🏰 **Raby Castle** This magnificent 14th-C fortress was altered considerably in the 18th–19thC. It has a splendid Great Hall, a fascinating medieval kitchen, a collection of carriages, and a lovely walled garden famous for its sweet peas. Venison from the estate is sometimes on sale. Open after-

noons – Sun–Fri, July–Aug. For other times telephone (0833) 60202.

🏰 **Staindrop** St Mary's church, which has Saxon origins, spans several centuries of architecture and contains some fine effigies of the lords and ladies of Raby Castle.

⑦ *Go back through village and turn right on to B6274. After ½ mile (0.8 km) turn left at T-junction (broken sign). Turn right on to A67, then left immediately on to B6274. Through Winston, turn right to Ovington.*

☆ **Ovington** Charming village with an old inn, The Four Alls.

Just beyond the village, on the Whorlton Road, lies Wycliffe Hall (not open to the public); a little further on there is one of the finest views of the Tees.

⌒ **Whorlton** A well-preserved iron suspension bridge leads into another nicely kept stone village.

⑧ *Turn left in village, and left again in about ½ mile (0.8 km). Both roads are signposted to Barnard Castle. Go across an old stone bridge to Egglestone Abbey.*

🅜 **Egglestone Abbey** Turner painted this romantic ruin which overlooks the Tees.

Continue along narrow winding road beside the river, then turn right on to B6277, which leads back to Barnard Castle.

Alnwick and the Northumberland Coast

G reat fortresses punctuate this tour. Some, such as the castles at Alnwick and Bamburgh, still dominate the towns that grew up around them. Others, such as Dunstanburgh, have only a bleak tower or keep to testify to their former strength.

Along the route there are two treats for those who prefer natural history. The Farne Islands provide sanctuary for a remarkable number of rare sea birds. They come and go as they please, but the wild cattle at Chillingham have been unable to seek new pastures since their ancestors were fenced in over seven hundred years ago.

Route: 83 miles (134 km)
In sequence from: Alnwick
Direction of travel: anticlockwise

☆ **Alnwick** Entered through the narrow stone arch of the Hotspur Tower (1450), the town is the main shopping centre for this corner of Northumberland. Even at peak holiday periods the crowds and coaches cannot hide the impressive stone-carved evidence of the town's long history. *Tourist information: tel. (0665) 603120.*

🏰 **Alnwick** The medieval mass of the outstanding castle is still the home of the Percy family, dukes of Northumberland; over the centuries, no fewer than nine peers died violent or mysterious deaths here.

Within the castle's solid walls, the richly decorated interior (the result of 18th–19thC restoration) comes as a magnificent surprise. Plenty to see including fine paintings, a museum of antiquities and the dungeon. *Open 1–5, Sun–Fri, May–Sept.*

☆ **Alnwick** Near the town centre, the Percy lion, tail outstretched, stands on top of an 83-foot (25-m) high monument nicknamed Farmers' Folly. Erected in 1816 by grateful tenants of the Duke, the latter then decided they could afford to pay more rent.

① *After 3¼ miles (5.25 km) take turning to right (signposted Littlehoughton) then almost immediately turn left on to Craster road.*

☆ **Craster** The stone piers seem too large for the tiny harbour and the village too small for its big reputation among connoisseurs

● *Bamburgh Castle: imposing, but, for purists, too freely restored in the 19thC.*

of kippers (Craster kippers are oak cured).

A bracing and thoroughly rewarding 1-mile (1.5-km) walk along the coast path leads to the fine ruins of 14th-C Dunstanburgh Castle, once a great fortress.

🏚 **Embleton** The 14th-C fortified rectory is a telling reminder of Northumberland's turbulent history. The large and interesting church dates from the 13thC.

⚔ **Embleton–Beadnell** Pleasant road across flat coastal farmland with views of the sea.

☆ **Beadnell** *Press on past the caravan park, following signs to the harbour.*

The port, which is as small as Craster, is dominated by what appear to be the ruins of another fort but are actually 18th-C lime kilns.

Return to B1339 for Seahouses.

⚓ **Seahouses** *Turn right in the town centre for the harbour.*

Every day, Apr–Sept, boats leave this small fishing port (now in danger of being swamped by candy floss and caravans) for the nearby Farne Islands, summer home of around 20 species of sea birds, including roseate terns, puffins, eider and guillemots.

The islands are also the headquarters of a large colony of grey seals.

A 14th-C chapel (restored *c.* 1845) commemorates St Cuthbert who lived on Inner Farne from 676 to 684. On one of the islands furthest from the mainland stands the Longstone Lighthouse; Grace Darling rowed to fame from here in 1838.

Bamburgh High up on its rocky promontory, the massive castle is one of the finest sights in England, and has often appeared in films and television dramas. The keep is 12th-C, but much of the rest was restored in the 19thC by Lord Armstrong of Cragside. *Open every afternoon from Easter to Oct.*

Bamburgh The Grace Darling Museum has the actual boat in which she made her heroic rescue, as well as mementoes of her family. *Open Apr to mid-Oct.*

② *Turn right at T-junction. After 1 mile (1.5 km), turn left at signpost to Belford, ignoring sharp left turn beside sign.*

Belford Coaches travelling from London to Edinburgh changed horses at the 18th-C Blue Bell Inn, and its atmosphere reflects its long history. Today's travellers can stretch their car-weary legs by taking a stroll around the flower garden which contains many old English varieties.

③ *Leave Belford on B6349 (near the Blue Bell), signposted to Wooler. Lovely views from this road towards high fells.*

④ *Turn left at signpost to Chatton. On entering village turn right at signpost to Alnwick, and after 400 yards (365 m) take left turning signposted to Chillingham.*

Chillingham The 14th-C castle is not open to the public, but its famous park contains England's only herd of wild cattle. These pure white beasts have bred in the park since 1220, when they found themselves on the wrong side of a wall built round the castle's perimeter. Visitors are advised to keep at a respectful distance. *Open Mon, Wed–Sat and Sun afternoon, Apr–Oct. Return to village and turn left.*

⑤ *Turn right at signpost to the Lilburns (mind the hares on the road!). Cross the small ford (if flooded, turn round and take right fork to Lilburn Tower and thence to A697, turning left to rejoin route just past Wooperton). At T-junction turn left, then when road divides take right fork (signposted to Wooperton). At junction with B6346, turn right, then left on to A697.*

⑥ *Turn right at signpost to Branton (do not take earlier turning to Brandon by mistake).*

☆ **Branton** The large church is now a shop selling antiques and secondhand goods, and the Breamish Valley Pottery welcomes visitors. *Leave village on Glanton road.*

⑦ *Turn right, then almost immediately take turning to left signposted Mountain/Whittingham. Go through the ford and then across the crossroads on Callaly road. (If ford is flooded, return to previous junction. Turn right for Whittingham and right again to Callaly.)*

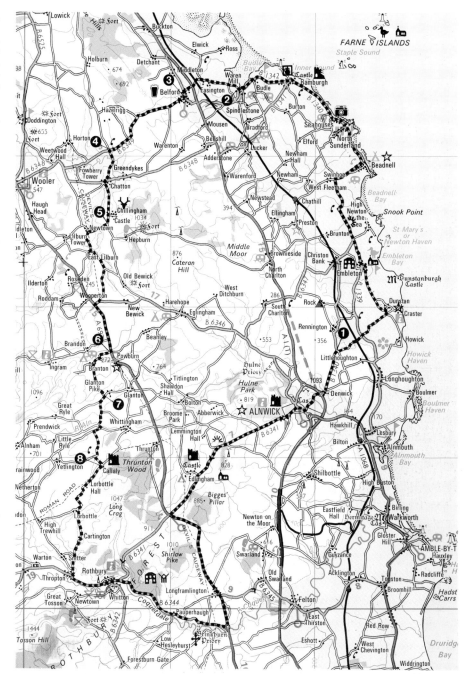

Callaly The big house is known as Callaly Castle, which is what it was in the 13thC. Although the original tower is still standing, drastic alterations in the 17th–19thC have turned the castle into a classical mansion with a splendid 18th-C saloon. *For opening times, telephone (066 574) 663.*

⑧ *On leaving castle, turn left. Turn right at signpost to Lorbottle. In Lorbottle village take left turning (signposted Thropton) beside telephone box).*

Rothbury Cragside, 1¾ miles (2.75 km) to the east of the town, off B6344, is an extraordinary, late 19th-C mansion designed by Norman Shaw for Lord Armstrong, the arms baron. Perched among trees on a steep hillside, it is more like a compressed village than a house. Its eccentric appearance, and the fact that it was the first house in England to be lit by electricity, moved John Betjeman to describe it as 'a . . . mixture of advanced technology and Wagnerian sentiment'. *For opening times, telephone (0669) 2033.*

Cragside's vast Country Park is famous for its lovely trees, lakes, waterfall and rhododendrons. *Open daily Apr–Oct; weekends only Nov–Mar.*

† **Brinkburn Priory** *Turn right off road for car park.* There is a walk of 200 yards (183 m) to this dignified 12th-C church, sympathetically restored in 1858 and prettily located beside the River Coquet.

Edlingham The ruined castle and part-Norman church with its stern little tower can be seen from the road. A little further on it is worth pausing at the lay-by for the views.

Local Tours: **Scotland**

Nine one- or two-day drives

The Galloway Hills

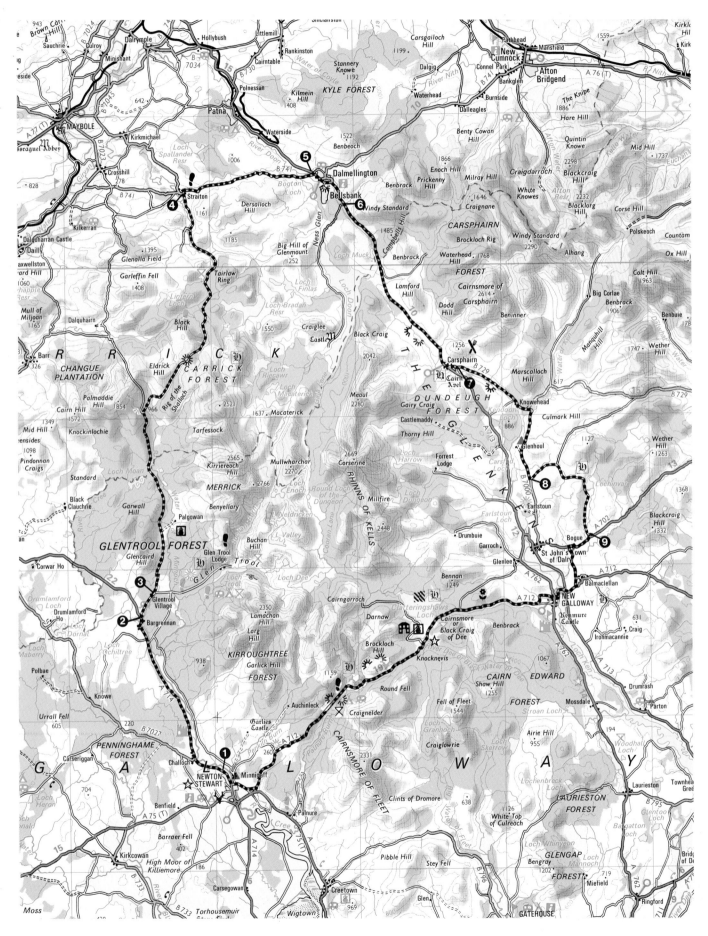

The name of Shangri-La has been applied to this country, although extensive forest clearance and a huge hydro-electric scheme (five power stations and seven reservoirs) give the landscape a distinctly man-made look today. It is, nonetheless, a peaceful region, not disturbed by the traffic which hurries along the main roads from England to the Scottish Highlands or to the ferry ports for Ireland. This route explores the National Forest Park lying at the heart of the hills, the historic land of Carrick and part of the Stewartry, so-called because for centuries it was ruled by a royal Steward.

Route: 88 miles (141 km)
In sequence from: Newton Stewart
Direction of travel: clockwise

☆ **Newton Stewart** Though a mere village by English standards, it is Galloway's most important market centre. Town houses crowd the banks of the River Cree. The bridge on which the road enters from the east replaced the 'Black Ford' of long ago, notorious for drownings. *Tourist information: tel. (0671) 2431.*

🍴 **Newton Stewart** On market days, look out for the 'belted' Galloway cattle, like bovine footballers in black jerseys with white hoops. Heavier imported breeds are replacing them and the famous Galloway pony, a rough stocky little cob, is also a rare sight.

① *Leaving Newton Stewart by the A714, signposted Girvan, the road follows the Cree upstream and almost immediately enters the Galloway Forest Park.*

② *At Bargrennan, cross river bridge and turn right on to unclassified road to Glen Trool.*

③ *In Glentrool Village take the minor road on right which ascends in 3 miles (5 km) to Loch Trool and Glen Trool Lodge. Fine views across loch; easy to park and picnic.*

🏛 **Glen Trool** Stone at west end of loch commemorates Covenanters 'most impiously and cruelly murthered' in 1685. Most Galloway churchyards contain such memorials. They recall the martyrdoms of Presbyterians in the 'Killing Times' which followed the restoration of the Catholic kings to the British throne. Scott's novel *Old Mortality* describes the aged wanderer Robert Paterson, native of Galloway, who went round the country tidying up the Covenanters' neglected tombstones.

🏔 **Glen Trool** At east end of loch a cairn and large boulder mark where Robert the Bruce defeated the English in a skirmish in 1307.

❢ **Glen Trool** The loch shore is a good starting-point for energetic walks to the hillstreams, snow-water lakes and heights of Merrick, the highest mountain in Scotland outside the Highlands.

🏠 **Palgowan** The farm-track on the right leads to Palgowan Open Farm, where the agriculture and working routines of a region of mild temperatures and copious rainfall may be observed. A full visit takes 2½ hours and prior notice is requested.

🏔 **Palgowan–Straiton** The route emerges from the Forest Park to the open moorland of the Carrick Forest: narrow winding road with passing places. A panoramic view-point at the 1,407-foot (429-m) summit, from which Ireland is often visible. The road twists down into woodland near headwaters of the Stinchar, a river much more beautiful than its name; useful picnic spots and a choice of short strolls or long walks.

🏛 **Palgowan–Straiton** This district of Carrick, through its association with Robert the Bruce, supplies a title to the British monarch's eldest son: the Prince of Wales is also Earl of Carrick. Here, after his encounter with the spider in a cave on Rathlin Island ('If at first you don't succeed . . .'), Bruce gathered his support for the campaign of liberation which ended triumphantly at Bannockburn in 1314.

④ *Leaving Straiton village by the B741, look out on the left for sign indicating 'Lady Hunter-Blair's Walk and Glen of the Lambdoughty Burn'. Here are numerous waterfalls and rapids or 'linns'. One of them, a favourite of Dante Gabriel Rossetti, is now called the Rossetti Linn.*

⑤ **Dalmellington** *Unnecessary to enter this mini-iron town: bear right on A713. A splendid view of serpentine Loch Doon and the high ridge of the Rhinns of Kells gradually opens out.*

⑥ *One mile (1.6 km) from Dalmellington, a detour on to an unfenced lochside road leads in 7 miles (11 km) to Loch Doon castle. The 14th-C fortress, formerly on an island, has been rebuilt at roadside. Return to A713 by same route.*

🏔 **Dalmellington–Carsphairn** As road gains altitude there are impressive views to the right and the rear.

🏛 **Carsphairn** The rough track on the right leads to old lead mines and passes the insignificant ruin of Lagwine Tower, home of a Highland MacGregor who, when the clan name was frowned on after the 1692 Glencoe massacre, called himself Macadam, arguing that 'all men are sons of Adam'. Or so the story goes. His son, John Loudon Macadam, born here in 1756, wrote the name into the language when he devised the tar-and-pebble composition which made roads fit for traffic.

🍴 **Carsphairn** Greystones, a small exclusive restaurant in the main street, serves local river trout; also bar snacks. The establishment appears in gourmet guides.

⑦ *Turn sharp left out of village and left again, taking the 'old road' to Dalry, the B729. Proceed between 'drystane dykes' (stone*

walls) and rhododendrons, with wide 🏔 views towards the Glenkens system of lochs, barrages and power stations.

⑧ **Lochinvar** *Two-and-a-half miles (4 km) beyond Knowehead, a moorland road on the left, signposted Lochinvar, leads to a 'lochan' (small lake) and a fragmentary* 🏛 14th-C ruin. Here is said to have been the island home of the Young Lochinvar who 'came out of the west' to steal his bride in the well-known ballad.

⑨ **Bogue** *Turn right on to the A702 and in ½ mile (0.8 km) left, signposted New Galloway. Continue ahead one mile (1.5 km) from this junction to view the pastel-coloured houses of local stone of St John's Town of Dalry, one of the most picturesque villages of Galloway.*

🏛 **Balmaclellan** The village, pleasantly sited on a hill slope, has quaint tombs in the churchyard and a monument to Robert Paterson, 'Old Mortality', and his family. He lived here in his younger days and his wife was the local schoolmistress.

🏛 **New Galloway** A tiny metropolis of the Stewartry, said to be the smallest royal burgh (population 300) in Scotland.

❢ **New Galloway–Clatteringshaws** In 3 miles (5 km) the road re-enters Forest Park among avenues of young conifers.

🏞 **Clatteringshaws Loch** Four-and-a-half miles (7 km) from New Galloway the road passes close to the flooded valley, now a large reservoir, but it is barely visible through the forest screen.

🏛 **Clatteringshaws** Near lochside on right, the Galloway Deer Museum is worth stopping at for its tableaux of red deer, wild goats and other fauna of the region, past and present. *Open daily Apr–Sept; car park and picnic area.*

🏛 **Clatteringshaws** Close to the museum stands a reconstructed Romano-British house, rescued from the drowned valley.

🏛 **Clatteringshaws** A short forest path from the car park, signposted Bruce's Stone, leads to the boulder on which the Scottish hero is said to have rested after the battle of Moss Raploch, 1307.

☆ **Clatteringshaws** The gravelled track on left, where the Black Water issues from a reservoir, is called the 'Raiders' Road'. The name is a reminder that S. R. Crocket, author of 19th-C best-sellers such as *The Raiders*, was a Galloway man.

🏔 **Red Deer Range** (not on map) At this point, 3 miles (5 km) from Clatteringshaws, there is a car park and a hilltop viewpoint.

🏛 **Red Deer Range–Newton Stewart** One mile (1.5 km) farther on, the granite monument on the right commemorates Alexander Murray, the 18th-C shepherd boy who became a leading Oriental linguist and ✗ scholar; picnic area at foot of hill; forest ❢ trail to summit (1,100 feet, 335 m) offers 🏔 fine views of the coast and prominent peaks of Galloway. From here it is an attractive descent to Newton Stewart.

The Scottish Borders

This is the trail of Sir Walter Scott, the land where he grew up, collected ballads, set the scenes of novels; and died. The eastern loop of the figure-of-eight covers well-wooded agricultural country and touches at Scotland's most famous medieval abbeys. The western loop embraces the wild, hilly Ettrick Forest which is not forest, but open moorland.

Route One: 51 miles (82 km)
Directions in sequence from: Selkirk
Direction of travel: anticlockwise

☆ **Selkirk** An ancient royal burgh of twisting hilly streets, with tweed mills and mill shops. *Tourist information: tel. (0750) 20054.*

🏛 **Selkirk** In the market-place stands a large monument to Sir Walter Scott, sometime Sheriff of Selkirkshire, and in nearby High St. a statue to locally-born Mungo Park, the African explorer. As you leave town centre, note the pillar with warrior and flag inscribed simply 'O Flodden Field'. Selkirk sent a hundred young men to fight the English at Flodden in 1513 and only one came home.

① *Leave Selkirk by the A7 signposted Hawick*

and in 4½ miles (7 km) turn left on to B6400, signposted Ancrum.

⚶ **Selkirk–Ancrum** Leaving Lilliesleaf, a view of Eildon Hills opens out, left. They say the triple peaks (about 1,300 feet/396 m) were split in a night by the familiar devil of 12th-C wizard, Michael Scot; however, the Romans called this place Trimontium or 'three hills'. In Scots folklore it was under the Eildon tree, which no longer exists, that Thomas the Rhymer, alias True Thomas, met the Queen of Elfland.

⚶ **Selkirk–Ancrum** Two-and-a-half miles (4 km) beyond Lilliesleaf a wide view of the Cheviot Hills opens on the right. The hills form the natural boundary between

---

● *The River Tweed curves gracefully through the Border country.*

Scotland and England and the 'Border Fence' runs along their crests.

🏛 **Ancrum** The name of this undistinguished village serves as the courtesy title of the heir to the Marquess of Lothian, principal landowner hereabouts. The village is a centre for exploring the local woodland (spring flowers) and the Teviot riverbank.

② **Ancrum–Monteviot** *Half a mile (0.8 km) beyond Ancrum, turn right on to the A68 Edinburgh–Jedburgh road, then sharp left, signposted to Nisbet.*

🏛 **Dryburgh Abbey** Here is the most beautiful of the Border abbeys in a ghostly setting beside the River Tweed. It contains tombs of Scott and Field-Marshal Earl Haig, whose descendants live at Bemersyde next door.

⑤ **Dryburgh–Leaderfoot** *Back-track 1 mile (1.5 km); follow signpost for 'Scott's View'.*

⚶ **Dryburgh–Leaderfoot** Panoramic indicator at Scott's View helps locate 43 (according to Scott) places famed in Border legend and history. At this point, in 1832, Scott's horses, leading his funeral cortège to Dryburgh, stopped of their own accord.

⑥ **Dryburgh–Leaderfoot** *Follow signposts for Melrose in the network of lanes, then turn right at signpost for Edinburgh and sharp left on to the A68. Cross the River Tweed and turn right under impressive (disused) Leaderfoot railway viaduct.*

🏛 **Newstead** Here the Roman Dere Street crossed the Tweed. Large roadside stone (left) marks site of Trimontium.

🏛 **Melrose** The 12th-C abbey in the town centre is the best-preserved of all Border abbeys.

❗ **Melrose** Road south to the golf course skirts Eildon Hills. Footpath to summits (40 mins) from club-house.

✗ **Melrose** Old Smiddy, opposite post office, serves good inexpensive quiches, curries, pizza, wines and coffee, and also displays local crafts and knitwear.

🏛 **Abbotsford** Custom-built pseudo-baronial home of Sir Walter Scott, stuffed with relics and heirlooms. *Open Mon–Sat and Sun afternoon, Mar–Oct.*

⚘ **Lindean Mill** *Half a mile (0.8 km) on right after joining A7, an unmarked track leads to the highly praised studio glassmakers Sandström and Kaplan; open to visitors.*

Route Two: 37 miles (59 km)
Directions in sequence from: Selkirk
Direction of travel: clockwise

🏛 **Selkirk** *Leaving by A707 and turning left on the B7009, is a fine view of Bowhill (Duke of Buccleuch); entrance on the A708; open 12.30–6 Wed, Thur, Sat, and Sun afternoon, May–Sept.*

⑦ **Ettrickbridge** *At end of village take steep, tortuous, unclassified road on right across Ettrick–Yarrow watershed; single lane with*

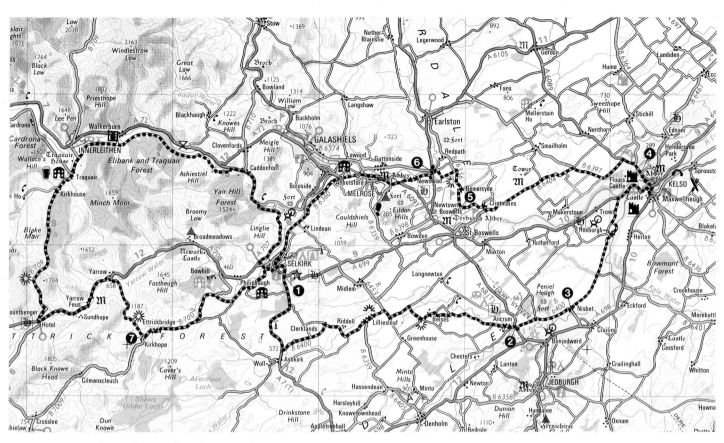

passing places (don't park in them). Wide all-round views at 1,187-foot (362-m) summit. Descend to the rushing Yarrow Water.

ᛗ **Yarrow–Gordon Arms** Fenced-in beside the road is the 6th-C Liberalis stone, a monument to ancient British warriors.

⌂ **Gordon Arms** On this old drovers' inn a plaque records the last meeting of Scott and his friend James Hogg, poet, the 'Ettrick Shepherd'.

⚘ **'Paddy Slacks'** This is the local name for the B709 through another mountain pass with views at the summit.

⌂ **Traquair** The gates of Traquair House on the Peebles road ¼ mile (0.5 km) left of this route were locked in 1745 against the day when a Stuart monarch returns. The house, continuously inhabited since the 13thC, brews its own ale and markets it commercially; craft fairs in summer; open afternoons, Easter–Oct.

⌂ **Walkerburn** Scotland's principal (though small) wool museum stands ½ mile (0.8 km) to the left of the route after the Innerleithen turn-off. Open daily Mar–Oct; knitwear for sale.

✗ **Walkerburn–Selkirk** Before the junction with the A72, this Tweedside backroad offers picnic spots in pleasant woodland.

ᛗ **Jedburgh** A detour of 3½ miles (5.5 km) down the A68, takes you to another historic Border town which, like Selkirk, bears scars of Anglo–Scottish wars. The ruined abbey in red sandstone dates from the 12thC, with a fine north transept surviving from the

14thC. The town houses of typical Jacobean Scots architecture with crow-stepped gables include a lodging of Mary, Queen of Scots, now a museum devoted to her relics. Jedburgh gave its name to Jethart justice (a sort of lynch law), the Jethart staff (a weighty fighting stick) and Jethart snails (mint candies).

⚘ **Monteviot** (not on map) Signs ¾ mile (1 km) from Ancrum indicate large woodland craft and visitor centre, on right. Open afternoons, Easter–Oct. daily except Mon and Sat.

③ **Monteviot–Roxburgh** Route continues through pastoral Vale of Teviot. At Nisbet leave B6400 for bumpy, unclassified road signposted to Roxburgh.

⌂ **Roxburgh** The row of sleepy farm cottages gives no hint that Roxburgh was once a royal residence, a town which minted coins and a citadel which, along with Edinburgh, Stirling and Berwick-upon-Tweed, formed Scotland's defensive 'quadrilateral' against England.

⚘ **Roxburgh** A fine craft pottery behind village street is signposted.

🏰 **Roxburgh Castle** Steep grassy mounds at the roadside (right) on the A699 where Teviot meets Tweed are remains of a once-powerful Border stronghold, six times English and seven times Scottish. On the left, across the Tweed, is a view of Floors Castle (Duke of Roxburghe) and river terraces or 'floors' where James II of Scotland, while besieging Roxburgh Castle in 1460, was killed by a cannon which 'brak in the shooting'.

⌒ **Kelso** Enter town by John Rennie's bridge over the Tweed, built 1803. Two lampposts are from Waterloo Bridge in London, created by the same engineer.

✗ **Kelso** is a market centre for the lower Tweed district with a spacious town square. The Cross Keys Hotel, on the square, was a renowned coaching inn. The Black Swan, opposite, of same period, with dark-oak décor, offers reasonable pub lunches.

ᛗ **Kelso** The 12th-C abbey in the town centre suffered badly in the last English assault in 1545, but part of the tower and façade survive, and the intricate Norman and early Gothic detail is worth a look.

⌂ **Ednam** Make a detour to this hamlet 3 miles (5 km) away on the B6461, which astonishingly produced the best-known patriotic song and one of the best-known hymns in the English language. A monument and a plaque commemorate James Thomson (Rule Britannia) and H. F. Lyte (Abide with Me), who were both local boys.

④ Leave Kelso by Edinburgh road (A6089) with the 'Golden Gates' of Floors Castle on the left. Turn left on to the B6397, signposted St Boswells. Public entrance to Floors Castle on left.

🏰 **Floors Castle** Started 1718 by Vanbrugh, completed by Playfair. Picture gallery, garden centre; open afternoons Sun–Thur, May–Sept.

ᛗ **Smailholm Tower** A 16th-C keep and viewpoint on the right of the B6404, was sentimentalized by Scott, and painted by Turner. A stiff climb, but the view is worth it.

Dunbar and the Lammermuir Hills

T his is a short day out on slow, narrow roads which are well surfaced and picturesque. Within minutes of leaving the busy A1, the route is crossing lonely trout streams and giving views over moors which echo only to the cries of lapwing, curlew and grouse.

Route: 61 miles (98 km)
Directions in sequence from: Dunbar
Direction of travel: clockwise

☆ **Dunbar** Inshore fishing port and holiday resort which claims the best sunshine record in Scotland; broad main street with country-style shops. Some steep labyrinthine 'wynds', boat trips in summer. *Tourist information: tel. (0368) 63353.*

🏰 **Dunbar** Use care when clambering round the red sandstone ruins of Dunbar Castle, a 13th-C stronghold which once occupied a chain of rocks enclosing one side of the harbour. The battlements, where countless sea birds nest, seem on the point of collapse – but they have been like that for four hundred years. The last notable resident was Mary, Queen of Scots, who took refuge there after Rizzio's murder in 1565.

🌾 **Dunbar** West of the harbour on the rocky esplanade, a flagged pavement leads to magnificent views of Bass Rock and islands in the Firth of Forth.

① At the end of High St. turn left, signposted Berwick-upon-Tweed, and 100 yards (91 m) past 'No Entry' street on right take right turn, signposted to Spott. After 1 mile (1.5 km), cross A1 at staggered junction, right then left.

🌾 **Dunbar–Spott** Wide views of Firth and East Lothian countryside open out behind as the road ascends.

🏘 **Spott** One of numerous East Lothian villages built in the time of the agricultural 'Improvers' to tempt Industrial Revolution workers back to the land. Fine carving on 18th-C pulpit in little church and, at gate, an old guard-room from which watch was kept for bodysnatchers.

② Continue through village and turn left for 'The Brunt' (signposted but not on map).
🌾 At top of hill, good views of May Island, Fife coast and North Sea.

③ After crossing Dry Burn (stream), turn left on to unsignposted road. Then follow signposts to Innerwick. After second turning, note the Jubilee statue (Queen Victoria, 1887) with disused drinking fountain and quaint poem.

📖 **Innerwick** At the first house on left there is a sundial, vertically mounted, with philosophical verse.

☆ **Innerwick** One of the prettiest of Lammermuir villages, quite close to the A1, but managing to stay in a world of its own.

🏰 **Innerwick** 13th-C castle, much knocked about by English invaders in 1547, is now an insignificant ruin.

🌾 **Innerwick** After passing through the village you have on the left a bird's-eye view of the controversial nuclear generating plant at Torness.

④ Half a mile (0.8 km) out of Innerwick take the first road on right, signposted Oldhamstocks.

🏰 **Thornton** (not on map) The castle above the stream, on the left, suffered the same fate as Innerwick Castle. You can see everything worth seeing from the road. *Bear right across stream and follow signs to Oldhamstocks.*

📖 **Oldhamstocks** Once a market-place of the hills, now very secluded; the church is worth a visit for its florid 16th-C sundial.

⑤ At road junction, with main part of village on right, turn left, signposted Duns. Then follow signs to Abbey St Bathans.

🌾 **Oldhamstocks–Abbey St Bathans** This lonely road, partly unfenced (watch for lambs in springtime), crosses the watershed of Lammermuir at about 1,000 feet (304 m) with excellent views of the coast of East Lothian and the Merse (water-meadows) of Berwickshire.

🏰 **Abbey St Bathans** Site of a former ancient monastic retreat.

✗ **Abbey St Bathans** Close to mill, on left at east end of village, is a trout farm and tearoom.

📖 **Abbey St Bathans** Footpath from mill leads downstream in 1 mile (1.5 km) to a footbridge and Edin's Hall, a Pictish fort and broch (dry-stone round tower) – the latter unique in southern Scotland.

⑥ Three-and-a-half miles (5.5 km) from Abbey St Bathans turn right.

🏰 **Cranshaws** Peel Tower on left, among trees, was originally a fortress of the Black Douglas, a medieval baron notorious in Scottish legend and history.

✗ **Cranshaws–Garvald** Follow B6355 signposted Gifford. At 2 and 2½ miles (3 and 4 km) picnic sites beside Whiteadder Water.

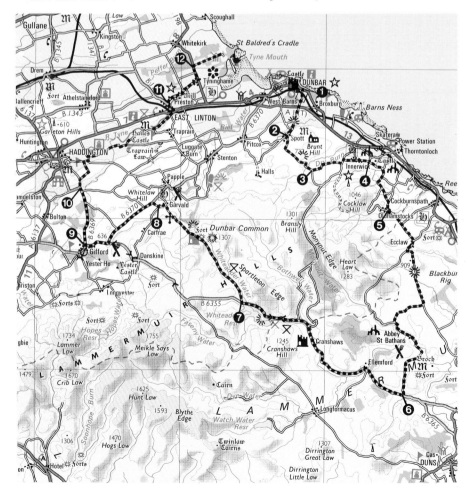

⚹ **Cranshaws–Garvald** Road ascends to Hungry Snout: lay-by at top with good views over Whiteadder Reservoir.

⑦ *Just beyond end of reservoir, bear right on unfenced, unclassified road signposted Garvald; narrow, undulating road with passing places; many sheep; watch for grouse in summer.*

✇ **Cranshaws–Garvald** One mile (1.5 km) beyond turn-off for Garvald, a high footbridge over the Whiteadder on right leads to a picnic spot, but beware of soggy verges.

⚹ **Cranshaws–Garvald** Two miles (3 km) beyond footbridge is a lay-by and information board for pre-Roman fort of White Castle, now a grass-grown mound 100 yards (91 m) on right of road.

⚹ **Cranshaws–Garvald** The 2-mile (3-km) descent from White Castle to Nunraw (not on map) offers a succession of varied views of the Firth of Forth, with Sancta Maria Abbey in the foreground.

✝ **Nunraw** The modern Cistercian abbey of Sancta Maria (on left) is severe and barrack-like, but welcomes visitors. A throne, built for the 1982 papal visit, is on show. Note: nearly all the monks are under a vow of silence. In ½ mile (0.8 km) on the right is a

---

● *The Lammermuir Hills, fine, open country easily accessible from Edinburgh.*

---

gatehouse admitting visitors to the 'old' abbey, which last century was an ordinary country house. A 16th-C painted ceiling in the chapel, with strange and exotic coats-of-arms, is readily shown to visitors when the chapel is not in use. The building is surrounded by cypress, eucalyptus and monkey-puzzle trees, rarities in Scotland.

🏠 **Garvald** Outside the church is a sundial dated 1633 and a set of jougs (neck cuffs for old-time malefactors).

✗ **Garvald** Garvald Inn, a historic building from 1780, serves real ale and inexpensive casseroles.

⑧ *Sharp right up steep hill, signposted Gifford; follow signposts to Gifford.*

✗ **Gifford** The Tweeddale Arms Hotel, one of numerous delightful local examples of rural architecture, has pleasant public rooms, traditional cuisine and a better-than-average cellar; but it is crowded at summer weekends.

⚘ **Gifford** At the workshops on Duns Rd. is Yester Wood, a small group of craftsmen specializing in solid hardwood furniture.

⑨ *Exit by B6369 signposted Haddington.*

⑩ *In 3 miles (5 km), where road forks left, continue straight ahead on unclassified road, then right and right again at road junction; follow signposts for East Linton.*

m **Hailes Castle** is worth a visit. Though de-militarized by Cromwell, it retains its evocative gatehouse, towers and dungeons. *Open Mon–Sat and Sun afternoon.*

⑪ *Cross A1 and River Tyne and pass under Edinburgh–King's Cross railway. Turn right in village on to B1407.*

☆ **Preston Mill** A pantiled grain mill in an idyllic situation; quality pottery in a small gallery. Site always visitable and *Mill is open and working Mon–Sat and Sun afternoon, Easter–Oct.*

🏠 **Tyninghame** A feudal hamlet; miniscule post office on left.

✿ **Tyninghame House** (Earl of Haddington) is at end of village, across the A198. *House private, but gardens open Mon–Fri, Jun–Sept.*

⑫ *From Tyninghame House main drive, detour by turning right on to A198 and in ½ mile (0.8 km) right again on to road not on map. This leads in 1 mile (1.5 km) to Tyninghame Links with car park and access to broad stretch of foreshore and Tyne* 🐦 *estuary, a famous haunt of sea birds and marine life. Return to A198 and turn left.*

🦌 **Tyninghame–Dunbar** *Join A1 and turn left for Dunbar. On left, just past roundabout, is a large country park named after local celebrity John Muir (1838–1914), the man who created national parks worldwide.*

Argyll

● *Kilchurn Castle stands on marshy ground that was once encircled by water.*

Here is an exploration of the wilds of the Clan Campbell domains. Their hereditary chief is the Duke of Argyll, and the roughest, hilliest part of this area is known ironically as 'the Duke of Argyll's Bowling Green'. But you pass quickly from the grandeur of chopped summits to the civilized botany of sheltered places.

Long fingers of both sea and inland lochs probe the hills: in spring their shores are carpeted with daffodils and primroses; in early summer they blaze with rhododendrons and azaleas – in fact there is colour in the landscape all year.

Route: 90 miles (145 km)
In sequence from: Inveraray
Direction of travel: clockwise

🏰 **Inveraray** Though a royal burgh and formerly known as the capital of the Highlands, this is a village of two streets, and it was small enough two hundred years ago to be shifted bodily to the loch shore to make room for the castle which dominates it. *Tourist information: tel. (0499) 2063.*

🏰 **Inveraray Castle** The splendidly ugly pseudo-Gothic seat of the Dukes of Argyll, chiefs of the Clan Campbell, was for ages almost a royal palace, so influential was this family in Scottish affairs. They were the Campbells (their name means 'crooked mouth') who set out to massacre their hereditary enemies, the MacDonalds, in Glencoe in 1692. Dr Samuel Johnson arrived 80 years later and drank his first glass of whisky. The current Duke and his family still inhabit the castle. Among many rich treasures – silver, paintings, plasterwork, furniture, arms – is the Armada chest which contains cannon-balls recovered from a sunken Spanish galleon in Tobermory Bay. (See the Isle of Mull page 222.) *Open Mon–Sat and Sun afternoon, July–Aug; Mon–Thur, Sat and Sun afternoon, Apr–June and Sept–Oct.*

🏛 **Inveraray** The Combined Operations Museum at Cherry Park in the castle grounds is a new venture and will no doubt expand as more material comes in. It re-creates Inveraray's World War II role as the first and principal training base of sailors, soldiers and airmen in combined opera-

tions – more than 250,000 of them. *Opening times same as for Inveraray Castle.*

① *Leave on road signposted Campbeltown.*

🏚 **Auchindrain** The Museum of Farming Life conveys a convincing impression of peasant hardships in a land rich in scenery, but little else. *Open Sun–Fri, Easter–May and Sept; daily Jun–Aug.*

🏚 **Furnace** A tiny port which *Para Handy* fans will remember as one of the sea-loch harbours served by the old-time 'puffers' or coal burning coasting vessels. Para Handy's creator, Neil Munro, was born on the shores of this loch.

🌿 **Furnace–Crarae** The road hugs the Loch Fyne shore with spectacular views towards the Duke of Argyll's Bowling Green. The laird of the castle across the water, and his address, make a good tongue-twister for English visitors: Lachlan MacLachlan of Strathlachlan, Castle Lachlan, Strathlachlan, Loch Fyne.

✿ **Crarae** On right, Crarae Lodge has one of the finest gardens in the west. Rhododendrons and azaleas in May and June are the speciality and there are many exotica. Crarae helps to explain why, in novels and plays about country-house life in England, the gardener was so often a Scot. *Open daily; plants sold 10–4.30.*

🏰 **Minard** The castle on the shore is modern, and privately-owned (*not open to public*).

🌿 **Minard–Lochgilphead** Beautiful seascapes open up on Loch Fyne and across Knapdale and Kintyre. Perhaps 'seascapes' is not the

right word because these channels are still 100 miles (161 km) from the real sea. There are notable views from Lochgair and on leaving Castleton.

🏚 **Lochgilphead** Another tiny west coast fishing town. The best kippers (Loch Fyne herring) were traditionally cured here. Many fish shops and fishing-tackle shops: sea angling is a growth industry.

② *Keep right at roundabout at end of town and follow sign for Oban.*

🚿 **Cairnbaan** A staircase of locks takes the Crinan Canal to its summit level. The 9-mile (14.5-km) canal, built for fishing craft, 1793–1801, is now used chiefly by motor-cruisers and yachts.

③ *Continue along B841 and follow the canal to Crinan.*

🌿 **Crinan** A village and yachting centre with a remarkable rock garden rising from Loch Crinan: from the rooftop restaurant of the Crinan Hotel there are memorable views over the Firth of Lorn, especially when the sun goes down in a clear sky, which does not happen every day.

④ *Backtrack 1 mile (1.5 km) and turn left on to the B8025.*

⚜ **Kilmartin** 'Kil' usually signifies a church or burial place and this neat village lies in a glen littered with Bronze Age monuments and chambered cairns. The sculpted grave-slabs and 8th-C carvings displayed at the church, on the left opposite the hotel, are well worth looking at. At Kilmartin Cross, the decorated pillar behind the Memorial Gateway, is one of the great Celtic relics.

𝔪 **Carnasserie** Only its castle, a ruin, is marked on the map, 1½ miles (2.5 km) past Kilmartin. Here in the 16thC lived the bishop who wrote and published the first Gaelic book.

⑤ *Turn right, signposted 'Ford'.*

⑥ *Continue along unclassified road signposted Dalavich.*

✗ **Ford–Inverinan** Numerous picnic spots on this minor road and several marked trails. You may see herds of Highland cattle hereabouts – they are fierce-looking but mild-mannered. On left, after Dalavich, the signposted track to Loch Avich and Avich Falls is a pleasant and not too strenuous walk of 1¼ miles (2 km).

⑦ *Straight on after Dalavich, signposted Kilchrenan.*

🌿 **Ford–Inverinan** At Kilmun (not on map), panoramic views back over the route.

🌿 **Annat** The mountain range which fills the northern horizon culminates in Ben Cruachan, 3,695 feet (1,126 m), the highest peak in Argyllshire. It gives its name to the war-cry of the Campbell clan: 'Cruachan!'

✗ Annat The minor road on right leads in half a mile (0.8 km) to Taychreggan Hotel in a charming lochside setting. This superior country inn, with admirable attention to detail in all its services, supplies bar or Danish buffet lunch and a gourmet dinner at a fairly (but not outrageously) high price.

☆ Kilchrenan has a useful store called Trading Post, run by a village co-operative.

❀ Detour: *From Kilchrenan a minor road on right goes to Ardanaiseig in 2½ miles (4 km). Georgian baronial house, colourful trees and shrubs; open daily, Apr–Oct.*

⑧ *Turn right, signposted to Crianlarich.*

☆ Falls of Cruachan Waterfall and footpath to reservoir are on the left as you emerge from the romantic Pass of Brander. On the right, an underground hydro-electric station offers visitors an exhibition and a mile-long (1.5-km) minibus trip through tunnel; *open normal working hours.*

ᴍ Lochawe After the right turn for Inveraray at head of Loch Awe, the much-photographed Kilchurn Castle (*not open to public*) is seen on its spit of land on the right. Part of the keep, built about 1440 by Colin Campbell, first of the Argyll dynasty, survives; disappointing at close range.

☙ Lochawe–Inveraray View of castle.

☆ Castle Fisheries (not on map) are 2 miles (3 km) from Inveraray on the left, well signposted. Here are trout ponds (with fish which eat from your hand) and fishing lakes with a tea-room, children's play area, fish hospital and a toy village on stilts, inhabited by small mammals: entertaining and educative in a modest way; *open daily.*

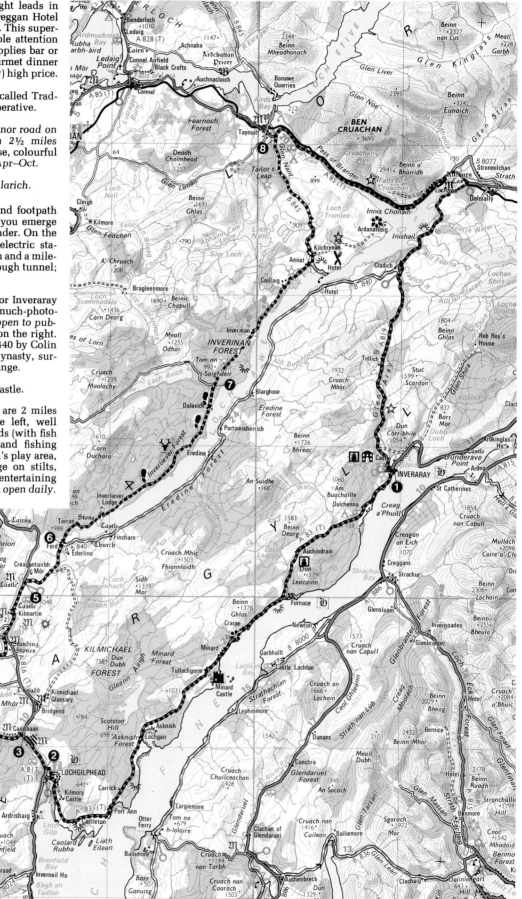

The East Neuk of Fife

● Crail, oldest of the 'East Neuk' fishing ports, was made a royal burgh by Robert the Bruce in 1310, with a charter that conferred the privilege of Sunday trading.

The fishing harbours of the 'East Neuk' are famed in Scottish history, and everyone has heard of St Andrews. Yet tourists often overlook the seaward corners of this area – formerly the Kingdom of Fife. The Stuart king's description of Fife, 'a beggar's mantle fringed with gold', hardly applies today for the mantle (the once-useless swampland) is richly agricultural while the gold (the harvest of the sea) has become tarnished with the decline of the herring fisheries.

Route One: 45 miles (72 km)
Directions in sequence from: Cupar
Direction of travel: clockwise

☆ **Cupar** County town and ancient royal burgh with a bustling Regency air.

Cupar The parish church, with early 15th-C tower, is one which escaped the Reformation. There are some quaint inscriptions on the gravestones.

Cupar Duffus Park contains the Douglas Bader Garden for the Disabled, an unusual kind of pleasure-ground adapted for the blind and handicapped.

① Leave town by the St Andrews road and in ¼ mile (0.5 km) turn right, signposted Pitscottie.

Pitscottie The name recalls the native historian whose accounts of Dark-Age turmoil gave Shakespeare the background for *Macbeth*.

Pitscottie The minor road labelled Dairsie enters a beautiful ravine called Dura Den, known to geologists as a rich source of fossils.

② Turn left on to the B939 for St Andrews. In

2 miles (3 km), an excellent view of this 'little city, worn and grey' (Andrew Lang).

St Andrews Enter town by South Street. On the south side is part of Scotland's oldest university, founded 1411. Other University colleges are on the north side of North St. At the junction of South St. and North St. stands Scotland's oldest cathedral. *Tourist information: tel. (0334) 72021.*

St Andrews Also at this junction (one-way system), Castle St. leads to St Andrews Castle, founded 1200. The ruins are widespread, with good views seaward. They include a Bottle Dungeon where John Knox was imprisoned, a secret passage and a ghost. *Open Mon–Sat and Sun afternoon.*

St Andrews The Scores, on seafront, leads to Golf Place, The Links and the Royal and Ancient Clubhouse. Anyone can play over the celebrated courses, including the Old Course, but some balloting for tee-off times is necessary in summer. The Clubhouse, ruling house of golf worldwide, is open only to members.

St Andrews Holy Trinity church on South St., opposite Town Hall, and the churchyard of St Regulus next door to the cathedral, have unusual monuments to Tom and Tommy Morris, 19thC golfing geniuses.

③ Turn right off South St. and leave town by Abbey Walk, signposted Crail, or by the vaulted Gothic 'Pends' (gatehouse). In 1 mile (1.5 km) bear right, signposted Grange (not on map).

④ Turn left at T-junction, signposted Dunino. Turn right at next junction and after 2 miles (3 km) left at crossroads.

Crail is the oldest of the 'East Neuk' fishing ports. At one period, a fleet of a hundred boats crowded the tiny harbour. They traded with Holland and Denmark and scoured the North Sea for herring. Local girls went down on foot to Yarmouth and Lowestoft to cure their catches and mend their nets.

Crail Museum depicts East Neuk's maritime history; *open afternoons, daily, in summer.* If this new venture flourishes, opening times will be extended.

Crail Leave by coast road, signposted Kilrenny. In ½ mile (0.8 km) on the left, is a wide view of the Firth of Forth, Bass Rock and May Island.

Anstruther (locally 'Anster') On left, entering village, the Fisheries Museum incorporates an aquarium, a library of the logbooks of whaling skippers and the North Carr lightship which was on station off Fife Ness from 1938 to 1975.

Pittenweem Just beyond the village on the left there is another brilliant panorama of the Firth.

⑤ In ¼ mile (0.5 km) bear right for Kellie Castle.

Kellie Castle, one mile (1.5 km) on right of the B942, is an interesting old house, well worth the short detour. Its tower dates back to the Siwards who came to Scotland in the time of Macbeth. *Open Sat–Thurs after-*

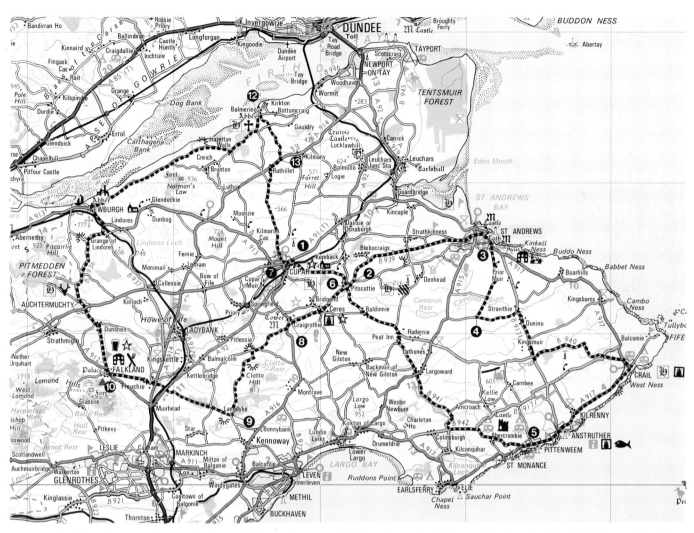

noon, Apr–Sept. Return to B942 and take the next right turn, signposted Cupar.

⑥ Continue on B940 for Cupar or turn left, signposted Leven, and join Route Two at Ceres.

> **Route Two: 41 miles (66 km)**
> Directions in sequence from: Cupar
> Direction of travel: clockwise

⑦ Leave by South Rd. and after crossing railway, fork left, signposted to Ceres.

🏛 **Ceres** The Fife Folk Museum displays domestic and farming life of long ago. You can see the whole thing in 20 minutes.

☆ **Ceres** At the corner of Main St. in centre of village, the photogenic 'Provost' sits with his tankard and keeps an eye on things. This comical stone statue was unearthed from a local garden. Its origin is unknown.

⑧ Turn left on A916 then right on unclassified road signposted Chance Inn.

🌿 **Craigrothie–Falkland** An attractive hilly road with views north to Firth of Tay and south to the Firth of Forth. You can see Arthur's Seat (a volcanically-formed hill) in Holyrood Park, Edinburgh.

⑨ Successive turns: left (no signpost), right (Cults), right (Burnturk) and straight on (Freuchie).

☆ **Falkland** A compact, old-fashioned township full of country shops and Jacobean 'wynds'. It has a kiltmaker's, violinmaker's, art gallery, craft shop, tearoom, pub and restaurant, all charming.

🏛 **Falkland Palace** This was the early Stuarts' favourite residence and the childhood home of Mary, Queen of Scots. As a prominent early example of the French Renaissance style it is a symbol of the 'Auld Alliance', the Franco-Scottish combination against England. Lovely walled gardens; a genuine historical experience; *open Mon–Sat and Sun afternoon in summer.*

⑩ Exit by road on right and follow signs to Auchtermuchty.

🏛 **Auchtermuchty** A jokey place-name (pronounced 'Auchmewty') for a dull village.

Y Auchtermuchty Half a mile (0.8 km) beyond the crossroads on the left is a deer farm. Visitors welcome; venison sold.

🌿 **Auchtermuchty–Newburgh** Fine views of Perth and the upper Tay estuary open out.

🏚 **Newburgh** A neat grey-stone village on one street, ancient despite its name. The Mugdrum Cross in the churchyard dates from early Christian times.

⑪ Exit by the unclassified road at the east of village, signposted Gauldry.

🌿 **Newburgh** In 1 mile (1.5 km) on the left are spread the barely-identifiable ruins of Lindores Abbey, founded 1178. More interesting architecturally is the water-mill.

🌿 **Newburgh–Balmerino** Several points along this peaceful Firth-side road offer good views of Dundee and its backcloth, the Sidlaw Hills. Six miles (10 km) from Newburgh the two Tay bridges, road and rail, come into view.

✝ **Balmerino** The ruined abbey on the left, atmospheric in its tranquil setting, has recently celebrated its 750th birthday.

🏛 **Balmerino** All the house-fronts on the row of cottages facing the Firth bear inscriptions recalling the Scots Guards' colonel's address to his troops before the Battle of Anzio, 1944.

⑫ Turn right at junction ¼ mile (0.5 km) past abbey and in 400 yards cross another minor road. Follow signs to Rathillet.

⑬ Cross the A914 and head for Cupar.

Tay and Tummel

In the middle of the last century, when the mail went up to Balmoral on a pony, when Queen Victoria regularly detoured to pause at her favourite view, and when her eldest son, afterwards Edward VII, gloried in the shooting around Aberfeldy, these quiet central Highlands knew royal pomp and ceremony. Then the railway and an improved main road were built, bypassing and draining away the traffic. Today, even in the holiday season, long stretches of this tour are peaceful and there should be no problems in stopping, picnicking and admiring the shifting panoramas of loch, forest and moorland.

Route: 90 miles (145 km)
Directions in sequence from: Killin
Direction of travel: anticlockwise

● *The Falls of Dochart, Killin: the River Lochay makes another fine set of falls nearby before joining with the Dochart to flow into Loch Tay.*

☆ **Killin** A small village clustered round the cascades of the River Dochart, which here drops into Loch Tay. *Tourist information: tel. (05672) 254.*

🏠 **Killin** If your name is MacNab, this is your ancestral heath. The islet of Inch Buie, in the river near Dochart bridge, was traditionally the burial place of the MacNab chiefs.

① *Leave by Falls of Dochart and take minor road on left signposted Ardeonaig.*

❀ **Killin–Ardeonaig** In 2 miles (3 km) there is a striking view of Ben Lawers, a mountain which, thanks to the 16-ft (5-m) cairn on top, permits the climber to stand at 4,000 feet (1,219 m) above sea level.

✗ **Killin–Ardeonaig** About ½ mile (0.8 km) past the viewpoint, Firbush picnic spot and parking.

❀ **Ardeonaig–Acharn** Views of Loch Tay in its cloak of variegated woodland grow increasingly impressive.

⛵ **Acharn** A cheerful little water-sports centre with canoes for hire and sometimes water-skiing.

☆ **Acharn** On right, about 200 yards (180 m) above the village is a waterfall on the Acharn Burn, turbulent after rain.

🏠 **Kenmore** Claimed as the prettiest village in Scotland, it was built last century by the Marquess of Breadalbane, heir to the powerful Duke of Argyll, to house estate workers at Taymouth Castle. Facing the village green (a rare feature in Scotland) are church, hotel and castle gates. Until fairly recently, the marquesses maintained a feudal life-style and in 1842 Kenmore saw the young Queen Victoria being entertained with fireworks, great slaughter of game and a procession of barges on Loch Tay.

❀ **Kenmore** As you cross the river bridge there is a good view on the left up the loch.

② *Passing through village, in ¼ mile (0.5 km) take the right turn signposted Tummel Bridge, and immediately bear right again.*

In 2¼ miles (3.5 km) turn right, signposted Aberfeldy.

🏰 **Castle Menzies** (on left) is an outstanding example of the 'Z-plan' fortified house of the 1570s. The castle was for three hundred and fifty years the seat of the chief of Clan Menzies, pronounced Mingus. The Clan society is restoring the building and *visitors are welcomed daily Apr–Sept.*

🏠 **Weem** On the left is a wall-plaque to General George Wade, the military engineer who opened up the Highlands with roads and bridges early in the 18thC. Along with Queen Victoria and Sir Walter Scott, Wade is considered a founder of Scottish tourism. He made Weem his headquarters and the well-known couplet says it all: 'If you knew these roads before they were made/You would lift up your hands and bless General Wade'.

③ *Continue along road signposted Strathtay.*

❀ **Weem–Logierait** Half a mile (0.8 km) after the Strathtay signpost, a good view to the rear embraces the Ben Lawers massif. To the right is Aberfeldy and its 'birks' (birchwoods) celebrated in a song of Robert Burns.

✿ **Weems–Logierait** Two miles (3 km) beyond the viewpoint on the left are Cluny House and gardens, a large woodland garden with some Himalayan trees and plants; fine views. *Open daily Mar–Oct.*

〰 **Strathtay** (no village, not on map) After Cluny the valley opens out and the route shows the typical character of Perthshire with mixed woodland, rhododendrons and dry-stone walls. *Keep to road on left bank of River Tay and join A827, signposted to Ballinluig.*

④ *Turn sharp left in front of the hotel, signposted to Dunfallandy: narrow road, steep ascent.*

⑤ **Logierait–Loch Faskally** At Dunfallandy pass under the new Pitlochry bypass and bear left, signposted Portnacraig. After ¼ mile (0.5 km) note signs on right to Faskally dam and fish ladder. Worth a detour spring and autumn when salmon are running.
☆ Also on right is the Pitlochry 'Theatre in the Hills', now rebuilt in a new setting, evening performances in summer.

❢ **Loch Faskally** An easy woodland walk, signposted, round this small artificial loch, offers access to Pitlochry, which has more hotels and souvenir shops per head of population than any place in Scotland.

⑥ *Turn right on to A9 and in ½ mile (0.8 km) right again at the Foss/Inverness signpost. In ¼ mile (0.5 km) the Coronation Footbridge gives access to Killiecrankie.*

❀ **Linn of Tummel–Foss** The whole route to Loch Tummel is well furnished with lay-bys and viewpoints. There is a particularly interesting viewpoint at the picnic site under Cammoch Hill.

📷 **Linn of Tummel–Foss** One mile (1.5 km) beyond the picnic site, on right, the imposing memorial arch of Clunie Power Station

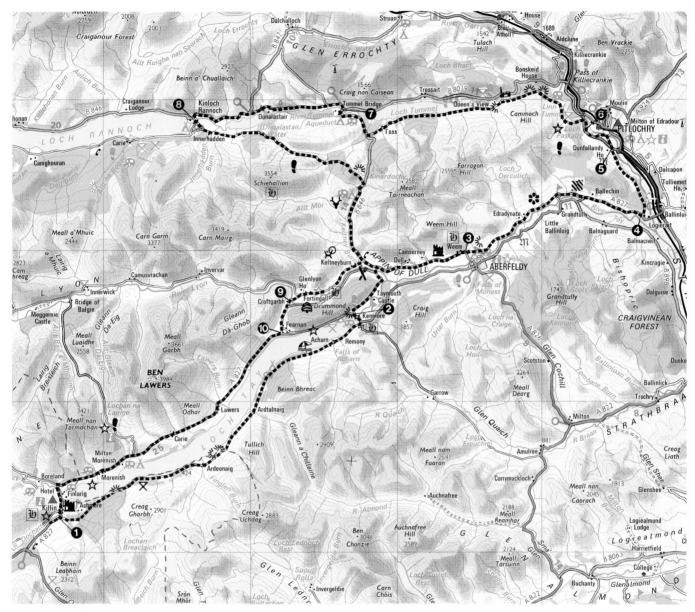

marks the completion in 1952 of the Tummel–Garry hydro-electric scheme.

Linn of Tummel–Foss Half a mile (0.8 km) from Clunie arch are lay-bys, tables and a view towards the Linn (waterfall) of Tummel with Ben Vrackie, 2,759 feet (841m), behind. Queen's View, on opposite bank of river, was the viewpoint which Victoria preferred above all.

⑦ *Cross bridge and turn left, signposted Kinloch Rannoch.*

⑧ *Bear left across bridge and left again after ¾ mile, both signposted Schiehallion.*

Braes of Foss (not on map) From the car park on the right is the footpath to Schiehallion, 3,554 feet (1,083 m), a prominent and graceful mountain popular with climbers. Note the cairn and plaque to the parson-astronomer Maskelyne who in 1774, on this mountain, experimented with the laws of gravity.

Loch Kinardochy Over Forest of Atholl,

just before you turn right on to the B846.

Kinardochy–Keltneyburn One mile (1.5 km) from previous turning, motorists may enter and park in the Deer Park on the right: red deer and other Highland fauna.

Coshieville (not on map) At road junction where you turn sharp right, the Coshieville Hotel is a useful lunch or dinner stop with better-than-average bar meals and a short but selective wine list; moderate prices.

Keltneyburn The old smithy has moved with the times and does a nice line in wrought iron and ornamental metalwork.

Fortingall Formerly a Roman garrison town, Britain's northernmost. Legend says that Pontius Pilate was born here, offspring of a centurion and a local girl, but the historical evidence is shaky.

Fortingall Nothing shaky, however, about the yew which has ramified all over the churchyard. It is the oldest living tree in Scotland.

⑨ *Leaving village, proceed straight on at road junction, signposted Fearnan/Killin, and cross River Lyon.*

⑩ *The road descends steeply to join A827, turn right.*

☆ Three-and-a-half miles (5.5 km) beyond Lawers, a road on the right offers an interesting detour to the Ben Lawers Visitor Centre in 2 miles (3 km): audio-visual displays, flora and fauna exhibition, guided walks, access to mountain summit (a 5-hour walk there and back). These slopes were the cradle of skiing in Scotland.

☆ **Ben Ghlas** (not on map) is one mile (1.5 km) from previous junction: weaving, tanning, wood-carving workshops, farm animals, soft-fruit market garden, sandwich bar; *open in normal working hours.*

Killin Re-entering the village, note Finlarig Castle near roadside on left, an ivy-covered ruin now closed and awaiting restoration. Its unique feature is the sole surviving beheading pit in Scotland.

221

Isle of Mull

Please bear in mind that on Mull the pace of life is gentle. It is not surprising that rock stars and politicians choose the island for their retreats, for it is another world, different even from the adjacent mainland. Roads seem to explore every hill in sight and these two routes involve much second- and third-gear work. In summer, there will be delays in passing places. The whole route, plus the ferry crossing, makes a long day.

Mull is 45 minutes from Oban on the large car ferry, or 15 minutes from Lochaline on the small, much cheaper ferry. On the latter, be prepared for a three-hour delay in summer.

Route One: 45 miles (72 km)
Directions in sequence from: Salen
Direction of travel: anticlockwise

Salen Its situation, where virtually all of Mull's roads are drawn to the narrow neck of the island, makes it a launching-pad for excursions by land and sea. Mull aerodrome (light aircraft) is also here.

① *Follow road signposted Tobermory.*

② *At entrance to glen, marked Glenaros House, bear right across river bridge.*

Aros Castle, now a poor ruin, was once a formidable fortress from which the Lords of the Isles exacted a toll on ships passing through the Sound of Mull.

Ardnacross Five miles (8 km) through outstanding scenery reach a climax at the splendid viewpoint of Lochan na Guailne Duibhe; parking area at roadside. The route ahead is bordered with rhododendrons.

☆ **Tobermory** Chief community of Mull; the name means Well of St Mary. *Tourist information: tel. (0688) 2182.*

✗ **Tobermory** Aros Park on left, before you descend to the harbour, has picnic places and signposted walks.

Tobermory Salvage expeditions work periodically between the harbour and Calve Island where in 1588 the Spanish galleon *San Juan de Sicilia* sank with treasure on board. Nothing much has been found and meantime the pride of the Armada sinks deeper into the mud.

Tobermory Print shop and Mull pottery.

③ *Turn right into Main St. and near end of street turn sharp left, signposted Calgary/Dervaig (but sign invisible from this direction). Bear left at top of steep hill*

● *Duart Castle, stronghold of the Macleans.*

and follow road signposted Dervaig. Though small, Tobermory is convoluted.

Dervaig Dramatic views as you approach village by a narrow bridge and a zigzag ascent; canal-like Loch Tor on right.

✗ **Dervaig** The smart little bookshop also sells toys, wines and coffee and offers lunches with a good cheese-board. The eating alcove consists of six chairs round a woodburning stove.

④ *At Bellacroy Hotel, where road divides, go straight on, signposted Calgary Sands.*

Dervaig–Calgary At road junction ½ mile (0.8 km) from Dervaig, the Old Byre Heritage Museum, signposted on left, is worth stopping at for its historical tableaux with vocal accompaniment. The restaurant boasts an island cuisine, chiefly seafood.

✗

Dervaig–Calgary Approaching Calgary you may catch a glimpse of Ardnamurchan Point across the sea on right. Ardnamurchan, 'Cape of the Great Storms', is the most westerly point of mainland Britain.

Calgary Emigrants from this hamlet founded Calgary in Canada.

Calgary Bay The pure colours of blue sea and white sand make Calgary Sands an idyllic spot on a sunny day.

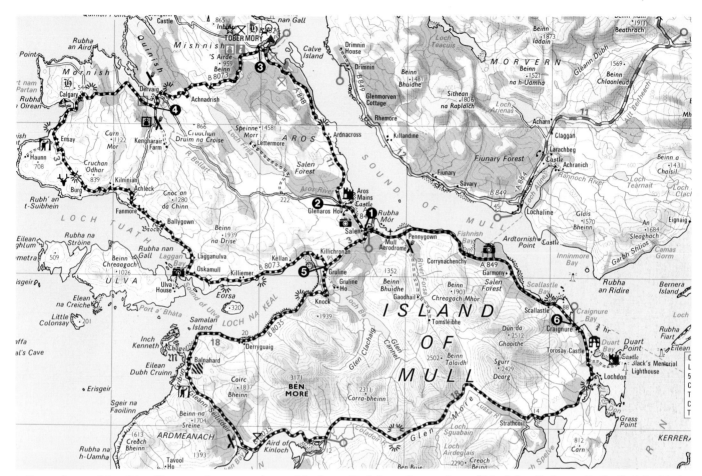

Ensay Approaching this village you have impressive views towards Coll, Tiree and the Treshnish Isles, beyond which the next land is America.

Ensay Rough track on right leads in ¾ mile (1 km) to the deserted settlement of Crakaig Treshnish and caves with flues cut in them, presumably to carry away the blue smoke of illicit whisky stills.

Burg Just before the descent, where Highland cattle are often roaming, there is a good view of the isle of Ulva.

Oskamull In 200 yards (183 m) on the right is the passenger ferry to Ulva. You could almost jump across. In summer, weather permitting, local boatmen take visitors to Staffa, for Fingal's Cave, 8 miles (13 km) away; but landing cannot be guaranteed.

Oskamull–Killichronan Superb views over Loch na Keal (said to be among Scotland's most enchanting sea lochs) to southern Mull including Ben More, 3,171 feet (966 m). There are often seals in the loch.

⑤ *For Salen turn left at road junction; if continuing on* **Route Two,** *go straight on and save 5 miles (8 km).*

> **Route Two: 47 miles (76 km)**
> Directions in sequence from: Salen
> Direction of travel: anticlockwise

Salen–Balnahard *Road traces the opposite*

shore of Loch na Keal from the one by which you returned on **Route One.** *For 6 miles (10 km) there is an unbroken series of spectacular views over the loch.*

Balnahard The formidable cliffs of Gribun stop short on the sea's brink and the road squeezes between. The islet 1 mile (1.5 km) offshore is Inch Kenneth. 'The most agreeable Sunday I ever passed,' said Dr Johnson after visiting it with James Boswell on their tour of the western isles in 1773.

Balmeanach is a farm (not on map) 1 mile (1.5 km) beyond Balnahard, from which there is a footpath to Mackinnon's Cave on the shore. Access is at low water only, and the cavern is so vast that legend says it goes right across Mull. The stone inside the entrance, called Fingal's Table, was perhaps an early Christian altar.

Balnahard–Lochdon Where the road arrives at Loch Scridain a roadside farm offers crabs, scallops and sea-urchins.

Balnahard–Lochdon One mile (1.5 km) on, nearly opposite Aird of Kinloch promontory, is a picnic area on Loch Scridain shore.

Balnahard–Lochdon The road penetrates into, then disentangles itself from, the massifs of southern Mull, with sensational mountain scenery in Glen More.

Lochdon Fine distant prospects of Loch Linnhe and the Lochaber district, towards Fort William.

Lochdon–Craignure In ¾ mile (1 km) is the entrance, on the right, to Duart Castle, an ancient coastal fortress, enlarged and improved down the centuries. It is the ancestral home of 30 generations of MacLeans, of whom one was recently Chief Scout and another lived to 101; *gardens open all year, house daily May–Sept; tearoom at castle, home baking.*

Lochdon–Craignure In ½ mile (0.8 km) past the Duart entrance is the entrance to Torosay Castle; another entrance is 1 mile (1.5 km) ahead at Craignure: a 19th-C baronial mansion. Miniature steam railway to Craignure; *gardens open daily; castle open daily May–Sept.*

⑥ *Ferry port for Oban: the crossing takes approximately 45 minutes.*

Craignure–Fishnish One of the very few stretches of double-lane road on the island. After Craignure, good views open up of Morvern on the mainland.

Fishnish (not on map) *In half a mile (0.8 km) on the right is the ferry port for Lochaline (15 minutes). Boards at roadside on ferry approaches indicate approximate waiting times – 2 hours, 3 hours and so on.*

Mull Aerodrome Close to the airfield on the right is the log-cabin-styled Glenforsa Hotel, one of the best on the island. The lunch menu often has local trout and salmon and a praiseworthy effort is made to provide traditional Scottish dishes, refined for modern tastes.

Donside and Dee

Donside – the area around and along the River Don – is a quiet country of farms and hamlets. Deeside – 'Royal' Deeside (for here, between Ballater and Braemar, close to the A93, is Balmoral Castle) – is one of the classic touring areas. It is lined with busy roads and holiday towns, but there are echoes of bygone days: proud cone-capped towers and grim medieval ruins mark the route, for this is Scotland's castle country, and was once the no-man's land of clan warfare.

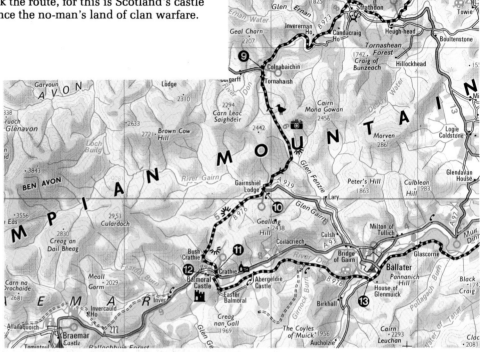

Route: 97 miles (156 km)
In sequence from: Banchory
Direction of travel: anticlockwise

☆ **Banchory** A clean little granite town on the Dee. The only real antiquity is the golf course, which was laid out in 1799. *Tourist information caravan: tel. (033 02) 2000 (summer only).*

① *Leave by A93, signposted Braemar.*

② *Bear right and after 1 mile (1.5 km) right again (no signpost).*

⚶ **Tillydrine** A fine view of the River Dee on the left, as it sweeps through a richly-wooded valley.

🏰 **Torphins** The name recalls Thorfinn of Norway, an ally of Macbeth. Not at Dunsinane, but at Lumphanan, 3½ miles (5.5 km) north-west on the A980, Macbeth died in battle, 1057. A cairn marks the spot.

③ *In Torphins continue straight on, signposted Inverurie. In 2 and 3 miles (3 and 5 km), there are extensive views to south and north.*

④ *At the next crossroads turn left, signposted Tarland. Two miles (3 km) on, turn right, signposted Tolmauds, then follow signs to Kintocher.*

⚶ **Kintocher** Approaching the A980 there is a sensational view of Craigievar Castle.

⑤ *Join A980 and turn right (no signpost) and in ½ mile (0.8 km), turn left for Craigievar Castle.*

🏰 **Craigievar Castle** is the supreme example of a late Jacobean tower house in the baronial style, tall and slender, poised, seeming hardly to touch the ground it rests on. This was Walt Disney's model for the fairy-tale palace in *Snow White*. It was lived in until fairly recently and old people remember how the maids gathered rushes from the meadows every morning to strew on the stone floors. The staircase bears the date 1668, with the Forbes coat-of-arms and the motto: 'Doe not vaiken sleiping dogs'. Furnishings match the beauty of the site and architecture. *Car park, gardens and picnic area are open daily all year; house opens Sun–Thurs afternoons, May–Sept.* This place is not to be missed.

⑥ *Return to main road and turn left.*

⑦ *Turn left, signposted Towie, and continue for 3 miles (5 km) along narrow undulating lanes; then bear right at crossroads signposted (sic) Milton of Kildromy. This is a very pretty road, but single-track with scarcely any passing places.*

⑧ *Bear left, signposted Kildrummy Hotel, and in ½ mile (0.8 km) left again, no signpost, on to A97.*

🏰 **Kildrummy Castle**, on right, is an enormous fortress, 'by Time's fell hand defaced'. It probably existed in the time of Macbeth but the most ancient remnant is the rounded 'Snow Tower' built about 1300 by its then owner, the Bishop of Caithness. On the subject of snow, Kildrummy is by an old tradition the coldest place in Scotland. *Open daily, Apr–Oct.*

🌊 **Glenkindie** Here begins the tortuous route upstream in the gorges of the infant Don, in increasingly impressive scenery.

🏰 **Glenkindie** The minor road on left leads in 1 mile (1.5 km) to Towie church and the ruined Towie Castle. An old Scots ballad sings of feuds between the Gordons and the Forbeses and of Adam Gordon's attack on Towie in 1571, when Alexander Forbes and his wife and children perished in the flames.

🏰 **Bridge of Buchat** The gaunt ruin on the right, just beyond the bridge, is Glenbuchat Castle, another of the many strongholds which line the course of the Don. This castle was a fortress of the Gordons who called themselves the 'Cocks o' the North'.

🏰 **Strathdon** Track on left at entrance to the village goes in ¼ mile (0.5 km) to Strathdon pottery and Old Semeil Herb Garden; craftwork and plants for sale.

⑨ *Keep left, signposted Ballater.*

🏹 **Colnabalchin–Gairnshiel Lodge** A wild, unfenced moorland road: grouse and capercailzie. You may be warned off if you stop to picnic during the nesting season. In 2 miles (3 km) on the right is an old military road going in 4½ miles (7 km) to Cock Bridge. It is now a public footpath, difficult after rain.

⚶ **Colnabalchin–Gairnshiel Lodge** At the summit of the road, 1½ miles (2.5 km) beyond the public footpath, there are exceptionally good views ahead over Royal Deeside and on the left to Morven.

⑩ *Turn right to another wild mountain pass, signposted Balmoral.*

⚶ **Gairnshiel Lodge–Crathie** From the summit, marked with cairns in 3½ miles (5.5 km) there are impressive views to the right, across the Grampian range, principally Ben Avon, 3,843 feet (1,172 m).

⚶ **Gairnshiel Lodge–Crathie** On the descent the route is bordered with extensive dry-stone dyking. In 3½ miles (5.5 km) Balmoral Castle is straight ahead – the best of all views of the Queen's Highland home, with 'dark Lochnagar', 3,791 feet (1,155 m), in the background.

⑪ *After turning left on to A93, signposted Aberdeen, turn sharp right, signposted South Deeside. Just beyond the turn are the car parks for Crathie church and Balmoral.*

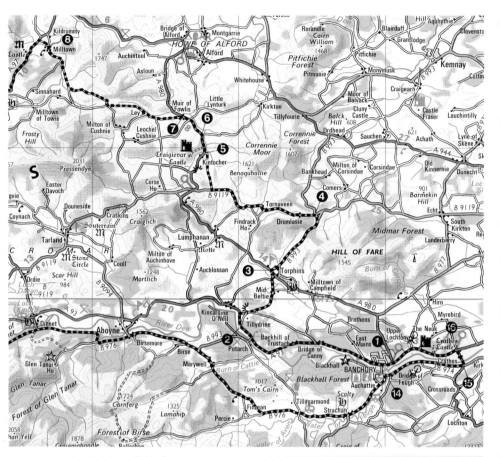

Crathie The well-kept, much-photographed church here is where the Queen worships when she is at Balmoral, normally August and September. On Sundays thousands line the road to see the Royal Family walk to church, and there used to be a scramble for seats; but pews are now reserved for parishioners.

Balmoral Castle The entrance is on the right, across the Dee bridge, ¼ mile (0.5 km) from Crathie car park. It is, of course, a uniquely interesting stately home, but visitors are restricted to the ballroom with its Landseer paintings and heavy Victoriana. Gardens on view; pony-trekking in park. *Open Mon–Fri, May–July, 10–5.*

⑫ *Continue past Castle entrance on South Deeside road.*

⑬ **Glenmuick** *Bear left after crossing river and follow signposts for Aboyne. In ½ mile (0.8 km) there are views of Ballater and the Morven massif on the left.*

⑭ **Glenmuick–Strachan** On the left, in 7½ miles (12 km), stands a florid monument with a Biblical inscription, commemorating Queen Victoria's Jubilee.

☆ **Glenmuick–Strachan** On the right, 2½ miles (4 km) beyond the Jubilee Stone, the minor road into Glen Tanar is worth a detour, especially when Glen Tanar House with its arboretum, lakes and Celtic chapel, *is occasionally open to visitors, generally in June.*

⑭ **Strachan** is a junction of old drove-roads. Here the Deeside routes were joined by the historic Cairn o' Mount highway from the south, a mountain pass well known to those who took part in reliability trials in early motoring days, and still something of an endurance test.

⑭ **Bridge of Feugh** *Bear right, signposted Aberdeen. In 1½ miles (2.5 km) on the right* is the Maryfield crafts complex.

⑮ *Sharp left at the crossroads, signposted Crathes, and in ½ mile (0.8 km) left again, signposted Banchory.*

Crathes Castle *is on the right, ½ mile (0.8 km) from the last turning.* This impressive tower house, famous for its painted ceilings, was built in the 16thC for the Burnetts of Leys, a family associated with Crathes for more than 600 years. The eight gardens are lined with yew hedges of great age. Picnic and play areas, shops and a restaurant cater for large crowds of excursionists: a deservedly popular destination. *Open Fri–Sat and Sun afternoon, May–Sept; gardens open daily all year.*

Crathes Castle Just inside the entrance-drive a road on the right turns back, dives under the A93 and emerges at the craft centre and gallery of Milton of Crathes: print-making, pottery and jewellery in a group of farm buildings; *open all year.*

⑯ *Rejoin A93 and enter Banchory.*

● *The River Dee.*

Speyside

This route takes in a corner of the 'whisky trail' – an invention of the tourist trade designed to introduce visitors to the great distilleries in this area. However, it is still relatively little-visited.

The circuit is centred where the Glens of Livet, Fiddich and Grant, and the rivulets of the Cromdale Hills all join Strath Avon and Strathspey. Here are the sites of the innumerable illicit 'sma' stills' of bygone days; and apart from being of consuming interest to devotees of the 'single malts' (the unblended Scotch whiskies), the drive takes in some of Scotland's wildest, most romantic scenery.

Route: 81 miles (130 km)
Directions in sequence from: Elgin
Direction of travel: anticlockwise

☆ **Elgin** A solid little market-town and a popular touring centre. *Tourist information: tel. (0343) 3388.*

♏ **Elgin** The cathedral which makes Elgin one of Britain's smallest cities stands in roofless decay on the banks of the River Lossie. When new in 1270 it was accidentally burned out and one hundred years later deliberately destroyed by fire. Later on the steeple fell down and the then Earl of Moray helped himself to all the lead on the roof to pay off debts. In 1711 the central tower collapsed and for many years the place was a stone quarry. But a surprising amount of graceful architecture has survived in the nave, choir and chapter house.

① *Leave by the Forres road and in ½ mile (0.8 km) bear left and soon afterwards right, both signposted Pluscarden.*

☆ **Elgin–Pluscarden** Two miles (3 km) from Elgin on the left is a large store for malt whisky in cask.

⚔ **Elgin–Pluscarden** The road enters Monaughty Forest: picnic spots, footpaths.

② **Barnhill** *At Pluscarden church the route bears right and then left, no signposts.*
✝ *(Detour straight on to Pluscarden Abbey, ½ mile (0.8 km). The Cistercian priory is well restored and once more lived in. On request the monks will show the 'Burgie Necklace' (a jet Bronze-Age diadem).*

③ **Barnhill–Dallas** *Turn left on to the B9010, no signpost.* Sign for Highland cattle and a
⚔ *good view to the right over Macbeth's 'blasted heath' and the town of Forres.*

☖ **Dallas** A hamlet on an innocent stream, as different as it could possibly be from the Texas city to which it gave its name.

✗ **Dallas** The Dallas Hotel offers a cheerful undemonstrative welcome and serves simple fare at all hours.

• *The Spey, second longest river in Scotland, and Mecca for salmon fishermen.*

---

④ *Leave Dallas by unclassified road on left, which climbs towards the source of the Lossie river. Here begins the spectacular scenery.*

⑤ *Turn right at junction.*

⑥ *The route goes down into Strathspey. In 3 miles (5 km) from previous junction turn left and cross the Spey.*

♞ **Marypark** Note the bagpipe-maker's shop on the corner as you turn right, signposted Tomintoul.

⚔ **Marypark–Ballindalloch** After a mile (1.5 km), a wide view of Strathspey and the braes of Moray opens up on the right.

♜ **Ballindalloch** Two miles (3 km) from Marypark, on the right, (not on map) are the baronial-style lodge and gatehouse of Ballindalloch Castle, a 16th-C tower house, not open to the public.

⑦ *At a mini-spaghetti junction of mountain roads turn right, then immediately left. In half a mile (0.8 km) there is a good view ahead of the Livet Water in its narrowing glen. In another half mile (0.8 km) is the Glenlivet distillery.*

☆ **Glenlivet Distillery** The best-known of the first licensed distilleries (1824, but operating illegally for a century before that date) has the privilege of describing its product as *The Glenlivet*, though half a dozen different malt whiskies depend on the River Livet for their water. *The reception centre opens Mon–Fri, Apr–Oct. The guided tour, which includes hospitality, takes about 40 minutes.*

⑧ *Exit by turning right at the Blairfindy Lodge hotel, then in one mile (1.5 km) left at next junction.*

⊼ **Glenlivet–Tomintoul** In one mile and 2 miles (1.5 and 3 km) are two useful picnic places, with amenities. Across the River Avon the hills rise to the heights of Cromdale, a 2,400-foot (730-m) ridge whose short sharp torrents help give Scotch malt whisky its magic formula.

☆ **Tomintoul** The highest village in the Highlands (but not in all Scotland) at 1,150 feet (350 m). There are fine views to the south on entering the village; picnic area on right.

⚘ **Tomintoul** The main-street shop called Whisky Castle is an emporium of local crafts and of the produce of the region, including whisky.

⑨ **Tomintoul** *Exit by road on left, signposted Braemar, then straight on, signposted Dufftown. (Road on right surmounts the Lecht and goes to Cock Bridge. At 2,100 feet (640 m) it is a notorious snow-trap, invariably the first British highway to be blocked in winter.)*

⚶ **Knockandhu** Splendid views on right to the Ladder Hills and ahead to Ben Rinnes. Bare granite and deep glens make this a dramatic route all the way to Dufftown.

⌂ **Dufftown** A model village of four streets meeting at a clock tower, founded in 1817 by Lord Fife (family name Duff) to provide work for soldiers returning from the Napoleonic wars.

⌂ **Dufftown** The clock tower has been gaol, council house and assembly room in its time and is now a museum and tourist information centre. The clock is 'the clock that hanged MacPherson' – a reference to a local villain condemned to death last century. Public opinion demanded a reprieve, but the sheriff of Banff advanced the clock to the time of execution, forestalling the arrival of the document.

☆ **Dufftown** The Glenfiddich distillery, where the world's best-selling malt whisky is produced, is just off the Elgin road, *open Mon–Fri all year.* It is one of seven malt distilleries which surround the little town. Another is Mortlach, off Fife St., the first licensed distillery in Scotland (1823), *not open to the public.*

⛪ **Dufftown** Mortlach parish church, at the end of Church St., has a strangely-carved Pictish cross and a symbol stone, also Jacobean graves and effigies. This has been hallowed ground since 566 AD, when St Moluag established a chapel.

m **Dufftown** *On the exit road A941, ¼ mile (0.5 km) past Glenfiddich distillery,* is the empty shell of Balvenie, a spacious courtyard castle known to Edward I, the 'Hammer of the Scots' and later to Mary, Queen

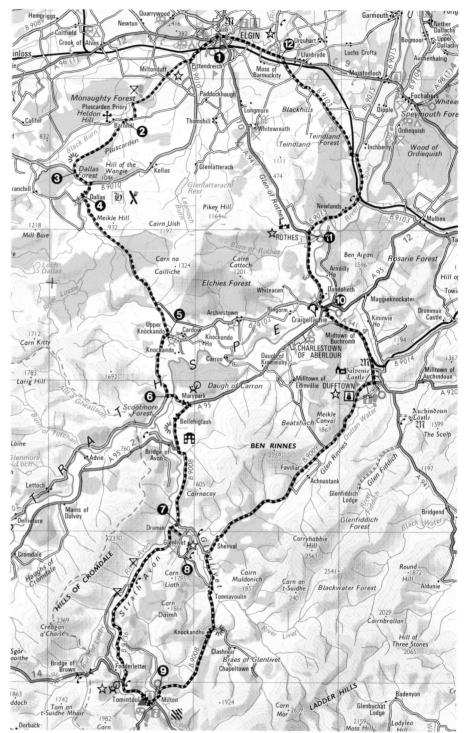

of Scots. The outstanding feature is the 'yett' or iron gate. *Open Thur, Fri and Sat and Sun afternoon, Apr–Sept.*

⑩ *Take right turn, signposted Elgin, then immediately left, signposted Rothes. After crossing Spey, straight on at crossroads, signposted Elgin.*

⌒ **Craigellachie** On the left of the bridge over the Spey is the handsome former road bridge, built in 1814 by Telford from local granite with a Welsh pre-fabricated cast-iron span. At £8,000 it was the costliest civil engineering job in the Highlands.

☆ **Rothes** On the left is another showplace distillery, the Glen Grant, with visitor centre and hospitality (no young children). *Open Mon–Fri, Easter–Sept.*

⛟ **Rothes** The large factory at the north end of the village turns distillery dreg and effluent into high-protein animal feed.

⑪ **Rothes** *Take the B9015 from the village, signposted Orton.*

⑫ *In 11 miles (17.6 km) from Rothes, turn left on to the A96, signposted Inverness. In 3 miles (5 km), enter Elgin.*

227

Index

This is a *combined* index: place names on the Routeplanner Atlas appear along with 'general' entries from pages 52–227. For example:

Beaumaris, (Gwyn) **28** SH 6076; *158, 159*

entry | county abbreviation | National Grid reference | other page references

Routeplanner page reference

Routeplanner references are always in **bold**.

Some entries are unique to pages 52–227, and so have no Routeplanner references.

County abbreviations are from the 1985 *Ordnance Survey Motorist's Atlas of Great Britain*.

PICTURE CREDITS

Geoffrey Berry 93; British Tourist Authority 73, 180; Fanny Dubes 158; Robert Estall 71, 100–1; Fotobank / Peter Kowal 55 / English Tourist Board 196 / Highlands and Islands Development Board 226 / D. Farquhar 220 / Andy Williams 68, 137 / Tom Wright 201; **Susan Griggs Agency** / Michael Boys 176 / David Beatty 131 / Rob Cousins 164 / Anthony Howarth 59, 208–9 / Simon McBride 113, 126 / Michael St Maur Sheil 167, 212 / Patrick Ward 102 / Adam Woolfitt Contents 60, 82, 104, 106, 182; **Robert Harding Picture Library / Ian Sumner** 57; **Robert Harding Picture Library** 175, 222, 225; **International Photobank / Peter Baker** 124; **Sarah King** 108, 114, 117, 118, 132; **Andrew Lawson** 146; **Gareth Lovatt Jones** 141; **Colin Molyneux** 87, 142–3, 151, 153, 154, 160–1, 162, 168, 169, 170; **Peter Phillips / Trevor Wood Library** 185, 190; **Scottish Tourist Board** 215, 218; **John Sims** 111; **Patrick Thurston** 88, 135, 139, 189, 198, 204; **Roger Vlitos** 63, 144; **Charlie Waite** 99, 120; **Simon Warner** 91, 97, 159, 193, 194, 206; **Noel Habgood / Derek C. Widdicombe** 122, 140, 156; **Derek C. Widdicombe** 186; **Trevor Wood** half title, title, 85, 172, 179, 203, 216.

EDITORIAL AND DESIGN

Editor **Gilly Abrahams**; editorial assistance and index **Rosemary Dawe**; art editor **Mel Petersen**; designer **Arthur Brown**, cartographic artwork **Roger Boffey, Brenda Breslan**, picture research **Jenny de Gex**.